http://www.wadsworth.com

wadsworth.com is the World Wide Web site for Wadsworth and is your direct source to dozens of online resources.

At *wadsworth.com* you can find out about supplements, demonstration software, and student resources. You can also send email to many of our authors and preview new publications and exciting new technologies.

wadsworth.com
Changing the way the world learns®

Advertising Titles from International Thomson Publishing

Jewler/Drewniany
Creative Strategy in Advertising, 6e
(1998, Wadsworth)

Mueller
International Advertising: Communicating Across Cultures
(1996, Wadsworth)

O'Guinn/Allen/Semenik
Advertising
(1998, South-Western)

Sivulka
Soap, Sex, and Cigarettes: A Cultural History of American Advertising
(1998, Wadsworth)

Woods
Advertising and Marketing to the New Majority:
A Case Study Approach
(1995, Wadsworth)

Soap, Sex, and Cigarettes

A Cultural History of
American Advertising

Juliann Sivulka

Wadsworth Publishing Company
I(T)P® **An International Thomson Publishing Company**

Belmont, CA • Albany, NY • Bonn • Boston • Cincinnati • Detroit • Johannesburg
London • Madrid • Melbourne • Mexico City • New York • Paris • Singapore
Tokyo • Toronto • Washington

Communication Studies Editor: Randall Adams
Assistant Editor: Michael Gillespie
Development Editor: Lewis DeSimone
Editorial Assistant: Megan Gilbert
Marketing Manager: Mike Dew
Print Buyer: Barbara Britton
Production: Melanie Field, Strawberry Field Publishing
Permissions Editor: Robert Kauser
Designer: Rob Hugel
Copy Editor: Tom Briggs
Cover: Rob Hugel
Compositor: TBH/Typecast, Inc.
Printer: Quebecor Printing/Fairfield

Printed in the United States of America
  2 3 4 5 6 7 8 9 10

For more information, contact Wadsworth Publishing Company, 10 Davis Drive,
Belmont, CA 94002, or electronically at *http://www.wadsworth.com/wadsworth.html.*

International Thomson Publishing Europe
Berkshire House 168-173
High Holborn
London, WC1V 7AA, England

International Thomson Editores
Campos Eliseos 385, Piso 7
Col. Polanco
11560 México D.F. México

Thomas Nelson Australia
102 Dodds Street
South Melbourne 3205
Victoria, Australia

International Thomson Publishing Asia
221 Henderson Road
#05-10 Henderson Building
Singapore 0315

Nelson Canada
1120 Birchmount Road
Scarborough, Ontario
Canada M1K 5G4

International Thomson Publishing Japan
Hirakawacho Kyowa Building, 3F
2-2-1 Hirakawacho
Chiyoda-ku, Tokyo 102, Japan

International Thomson Publishing GmbH
Königswinterer Strasse 418
53227 Bonn, Germany

International Thomson Publishing Southern Africa
Building 18, Constantia Park
240 Old Pretoria Road
Halfway House, 1685 South Africa

Library of Congress Cataloging-in-Publication Data

Sivulka, Juliann.
        Soap, sex, and cigarettes : a cultural history of American
    advertising / Juliann Sivulka.
            p.   cm.
        Includes bibliographical references (p.   ) and index.
        ISBN 0-534-51593-2
        1. Advertising — United States — History. 2. Advertising — Social
    aspects — United States. I. Title.
    HF5813.U6S55   1997
    659'.1'0973—dc21   96-51949

This book is printed on acid-free recycled paper.

To my parents, John and Julia Sivulka,

for their continued encouragement.

Brief Contents

Contents

Introduction

From the moment our clock radio awakens us in the morning, we are inundated with as many as three thousand commercial messages a day. Advertising is an inescapable part of modern life—on radio and television, in newspapers and magazines, on city streets and subways, and even on computer screens.

The "trade of advertising is now so near to perfection that it is not easy to propose any improvement" wrote Dr. Samuel Johnson in 1759. Astonishingly many of the ways yesterday's merchants tried to catch people's attention, convince them that what they were selling was desirable, and persuade them to purchase the products are still in use today. But advertising is not stagnant. It is constantly changing, even as our culture is ever changing. On the threshold of the millennium, some observers even predict that emerging technologies will dramatically alter not only our lives but also the very process of advertising. To understand where advertising might be headed, it is important to examine how advertising in America got to be what it is today.

This book presents a broad overview of how advertising both mirrors a society and creates a society. Modern advertising couldn't have developed without the printing presses, the Industrial Revolution, urbanization, and the rest of the tools of social organization and mass communication that evolved over the centuries. These forces eventually led to the emergence of advertising agencies a little more than a hundred years ago, further fueling the growth of advertising. As an element in consumer culture, social trends also altered people's buying habits, and advertising responded by altering its messages to reach the new audience.

In addition, advertising has provided a means by which people have learned about new products and, in the process, shaped mass behavior and desires—desires that are a driving force in a consumer economy. Advertising taught women ways to attract a husband and manage a home. Advertising also showed the pleasures of owning bicycles, cameras, and motorcars; of drinking beer and orange juice; and of smoking cigarettes. But advertising made its greatest contribution by showing how the endless stream of new inventions—toothbrushes, light bulbs, vacuum cleaners, refrigerators, washing machines, cars, computers—fit into ordinary people's lives.

A huge and powerful industry, advertising expenditures approached $150 billion in 1995 and continue to reach record levels every year. The biggest advertisers are the nation's manufacturers of automobiles, food, soft drinks, beer, and tobacco. Advertising expenditures pass through the six thousand or so advertising agencies that primarily create the ads and buy the space or time in the media. However, 57 percent of the domestic billings pass through the forty-six U.S.-based agencies that form global corporations with worldwide connections. Other smaller agencies have chosen to specialize in retailing, direct mail, and minority markets, among other services.

Advertising stands with TV, sports, movies, and music as an icon of American popular culture. Brand names of products have become so familiar that they are synonymous with similar products. For example, Kleenex could refer to any facial tissue, and Xerox describes all types of photocopying processes. Likewise, advertising slogans and jingles have been assimilated into our national lexicon; examples include Wendy's "Where's the beef?" and Alka-Seltzer's "I can't believe I ate the whole thing." Advertising collectibles also re-create the familiar image of immortal characters such as Tony the Tiger, Joe Camel, and the Pillsbury Doughboy. Items also popular with collectors include Absolut Vodka ads, Coca-Cola trays, and numerous other objects with a company's logo or trademark—store displays, statuettes, coffee mugs, squeeze toys, banks, radios, dolls, inflatables, and so on.

Yet few students and professionals in the trade can identify the major developments and figures in the history of American advertising. To fill this need, this book is aimed at undergraduate college students enrolled in marketing, journalism, advertising, communications, and popular culture courses, for which little survey material exists on the history of advertising. This book is designed to stand alone as a text on the history of advertising or to be used as a supplement in a survey course. It should also be required reading for any advertising professional. And the growing number of collectors who treasure old ads will find this history of interest.

The book is organized as follows. Chapter 1 gives a brief history of advertising, laying a foundation for a more detailed examination of the growth of advertising over the past century or so. Chapters 2 and 3 examine how the Industrial Revolution enabled manufacturers to produce an ever-increasing variety of products and to distribute and advertise through a variety of media, including newspapers, magazines, and direct mail. The Industrial Revolution also created a whole new generation of customers who previously had bought few things from a store. Chapters 4–6 explore how admakers refined their selling techniques to stimulate mass consumption. Chapters 7–9 carry the story through to the present day. In the last half of this century, a cornucopia of new products have flooded the marketplace, and the number of advertisements has increased proportionately. The book ends by tracing how the emergence of new technologies and the growth of international trade signal the end of one major epoch in American advertising history and the beginning of another.

Integrated throughout the chapters are examples of how advertising works, how it uses the skills of the creative artist and writer, and how it tries to get our attention and convince us to buy a product. Unfortunately, as of this writing, we were unable to obtain permission to reproduce ads for Absolut Vodka, Calvin Klein, Norwegian Cruise Lines, Marlboro, Virginia Slims, and Benson & Hedges cigarettes, as well as certain Coca-Cola ads. In any case, with this narrative outline in mind, let's take a look back at how advertising began in America.

Acknowledgments

A decade ago I began to write this book as a way of presenting material for a course on the history of American advertising. Along the way many individuals have provided helpful suggestions, references, and clippings, including Patricia Berns, Don Davidson, Michael D. Hamilton, John Heaphy, Mark Dixon, Lillian Hetherington, Tatsuko Martin, Dan Max, Deanne Berger-Moudgil, George Pouridas, Roxanne Farrar, Jan Morse Schroeder, Carrie A. Z. Smith, and my students. Thanks, as well, to Mel Warenback, who introduced me to the advertising profession, and to Mike Dattel, who first asked me to teach the subject. I am also deeply grateful to Leslie C. Kranz, whose ideas, critical insights, and suggestions were invaluable in preparing this book.

At Wadsworth, a special thanks to editor Todd Armstrong, who never lost enthusiasm for the project, Michael Gillespie, Melanie Field, Tom Briggs, Bob Kauser, as well as to the company's design and technical staff. Thank you, too, to the following for their insightful comments: Sharon S. Brock, The Ohio State University; Henry B. Hager, School of Journalism, University of Missouri; Nancy Mitchell, University of Nebraska–Lincoln; Barbara Mueller, San Diego State University; and Tommy V. Smith, University of Southern Mississippi.

Historical Overview

1492

The first printing press arrives in colonial America (at Harvard College).
1639

1704
The first regularly published newspaper in America appears, the *Boston News-Letter;* the third issue contains the first paid advertisement in the colonies.

America declares its independence from England.
1776
The first magazine advertisement appears in the May issue of Benjamin Franklin's *General Magazine.*
1741

1839
The first photographs appear, called "dagguereotypes."

1840
The first telegraph message is transmittd between two cities.

Chapter 1

1492–1880 The Beginnings

The Emancipation Proclamation frees the slaves.
1863

The Civil War divides the country.
1860–65

The first advertising agent in America, Volney Palmer, sells newspaper space in Philadelphia.
1843

The J. Walter Thompson and Lord & Thomas (later Foote Cone & Belding) advertising agencies open for business.
1871

The first federal trademark protection law is enacted, encouraging the use of heavily advertised commercial symbols.
1870

1867
Mathilde C. Weil starts working in advertising in New York and later opens her own agency, M. C. Weil.

1869
The railroad spans the continent from coast to coast.

1876
The Philadelphia Centennial Exhibition presents such wonders as the telephone, the light bulb, and the typewriter.

1880

Although advertising as we know it has its roots in the nineteenth century, advertising has been part of the American cultural landscape since it enticed European settlers to the New World. Ever since, this unique institution has played an ever larger role in our economy, helping to create a powerful new medium of information, entertainment, and selling that both mirrors a society and creates a society.

A modern world without advertising is unimaginable. Advertising has enabled people to learn about and to publicize products and services. An endless stream of ads and commercials pitches the wonders of microwavable foods, miracle cleaning agents, and soothing remedies. Ads give us hints on the latest trends in diet, fashion, gadgetry, electronic equipment, housing, automobiles, travel, and books. Looking for a job, an apartment, or a sale? Simply leaf through the newspaper or check the classified ads.

Yet the idea of advertising can be traced back to ancient times. Over the centuries technological and cultural changes have affected the evolution of American advertising—both the medium and the message. But the general purpose of advertising—to inform and to persuade—has not changed. By surveying the roots of modern advertising, we can establish a foundation for a more detailed examination of advertising over the past one hundred years.

Advertising in the Old World

For thousands of years tradespeople used public criers and pictorial signs to attract attention because few people could read. For example, in ancient Babylon, as in other lands, barkers enticed buyers with florid descriptions of cargoes such as wine, spices, rugs, and other wares from newly arrived ships. Like shopkeepers of later periods, early Egyptian, Greek, and Roman merchants hung carved signs and painted shop fronts, using symbols and pictures instead of words so that even illiterate passersby could identify the nature of the business. In medieval England customers could find the shoemaker by a golden boot, the baker by a sheaf of wheat, or the optician by a pair of spectacles. Advertisers also used hand-lettered flyers and posters to attract attention. And in the 1400s clergymen, lecturers, teachers, and other professionals promoted their services on tacked-up handbills—a practice similar to today's want ads.

If it plese ony man spirituel or temporel to bye ony pyes of two and thre comemoracios of Salisburi use enpryntid after the forme of this preset lettre whiche ben wel and truly correct, late hym come to Westmonester in to the almonestrye at the reed pale and he shal habe them good chepe ⁘

Supplico stet cedula.

Figure 1.1   In 1477 the first English-language ad appeared, promoting a prayer book.

The Impact of the Printing Press

The most important development in the history of advertising was the introduction of the printing press around the mid-1440s. In Germany Johannes Gutenberg perfected a system of printing with independent, movable type that could be used again and again to produce books and other printed matter. The first typographic book issued by Gutenberg, the Bible, set a high standard for later printers. Within fifty years presses were in operation all around Europe, replacing slow hand replication with more rapid, volume printing.

This extraordinary invention changed the way people worked and communicated. Before the invention of the printing press, only a few learned monks and scholars could read and write, and news traveled by word of mouth. However, "the word" seldom carried more than fifty or so miles, because dialects varied from region to region.[1] Printing provided a way to record facts and important information on documents so that people no longer had to rely on their memories. Many more people learned to read and write, and ideas spread quickly. The new technology also enabled the development of the first forms of advertising—printed handbills, posters, and trade cards—and the first mass medium—newspapers.

With printed advertising tradespeople and merchants could now reach thousands of potential customers far beyond their immediate neighborhoods. In 1477 William Caxton, a London printer, posted the first printed advertisement in English, a 3- by 5-inch handbill announcing his prayer book for sale (Figure 1.1). The church used printed material to spread its liturgy, solicit contributions, and recruit clergymen. Tradespeople handed illustrated shopbills out over the counter or door-to-door to prospective customers (Figure 1.2). And producers of medicinal remedies began to attach posterlike labels to their bottles, a forerunner of modern packaging.[2] Other printed communication also appeared in the form of official announcements, programs, menus, and guides to exhibitions, museums, churches, towns, and inns.

Figure 1.2   This eighteenth-century illustrated shopbill promoted a London scale maker.

The technology of printing also led to the dramatic development of newspapers and magazines, which carried advertisements into the surrounding community. Of the two print media, newspapers are the oldest.

From News-Letters to Newspapers

The first newspapers in the world appeared during the sixteenth century. Professional writers penned handwritten manuscripts, or "news-letters," for sale to noblemen or other exalted personages requiring news of the day. These letters eventually appeared irregularly in mass-produced, printed form. News periodicals printed on a regular basis later took the form of a pocket-size publication, called a "newsbook." In 1625 the first newspaper advertisement published in English appeared on the back page of a newsbook; it also promoted a book.[3] In subsequent editions advertisements appeared on the last page or sandwiched in among the news. To catch the reader's attention, news-book publishers headed these commercial announcements with the word *advertisement,* which was derived from the Middle English word *advertisen,* meaning "to notify."

Single sheets later replaced the book form, and by the early 1600s "newspapers" were available in many major European cities. In Italy the publications became known as "gazettas," from an old Venetian word for a certain coin (the price of the pamphlet)—hence the origin of the modern word *gazette.* In England the first officially recognized newspaper initially refused advertising, stating that the paid notices of books, medicine, and other such items were "not properly the business of a paper of intelligence."[4] The publication eventually carried text-only advertisements similar to today's want ads, but they appeared on a separate sheet. Over the course of the next century, advertising emerged as a major source of newspapers' revenue. This was also the period in which modern American advertising has its roots.

Selling the New World

The efforts by English entrepreneurs to attract new settlers to America was "one of the first concerted and sustained advertising campaigns in the history of the modern world," according to historian Richard Hofstadter.[5] Throughout the seventeenth and eighteenth centuries, enterprising Englishmen printed a variety of books, brochures, and posters to promote America to their countrymen.

Like their counterparts throughout history, the promoters spun fanciful tales that often tapped into the hopes and dreams of their listeners, but their stories were often far from reality. The English entrepreneurs lured potential colonists to the New World with promises of the good life: gold and silver, fountains of youth, abundant fish and game, productive land. Reports of earlier explorers also had portrayed the New World as a Garden of Eden—an idyllic place where food could be effortlessly plucked, where clothes and shelter were hardly needed, and where docile natives could be put to work and converted to Christianity. The idea of America as a land of staggering opportunity had an understandable appeal and fueled the early settlement of America.

One theme runs through all the promotions aimed at attracting investors and settlers—the promise of free land. Companies induced prospective colonists to sign up for the venture, offering land in exchange for labor or other services. To the millions of Englishmen who only rented their land, owning land was equated with wealth, income, a higher social position, and more rights. In one early promotion the Virginia Company published a pamphlet in London in 1609, offering an investment opportunity in its colonial enterprise. The title page headlined, "Nova Britannia. Offering most excellent fruites by planting in Virginia." The leaflet went on to offer stock options, housing, vegetable gardens, orchards, and clothing (Figure 1.3). In fact the Virginia Company's coastal town at Jamestown survived as the first American settlement, and it eventually flourished by growing tobacco.

Promoters also made special efforts to attract women to the colonies because as late as the mid-1600s in Virginia and Maryland, men outnumbered women by six to one. The Virginia Company provided one solution: any planter could buy a wife from the enterprise for 120 pounds of "the best leaf tobacco."[6] Another Carolina promoter used advertising to encourage women to make the New World their home. The company's leaflet explained how a woman might have a better life in America:

> *If any maids or single women desire to go over to Carolina, they will think themselves in the Golden Age, when men paid dowries for their wives, for if they are only civil and under fifty age, some honest man or other will purchase them for their wives.*[7]

Figure 1.3   In 1609 a pamphlet printed in London promoted the New World to prospective colonists.

From Colony to Nation

Once in the New World, the colonists struggled to survive in an environment that, while rich in natural resources, hardly lived up to its glossy billing. They made the first colonies viable, organized local governments, and adapted their Old World ways to the New World. By the 1750s about 1.3 million people populated a string of coastal settlements extending from Maine to Georgia.

Colonial Advertising

European colonists brought the idea of advertising with them to America, but the concept was slow to take hold. Colonists simply had little need to advertise their goods and services for sale over a wide area. They also found printing equipment and supplies to be both scarce and expensive in the New World. The English government licensed printing presses and restricted what the colonists could print in order to suppress any criticism of the government. Without printing presses to produce newspapers, news spread primarily through gossip or by the town criers. Every book or other printed matter had to come from Europe, and even then, few colonists could read. Despite these limitations the first printing press in America arrived in the Massachusetts Bay Colony (at Harvard College) in 1639. The sponsors planned to turn out mainly Puritan theology and some classical writings.

An enterprising few made a living by penning news-letters filled with information collected from a few foreign newspapers, incoming ships, travelers, and local residents. One such newswriter was Boston postmaster John Campbell, who in 1704 secured a license to publish the *Boston News-Letter,* the first regularly printed newspaper in America. It was a single sheet of paper (8 by 12 inches) printed on both sides.

The third issue of the *Boston News-Letter* carried the first known paid advertisement in America (Figure 1.4). Three announcements appeared on the back page of the *News-Letter* under the heading "Advertisements." Two of the notices offered a reward, one for some stolen goods and the other for the return of two anvils. The third offered something for sale, real estate:

> *At Oysterbay, on* Long Island *in the Province of* N. York, *There is a very good Fulling-Mill, to be Let or Sold, as also a Plantation, having on it a large new Brick house, and another good house by it for a Kitchin & workhouse, with a Barn, Stable & c. a young Orchard and 20 acres clear Land. The Mill is to be Let with or without the Plantation: Enquire of Mr.* William Bradford *Printer in* N. York, *and know further.*

As founder of the *Pennsylvania Gazette* in 1728, Benjamin Franklin became the first known American to use illustrations in newspapers ads. With its lucid writing, appealing typography, and pictorial details, the *Gazette* quickly became widely circulated. With its

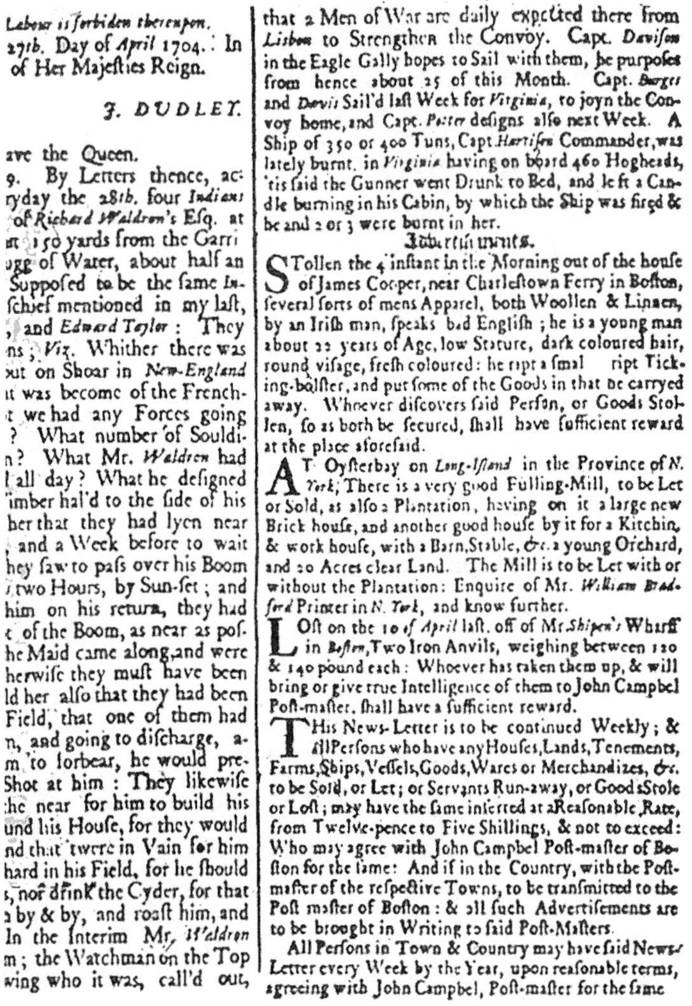

Labour is forbiden thereupon.
27th. Day of April 1704. : In
of Her Majesties Reign.

J. DUDLEY.

ave the Queen.
9. By Letters thence, ac-
ryday the 28th. four Indians
of Richard Waldron's Esq. at
at 150 yards from the Garri
ogg of Water, about half an
Suppofed to be the fame In-
fchief mentioned in my laft,
and Edward Tayler : They
ns ; Viz. Whither there was
ut on Shoar in New-England
it was become of the French-
t we had any Forces going
? What number of Souldi-
n? What Mr. Waldron had
all day? What he defigned
imber hal'd to the fide of his
her that they had lyen near
and a Week before to wait
hey faw to pafs over his Boom
two Hours, by Sun-fet ; and
him on his return, they had
t of the Boom, as near as pof-
he Maid came along, and were
herwife they muft have been
ld her alfo that they had been
Field, that one of them had
n, and going to difcharge, a-
m to forbear, he would pre-
Shot at him : They likewife
he near for him to build his
und his Houfe, for they would
nd that twere in Vain for him
hard in his Field, for he fhould
s, nor drink the Cyder, for that
a by & by, and roaft him, and
In the Interim Mr, Waldron
m ; the Watchman on the Top
wing who it was, call'd out,

that 2 Men of War are daily expected there from Lisbon to Strengthen the Convoy. Capt. Davison in the Eagle Gally hopes to Sail with them, he purposes from hence about 25 of this Month. Capt. Burges and Davis Sail'd laft Week for Virginia, to joyn the Convoy home, and Capt. Potter defigns alfo next Week. A Ship of 350 or 400 Tuns, Capt Harrison Commander, was lately burnt, in Virginia having on board 460 Hogheads, 'tis faid the Gunner went Drunk to Bed, and left a Candle burning in his Cabin, by which the Ship was fired & be and 2 or 3 were burnt in her.

Advertisements.
STollen the 4 inftant in the Morning out of the houfe of James Cooper, near Charleftown Ferry in Bofton, feveral forts of mens Apparel, both Woollen & Linnen, by an Irifh man, fpeaks bad English ; he is a young man about 22 years of Age, low Stature, dark coloured hair, round vifage, frefh coloured: he ript a fmal ript Ticking-bolfter, and put fome of the Goods in that he carryed away. Whoever difcovers faid Perfon, or Goods Stol-len, fo as both be fecured, fhall have fufficient reward at the place aforefaid.

AT Oyfterbay on Long-Ifland in the Province of N. York, There is a very good Fulling-Mill, to be Let or Sold, as alfo a Plantation, having on it a large new Brick houfe, and another good houfe by it for a Kitchin, & work houfe, with a Barn, Stable, &c. a young Orchard, and 20 Acres clear Land. The Mill is to be Let with or without the Plantation: Enquire of Mr. William Bradford Printer in N. York, and know further.

LOft on the 10 of April laft, off of Mr Shipen's Wharff in Bofton, Two Iron Anvils, weighing between 120 & 140 pound each: Whoever has taken them up, & will bring or give true Intelligence of them to John Campbel Poft-mafter, fhall have a fufficient reward.

THis News-Letter is to be continued Weekly ; & all Perfons who have any Houfes, Lands, Tenements, Farms, Ships, Veffels, Goods, Wares or Merchandizes, &c. to be Sold, or Let; or Servants Run-away, or Goods Stole or Loft ; may have the fame inferted at a Reafonable Rate, from Twelve-pence to Five Shillings, & not to exceed: Who may agree with John Campbel Poft-mafter of Bo-fton for the fame: And if in the Country, with the Poft-mafter of the refpective Towns, to be tranfmitted to the Poft mafter of Bofton : & all fuch Advertifements are to be brought in Writing to faid Poft-Mafters.

All Perfons in Town & Country may have faid News-Letter every Week by the Year, upon reafonable terms, agreeing with John Campbel, Poft-mafter for the fame.

First known ad in America

Figure 1.4 Detail from the third issue of the *Boston News-Letter,* published in 1704, the back page carried the first known ad in America.

large readership the *Gazette* attracted more advertising than any other colonial newspaper.

The pictorial details of Franklin's advertisements attracted a new class of advertisers, particularly in the retail field. To make the notices pleasing to the eye, Franklin separated each announcement with white space, centered large 14-point headlines over the copy, and added stock, 1-inch woodcut illustrations. For special customers he created custom engravings such as spectacles, a clock face, and occasionally an ornamental heading. The illustrations enabled readers to instantly identify the nature of the advertisements (Figure 1.5). Franklin also printed ads on the front page, in marked contrast to the common prac-

Figure 1.5 As this page from a 1760 issue of his *Pennsylvania Gazette* shows, Ben Franklin made ads readable by using large headlines and illustrations.

tice of starting notices in the last column of the back page. The paid announcements later appeared next to news matter on every page.

Franklin's *General Magazine* was the first magazine to be conceived in the colonies, but rival Andrew Bradford issued his *American Magazine* three days earlier. Although both periodicals were short-lived, the first magazine advertisement appeared in the May 1741 issue of Franklin's publication:

> *There is a Ferry kept over Potomack (by the Subscriber), being the Post Road, and much the nighest Way from Annapolis to Williamsburg, where all Gentlemen may depend upon a ready Passage in a good*

> *new Boat and able Hands. By Richard Brett, Deputy-*
> *Post Master at Potomack.*

Yet prior to the Industrial Revolution, businesses had little need to advertise to attract customers, and most people had little money to spend. Small family operations produced items in modest amounts and found buyers in the village marketplace. Most of the nation's households made a living from their farms, growing and making nearly everything they needed. If they sold their small surplus, the proceeds mostly went for coffee, salt, clothes, and tools. And workers earned little cash, because employers often provided room and board in exchange for labor, with perhaps a very small amount of money thrown in.

The majority of advertising centered on land, runaways (apprentices and slaves), and transportation; lost articles, books, and merchants' lists of goods accounted for the rest. These notices made simple announcements that answered two basic questions: Where? and When? (Has anyone got any flour? Will there be a stagecoach to Savannah? When is the ship arriving with the cargo of farm tools?)

Notices selling slaves also constituted a good percentage of these advertisements. Posters, flyers, and newspaper ads advertised slaves in the same way a merchant sold goods—as an inanimate article for sale. From the legalization of slavery in 1611 until its abolishment in 1863, traders kidnapped or purchased millions of Africans, packed them on ships, and transported them to the colonies. Slavery formed the foundation of the Southern economy, which plantation owners argued might collapse if they paid fair wages to the enslaved workers. Yet the practice of slavery "would not have been such an effective institution without the vehicle of advertising," according to Marilyn Kern-Foxworth.[8]

Advertising human merchandise involved a number of innovative techniques. Promoters marketed newly arrived cargoes of "fine, healthy Negroes" with eye-catching graphics, illustrations, "product" liability disclaimers, and descriptive copy (Figure 1.6). Traders often used red-hot branding irons to mark slaves' bodies so that each owner could easily distinguish his property. Advertisements offered "a lusty negro man-slave," "a likely young Negro wench," and a "good House-Negro who can do all manner of house work, and can knit and spin, said one of them is an extraordinary cook."

For runaways the ads generally emphasized any noticeable characteristics that could identify the slaves, the kind of work they performed, and other features of their lifestyle. The detailed descriptions increased the chances of capturing the runaway.

The Effect of Paper Shortages

By 1765 an estimated 2 million people lived in the colonies. This audience noticed almost anything in print, because cheap reading matter

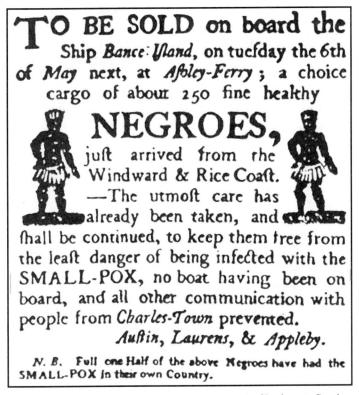

Figure 1.6 This 1765 ad promotes a slave auction in Charleston, South Carolina.

was still a rarity. A mere twenty-five publishers printed approximately 15,000 four-page weekly newspapers that had an even larger second-hand circulation. Colonists commonly read newspapers aloud in group gatherings. They gave primary attention to local news and to advertising rather than foreign events, because these matters affected their daily lives. They read and reread announcements about the arrivals of new shipments of tools, food, and drink.

The demand for news about the American Revolution enlarged newspaper circulation, which made the chronic paper shortage even more acute. At that time paper was made exclusively from rags. Yet the lack of papermaking rags made this type of paper hard to come by. People typically used the same fabric over and over, because the home production of cotton and linen involved laborious spinning and weaving. They used remnants to patch old clothing, to fashion quilts, and to braid rugs; but even then the rags took years to deteriorate before people sold them by the pound to printers. Despite editorial pleas for people to save their rags to make newsprint, the paper shortage often limited many major city newspapers to a mere 300–400 copies per day.[9] Others were forced to suspend publishing.

To solve the chronic paper shortage problem, publishers crammed more type into less space and restricted advertising (Figure 1.7). As many as seven or eight columns crowded a page, where before there had been three to five. Publishers also dropped rules between columns, shrank type sizes from the standard 12-point down to an almost illegible 6-point in both news and advertisements, and virtually eliminated white space. And advertisements were limited to abbreviated announcements of product lists, with an occasional exception such as a thumbnail-size illustration of a ship or stagecoach in transportation announcements.

Many advertisers responded by moving their creative announcements to posters called "broadsides," handbills, and trade cards. The broadsides typically were twice the size of a newspaper page, providing plenty of space to announce the arrival of new merchandise and to list merchants' products. Broadsides also proved a popular news medium. Publishers printed their message on single sheets and hired runners to distribute them throughout the city. Selling for a penny, the notices contained official declarations, political propaganda, dying confessions of convicted criminals, and even poetic verses.

Despite chronic paper shortages the United States boasted more newspapers than Great Britain by the early nineteenth century. Although publishers also attempted to put out a number of magazines, few were successful initially. The Industrial Revolution then changed both production economics, consumption patterns, and advertising.

The Impact of the Industrial Revolution

The Industrial Revolution, which began in England in the mid-1700s and reached North America in the early 1800s, affected both businesses and households. For the first time it cost people less to buy a product than to make it themselves, and customer demand was increasing. The introduction of steam power, interchangeable parts, assembly lines, and factories to the production process enabled manufacturers to turn out a stream of goods at both a low cost and uniform quality. Advertising provided American manufacturers with a way to stimulate demand for their output, and retailing provided new outlets for the ever increasing flow of goods.

Mass Production Spurs Economic Growth

By 1850 the economy was booming. A network of waterways, roads, and railroads opened new markets and reduced transportation costs dramatically. For example, between 1820 and 1860, the cost of shipping a ton of goods one mile dropped from 20 cents to a penny, and the goods arrived five to ten times faster. The railroads themselves became a big business, hauling lumber, coal, and farm goods to the growing consumer and industrial markets. And innovations like the steel

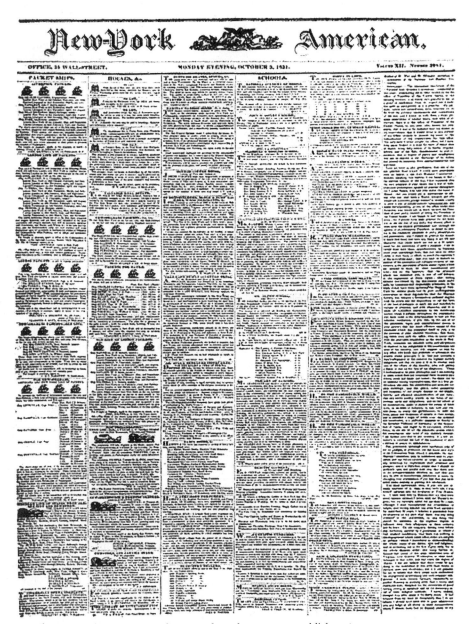

Figure 1.7 Chronic paper shortages forced newspaper publishers to cram as many as six columns of 6-point type onto a traditional 9- by 12-inch page.

plow and the horse-drawn reaper increased food production 400–500 percent by midcentury.

Farm and factory operations, railroad and telegraph construction, mining and lumber enterprises, and the building of towns all required heavy labor. But the swelling flood of immigrants did not begin

A Taste of the Times

The Victorian Era spanned the long reign of Victoria (1837–1901), queen of Great Britain and Ireland. During this period the opening of the American frontier and America's reaction to the rapidly emerging industrialized world had a profound effect on American culture. The economic prosperity of the 1820s and 1830s created an affluent urban class, which gladly supported the arts, architecture, museums, science, sports, and urban parks in the burgeoning cities.

Yet these Victorians yearned for the cultural trappings of bygone eras. This "romantic movement" inspired authors and artists to re-create the past—foreign in place, medieval in time, and Gothic in style. James Fenimore Cooper's *Last of the Mohicans,*

Henry Wadsworth Longfellow's *Song of Hiawatha,* and William Jennings Bryant's poetry reflected the sentiments of the period. Romanticized natural scenery and western grandeur became firmly established artistic themes. Architects revived medieval styles, designing Gothic cottages in natural settings that became affordable to middle-income families. Designers found inspiration in Owen Jones' popular *The Grammar of Ornament* (1856), which catalogued large color plates in classical, medieval, and renaissance styles. The overelaborated look also was reflected in extravagant new typefaces and cluttered graphics, influencing magazine covers, posters, and advertisements of the period.

Paris set the style for fashion. For the fashionable woman tightly laced corsets, puffed sleeves, ruffled bosoms, and voluminous

to fill the need for workers. The labor shortage steadily drew poor women and even children into factory work for the first time. Despite this social advance, however, women still could not vote, own property, sign a legal contract, earn equal pay, or spend their wages without getting permission from their husbands. In addition, many families expected young, unmarried women to contribute their earnings to the household.

The Far West also presented new opportunities. For example, in 1848 miners discovered gold in California. Once newspapers declared that there was "gold in them thar hills," tens of thousands of people rushed West seeking their fortune. This westward exodus, one of the greatest migrations in American history, completed the nation's expansion to the Pacific coast.

Despite the nation's remarkable industrial growth, 60 percent of America's labor force still made a living from agriculture. Small factories dominated manufacturing, employing on average about ten work-

The cluttered graphics of this 1884 ad reflected the influence of the overelaborate look of the Victorian era.

skirts further emphasized her curves. The resulting wasp-waisted silhouette embodied the Victorian ideal of the "feminine" woman—delicate, graceful, and helpless. As for the men, they favored "working-class" trousers, wore "long-john" underwear year round, and rarely left home without a vest and brown derby hat.

Romantic freedom, however, did not extend to contemporary standards of decorum. During this arch-conservative period prudery became a mark of refinement, because Victorians considered frankness about sex to be a sin against morality. Restrictive social conventions resulted in a proliferation of euphemisms: "limb" for leg, "white meat" for chicken breast, "white-sewings" for women's undergarments, and "deceased" or "departed" for dead. The mere mention of marital discord and divorce also remained taboo.

ers each. These factories initially focused simply on processing food products, rather than on the heavier, labor-intensive production of steel and iron. Amidst this surge of economic activity, America simply could not meet its own demand for heavy industrial products. Therefore the country continued to import many foreign manufactured goods.

The Civil War Fuels a Consumer Economy

The Civil War (1860–1865) advanced the advertising profession and dramatically changed manufacturing, giving rise to a consumer economy. The federal government launched the first national advertising campaign when it enlisted an advertising agent to help sell war bonds and promoted the issue in more than five thousand publications. Posters also recruited army volunteers (Figure 1.8). And wartime shortages and the demand for war news spurred innovations in

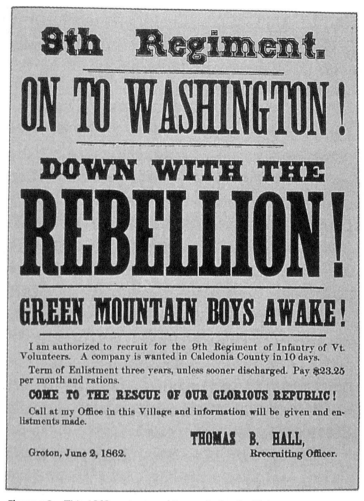

Figure 1.8   This 1862 poster sought recruits for the Union army.

publishing, including new methods of illustration, improved printing techniques, and advances in papermaking technology.

The Civil War also forced significant changes in manufacturing practices. Previously food and dry goods had been shipped, stored, and sold in bulk, self-serve style. With the onset of war, the need to feed hundreds of thousands of soldiers in sometimes remote locales led to innovations such as modern packaging and canning. The unavailability of cotton-cloth sacks spurred the creation of the familiar paper bag, which became a popular method of packaging retail goods. Although canning techniques to preserve goods had been developed in the early 1800s, consumer use lagged until a generation of soldiers became accustomed to eating canned vegetables and fruits and drinking canned condensed milk. The invention of the can opener removed another troublesome obstacle to the widespread use of processed foods. During the 1860s the sales of canned goods increased six-fold.[10]

The necessity to mass-produce thousands of uniforms, as well as underwear and shoes, also brought the labor-saving sewing machine into wider use. Although the sewing machine actually was invented in 1790 in Britain, New Yorker Isaac Merritt Singer refined the technology and offered the first reliable "family sewing machine" for home use in 1856. An early Singer cost $125, about one-fourth of an average family's annual income. To enable families to purchase his device, Singer created installment buying, selling the machine for $5 down and $3 a month. The sewing machine became the first heavily advertised machine made for the American home. And when Ebenezer Butterick introduced reusable clothing patterns for sew-at-home fashions in 1863, dressmakers were able to duplicate the fancy garments pictured in colorful fashion magazines for a fraction of the cost.

At the same time, ready-made clothing evolved into a big business. Beginning in the 1850s, the sewing machine enabled textile manufacturers to mass-produce clothing for a limited market. The Civil War had introduced many men to machine-made uniforms, and thereafter the industry found a more accepting public. Many men preferred the factory-made suit to the clothing made at home, and they bought more moderately priced men's shoes through the mail and from shoe stores than from cobblers. Apparel manufacturers relied heavily on newspaper and magazine advertisements to promote their latest fashions.

The Civil War also fueled the rise of a consumer economy. Prior to the war American families living on farms formed a tightly knit economic unit. Husbands, wives, and children lived and worked together. The women performed such important functions as preserving foods, spinning, sewing, making clothes, and processing ashes into soap. The men worked in the fields, managed the family's money, and made most of the purchases. And the children pitched in wherever they were needed—in the fields, the barnyards, and the home.

With the men gone to war, the women did a "man's" work in the fields and the factories. Now, instead of the men, it was the women with their wartime earnings who shopped in the stores and purchased goods from peddlers. With less time for household tasks, women bought clothing, canned goods, bakery items, and soap that they previously would have made themselves. In the process women became consumers, assuming responsibility for choosing what and how much to buy.

After the war this purchasing trend continued as many people left the farms to work in urban factories. As a result they came to rely less on their own production and more on the purchase of affordable, mass-produced goods. They simply could not match the variety, attractiveness, and particularly the prices of the goods produced by American manufacturers—from clothing and furniture to food and drink. For example, in 1790 people fashioned 80 percent of all clothing; a century later manufacturers produced 90 percent of men's and boys' clothing.[11]

The explosive growth of urban areas following the war also created new opportunities for women. The opening of department stores, the swelling school population, and the invention of the typewriter, telephone, and other business machines meant thousands of new jobs (Figure 1.9). Thus by 1870 one in every six paid workers was a woman, almost all young and unmarried—and with money to spend.[12]

Urbanization Changes the Face of Retailing

By 1840 Americans shopped in more than 55,000 stores, and retailers began to use advertising as a key selling tool. General stores sprang up as communities grew and the demand for goods increased. Usually located at the crossroads of a small rural town, the general store had a near monopoly in the community. On the farm a family could raise animals for meat, grow a variety of foods, and make furniture, clothing, soap, and shoes. Therefore the general store's customers not only supplied the goods it stocked but also bartered their surplus for other goods or services. The small, windowless stores crammed everything consumers needed under one roof: food, clothing, hardware, kitchenware, medicines, saddles, and so on. The scent of peppermint mingled with the aroma of pickles, crackers, molasses, and strong tobacco. The shopkeeper portioned out bulk food from open containers and sold it by weight.

City dwellers had other concerns. Their rising numbers created a constant demand for fresh food and other necessities that they no longer either made or grew themselves. However, self-service supermarkets with attractive, packaged merchandise on easy-to-reach shelves had yet to be invented. Therefore people depended on noisy, smelly, crowded, and sometimes filthy city markets. Urban groceries also lacked marked prices, so city shoppers had no real way of knowing what products cost from one week to the next. And perishable products lasted only a few days, because refrigerators did not become common until the 1920s. To preserve food supplies, kitchen "iceboxes" became as much a household necessity as the dining room table. The iceman became a common sight, delivering ice door-to-door six or seven days a week.

Urban food retailing evolved from city markets to specialty food stores as manufacturers began to mass-produce foodstuffs in the mid-1800s. In the larger cities a shopper might visit as many as a half dozen "specialty stores" to obtain basic foods: produce, dairy products, meat,

Figure 1.9 This 1875 ad for the typewriter helped pioneer larger newspaper advertisements that spanned two columns and more.

baked goods, tea, coffee, liquor, and candy. The shopper typically found goods placed behind a counter; a salesclerk searched the shelves or portioned out goods from open containers. These specialty stores established the foundations for today's self-service supermarkets.

Meanwhile a new breed of merchandisers brought the European idea of large retail shops—or "department stores"—to America. A. T. Stewart, R. H. Macy, and Lord & Taylor in New York, John Wanamaker in Philadelphia, and Marshall Field in Chicago set up department stores and tried to outdo one another, offering customers elegant surroundings, selection, and service. Previously the finer stores had kept their goods out of sight behind counters and displayed them only for the most serious customer. In these new, glossy showrooms any shopper could examine fine furniture, clothing, and dry goods; ask questions; and compare prices. To facilitate sales, the age-old practice of negotiation eventually gave way to a system of uniform, fixed prices.

Shopping became a grander experience. Grim treks through muddy streets in search of merchandise gave way to leisurely strolls downtown along sidewalks to shop in block-size establishments. "Window-shopping" became a new pastime. Enclosed, multitiered arcades followed, with space for shops, restaurants, doctors, and lawyers. At night people returned to these complexes to dine, listen to music, or attend assemblies. These enclosed arcades have since evolved into twentieth-century suburban shopping centers.

Department stores did not become major advertisers in America until a decade or so after the Civil War, when their size and sales increased. Macy's and Lord & Taylor pioneered store newspaper advertising that spanned three columns and even greater widths, but this practice remained rare in the 1870s (Figure 1.10). Such ads generally appeared when the stores made special announcements such as for a Christmas promotion. More typically, however, individual store advertisements expanded down the column rather than across adjoining columns. In 1879 the first full-page store advertisement appeared; yet ten more years passed until such ads ran with regularity.[13]

General Merchandisers Pass on Economies of Scale

The next big step in modern retailing came in 1879, when F. W. Woolworth opened his 5-cent store in Lancaster, Pennsylvania, offering a number of useful items at a low price. Woolworth defined his product line by how much things cost, not by category or potential purchaser. His store featured a welcoming interior similar to that of the department store; it was filled with glass display windows and cases that allowed the shopper to choose from tin cookware, sewing notions, and hundreds of other items. Pleasant clerks offered help, completed transactions, and placed purchases in bags. When Woolworth later added 10-cent items in the 1890s, he judiciously kept them in a different part of the store to avoid confusion. Woolworth's Five-and-Dime stores went up across the country.

Meanwhile in rural America mounting dissatisfaction with high prices and limited choices, coupled with the introduction of free delivery service, eventually led to the idea of shopping by mail. In 1872 Chicago-based Montgomery Ward began the first mass-marketed, general-merchandise catalog with $2,400 in capital and a flyer listing 163 items. Shoppers loved it. Montgomery Ward used the mail to advertise its wares and to receive orders; the railroads shipped the goods. Basic necessities often were hard to come by out in the country. Thus farm

Figure 1.10   These 1865 newspaper ads for Macy's and Lord & Taylor department stores were typical of the times.

folks eagerly awaited the arrival of the catalog, often known as the "wish book."

If Montgomery Ward was out of stock, the mail-order shopper would try Sears. Although Montgomery Ward resisted selling C.O.D. (cash on delivery), Sears built a retail empire on the practice and ran advertisements carrying the magic three-word message: "Send No Money," followed by the simple directions, "Cut out and return this ad." By the turn of the century, Sears, Roebuck and Co. and Montgomery Ward had both become trusted names in retailing.

The Communications Revolution

The Industrial Revolution brought technological advances that led to the greatest changes in communications since the introduction of the printing press. The invention of photography in 1839 and the ability to print detailed illustrations gave advertisers a new way of showcasing their products. Railways, postal routes, telegraphs, typewriters, and telephones speeded personal and business communication. Newspapers and magazines broadened circulation and reached into the urban areas and beyond to bring news and advertising to millions of people.

The age of mass communications had arrived. Society became more urbanized and industrialized, people were better educated, and life was faster paced. The combination of rising literacy and falling printing costs expanded the reading audience, which developed an insatiable appetite for written news and entertainment. This literate audience, concentrated in cities and larger towns, became the target of what we now call the mass media—newspapers, magazines, books, "dime" novels—and advertising.

Go West, Young Man

With the development of a nationwide railroad system in the post–Civil War era, the United States entered a period of spectacular economic growth. The rails made it possible to move raw materials from coast to coast swiftly and cheaply, thereby reducing manufacturing costs. The savings in turn enabled manufacturers to deliver lower-priced goods to distant markets. People could travel more quickly and easily, too. For instance, a trip from the East to Chicago or St. Louis took only 48 hours instead of two or three weeks. The Union Pacific and Central Pacific railroads were connected in 1869, and for the first time the railroad spanned the continent. Over the next several decades four more transcontinental lines quickly laid tracks to nearly complete America's railroad network. These developments also encouraged miners, cattle ranchers, and farmers to settle the West.

As with the New World several centuries before, promoters sold the West as offering opportunity, freedom, and above all, land. For example, the 1862 Homestead Act offered any person who applied 160 acres of public land free, requiring only that the individual live and farm on it for five years. By the end of the century, the U.S. government had given away 80 million acres under this legislation (Figure 1.11).[14] Other large landholders advertised to attract settlers, particularly the railroads. Having invested millions of dollars to build lines across the country, the railroads wanted to make sure that their investment returned a profit. Rail companies explored strategies to lure new customers, who would ship their farm goods via rail to market. These promoters widely circulated ads in the East and in Europe, offering various inducements to attract settlers such as land-exploring tickets, low prices, credit, and deferred payments. The following notice, which appeared in England in 1871, was typical. It promised a fast passage to and a good life in the American West:

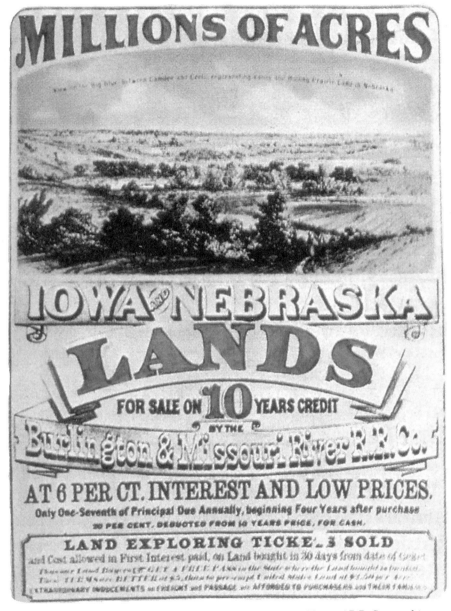

Figure 1.11 This 1873 ad sponsored by the Burlington & Missouri R.R. Co. sought to lure settlers to the West.

To the West, to the West, to the Land of the Free . . . Emigration to Iowa and Nebraska, U.S. . . . HOMES FOR ALL! More Farms than Farmers! More Landlords than Tenants! Work for all workers!

Print Media Timeline

c. mid-200s B.C.

The Chinese invent paper as we know it today; six centuries later they produce the earliest known printing.
A.D. 105

The Romans modify the Greek alphabet to give it the form we know today, changing the letter shapes and adding letters.
c. mid-200s B.C.

The first newspapers in the world appear in the form of handwritten manuscripts, or "news-letters"; eventually newspapers appear on a regular basis as mass-produced, pocket-size publications, called "newsbooks."
1500s

c. mid-1440s
Johannes Gutenberg perfects a system of movable type that can be used again and again to print the first typographic book, the Bible.

1704
The first regularly published newspaper in America appears, the *Boston News-Letter;* the third issue contains the first paid advertisement in the colonies.

The West's rapid settlement also created the need for a reliable mail service. In 1860 America's first rapid communication service to the Pacific region was established. The Pony Express Service, organized by the Central Overland California and Pike's Peak Express Service Company, offered a ten-day delivery time between Missouri and California, fifteen days faster than the two-year-old Overland Mail stagecoach line. Only the daring needed apply for a job with the Pony Express. "Wanted," read an 1860 newspaper advertisement, "Young, skinny, wiry fellows not over 18. Must be expert riders, willing to face death daily. Orphans preferred." The Pony Express ceased operations eighteen months later when telegraph lines connected the East and West. The new telegraph system also monitored movement of trains and traffic, enabling firms to communicate directly with their buying offices and suppliers. To make it easier to keep in touch, the U.S. Postal Service introduced the 1-cent postcard in 1873 and the 2-cent letter rate in 1883.

Extra, Extra, Read All about It!

The Industrial Revolution brought bigger and faster steam-powered presses, lithography, new methods of paper-making, and color reproduction techniques that made volume printing cost-effective by the mid-1800s. At the same time, the country's burgeoning population, booming economy, and western expansion created a demand for news about business, travel, entertainment, and the availability of goods and services. This led many newspaper publishers to consider advertisements as a vital source of revenue; some even included "Advertiser" in the paper's name. The combined income from advertising

Benjamin Franklin conceives the *General Magazine,* but rival Andrew Bradford issues the *American Magazine* three days earlier; the May issue of Franklin's periodical carries the first magazine advertisement.
1741

Magazines emerge a major force in the American media landscape.
1880s
Congress creates special, low postage rates for magazines, the better to increase their national distribution.
1879

USA Today is introduced as a full-color, national newspaper.
1982

1833
The New York Sun, a "penny paper," sells for 1 cent as opposed to the more common 5 or 6 cents; advertising subsidizes the paper's subscription revenue.

1883
Joseph Pulitzer starts the *New York World,* basing ad rates on circulation figures.

1990

and subscriptions could support a paper whose circulation ran a mere 300–400 copies in business.

The typical newspaper page looked much the way our present-day want ads or legal announcements do, with little white space and few illustrations to separate the ads from the text. In 1827 a typical newspaper cost $10 a year (or 6 cents a copy), and advertisers could buy almost any number of lines daily for a flat rate of $32 a year.

A key development in the newspaper world was the introduction of the "penny paper." In 1833 former publisher and printer Benjamin Day issued *The New York Sun,* which cost only 1 cent as opposed to the more common 5 or 6 cents. At this low price Day planned to sell a lot of advertising to subsidize the paper's operation. The paper measured 9 by 12 inches, about one-third the width of other papers of that era. The *Sun* also had a flat advertising rate of $30 a year, like its contemporaries, but instead of selling unlimited space, the paper sold only square, one-column-wide, ten-line units that ran daily. This lively paper did not carry the usual political articles and editorials. Rather, it printed "human interest" stories, sensational crime and horror accounts, and humorous police-court items. Other penny papers soon hit the streets.

These publications had one thing in common. Instead of targeting "elite" Americans, they reached a new class of reader—the common man. However, most were short-lived, except for the *New York Herald,* which James Gordon Bennett started in 1835. While the *Sun* and *Herald* appeared similar in size and price, they differed in content. Bennett's penny paper presented news of foreign affairs, politics, business, high society, sports, and theatrical events. Unlike other newspapers of the time, Bennett did not offer advertisers unlimited space; he sold space by the square unit and charged a daily rate. An advertiser could buy space for 50 cents a day or $2.50 for two weeks (two-days' pay for a working man), but the ad copy could run no longer than two weeks to keep the announcements fresh. Bennett also boldly banned all display advertising in 1847, stating it was unfair to the daily small-space advertisers. Other papers soon followed suit.

By 1850 illustrations had almost disappeared from penny papers although the 6-cent papers occasionally used thumbnail-size engravings. To overcome this limitation, creative advertisers like Richard Bonner maneuvered around the stringent restrictions. Bonner had demonstrated skill in typography as a compositor that brought him work from several small publications when he opened a shop of his own. In 1851 Bonner bought one of these sheets, the *Merchants Ledger,* and turned it into a family paper, changing the name to the *New York Ledger.* Bonner aggressively promoted his publication and sought ways around the stringent newspaper ad rules. Drawing inspiration from the repeated phrases that appeared in London newspaper ads, Bonner submitted ninety-three identical advertisements in the want-ad style accepted by the *New York Herald,* filling a column in an 1856 issue by repeating this announcement:

> *ORION, THE GOLD BEATER is the title of Cobb's sensational story in the New York Ledger.*

Anybody who read the *New York Herald* that day could not miss the *Ledger* ad. Next Bonner filled two columns with his ads. Eventually he ran full-page ads that repeated a single message six hundred times, such as "See the New York Ledger with Cobb's new story" or "Don't go home tonight without the New York Ledger." From then on, Bonner invested heavily in newspaper advertising to promote his publication, yet he adamantly refused any paid notices in his own periodical. The *Ledger* became the first weekly publication to reach a national circulation of 400,000.

Bonner's huge expenditures and display methods immediately affected advertising practices. The success of Bonner's repetitive style also led to a variety of "type tricks." Advertisers attracted attention by cleverly using white space and built-up type to form novel images. For example, Brady's Gallery formed the tiny type into three 1-inch numerals, which represented the gallery's street address on Fifth Avenue (Figure 1.12). Another store ran its holiday message in the shape of a Christmas tree. Readers may have found such advertisements hard to read, but the ads did attract attention. Other advertisers, who sold the same kind of goods over and over, simply reminded readers of their existence using slogans and catch phrases to fill a line of type. The repeated line made the copy block look different from the adjacent announcements, starting the idea of ad slogans such as "Use Sapolio" and "Eat H-O," later seen across the country (Figure 1.13).

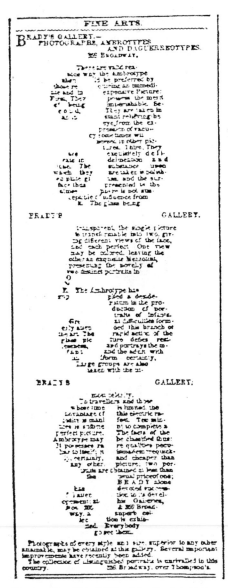

Figure 1.12 This 1856 ad for Brady's Gallery used built-up type images to get around the stringent "agate-and-no-display" rule.

By the late 1860s publishers recognized that retailers and other advertisers were willing to spend a lot of money to attract attention and eventually gave them greater freedom. When Bonner's repetitive style became too common and no longer "pulled," advertisers knew they had to try something different. The promoters of sewing machines and typewriters became the first to picture their products in large newspaper ads; these were also the most heavily advertised machines of the era. However, full-page newspaper advertisements did not become common until the end of the century.

Two other New York publishers, Joseph Pulitzer and William Randolph Hearst, also encouraged advertising. Pulitzer, "a friend to advertisers," wisely recognized the importance of advertising revenue when he started the *New York World* in 1883. His paper, the first to base ad rates on circulation figures, sold advertising space at extremely low prices and encouraged display ads. Pulitzer also illustrated the *World,* made the copy easier to read, and introduced light features for the less serious-minded. Like Pulitzer, Hearst also recognized the commercial possibilities of journalism. Soon after Hearst purchased the *New York Morning Journal* in 1895, he added the Sunday comics section, moved the funny strips into the dailies, and included sensational illustrated news stories sure to boost circulation. Both Hearst and Pulitzer also reported on sporting events every day to appeal to men, offered women's features, and built up department store advertising to attract the female reader.

These and other newspapers gradually converted millions of people to the daily reading habit and brought advertisers' messages into many more homes.

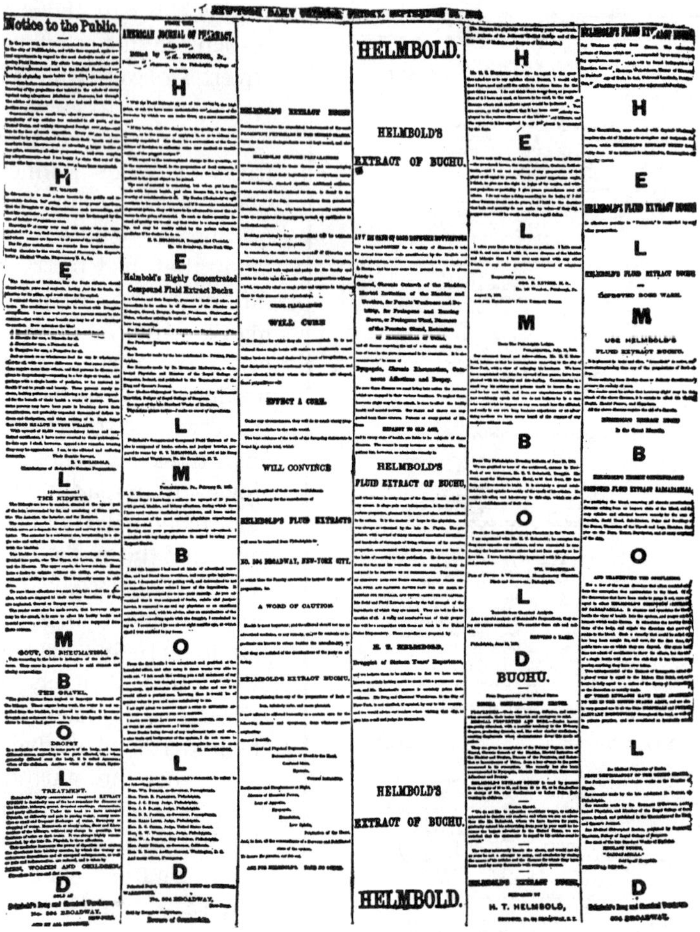
Notice to the Public.

HELMBOLD.

H

HELMBOLD'S

EXTRACT OF BUCHU.

E

L

WILL CURE

M

EFFECT A CURE.

B

WILL CONVINCE

HELMBOLD'S

FLUID EXTRACT OF BUCHU,

O

A WORD OF CAUTION

L

BUCHU.

D

HELMBOLD'S

EXTRACT OF BUCHU.

HELMBOLD.

H. T. HELMBOLD,

Figure 1.13 Dr. H. T. Hembold creatively promoted his patent medicine with this 1865 full-page newpaper ad that repeated the name of the product.

Advertising Gets Creative

Interest in other forms of advertising also developed, due in part to the newspaper's strict limitations. Creative display advertising appeared in the form of posters, handbills, trade cards, pamphlets, and outdoor signs. Promoters posted notices at taverns and other gathering places. Handbills and broadsides advertised theaters, museums, patent medicines, clothing stores, and auctions. Advertisers painted notices on walls and on the sides of barns. The walking billboard, or "sandwich man," became a common sight. Horse-drawn wagons carrying advertisements paraded along downtown streets, and announcements later appeared on rail cars.

Advances in pictorial printing also added realism and spurred a new wave of creativity. Before the introduction of photography in

P. T. Barnum: The First Great Adman

P. T. Barnum.

New York showman P. T. Barnum (1810–1891) set out to attract public attention and ended up as the first advertising genius. Barnum harnessed the power of virtually every form of media and grouped them under one word—advertising. Posters, handbills, newspapers, dramatic illustrated signs, brass bands, parades, stunts—Barnum used them all to promote his shows. "I owe all my success," Barnum confessed in his autobiography, "to printers' ink."

Barnum's rousing posters and startling newspaper headlines lured the public with such curiosities as a 161-year-old slave who had been present at George Washington's birth and had been "first to clothe the unconscious infant" (in truth she was no more than 80 years old); a "Real Mermaid!" (actually a monkey's head joined to the body of a large fish); and the midget "General Tom Thumb . . . but one foot and ten inches high" (in fact a 5-year-old boy who had stopped growing at a few months of age). Barnum also promoted Jumbo the Elephant, the Siamese Twins, the Missing Link, and other "natural" oddities. In effect Barnum owed his success to his ability to excite the common man.

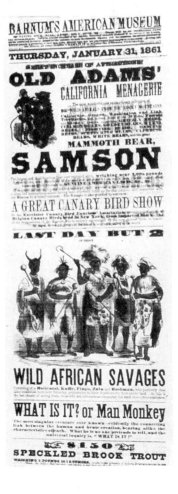

Figure 1.14   This 1884 trade card by the Domestic Sewing Machine Company used chromolithography to achieve realistic images.

1839, woodcuts or metal engravings reproduced illustrations. After 1860 chromolithography, or "chromos," quickly became the dominant printing medium to achieve convincingly real images. Most chromos were gaudy and short-lived, what collectors today call "paper ephemera," but people displayed the treasured pieces of this art in albums. Chromos appeared in such forms as Christmas and Valentine's Day cards, book markers, paper dolls, and linings for suitcases and trunks.

Yet it was the advertising industry's commercial application, more than anything else, that pushed printers to use chromolithography to print striking designs, bright colors, and innovative forms (Figure 1.14). In the 1870s printers began to run large quantities of the vibrant cards with a blank area to imprint the client's advertising message. Often picture calendars and posters looked appealing enough to put up on the kitchen wall or to frame for the parlor. Images of the home with women and children proved especially popular. Tobacco companies circled individual cigars with colorful labels and lined boxes with elaborate and colorful art. The popularity of chromos declined around the turn of the century, however, as advertisers turned to popular illustrated magazines and expanded their use of photographic reproduction.

The Modern Magazine Debuts

Unlike newspapers, magazines made most of their money from subscriptions and did not accept paid notices until the 1870s. These publishers depended on their subscribers who, being refined or aspiring to be so, regarded publicity as vulgar and dismissed most product advertising as a sham. And for the most part it was.

A few quality monthly magazines enjoyed moderate success without advertising. For the news people read *Harper's Weekly* and *Frank Leslie's Illustrated Weekly*. The picture-filled *Graham's Magazine* offered entertaining literature, detailed illustrations, and popular fashion plates. And for women *Godey's Lady's Book* and *Peterson's* featured articles on dressmaking and housekeeping and included lavish hand-colored fashion plates that promoted the season's latest collections. The rest of the literary magazines started as promotional vehicles for book publishers. In 1850 *Harper's New Monthly* began to publish serialized fiction accompanied by numerous woodcut illustrations, and *The Atlantic Monthly* came along in 1857. These magazines contained no advertising other than a list of forthcoming book titles.

Patent medicine manufacturers looked greedily on the magazines' national audience, but the better publications turned up their noses at the advertising revenue. One enterprising bottler, F. G. Kinsman of Augusta, Maine, decided to start his own magazine, a religious periodical that also served as an advertising vehicle to promote his patent medicine. Kinsman supplied different church denominations with individualized inspirational Sunday school journals—all of which carried patent medicines discreetly advertised in the back of the publication. This venture proved to be extraordinarily profitable for Kinsman, as well as for other agents, such as F. Wayland Ayer and William J. Carlton, who began to specialize in religious advertising. By 1870 advertisers promoted products in some four hundred monthly periodicals and more than four thousand secular weeklies with a circulation of approximately 15 million copies each week.[15]

Many literary periodicals that initially had refused to sell advertising space began to accept paid announcements around 1870. Yet most magazines still restricted advertising to special sections at the front or back of the issues so that readers would not confuse ads with the editorial matter. Even after *The Atlantic* and *Harper's* consented to carry ads for something other than their own books, the volume remained small—perhaps five to twenty advertisements covering two or three pages. The magazine *Century*, however, broke away from this high-brow tradition and actively sought advertisers by offering moderate rates.

Youth's Companion began as a Sunday school magazine in 1827 and later moved advertising from the era of space peddling into the beginnings of a service business—planning, creating, and executing ad campaigns. Although the magazine was intended for family reading, its

Figure 1.15   This ad in the magazine *Youth's Companion* featured art and design far ahead of its time.

in-house copy-planning department sold full-page advertisements, complete with text and illustrations, to manufacturers who previously had used less space or had not advertised at all. The high-quality art and design of these ads were far ahead of their time (Figure 1.15).

In the following decades magazines enabled manufacturers to sell their products nationwide. For example, *The Delineator* (1873) pictured sew-at-home fashions made with Butterick patterns, and competitor *McCall's* (1876) also started as an advertising vehicle. The *People's Literary Companion* later pushed soap powder by mail. Other popular periodicals also started as advertising vehicles to subsidize subscription revenues.

The Advertising Agent: A New Occupation

Advertising as a "profession" did not exist until the mid-1800s. There were no copywriters, art directors, account executives, or marketing professionals. As long as advertising was aimed only at local readers, advertisers had little need for outside assistance and dealt directly with newspapers.

With improved methods of transportation, manufacturers distributed their goods over wider areas and thus required sales promotions that reached beyond their local region. Advertisers often found that the media arrangements needed to print their announcements involved a myriad of details and time-consuming tasks. These included identifying effective newspapers, negotiating rates, directing the printer, confirming the insertion, and sending in payment. To fill this need, newspapers began paying agents to sell space to advertisers and thereby gave birth an entirely new business, the advertising agency.

The earliest known advertising agent in America was Volney B. Palmer, who set up shop in Philadelphia in the early 1840s. Palmer called himself an "agent for country newspapers." He worked for the newspapers that he represented and also acted as an agent for the advertisers. When he persuaded a firm to buy advertising space, he passed along the copy that he received, and the newspapers paid him a part of the revenue (usually 25 percent). Following in Palmer's footsteps, a number of agents operated as authorized representatives for the newspapers. By the beginning of the Civil War, there were about thirty such agencies, with more than half located in New York.

Among these advertising agents, John L. Hooper, George P. Rowell, and F. Wayland Ayer did things a little differently. Hooper started business in the 1840s and bought advertising space cheaply from newspapers and then resold it at a profit to advertisers. When George P. Rowell opened a Boston office in 1865, he followed Hooper's example and wholesaled newspaper space, but he standardized his commission at 25 percent. He also agreed to pay cash to any publisher who gave an additional 5 percent discount for large orders of space, which he bought at a substantially lower price. He then divided the space into smaller units and resold them at a higher price—yet still a considerably lower price than what advertisers could obtain elsewhere. Rowell's approach proved an immediate success. He earned a handsome profit, while advertisers benefited from his shrewd bargaining. Today, U.S. agencies still follow this practice of paying the media for space and time and then billing the advertisers.

Rowell later moved on to New York and published the *American Newspaper Directory,* providing agencies and advertisers with the first sound basis for estimating a fair value for media space. The directory listed more than five thousand newspapers in the United States and rated the accuracy of the circulation estimates. A number of agents criticized Rowell's efforts, because the directory devalued their own tabulations of paper locations and circulations. But Rowell outraged the newspapers even more. Previously newspaper publishers had tended to inflate circulation numbers up to five times more than the actual figure to justify their high advertising rates. Rowell's directory now forced many papers to reform their deceptive reporting practices. In addition, Rowell distributed information on how to use the directory and how to advertise effectively to advertisers and newspaper publishers.

Francis W. Ayer started his New York agency, N. W. Ayer & Son, in 1869. Although Ayer adopted Rowell's basic approach, he added another strong selling point—the "open contract." Other agents had kept advertising rates strictly confidential so that the customer never knew the net publication prices. Ayer, however, fixed his commission at 15 percent, giving the advertiser the benefit of both all discounts and his own shrewd bargaining.

The field of advertising also expanded when agencies started directing the artistic side of print advertising, specifying type styles and creating artwork for ads. In the 1850s New York–based S. M. Pettengill, who learned the trade from Palmer, added another service to his agency when he offered to write ad copy. This practice soon evolved into an important function of the advertising agency.

At the same time, the manpower shortages caused by the Civil War created opportunities for women in advertising, but these professions closed up around the turn of the century. For example, in 1867 Mathilde C. Weil started working in advertising in New York; she later opened her own M. C. Weil agency. Mary Compton placed ads for a drug account, Vapo-Cresline, beginning in 1870. A woman managed advertising for Peruna, one of the largest patent medicines, and another drug company, Swamp Root, employed a woman as a space buyer. And in the 1890s a number of women operated agencies, edited trade journals, wrote campaigns, illustrated jingles, and prepared ads. In particular, women trained as stenographers and "type writers" had found themselves in demand in the business world in the decades following the Civil War. By 1900 women accounted for about three-quarters of office workers, which inevitably sparked a backlash. According to Nancy Woloch, "Male critics charged in the press that business work imperiled femininity and disqualified women for marriage and motherhood." Critics also asserted that "women were incapable of office work. They were flighty, temperamental, and unsystematic."[16]

Puffery and Patent Medicines

Between the end of the Civil War and the beginning of the twentieth century, advertisements for dubious health remedies, get-rich-quick schemes, and other outrageous fakery filled the pages of newspapers and magazines. The ad copy, commonly called "puffing," had virtually no limits to the claims it made to stimulate demand for often worthless merchandise.

Although critics blasted the ethics of these advertisers, their extraordinary success demonstrated the possibilities of selling through various media. In particular patent medicine manufacturers pioneered new techniques for advertising brand-name, packaged goods. They also established the foundations for today's multimillion-dollar health

New Brand Names

1796 Old Grand-Dad, a Kentucky distiller named Basil Hayden Sr. fills his first barrel of bourbon whiskey.

1801 Crane & Company manufactures fine stationery and currency paper for the U.S. government.

1822 William Underwood preserves fruits and condiments; later he cans deviled ham.

1834 Cyrus McCormick patents his grain-reaping machine.

1835 Samuel Colt patents a handgun that fires up to six shots in rapid succession, with no need to reload after each shot.

1837 Harley T. Procter and James Gamble begin shipping soap and candles from Cincinnati to cities along the Mississippi River.

1839 Charles Goodyear accidentally discovers a new way to treat rubber and patents some five hundred uses for "vulcanized" rubber.

1842 Stephen F. Whitman markets chocolate in Philadelphia, and Gail Borden sells condensed milk from a pushcart in New York City.

1847 James Smith's cough drops soothe sore throats.

1853 Levi Strauss sells pants made of the durable cloth known in France as "genes."

1858 John L. Mason's jar uses a rubber seal and a screw top to preserve food for long periods of time.

1865 John B. Stetson designs a big, wide-brimmed hat for life on the western plains.

1868 Charles Fleischmann's standardized yeast makes baking easier.

1869 Joseph Campbell cans vegetables, condiments, jellies, and, later, soups.

1869 Henry J. Heinz bottles horseradish, the first of "57 varieties"; eventually Heinz puts out more than three thousand different products.

1870 Charles E. Hires combines dried roots and herbs to make a home-brewed "root beer" drink.

1873 Adolph Coors brews beer with "pure Rocky Mountain springwater" in his Golden, Colorado, plant.

1874 Joseph Schlitz adopts the Schlitz name for his beer, first brewed in Milwaukee.

1876 Anheuser-Busch brewery in St. Louis creates Budweiser, "The King of Beers."

industry with their promotion of over-the-counter medicines, mail-order remedies, and "cure-all" aspirins.

Patent medicine advertising was a centuries-old tradition in England, where the medicines had already become the leading advertised product in the mid-1800s. The "patent" referred to the fact that the Crown had granted a "patent of royal favor" to purveyors of certain remedies sold in the mid-1700s; these bottles carried the patent or crest of the king. The remedies contained ingredients alleged to treat specific ailments or cure a wide variety of illnesses. Often intoxicating, many did not do one's health any good.

Advertisers, evangelists, peddlers, quacks, and respected doctors and druggists all stimulated demand for patent medicines, pitching promises of "instant relief." With the colonization of North America, settlers often were far removed from physicians; the English responded by shipping medicines to the settlements. Immediately before the Civil War patent medicine advertisements accounted for more than half the advertising lineage in many papers, and annual sales totaled about $3.5 million. The remedies became tremendously popular after the Civil War. Sales soared to $75 million annually by the turn of the century and accounted for one-third of American publishers' revenues.

Several factors accounted for this explosive growth of patent medicines. During the Civil War army doctors routinely treated wounded soldiers with doses of highly addictive compounds. While some were harmless old folk cures, the more successful ones contained 20–40 percent alcohol, as well as roots, herbs, cocaine, opium, and morphine. After the war the men continued their use (or addiction). Inadequate diets, high rates of disease, and hordes of new settlers who pushed westward into doctorless territories also fueled the demand for these medicines.

Many newspapers and magazines did not want to sully their pages with such lurid advertisements. Their strict policies forced many medicine-makers to search for other ways to promote their products. Thus bottlers poured their profits into printed announcements, bill postings, and outdoor coverage. Painted messages, a conspicuous feature of early American advertising, appeared on barns, fences, and even rocks, particularly where trains passed—sites that conventional advertising had yet to utilize. Promoters even offered to give farmers' barns a much-needed coat of paint; when this inducement was not enough, they offered money and/or free samples. Enterprising Dr. Helmbold, Plantation Bitters, and St. Jacob's in particular set a pace for outdoor coverage unequaled by other advertisers.

Other bottlers believed that an easily remembered name ensured success. Thus Radway's Ready Relief, Cascaret's Candy Catharic, and dozens of others vied for attention and sales. Powerful suggestions and an aura of mystery also were effective promotional devices. An outstanding example is Dr. J. H. Drake's Plantation Bitters, which conspicuously bore the mysterious, scientific-sounding "S. T. 1860 X." Dr. Drake asserted that the slogan had no meaning and served only as a device to arouse curiosity. Another theory was that the phrase stood for "Started Trade in 1860 with $10." Advertising agent George P. Rowell suggested an even more interesting solution to the puzzle: Dr. Drake simply rebottled Santa Cruz rum so that the "1860" actually substituted for "CROI." Thus the phrase translated as St. Croix, referring to a site in the Caribbean. In any case Drake aroused people's curiosity and stimulated sales.

Other medicine makers knew how to tell a good product story. Some companies professed to know the secret wisdom of Native American medicine men. For example, Dr. H. T. Helmbold, responsible for the remedy Extract of Buchu, tapped into the primitive and the exotic with illustrations of the "Hottentot" Indians gathering buchu leaves in the Cape of Good Hope in South Africa. The powerful images made Helmbold a household word (Figure 1.16). Other sales campaigns revolved around full-scale medicine shows. One such peddling performance introduced a high-profile product known as Kickapoo Indian Sagwa. Before the extravaganza the targeted town was plastered with broadsides that promoted a not-to-be-missed encounter with savagery and adventure. These shows proved particularly popular in the East, where encounters with Native Americans were a rarity. Still other medicine-makers used sensational "news"-type headlines in their advertising, a common practice in the 1880s. A Safe Cure advertisement, for example, headlined, "Drops 'Dead' in the Street," followed by a chronicle of how a dose of the medicine revived a fallen man from the dead.

Lydia Pinkham's Vegetable Compound became one of advertising's first widely publicized success stories. On her kitchen stove in Lynn, Massachusetts, Quaker housewife Lydia Pinkham brewed a folk remedy for "female complaints," a mixture of roots and alcohol. For years she shared it just with her friends. In the hard times after the 1873 depression, however, her sons Dan and Will persuaded her to bottle the remedy for sale and promote it in a pamphlet. Sales took off when the family decided to include Lydia's face in the advertisments (Figure 1.17). The ads stressed that "woman can sympathize with woman"; the copy assured the reader that the compound was "pleasant to the taste, effective, and immediate in its effect"—that is, a sure cure for everything from female weakness to painful menstrual problems to a prolapsed uterus. Pinkham also urged ailing women to write her for answers about their most intimate health problems, suggesting that men just didn't understand. Orders and letters poured in, and the best responses subsequently appeared as testimonials in the ads. These personal statements proved a potent device to build reader's confidence.

Figure 1.16 Enterprising Dr. Helmbold tapped into the primitive and the exotic to promote his patent medicine.

WOMAN CAN SYMPATHIZE WITH WOMAN.

HEALTH OF WOMAN IS THE HOPE OF THE RACE

Yours for Health—

Lydia E. Pinkham

LYDIA E. PINKHAM'S
VEGETABLE COMPOUND.

A Sure Cure for all FEMALE WEAK-
NESSES, Including Leucorrhœa, Ir-
regular and Painful Menstruation,
Inflammation and Ulceration of
the Womb, Flooding, PRO-
LAPSUS UTERI, &c.

Figure 1.17 When Lydia Pinkham's image began to appear in the ads in the 1880s, sales of her home remedy skyrocketed.

Although Pinkham died in 1883, her famous face continued to appear in newspapers and magazines, on billboards, and in streetcar ads. In 1890, however, the Pinkhams slashed advertising expenditures, and annual sales tumbled by nearly 80 percent. In response the family resumed heavy advertising over the next decade and succeeded in increasing their annual sales by 2500 percent.[17] The campaign effectively demonstrated to businesspeople a simple principle: It pays to advertise.

By the dawn of the twentieth century, advertising had become a social and economic fixture in the United States, despite its lingering dubious reputation. The next chapter focuses on the evolution of American advertising around the turn of the century.

Early American Advertising

(my mama used Wool Soap)   (I wish mine had)
WOOLENS will not shrink if
WOOL SOAP
is used in the laundry

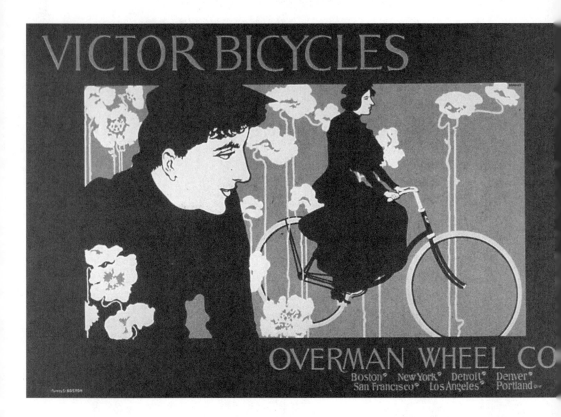

VICTOR BICYCLES

OVERMAN WHEEL CO
Boston° New York° Detroit° Denver°
San Francisco° Los Angeles° Portland°

1880

Wabash, Indiana, is the first city to use electric streetlights, and Cleveland, Ohio, runs the first electric streetcars; a year later, Edison turns on the lights in New York City.
1880

The half-tone screen process makes picture printing practical for magazines and for general use by advertisers in the 1890s.
1885

1884
Chicago's ten-story wonder, John W. Root's Montrauk building, is the first "skyscraper."

1890
The population of the United States reaches 63 million.

Chapter 2

1880–1900 Selling the Goods

George Batten starts his
advertising agency, initially known
as George Batten Co. and later as
BBDO (Barton, Batten, Durstine,
Osborne).
1891

The first moving picture, Thomas
Edison's "The Sneeze," is shown.
1894

1893
Advertising agent Charles Austin
Bates opens the Bates agency.

Chicago's Columbia Exposition
exhibits telephones and electric
power.

Frank Duryea drives the first
working automobile on the streets
of Springfield, Massachusetts.

The first full-page color
advertisement appears in the
American periodical *Youth's
Companion.*

1896
Guglielmo Marconi sends the first
wireless message across America.

The federal government
inaugurates rural free delivery,
boosting direct and mail-order
selling.

1900

By the 1880s a number of manufacturers had realized unprecedented scales of economy, expanded distribution, and reached for coast-to-coast markets. Dramatic changes accompanied the enormous economic growth. For example, coal replaced wood as the major source of energy. Mechanized reapers, sewing machines, and other new machinery replaced older tools and enabled new production processes. Factories increased in size, and raw materials flowed in and finished products flowed out at a faster rate and lower cost than ever before. Entirely new inventions appeared, such as the light bulb, the telephone, powered streetcars, the phonograph, and moving pictures. Direct and mail-order selling flourished with the development of the national railroad system and the 1896 introduction of rural free delivery. Getting goods to out-of-the-way places no longer was a problem. Yet manufacturers also found themselves with surplus products and increased competition for markets.

Continued economic progress therefore depended on the addition of new customers. When America industrialized in the mid-1800s, manufacturers gained larger markets while advertisers zeroed in on a swelling consumer population that increasingly could understand print ads. As late as 1860, only one white child in six attended school while hardly any African American children received schooling.[1] The 1880 census, however, revealed that the illiteracy rate had dropped to 17 percent due to the emerging system of free public elementary schools and compulsory attendance. Meanwhile, even as pioneers settled the wide-open western lands, America became more urban. Struggling farmers moved to cities looking for work and floods of immigrants made the Atlantic crossing, all searching for land, jobs, and the opportunity to forge a better life. The populations of New York City and Philadelphia, and inland cities such as Cincinnati, Chicago, and St. Louis also grew rapidly.

To gain new customers, manufacturers had to persuade these formerly self-sustaining households to purchase soap, bread, clothes, and other necessities instead of making their own, as well as convince potential customers to select their products over a competitor's. Furthermore, businesses began to recognize that advertising could do more than reduce overall production costs by increasing sales. It could also create desires—desires that could fuel a consumer economy. People bought articles that they did not know they wanted until advertising pictured the product's benefits and told them why they couldn't live without it. The great expansion of mail-order houses like Montgomery Ward and Sears, Roebuck & Co. demonstrated the possibilities for sales on a national scale. Patent medicines also realized spectacular growth in sales by advertising in closely read country weeklies and mail-order magazines. As for city dwellers, they relied on department store newspaper advertising to identify products to purchase.

Advertising emerged as only one aspect of a national marketing effort. Early mass marketing firms also developed national organizations of managers, distributors, salesman, and buyers. Hierarchies of responsibility made possible corporate organizations that managed administration, manufacturing, and marketing. Firms also set up extensive marketing organizations and established ties between managers, staffers, and retailers. This enormous market power forced many retailers into distributing their product without any price breaks, often creating a monopoly.

One leading company or a handful of firms typically controlled the national product market of an industry. In 1878, for instance, Gustavus Swift began shipping beef in refrigerated railroad cars from Chicago to eastern markets; ten years later he dominated the industry. Andrew Carnegie became the world's leading producer of steel by the century's end, and what Carnegie was to steel, John D. Rockefeller was to oil. No doubt their efforts to consolidate manufacturing and marketing into a single company limited competition. Small firms simply could not compete for long against the larger ones without substantial capital investments, especially in the rapidly changing late nineteenth century.

Another group of relatively new manufacturers used innovative, continuous-process machinery to produce low-priced, packaged consumer goods. In 1898 the biggest advertisers produced the nation's medicines and remedies, household articles and furniture, apparel, food and drink, construction equipment—and interestingly, bicycles and bicycle accessories. The volume of advertising increased from $200 million in 1880 to $542 million in 1900.[2]

In this period large-scale advertising helped lay the foundations for the growth of such present-day companies as American Express, American Tobacco, Borden, Campbell Soup, Carnation, Coca-Cola, Colgate-Palmolive, Eastman Kodak, Sears, Roebuck & Co., Quaker Oats, Heinz, Libby, Pillsbury, Procter & Gamble, National Biscuit Company (later Nabisco), and Spalding, to name just a few.[3]

A New Role for Advertising

What was new about advertising in the 1880s and 1890s? National advertising of mass-produced, brand-name packaged goods emerged as the most significant development of this era. Manufacturers packaged food, drink, and nearly everything else consumers bought. To sell their enormous output, manufacturers explored new ways to encourage the public not only to buy more but to purchase their goods again and again. Marketers reached from coast to coast for new markets, using advertising to deliver their message through a wide variety of media—

newspapers, magazines, direct mail, and outdoor. And in the process they helped create a new culture of consumption.

The Packaging Revolution

Before the 1880s the names of most manufacturers had been virtually unknown to the people who bought their products. Tobacco was tobacco and flour was flour until manufacturers started promoting their brand names to customers. Individually packaged goods began to replace bulk-packed merchandise, providing marketers with an advertising vehicle in the form of labels, wrappers, and boxes. The makers of patent medicines pioneered the merchandising of brand-name, packaged goods in the first half of the 1800s, bottling and labeling their potions. To make sure buyers picked the right bottle from the store shelf, the medicine-makers experimented with elaborate and distinctive labels, often featuring their own portrait. Strange-sounding names like Swaim's Panacea, Robertson's Worm-Destroying Lozenges, and Hamilton's Grand Restorative became well known to the public through advertising.

Tobacco manufacturers also advanced the use of appealing brand names, commercial symbols, and packaging. Manufacturers packed bales of tobacco under labels and began literally to "brand" their products with hot irons that burned the maker's name (or brand) into wooden packages—hence "brand names" such as Smith's Plug and Brown and Black's Twist. This was hardly a new idea—since antiquity people had branded symbols or their name on livestock, barrels, boxes, or wood tools to mark ownership. But branding as a marketing tool was a relatively new development. Still other manufacturers burned "X's" on barrels of whiskey and sugar to aid clerks who could not read.

In the 1850s tobacco companies had found that more creative names helped sell their product; Cherry Ripe, Wedding Cake, and Rock Candy sold rich, aromatic tobacco, and Bull Durham meant a stronger smoke. In the next decade they began to package their goods for sale directly to the consumer. Like the patent medicine bottle they also experimented with picture labels and decorations to ma. the packages attractive.

Other manufacturers soon followed the strategy of packaging brand-name goods established by patent medicines and tobacco. During the sixty-year period from 1860 to 1920, factory-produced and -packaged merchandise largely replaced locally produced goods sold in bulk from containers. At first most people considered packaged goods to be luxuries suitable only for gifts or as a personal indulgence. Decorative bottles suggested the allure of Pears' toiletries. Printed labels on pottery jars enhanced the appeal of Keiller's Dundee marmalades. Foil-wrapped individual candies created an elite image for imported British Cadbury chocolates.

The next development in the move to standardized packaging of goods began with the simple paper bag. The paper bag helped popularize the concept of packaging simply because it made things easier to carry. The grocer could scoop small quantities of rice, flour, or other bulk items from a barrel into a paper bag, so that shoppers no longer had to bring their own containers to the store to be refilled with such staples. The next significant innovation in distribution and marketing was the folding box. In 1879 the cereal industry mechanized the printing, folding, and filling processes.[4] Over the next two decades marketers recognized that packaging accelerated retail sales.

Marketing's first success with brand-name, packaged goods was Quaker Oats oatmeal, which still appears on today's breakfast menu. In 1856 Ferdinand Schumacher built his first mill, shipping his oats in small glass jars and then in 180-pound barrels from which the grocer would sell in bulk. Demand eventually became substantial enough that Schumacher constructed a five-story mill in Akron, Ohio. In 1888 Schumacher merged with seven of the largest mills, creating the American Cereal Company. However, the new company found that it was producing far more cereal than the market could bear, because consumers still generally considered oatmeal to be food for invalids and for Scottish immigrants. Here's where advertising took center stage.

The idea of marketing oatmeal as a brand-name, packaged breakfast food for the general public originated not with Schumacher, but with his formal rival, Henry Parson Crowell. The entrepreneur recognized that the key to the product's success lay in packaging and advertising. First, Crowell transformed the raw oats into a more desirable product by packaging them in a cardboard box printed with the picture of a Quaker man and a recipe for cooking oatmeal. Next, he began extolling the virtues of Quaker Oats through advertising. In 1888

Crowell's first newspaper ad pointed to the remarkable properties of oatmeal: "One pound of Quaker Oats makes as much bone and muscle as three pounds of beef. Is it worth trying?" Indeed, "Oats . . . supply what brains and bodies require." Subsequently the pioneering cereal carried its message of health through a variety of forms: newspapers, magazines, streetcar signs, billboards, booklets, samples, cooking demonstrations, store displays, premiums inside the carton, calendars, cookbooks, and picture cards. Within a few years the Quaker Oats trademark character became familiar nationally (Figure 2.1). If Quaker Oats had tried to sell its cereal door-to-door, the cost would have been astronomical; but by taking out a full-page national magazine ad, it was able to reach millions of subscribers for pennies each. And when the company began rolling the oats into flakes instead of grinding them, cutting the overnight cooking time in half, an 1897 ad explained the advantages:

Strong and serene, as mighty forest tree
That braves the blast and dares the storm, is he
Who wisely lives, and living, learns to know
The health and strength which Quaker Oats bestow.

AT ALL GROCERS IN 2-LB. PACKAGES ONLY.

Figure 2.1 This 1897 ad for Quaker Oats promoted the health benefits of the cereal.

"The Easy Food, Easy to Buy, Easy to Cook, Easy to Digest: Quaker White Oats."

Quaker Oats is a prime example of how marketers could turn relatively generic bulk goods into far more popular and identifiable products. A manufacturer put a commodity in a small box, injected a "personality," added information to increase its usefulness, and turned the goods into something both desirable and extremely profitable. The success of selling standardized, small-packaged goods also depended on advertising a "name." Yet it was something more than a name—it established identification of a "brand name." This identity differentiated the product from others in the market and enabled buyers to appraise the value of the merchandise before buying.

Brand-Name Advantages

Other manufacturers soon recognized that with a memorable brand name and attractive packaging they could charge a higher price for goods; in turn, they urged consumers to accept no substitutes. But the brand name had to be one that people could remember, feel comfortable with, and believe represented a well-established firm and a quality product. If manufacturers could inspire confidence, this gave customers a reason to choose their product instead of a competing brand. Joseph Campbell, for example, used advertising to identify his concentrated soups, preserved vegetables, condiments, and mincemeat as part of the Campbell family of food products, which reinforced a sense of superior quality.

Thus early manufacturers boxed hundreds of cereals; packaged soaps, flour, cigarettes, and matches; and canned vegetables, fruits, milk, and soup. Then they put their name on the package and strove to develop a loyal following. Procter & Gamble soap, Pillsbury flour, Heinz condiments, Borden dairy products, Levi-Strauss jeans, Hires root beer, and Hills Bros. coffee are just a few examples.

Other marketers believed that the brand name should suggest something desirable about the product or its performance. For example, Carnation condensed milk suggested freshness and sweetness. Cream of Wheat cereal implied a healthful grain product. And Brad's Drink became Pepsi-Cola to emphasize that the beverage relieved dyspepsia and peptic ulcer pain.

Advertising also could help manufacturers sell an enormous amount of products both at a lower cost and at a profit. The challenge, however, was to convince buyers that they could not pass up the advantages of the brand-name products, which usually cost more than the generic ones. To distinguish one product from another, marketers advertised both a specific brand name and a graphic image or symbol for visual identification, called a "trademark," that identified the source of the goods in trade.

Packaging, too, proved an effective medium to display the brand name and trademark and to explain why the product was superior. Patrick J. Towle, a grocer in St. Paul, Minnesota, provides an outstanding example. He recognized the need for a blended table syrup with the flavor of maple but without the high price of pure maple syrup, a principal sweetener at the time. Thus in 1887 his Log Cabin Syrup blended cane and maple syrups. While other grocers were filling cheap tin cans with syrup from a barrel, Towle ordered a trial supply of miniature log-cabin-shaped containers to package his syrup. Towle soon found that customers willingly paid extra for the novelty, as well as for the convenience and product assurance they gained.

As the use of brand names and commercial trademarks spread, so did the practice of imitation. Until 1870 the U.S. Constitution protected rights of ownership in copyrights and patents but did not grant manufacturers exclusive rights to some mark placed on their wares. With the enactment of the nation's first federal trademark law in 1870, however, manufacturers could register their mark with the federal patent office in Washington, sending a clear drawing of their mark and a description of the type of goods on which it was used along with a $25 fee. Interestingly one of the first marks submitted under the new law was the "Underwood devil," which was registered to William Underwood & Company in Boston for use on "Deviled Entremets." With subsequent revisions of the trademark law, protection was expanded to cover symbols used in interstate commerce and to designate services as well as products, such as union labels and club emblems.

The protection provided by the new trademark laws encouraged manufacturers to rely more heavily on well-advertised commercial symbols. All things being equal, brands from well-known companies proved more valuable than those from unknown companies. Branding also protected many manufacturers from price competition to some degree as consumers came to accept no substitutes rather than settle for the least expensive brand available. Manufacturers who advertised could bring customers to the point that they would ask stores for the brand by name. With brand-name products so appealing and in such demand, national advertisers could set their price at the factory instead of in the marketplace. People came to rely on these labels for assurance that the food they ate and the products they bought came from a reliable source. This perception remains in force even today.

The New Culture of Consumption

After the Civil War rapid industrialization and urbanization created new patterns of social life and changed the character of the American middle class. Influenced by its English counterparts, the urban, middle-class American family embraced the sociocultural standards of the Victorian era.

Victorian society was based on clear-cut boundaries between men's and women's spheres. The man earned a wage away from the home in an office or factory, while the woman remained at home, cleaning, cooking, and raising children. Instead of producing their own everyday necessities, households increasingly purchased such items outside the home. With the men toiling at work, women became consumers as they chose what and how much to buy. This practice, however, also served to increase women's economic dependency, because the woman traditionally spent money given to her by her wage-earning husband or parents. Even poor married women who earned a wage out of economic necessity still looked to their husbands for money to spend.

The mass media and advertising played a major role in creating and sustaining this idealized image of the Victorian middle-class family and the woman's role in it. In particular the culture promoted strict adherence to the traditional role assigned to women in society. Literature fostered the sentimental view of home as a sacred place or a haven where women cultivated nurturing relationships. Moralizing tales preached against leaving the home, accumulating possessions, and having social aspirations. Poems, songs, stories, books, and dramas invoked the hopes and joys associated with romance and wedded bliss—a woman's wealth, social standing, home, and happiness all came through marriage.

Advertisements popularized this way of thinking by urging women to attract a man rather than become an old maid. Ads for tightly laced corsets, fashionable clothing, and perfumes offered one means to do so (Figure 2.2). Promotions for beauty soaps, cosmetics, and creams also promised love and romance as a prelude to marriage, although sex did not become a focus of advertising until the 1920s. Ads influenced tastes for ornate homes and furnishings and promoted such labor-saving devices as the sewing machine to ease the burden of daily chores. Collectively these ads fostered the illusion of wedded bliss as a social ideal. Few women, however, could measure up to the idealized images that advertising portrayed. (It was not until the 1960s that women seriously questioned the role advertising played in creating and sustaining this standard.)

Brand-name goods also provided status and identity for the individual with social aspiratations. But in the 1880s people still found themselves more dazzled by the variety of goods than by the brand name.

Manufacturers began to exploit people's desire for fashionable things as material goods became visible symbols of personal worth and an index for income after the Civil War—particularly amidst the growing urban class within which social mobility became a possibility. Possession of material objects provided aspiring Victorians with an entry into a desired social world and a means to differentiate themselves from other social groups. Victorian extravagance encouraged men and women not just to dress, but to overdress. The well-off also cluttered their homes with overornate, overstuffed furniture and other mass-produced items.

Yet not all Victorians found themselves wealthy enough to enjoy all that advertisements portrayed. Although advertisers could not

Figure 2.2 This 1882 ad for tightly laced corsets promoted the idealized Victorian hourglass figure for women.

ignore the ever-widening differences between the "haves" and "have-nots," they rarely directed advertising campaigns with overt appeals to particular social classes or ethnic groups. (Not until the 1950s did the industry widely embrace market segmentation by targeting sub-groups of consumers.) Rather, they experimented with different styles of selling aimed at all consumers.

The Selling Style: Hard or Soft?

In this era the selling message changed—from blaring "hard sell" to subtle "soft sell"—as the volume of both products and advertisements increased. The patent medicine peddlers had perfected one of the oldest selling styles, the hard sell. They recognized early on the enormous importance of getting noticed by claiming to be the best, the greatest, or the most wonderful product in the world. Their straightforward, fact-filled product announcements screamed, "send no money," "money-back guarantee," and other attention grabbers.

In the new era of packaged, brand-name goods, advertising no longer focused on providing product information, because people already were familiar with most of these commodities. Instead, the selling emphasis shifted to a soft-sell, feel-good style that focused on establishing the brand name, that is, the reputability of the manufacturer. The idea that a brand name might affect sales ripened into soft-sell advertising strategies. The goal was to link together the all-important trademarks and symbols for the brand name with favorable and memorable associations powerful enough to build up desire for the product. For example, patent medicine advertisements built a distinct product personality to justify a relatively high price by relating the product to something exotic, mystical, ancient, and even romantic.

These hard-sell and soft-sell approaches tend to be associated with eras, in which each new marketing idea replaces an old strategy. This suggests a fundamental aspect of the history of advertising. Whenever a certain style appears to work, it is constantly copied until buyers stop responding. Inevitably consumers express interest when shown a novel style. The late nineteenth century was no exception: advertisers followed "hot" marketing trends, as well as popularized even more diverse experiments. Admakers became very skilled at capturing attention, telling stories, and persuading people to buy their products. In fact a number of familiar advertising ideas—slogans, jingles, trade characters—first appeared over one hundred years ago.

Honesty Takes Its Turn

Newspaper advertising by department stores typically appeared either as blaring overstatements or lists of merchandise until copywriter John Powers introduced something new to advertising, honesty. In the late 1870s Powers wrote ads part time for the Lord & Taylor department store in New York, and in 1880 he moved on to Wanamaker's in Philadelphia. Once there Powers experimented with different styles of newspaper ads to attract attention.

While other advertisers were using detailed hard-sell copy to promote dry goods, Powers decided that this approach simply did not work. Instead, Powers printed his ad copy as straight text, in sharp

A Taste of the Times

During the High Victorian period, called the "Gilded Age," extravagance became the order of the day. Architecture, fashion, furnishings, and decorative arts featured an eclectic style that knew no bounds.

The exuberant 1876 Philadelphia Centennial Exhibition, then the largest world's fair to date, played an important role in fashioning public taste. Exhibits displayed such wonders as the light bulb, telephone, typewriter, sewing machine, and carpet sweeper. The exotic bronzes, ceramics, screens, and lacquerware displayed by Japanese presenters astonished visitors and popularized the style. Another exhibit building replicated the English dwellings built for the gentry during Queen Anne's reign (1702–1714) and inspired new architectural styles. Plain facades gave way to bold colors and uninhibited decoration. Homes turned into museums cluttered with an eclectic mix of overstuffed, over-elaborated furniture, beloved knick-knacks, and pictures.

Affluent people also treated food as more than sustenance; it became a sign of affluence as Victorian extravagance might suggest. Whether an elegant dinner party, a sumptuous banquet, or a costume ball, multicourse meals were served in magnificent settings with flamboyant amusements. Diners might sit down to sumptuous ten- to fourteen-course meals and quickly *bolt* them down. This custom had its roots with the Puritans, who condemned all sensual pleasures as sinful and so gulped down their meals rather than savor them. Women of the period were not afraid to indulge in heavy meals, too. Singer and actress Lillian Russell, the reigning American beauty of her time, tipped the scales at an ample 186 pounds. A less well endowed woman could read popular beauty books like *Plumpness: How to Acquire It* or discreetly purchase remedies through the mail, like Loring's Fat-Ten-U and

contrast to the standard news-type headlines and lengthy exaggerations. Readers came to immediately recognize Powers' advertisements. One- to three-word headlines, brief anecdotes, and catchy slogans lured people into simple, easy-to-read announcements. The selling points revolved around what the product could do for the purchaser and nothing else. Powers' chatty advertisements appeared in a single column of 12-point Caslon type, with no eye-catching display lines, pictures, or ornaments, which only wasted space (Figure 2.3).

Powers' sincerity, understated approach, and skillful support for his claims quickly overcame consumer resistance. For Wanamaker's, Powers wrote that the department store "never quite leads in new styles of dresses." About a sale of summer suits, he wrote, "They are

Corporular Foods that "make the Thin Plump and Comely."

A host of entertaining new inventions came on the scene: player pianos, cameras, phonographs, bicycles, and moving pictures called "flickers." These flickers typically were shown at the nickelodeon, postered storefronts that housed a screen, several rows of chairs, and a piano. The makeshift theaters usually offered a series of 10-minute films accompanied by a soloist.

Popular fiction such as *Little Lord Fauntleroy* (1886) reflected the Victorians' sentimental ideals. Escapist fiction such as *King Solomon's Mines* (1886), *The Prisoner of Zenda* (1894), and *When Knighthood Was in Flower* (1898) also sold well. Even the "bad English" of *Tom Sawyer* (1876) and *Huckleberry Finn* (1884), which was contrary to the tone of the times and offended many "proper" people found an audience. At the same time, prolific author Horatio Alger turned out more than a hundred action-filled books for boys, all based on the principle that any young man could rise above poverty and temptation to attain wealth, power, and happiness. Most of Alger's generation believed the premise, and his books found a wide audience.

Yet with the "haves" came the "have-nots." America's booming economy led to vast fortunes for some, and palatial mansions were constructed in significant numbers after the Civil War. Although available only to the affluent, early luxuries included running water, indoor bathrooms, and gaslights; yet another generation would pass before the masses enjoyed these luxuries. Public services such as sanitation, water, and utilities often proved inadequate for the burgeoning cities, where overcrowding became the standard. Even after multistoried apartment buildings began to appear in New York City around 1870, middle-class families often were crammed into crowded flats and boarding houses. And the less fortunate managed in far more primitive quarters.

cool!—we are not stupid enough to offer you anything else in this weather." In another soft-sell ad Powers even promised that dissatisfied buyers could get their money back:

> *The tidy house-keeper banishes flies; but one persistent buzzer sticks. The fly-fan keeps him off while you dine or doze in peace. It IS a luxury!!*

> *Winds like a clock, goes an hour-and-a-half, and costs $3.00—best machine, $4.00; the latter with nickeled base, $6.50; with decorated-china base, $7.50. It is worth a hundred dollars; send it back if it isn't.*

> 'One of the minor troubles of house-keeping is the breaking of lamp-chimneys. Chimneys cost but little apiece, and break but one at a time. You class these little surprises among "mysterious providences," and bear them, meekly resigned.
>
> All wrong! the chimneys are wrong; the glass was ready to pop the minute it cooled.
>
> The maker saved two cents on a chimney, and put this loss and annoyance on you.
>
> "Pearl-top" chimneys do not break in use.

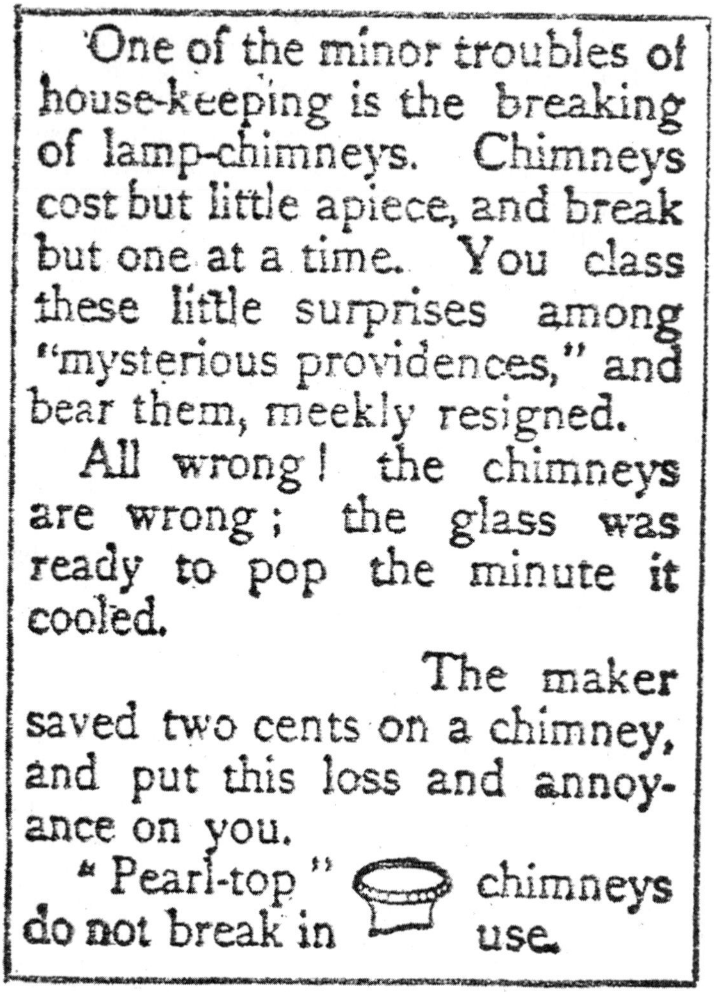

Figure 2.3   In the 1880s copywriter John Powers used understated honesty instead of exaggeration and overstatement to sell products.

Customers liked Powers' candid style, and Wanamaker's heavy advertising expenditures paid off as sales doubled from $4 million to $8 million in the early 1880s.[5]

After leaving Wanamaker's in 1886, Powers used his honest advertising style to sell a number of other products that became well known, including Beecham's Pills, Murphy Varnish, Scott's Emulsion, and the George A. MacBeth Company in the 1890s.

Other professional freelance copywriters adopted Powers' approach and raised the standards of advertising. Nathaniel C. Fowler, a Boston reporter turned adman, published the first books on advertis-

Printer's Ink

George P. Rowell.

The fundamentals of good advertising were spread through a weekly trade publication called *Printers' Ink* (1888–1967),

founded by advertising agent George P. Rowell and, beginning in 1890, edited by John Irving Romer. Rowell originally designed the periodical to publicize his business; the idea for the title came from the agent's recognition that he was also a dealer in "printers' ink." The publication disseminated ideas to various businesses, informing them why they should advertise and how to do it. It also analyzed industries, markets, and competition; supplied media and agencies with leads for new advertisers; and offered commentary on current copy, typography, and design.

Other publications devoted to advertising arrived after *Printers' Ink,* including *Standard Rate and Data Service* (1919), which compiled information on magazine, newspaper, and other media rates, location, closing dates, and so on; *Advertising Age* (1930); and later, *AdWeek* (1960).

ing: *Advertising and Printing* (late 1880s); *Building Business* (1893), a manual on copy, media, and typography; and *Fowler's Publicity* (1897). Among his rules for advertising, Fowler stressed continuity: "Do not begin to advertise unless it be the intention to stick to it." And he advocated, "Advertise one article at a time." Charles Austin Bates, another early copywriter, issued *Good Advertising* (1896) and *Short Talks on Advertising* (1898). Between 1885 and 1910 a number of trade journals were launched that dispensed information on methods of advertising, cultivated economic interests, and provided an industry forum. One of the first was *Printers' Ink,* by agent George P. Rowell, a weekly journal that guided advertisers for the next forty years. Another large-circulation journal was begun by C. F. David of Boston and taken over in 1897 by Kate F. Griswold, one of the most well known women in turn-of-the-century advertising.

Slogans and Jingles Catch On

Advertising slogans evolved from the midcentury and reiterated the Bonner style of repeated phrases used to get around newspaper advertising limitations that banned display ads. Constant repetition of two-word phrases such as Royal Baking Powder's "Absolutely Pure," Hornby's Oatmeal's reminder to "Eat H-O," and Sapolio soap's "Use Sapolio" made the products into household names and boosted sales. Admakers set the brief copy in large, boldface type with a few lines of accompanying text and attention-getting white space. Thus the modern advertising slogan was born.

Soon slogan making developed into a specialty. Some phrases were quickly dashed off, a few were excerpted from earlier advertisements, and others were laboriously worked out. Ad expert Charles M. Snyder penned the witty query "See that hump?" for Richardson and De Long Brothers to promote the De Long Hook and Eye fastener, which took the place of buttons. The popular phrase also provided a model for the essentials of a good slogan: it should be brief, appropriate, simple, memorable, and easy to repeat, and it should encapsulate a key theme or idea about the product.

Advertising agencies developed still other catch phrases, such as Prudential's "Rock of Gibraltar" from J. Walter Thompson and "Do Uneeda biscuit?" from N. W. Ayer & Son. Also, Lord & Thomas developed the Wool Soap ad that ran with a picture of two children, one with a conspicuously shrunken shirt: "My mama used Wool Soap. I wish mine had." The text explained the line: "WOOLENS will not shrink if WOOL SOAP is used in the laundry" (Figure 2.4).

In addition to creating slogans, admakers revived the jingle. The jungle was hardly a new idea; advertising rhymes had appeared in England nearly a century before and met with great success. In the United States advertisers picked up on the idea of jingles and used them extensively.

Often charming, the jingle became an easily remembered ad. In 1890, for example, Hires root beer ran this ad for their "Delicious Temperance, Thirst-quenching, Health-Giving Drink":

> *Said the owl to himself,*
> *"If the moon I could get,*
> *whenever I'm dry*
> *my throat I could wet;*
> *The moon is a quarter—*
> *with a quarter I hear;*
> *you can purchase five gallons of Hires Root Beer."*

Famed sloganeer Charles M. Snyder set the style for the jingle era with his verses for the De Long Hook and Eye. The rhymes, most of them absurd, initially appeared on white streetcar signs printed in black and red type. Here is one of them:

(my mama used Wool Soap)   (I wish mine had)
WOOLENS will not shrink if
WOOL SOAP
is used in the laundry

Figure 2.4 This memorable 1890s ad immediately reveals the benefit of the product.

The cable cars may lose their grips,
The horse cars they may jump,
But there's one thing that never slips,
It's name is on the million lips
That murmur "See that hump?"

And Plymouth Rock Pants contributed this tongue twister:

A pant hunter pantless
Goes panting for pants
And pants for the best pants

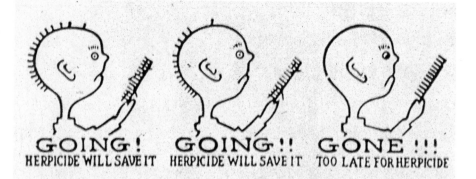

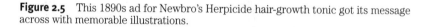

Figure 2.5   This 1890s ad for Newbro's Herpicide hair-growth tonic got its message across with memorable illustrations.

> *That the pant market grants*
> *He panteth unpanted*
> *Until he implants*
> *Himself to a pair*
> *Plymouth Rock Pants!*

Some jingles were so popular that people adapted them to current hit songs. For example, the hair-growth tonic Newbro's Herpicide already had a successful print campaign (Figure 2.5). But fans of the product's jingles also fit the words to the melody of the song "Harrigan, That's Me":

> *H-E-R-P-I—C-I-D-E spells Herpicide*
> *That's the bloomin' stuff that makes your hair grow*
> *Makes you look just like a human scarecrow.*
> *H-E-R-P-I—C-I-D-E you see*
> *First I rub it, then I scrub it, and I scrub and I rub it,*
> *Then there's HAIR AGAIN—on me.*

Despite the fact that radio did not yet exist, scores of such jingles delighted the public into the twentieth century. Like the advertising slogan these rhymes also contributed to the growth and acceptance of advertising. But creating a visual identity emerged as the key to successful brand-name advertising.

Trademarks Come to Life

New printing technology brought the trademark to life in the 1890s, and trademarks evolved from simple marks and names into a variety of pictorial symbols. One of the earliest trademarks came from Walter Baker & Company, which identified its cocoa and chocolate with the demure Baker Cocoa waitress bearing a tray of hot chocolate. The

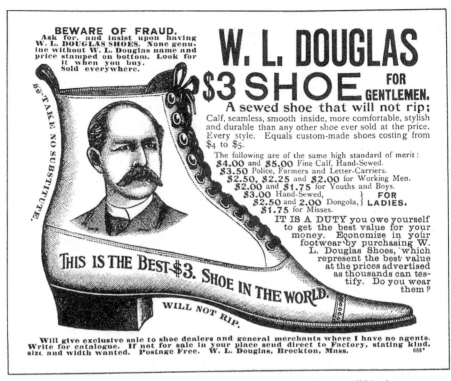

Figure 2.6   This 1892 ad featured W. L. Douglas' trademark face to sell his shoes.

Quaker Oats trademark character appeared on a cereal package. Several other advertisers used their own appealing faces: Lydia Pinkham for her patent medicine, John H. Woodbury for his facial soap, Sir Thomas Lipton for his packaged tea, and W. L. Douglas for his shoes (Figure 2.6). The Smith Brothers (William and Andrew), attracted a lot of attention for their cough drops with the words "Trade" and "Mark" beneath their pictures. Following the success of Aunt Jemima, the Cream of Wheat chef, the Underwood Devil, and the Wool Soap children, other trademark characters arrived on the scene just as the new century began.

Advertisers also used sex to catch the public's attention. In the 1850s admakers had used the heads of beautiful women, and after the Civil War the heads acquired bodies. In particular, circus ads featured women clothed in tights that could be quite revealing, while patent medicine ads often emphasized low-cut bodices, a common practice during the reign of Napoleon (1804–1821). The new ability to print high-quality illustrations popularized "pretty girl" pictures in the 1890s. Full-page black-and-white ads quickly appeared in some magazines. Because the Victorians covered their bodies from chin to toes, advertisers found that a peek at the forbidden could bring readers to a

Advertising Characters

An advertising character may be a real person, an animal, or a fictional being with human attributes who exclusively endorse products, brands, services, or companies. Leo Burnett's Chicago ad agency developed some of the most memorable ad characters, which they affectionately referred to as "critters." Here are some of the classics with their birth dates:

1877 Quaker Oats Man

1895 Michelin Man ("Bibendum")

1904 Buster Brown

1905 Aunt Jemima

1911 Morton Salt Girl

1916 Mr. Peanut

1921 Betty Crocker

1926 Jolly Green Giant

1926 Reddy Kilowatt

1936 Elsie the Cow

1941 Snap, Crackle & Pop

1945 Chef Boyardee

1949 Smokey Bear

1951 Speedy Alka-Seltzer

1957 Mr. Clean

1966 Ronald McDonald

The Michelin Tire Man.

halt. Prior to World War I it took only a hemline lifted to the ankle to arrest the viewer—a far cry from Calvin Klein's deliberately titillating and even shocking graphics of today.

One of the first lifelike advertisements featured the smiling "Sozodont Girl" for Sozodont toothpaste, who appeared in the 1880s as a woodcut portrait and in the next decade as a halftone photograph (Figure 2.7). Other "pretty girls" quickly followed. For instance, the owners of the White Rock Springs Company put an image of the half-clothed fairy Psyche (later called "The White Rock Girl") kneeling on a stone and peering at her reflection in a pool of water on the labels of their bottles. Coca-Cola also associated its products with fashionable women, and for Kodak camera the "Kodak Girl" popularized the striped skirt with style and taste.

Figure 2.7   This 1884 woodcut of the "Sozodont Girl" was one of the first life-like images in advertising.

Pictures Show the Way

New technology also provided inexpensive, high-quality illustrations for national magazines. The first full-page color advertisement appeared on the back cover of an 1893 American periodical, *Youth's*

Companion, which carried the lithograph of a popular painting of Cupid that it prepared for the Mellin's Food ad at a cost of $14,000.[6] Other colorful advertisements quickly followed.

Admakers reproduced original paintings, delicate oil-and-water drawings, and sketches as full-page advertisements that quickly became important sources of product image building. These ads sought to combine style, design, and tone to create an instantaneous impression—"picture magic."[7] Placement of the all-important product name and identifying symbols, trademarks, and slogans also became an important part of the advertisement.

One popular motif captured the attention of most people, especially women—the picture of a healthy, happy child. If the picture also interested children, and if women exclaimed, "How darling!" it was a winner. Special products for children such as food and soap frequently were advertised in this manner. By portraying cheerful children involved in everyday activities, these advertisements drew the attention of mothers and communicated the message "If you buy this product, your child could look like this."

Mellin's Food, Pears' soap, Pyle's Pearline soap, and Ivory soap popularized soft-sell art in American advertising.[8] In the United States Pears' soap, made in England, introduced popular "family appeal" paintings to illustrate an advertisement, a common practice in England at the time. In 1888 early woodcut reproductions pictured an infant reaching for the bar of soap: "He won't be happy till he gets it." It communicated to parents that Pears' soap would make for a clean and happy baby. Other family images followed. In one a mother asks a child, "How do you spell soap, my dear?" The child replies: "Why, Ma, P-E-A-R-S, of course." A full-page series of paintings also appeared with this famous caption: "Good morning, have you used Pears' soap?" (Figure 2.8). And one amusing ad portrayed a Christmas scene with a cheerful child querying a surprised Santa Claus.

These illustrated ads first appeared at a time when the posters coming out of London and Paris fascinated the art world. This work set the stage for the illustrators who would dominate advertisements well into the twentieth century. Their work would appear on magazine covers and literary posters and in magazine articles and higher-brow advertisements. Among the early American artists were Frederick Remington, who painted western scenes for Smith & Wesson guns, and Jesse Wilcox Smith, who created original art for Ivory soap and Kodak.

Unfortunately advertisements, package illustrations, and trademarks also perpetuated grotesque racial caricatures and stereotypes. At the time, Americans accepted these images as everyday humor. For example, African Americans commonly were portrayed as dancing minstrels, shuffling servants, polite porters, and cheerful cooks, reinforcing the popular misconception that they were suitable only for menial jobs. To reinforce the brand-name image for its pancake mix, one company hired Nancy Greene, a black cook, to be "Aunt Jemima."

Figure 2.8 In the 1890s Pears' soap popularized the use of original paintings in ads.

In this persona she traveled around the country and cooked thousands of pancakes at fairs, inspiring the line "I's in town, honey." The Cream of Wheat chef Rastus, another famous trademark, appeared on one advertisement with the caption "de bes' known man in de worl'" (Figure 2.9).

Other racial stereotypes commonly appeared in advertising as well. Commercial artists often stereotyped Asian Americans with long braids, swallowing live rats to sell such vermin exterminators as Rough

"AH RECKON AS HOW HE'S DE BES' KNOWN MAN IN DE WORL'"
Painted by Rowland M. Smith for Cream of Wheat Co.

Figure 2.9   This 1897 ad for Cream of Wheat helped perpetuate the stereotype of African Americans as smiling chefs, minstrels, porters, and servants.

on Rats and Chinese Rat Destroyer Poison (Figure 2.10). Similarly the portrayals of Native Americans were simplistic caricatures. Native Americans appeared as fierce warriors for the Savage Arms gun company or as noble primitives for Calumet baking powder, Red Cloud Tobacco, and Hiawatha canned corn, to name a few. Many of these objectionable portrayals continued to circulate into the 1960s, when the civil rights movement brought attention to these demeaning images.

Figure 2.10 This 1890s ad for rat poison helped reinforce the stereotype of Asian Americans as long-braided, oddly attired people.

Whatever the content or selling style of advertisements in this era, a common denominator was the all-important trademark. With the taming of the West, advertising went national.

The First National Advertisers

Packaged, brand-name household goods became the first nationally advertised products—cereals, soaps, baking ingredients, and foodstuffs. Many of these small businesses quickly became big-time ventures, with annual advertising expenditures skyrocketing from several thousand dollars a year to multimillion-dollar sums in the following decades. These successes further demonstrated the power of advertising.

A Trio of Household Staples

Catchy slogans and a flood of advertising made Royal Baking Powder, Sapolio soap, and Ivory soap three of the most recognized brand names of the day. By the early 1890s Royal Baking Powder commanded the largest advertising budget in the business, spending $600,000 a year.[9] Druggist J. C. Hoagland in Fort Wayne, Indiana, first mixed a batch of the compound in 1868. Before this time recipes that called for baking soda required the addition of an acidic substance, such as sour milk or vinegar, to activate the soda. The new formula, called "Royal Baking Powder," premixed its own activator and soon became very popular.

Reaching for new markets, Hoagland placed ads in religious and women's periodicals. In the 1870s Hoagland became the first advertiser to include a picture of the package in his ads—a can with the motto "Absolutely Pure"; his newspaper ads featured frequent repetition of the slogan. Sometimes his ads contained a few lines of text in small type: "This powder never varies, a marvel of purity, strength, and wholesomeness." In contrast, the name and the slogan stood out in large, boldface type (Figure 2.11).

Soapmakers, however, took the lead in enterprising advertising on a large scale (along with patent medicines). In the United States, Sapolio and Ivory, along with Pears', Lever Brothers, and Kirk, set the trend. For example, New York's Enoch Morgan and Sons already had an extensive line of soaps when they produced Sapolio, a small gray cake of scouring soap for heavy cleaning. The company first advertised Sapolio in 1869. An early newspaper included an illustration of a man using the bottom of a shiny-clean pan as a mirror. The accompanying copy made such claims as "Better and cheaper than soap" and the best for "polishing metal and brass." The soapmakers' first selling efforts also included distributing promotional material to retailers. Sapolio hired writer Bret Harte to anonymously pen one such brochure that outlined the scope of the promotion plans for Sapolio. Each page pictured one form of publicity, accompanied by a verse. Here's one example:

> One Sabbath morn, as heavenward
> White Mountain tourists slowly spurred
> On every rock, to their dismay,
> They read that legend, always
> SAPOLIO

Sapolio next shifted its promotion focus to a variety of media. In 1884 the soapmaker hired advertising manager Artemas Ward, who

Figure 2.11 In 1870 Royal Baking Power became the first advertiser to feature a picture of its package in the ad.

over the next two decades made Sapolio into a household name. Faced with a seasonal product that sold most heavily for fall and spring cleanings, Ward succeeded in using various inventive devices and steady advertising to increase sales in slow months. Ward placed catchy slogans in country weekly newspapers and on the sides of streetcars, such as "Be Clean!" or "Sapolio Scours the World." The master of publicity also circulated the mysterious legend that "Oilopas Esu" had been found in an Egyptian tomb—a ploy that delighted people when they recognized what it spelled backwards. Yet it was the famous Spotless Town campaign that made Sapolio synonymous with cleanliness.

A series of lighthearted streetcar ads for Sapolio began to appear in 1900 (Figure 2.12). Artemas Ward dreamed up the idea, and James Kenneth Fraser wrote and illustrated the stories about "Spotless

This is the butcher of Spotless Town,
His tools are bright as his renown.
To leave them stained were indiscreet,
For folks would then abstain from meat,
And so he brightens his trade you know
By polishing with

SAPOLIO

Figure 2.12 Beginning in 1900 and running for 6 years, Sapolio's famous series of Spotless Town ads made the soap a household name.

Town," a quaint, cobblestoned Dutch village whose inhabitants praised the qualities of Sapolio. After a few months the public recognized that each new piece was an installment in a series. The ads introduced new characters, eventually totaling twelve in all, as the series progressed. The ads gained such public favor that many people actually looked forward to each new chapter, as they met the doctor, the mayor, the butcher, and so on.

Allusions to Spotless Town soon became a familiar sight in newspapers, on the streets, in public speeches, and even on stage. Cartoons, toys, books, plays, and political speeches borrowed the Spotless Town phrases and scenes. Ward even created a special play with music based on the advertisements and supplied the scenery. The show played all over the country to raise money for charity, and as a result over a thousand proud towns featured Sapolio in their local clean-up campaigns. After the beloved campaign had run for six years, Ward deliberately wound up the promotion rather than let it fall out of fashion.[10]

Harley Procter, from Procter & Gamble in Cincinnati, Ohio, strategically created Ivory hand and bath soap for national marketing. At the time soapmakers typically made the product from animal fats, but this proved too perishable to sell outside of regional markets. To solve this problem, Procter perfected a white, perfumed soap, made from vegetable fats, that was mild enough for the laundry or the nursery. With a need for a distinctive name, Procter received a heavenly suggestion in church one Sunday morning in 1879, as the congregation read a psalm: "All thy garments smell of myrrh, and aloes, and cassia, out of the ivory palaces whereby they have made thee glad." It became "Ivory" soap then and there.

While a divine inspiration named the soap, a manufacturing accident provided the key to its success. In 1881 a plant worker apparently left a batch of soap inside the stirring machine too long, and the mixture hardened with a pocket of air inside. The resulting soap had a curious property: it floated in water. Customers apparently liked the "soap that floats," so Procter adjusted his manufacturing process to produce nothing but floating bars of Ivory. Thus Procter & Gamble launched Ivory soap in 1882.

From the start Ivory soap blazed a trail in advertising art. The advertisements always contained an idea and attractive illustrations. During this era two memorable slogans first appeared in ad copy, slogans that have endured for more than a century: "Ivory Soap's 99$^{44}/_{100}$ pure" and "It floats" (Figure 2.13). Ivory soap also occasionally included jingles in full-page magazine ads. Noting the popularity of jingles, Procter & Gamble began offering prizes for the best rhymes submitted praising its soap in 1892. The response was overwhelming: prize-winning jingles appeared in monthly magazine ads over the next year and a half.

Try It! You'll Like It!

In the latter part of the nineteenth century, Heinz and Coca-Cola both started advertising with trade cards. Henry J. Heinz came first, peddling bottled horseradish from a wheelbarrow in the streets of Pittsburgh in 1869. By century's end Heinz put out over sixty varieties of condiments and preserved foods, but he settled on the "57 Varieties" slogan simply because it appealed to him.

For a quarter century Heinz invested heavily in booth, outdoor, and novelty advertising. A distinctive label, the "57 Varieties" slogan, and the pickle—along with the Heinz name—identified Heinz products. The pickle symbol appeared on the keystone-shape label of Heinz products, representing the company's specialty in pickles. Over the years Heinz distributed millions of tiny green pickle-shaped pins, watch charms, and brooches to the public at country fair stands and exhibit booths and to visitors at his Pittsburgh plant. Posters and streetcar signs also appeared all over the country. And Heinz made a big splash at both the Chicago's World Fair in 1893 and the Paris Exposition in 1900.

As Heinz's business grew, so did his advertising campaigns. In 1898 the "Pickle King" built the Heinz Ocean Pier at Atlantic City. A few years later in New York, the Pickle King erected what was then the largest electric sign on Broadway. The spectacular billboard displayed a 50-foot-long pickle lit in green lights with the name "Heinz" blazoned across it in white. Additional panels spelled out other product names in different colors, flashing one at a time. However, Heinz did not become an extensive print advertiser until the turn of the century.

Drawn for The Century Co.

Ivory Soap   It Floats

Figure 2.13 Ivory soap's memorable slogan "It floats" first appeared in this 1891 ad.

Like Heinz, Coca-Cola started out with a product, a few dollars, and some trade cards. In 1886 John S. Pemberton, an Atlanta pharmacist, tested a glass of his new syrup mixed with carbonated water and declared the results refreshing. The drink went on sale at once. The exotic ingredients of the beverage—the South American coca leaf and the African cola nut—suggested the name "Coca-Cola." Pemberton's bookkeeper, Frank Robinson, penned the trademark name in the familiar graceful script. Pemberton then began advertising with trade cards entitling the bearer to a free Coke (Figure 2.14).

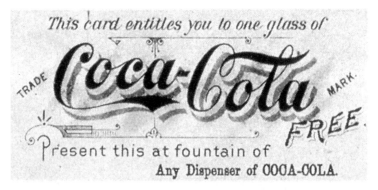

Figure 2.14 In the late 1880s Atlanta pharmacist John Pemberton began advertising with store cards that featured the graceful trademark name.

When Pemberton died two years later, Atlanta businessman Asa Candler bought up the rights to the name and the secret formula. At first Candler sold the syrup to fountains, but after a decade he began bottling the drink to sell to outlying areas.

Sipping soda had already become an established American tradition. Sparkling water beverages date back to 1825, when a Philadelphia drugstore stocked soda water. Over the years millions of gallons of carbonated beverages were dispensed from pharmacists' counters. The bubbly drinks initially were touted as health drinks, including Hires' root beer, Dr. Pepper, Pepsi-Cola, ginger ales. Coca-Cola, too, first tried promoting the tonic effect of the drink as an energy source. One early 1892 print ad headlined: "The Ideal Brain Tonic, a Delightful Summer and Winter Beverage! . . . For Headache & Exhaustion" (Figure 2.15).

At the turn of the century, Coca-Cola shifted its sales focus away from health benefits, making "refreshment" the central theme of its advertising. To convey this idea, the company linked the product with wholesome images of the pleasant things in life, showing beautiful people drinking Coca-Cola while lounging in elegant surroundings playing golf and tennis or swimming at resorts, which in those days were rich people's sports. The slogan "Drink Coca-Cola Delicious and Refreshing" appeared everywhere—on posters, store signs, trays, clock faces, fences, walls, playing cards, advertisements, and so on.

The first of dozens of beautiful "Coca-Cola girls" also appeared at this time, as actress Hilda Clark and Metropolitan Opera star Lilian Nordica posed for early promotional pictures (Figure 2.16). In 1906 Coca-Cola switched from the Massengale agency to the D'Arcy agency, which handled the account for the next fifty years. Although the continuity of the advertising theme was maintained, the kinds of people depicted subtly shifted to appeal to all classes, ages, and sexes. Thus

Figure 2.15   This 1892 ad promoted the tonic effects of Coca-Cola.

the images of pleasant, wholesome, but always beautiful women reflected the ideal of the middle-class American woman.

In the latter nineteenth century many already familiar products became household names—and sources of huge profit—through the power of advertising. But in this era of industrialization and unprecedented technological growth, advertisers also faced the challenge of promoting entirely new products such as cameras and bicycles.

Figure 2.16 Around the turn of the century, actress Hilda Clark became the first "Coca-Cola Girl."

Selling Entirely New Products

National advertising of cameras and bicycles, like department store advertising, demonstrated that people would buy something they did not even know they wanted until advertising pictured the product and sang its praises. And they would do so even if the cost of the item exceeded their standard of living.

New Brand Names

1880 Sherwin Williams introduces the first popular premixed paint.

1880 Samuel Bath Thomas treats New Yorkers to a round, flat cake he dubs the "English Muffin."

1886 Coca-Cola is prepared by mixing a syrup with carbonated water.

1888 Johnson & Johnson adopts the red Greek cross for its health care products.

1888 Sir Thomas Lipton pioneers packaged tea.

1888 Kodak camera makes photography as easy as "You push the button, we do the rest."

1890 Aunt Jemima's smiling face appears on the packaged pancake mix.

1891 Del Monte cans fruits and vegetables.

1891 Fannie Farmer's *Boston Cooking-School Cook Book* urges cooks to purchase measuring cups and spoons.

1892 Maxwell House coffee debuts as the namesake of the Nashville hotel where the famous blend was first served.

1893 Cream of Wheat's smiling chef Rastus brightens the package.

1894 Our Pet evaporated milk cans with a cow logo appear in stores.

1894 Milton Hershey of Lancaster, Pennsylvania, develops a chocolate treat in the form of a slab, called the Hershey Milk Chocolate Bar.

1895 Postum introduces a caffeine-free coffee substitute.

1897 Jell-O gelatin dessert debuts.

1898 Dr. John Harvey Kellogg's toasted corn flakes are available as a mail-order health food.

1898 Pepsi-Cola claims to relieve dyspepsia and peptic ulcer pain.

1899 Carnation condensed milk adopts the name of a flower to suggest freshness and sweetness.

In 1888 a Rochester, New York, inventor named George Eastman introduced his camera, which he called a "Kodak" (a meaningless invented word). The first Kodak was a small black box loaded with a 100-exposure roll of film; it had no viewfinder, but merely a line on the top of the box that indicated the direction in which to point the device. The camera cost $25 and came with a booklet of simple instructions. After customers used up the roll of film, they simply shipped the entire camera back for developing and reloading of new film. But the booklet that came with the camera also explained how hobbyists could develop the film themselves.

Eastman immediately began advertising his innovation in magazines that catered to readers who could afford the $25 price. (At the time, $25 amounted to more than two weeks' pay for the average shop clerk or office worker.) Here's the text of one 1889 ad:

The KODAK:

Anybody can use the Kodak. The operation of making a picture consists simply of pressing a button. One hundred instantaneous pictures are made without reloading. No dark room or chemicals are necessary. A division of labor is offered, whereby all the work of finishing all the pictures is done at the factory, where the camera can be sent to be reloaded. The operator need not learn anything about photography. He can "Press the button"—we do the rest.

Send for a copy of KODAK PRIMER with sample photograph.

The phrase "you press the button, we do the rest" struck the public's fancy, and the slogan quickly became part of everyday conversation. The simple message effectively conveyed the idea that anyone could now do photography without technical knowledge and the elaborate equipment required by Daguerre's complicated process. Over the years the simple button-pressing idea was featured in many Kodak advertisements (Figure 2.17).

Bicycle manufacturers were the first to demonstrate that a luxury item costing $100 or more could be sold to the masses. The high-wheel bicycle, called a "bone-shaker," first attracted attention at the 1876 Philadelphia Centennial Exhibition, but it proved difficult for the average rider to master. The 1889 introduction of the "safety bicycle" represented a major improvement over the earlier models. The new bicycle featured equal-sized inflatable rubber tires, a cushioned seat, a balanced frame, and a chain drive.

With the development of the safety bike, the Columbia and Victor bicycle companies began to advertise widely and set the bicycle craze in high gear. The manufacturers pioneered advertising strategies that many automakers would later adopt. Early cycle ads soberly focused on the mechanical aspects and the fine points of design. Before a Columbia bicycle left the shop, it was "inspected in every detail by 21 engineers and mechanics." Bicycle enthusiasts analyzed the mechanical differences touted by bicycle manufacturers, and their discussions added valuable "word-of-mouth" advertising.

Once the bicycle craze took hold, however, the focus shifted. Manufacturers no longer had to present arguments and claims to generate sales; they simply had to convey the idea of sporty, exhilarating fun.

Figure 2.17   Beginning in 1890 Kodak ads stressed the button-pressing slogan, emphasizing that anyone could now take photographs.

Scenes appeared depicting the delight of countryside tours. Dry images of tubular frames gave way to pictures of pretty girls, and technical descriptions gave way to engaging copy. These advertisers also were among the first to commission famous artists to create art posters (Figure 2.18).

Millions of Americans took up the new sport: between 1890 and 1896 the number of cyclists soared from 100,000 to 4 million.[11] The cycling craze inspired clothing, songs, stories, and even advice on bicycle etiquette. Daring women wore divided skirts and bloomers, and for the more "fragile" ladies there were bikes equipped with folding screens to demurely hide their exposed ankles and feet. The new cycling pastime also provided an impetus for the development of smoother, paved roads.

Whether old or new, products jammed the marketplace, and advertisers sought new ways to reach potential consumers. Two trends in particular reflected this effort: the emergence of magazines as an advertising vehicle and the expansion of agency services.

Magazines and Agencies

With the rise of national advertisers and the advent of new media, advertising agencies changed to meet the demands of American businesses. Agencies expanded far beyond their initial role as sellers of newspaper space. Some agents formed bill-posting companies, which

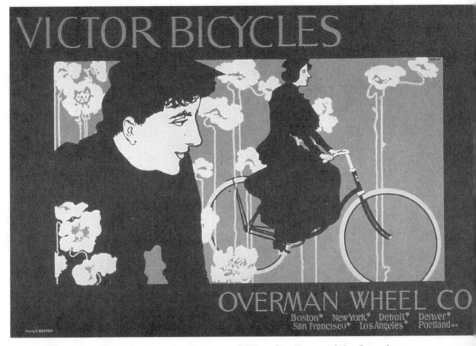

Figure 2.18   For Victor Bicycles illustrator William Bradley used the flat colors, minimal lines, and dynamic curves of Art Nouveau design in this 1895 ad.

erected their own boards and leased space. Others organized streetcar and magazine advertising, selling the media on a national basis. Agencies also learned how to create advertising campaigns and plan marketing strategies.

These efforts solved many of the staggering problems that entrepreneurs faced when they set out to advertise beyond their community. The selling of newspaper space alone became increasingly complex. The number of daily newspapers increased nearly nine-fold, from 254 in 1850 to 2,226 in 1900; weeklies increased at even a faster pace, from 991 in 1838 to 13,513 in 1904.[12] With circulations soaring publishers gradually released more reliable readership statistics to further boost advertisers' confidence and encourage them to buy space.

This activity led to the creation of national, and sometimes global, advertising organizations. New York City, the nation's leading city in domestic and foreign trade, emerged as the center of advertising as major agencies opened up shops: N. W. Ayer & Son (1869); J. Walter Thompson (1871); Lord & Thomas, later Foote Cone & Belding (1871); George Batten Co., later BBDO (1891); and Bates Agency (1893). Pioneers Mathilde C. Weil, Mary Compton, and Meta Volckmann also operated their own agencies in New York. Other women found places in the business as copywriters, advertising artists,

Memorable Slogans

Absolutely Pure. (Royal Baking Powder)

It floats. (Ivory soap)

$99^{44}/_{100}$% pure. (Ivory soap)

You press the button; we do the rest. (Kodak camera)

Good morning, have you used Pears' Soap?

See that hump? (De Long Hook and Eye fastener)

The Prudential has the strength of Gibraltar. (Prudential Insurance)

My Mama used Wool Soap—I wish mine had.

Children cry for it. (Fletcher's Castoria laxative)

Millions use Pearline. (Pyle's Pearline soap)

Don't be a clam. (Frank Siddall's soap)

Do you know Uneeda biscuit?

All the news that's fit to print. (*The New York Times*)

publishers, agents, advisers, and representatives. However, women would not again enjoy such a range of opportunities until the latter part of the twentieth century.

A few agency leaders like George P. Rowell, Francis W. Ayer, and J. Walter Thompson, as well as several copywriters, made fortunes in advertising. The typical advertising professional, however, struggled to get by in a still dubious profession. Charles Austin Bates put it this way: "It is a notorious fact there has been so much trickery and dishonesty in the advertising business that a man engaged in it sometimes feels embarrassed when he is asked what business he is in."[13] Nevertheless, advertising was a growth industry, with magazines becoming an increasingly important source of revenue and agencies broadening their services.

Magazines Emerge as Advertising Vehicles

During the 1890s a new generation of magazines appeared as advertising vehicles. Their styles ranged from the *Ladies' Home Journal* to the reformist *McClure's Magazine* and the impassioned *Munsey's Magazines*. Although they varied in content, these magazines had one thing in common: they depended on a new class of subscribers—the middle-class readers who were ready to buy consumer goods advertised in an appropriate fashion.

Yet it was Boston advertising solicitor Cyrus H. K. Curtis who truly expanded the magazine as an advertising vehicle. Curtis began with the weekly four-page *The Tribune and Farmer* and invited his wife to edit a women's column. The column stirred so much interest that Curtis turned the page into the *Ladies' Home Journal* in 1883. It proved an immediate success. The *Journal* offered the right mix of abundant reading on decorating tips, needlework patterns, fiction, and plenty of romance. Curtis also wisely accepted only high-grade advertising and reset many ads for a more pleasing appearance. A different illustration on the cover every month attracted attention. Moreover, at 25 cents per issue, the periodical reached the average woman in terms of not just content but also price (other fashion books typically cost $2 or $3). In 1897 Curtis purchased the failing *Saturday Evening Post* and revamped it into one of the most widely read magazines ever produced. As a result, in 1903 the *Journal* became the first American magazine to reach a circulation of one million.

The booming Curtis publications reflected other changes underway in the magazine field. New York advertising agent J. Walter Thompson also transformed magazines into eye-catching issues that were underwritten by advertising and that reached millions of homes. It began when Thompson took over the Carlton & Smith agency (founded in 1864). Once there, he focused his attention on soliciting business for general magazines. Thompson, more than any other agent, worked up a vast amount of advertising revenue for an array of magazines such as *Good Housekeeping* (1885), *Vogue* (1892), and *House Beautiful* (1896). In fact Thompson bought virtually all the magazine space available to advertisers and controlled nearly all the advertising space in American magazines as late as 1898.

Agencies Widen Their Services

These new magazines created new opportunities for national advertisers as well as new demands on agencies. Although agents constantly warned advertisers that they lacked bargaining power and knowledge of circulation, some of the era's earliest advertisers did not rely on an independent agent's services to buy media. However, the needs of companies like Royal Baking Powder and Singer, the patent medicine manufacturers, and other large national advertisers reshaped the advertising business.

Previously agencies had not employed full-time personnel who specialized in writing ads. From the start agents like S. M. Pettengill had prepared the copy for advertisements, but this work was merely a sideline. The large department stores, however, emerged as the first important advertisers requiring such skilled assistance. Another impetus for skilled advertisement preparation came from the manufacturers of brand-name consumer goods, who frequently mounted extensive promotion. The need for persuasive advertising became a pressing concern. Art, copy, and layout had to be carefully considered to reflect the broader marketing strategy of product image, pricing, and distribution.

In response some agencies began to offer services other than space brokerage to justify their commissions and attract more business. One of the earliest such agencies was N. W. Ayer & Son, which hired its first full-time copywriter in 1892. The Bates agency had an art department, one of the first in the business. And when Albert D. Lasker started working at the Chicago agency of Lord & Thomas in 1898, he hired both a copywriter and a commercial artist. By 1900 copy preparation had become a standard part of the agency practice, and ad preparation soon followed. Accompanying this expansion of agency functions was the emergence of a new wave of ad designs.

A New Wave of Design

Maintaining a fashionable appearance became an important component of a product's image. Marketers recognized early on that the visual style of packages, labels, and advertisements gave a product either an up-to-date or an out-of-date appearance. Printing innovations, design ideas, and prevailing attitudes could spur a wave of changes in the combination of colors, typefaces, and general design approaches that were generally identified with that product.

One of the first attempts to break away from the prevailing cluttered Victorian style occurred in the 1880s. William Morris, a leader in the English Arts and Crafts movement, advocated a return to sturdy medieval craftsmanship and a retreat from the tastelessness of mass-produced goods, furniture, and houses. As early as 1868, English writer Charles Eastlake's *Hints on Household Taste* pointed out the importance of avoiding ornate embellishments in Victorian homes and offered advice on designing, constructing, and decorating everything in the household from furniture and wallpaper to clothing to jewelry. Like Morris, Eastlake stressed the need to emulate the unadorned and solid handcrafted art of the Middle Ages. The Arts and Crafts movement also reflected an interest in the quality of materials, typography, graphic design, and printing. The movement influenced design and the look of advertising well into the twentieth century (Figure 2.19).

At the same time, the Art Nouveau movement began to influence the art world. Art Nouveau emerged as a transitional style that encompassed all the arts: architecture, handicrafts, furniture, fashion, product design, and graphics. The style represented the new wave of aesthetic thinking and prepared the way for the modern artistic movements of the twentieth century. Ornamental Art Nouveau's underlying theories encompassed more than a protest against sterile realism. The decorative art also expressed a romantic statement about industrialization and mechanization and the unnatural objects they

Figure 2.19 The 1890s renaissance in design aesthetics as advocated by the Arts and Crafts movement is realized in this ad for Fairy soap, which featured classic typefaces, meticulous borders, and realism.

produced. Art Nouveau's sinuous natural forms and graceful lines sharply contrasted with the mass-produced objects that cluttered homes. The sources of Art Nouveau design ideas lay in the art of the Japanese print, the careful craftsmanship of the English Arts and Crafts movement, and the curves of the eighteenth-century Rococo period in France. The exotic yet simplified designs of artists Vincent van Gogh, Paul Gauguin, Henri Matisse, and their contemporaries also influenced the style.

The first illustrated ads appeared in the 1890s. At about the same time, the American art world became fascinated with the brilliant Parisian Art Nouveau posters turned out by leading artists and print-makers. In contrast to Victorian complexity, the Art Nouveau posters were characterized by sweeping, exaggerated lines; by bold, flat blocks of color, and by comparative simplicity—all of which have influenced poster design ever since. Manufacturers vied with one another for the poster artists' services, and the public frequently followed bill posters to obtain copies even before they were pasted up.

Art posters first became noticeable in America about the same time as the first illustrated ads. Innovations in lithography had enabled the printing of pictures up to 28 by 44 inches as early as the 1860s. In the following decade lurid dramas, flamboyant circuses, and burlesque shows first made use of the beautifully printed posters. As an art form, however, the American poster developed slowly compared to its European counterpart.

The idea for the "modern" art poster first came to French artist Jules Cheret in 1867. Cheret also worked as a lithographer, printing labels and perfumery show cards. The artist recognized the advertising value of the poster after seeing a garish notice posted for an American circus appearing in Paris. Cheret's first boldly colored poster promoted the appearance of the famous actress Sarah Bernhardt in a play. Although France had displayed posters before, none proved so artistic that people actually stopped and looked. With dazzling color schemes and flowing curves, Cheret created a sense of action in his illustrations—one could almost see children rollicking or hear the sounds of rustling silk skirts. During his career Cheret designed more than a thousand posters, selling everything from cough drops to world expositions (Figure 2.20).

Other poster artists followed Cheret, including Henri de Toulouse-Lautrec and Theophile-Alexendre Steinlen, who chronicled French life. But it was a Czech named Alphonse Mucha, working in Paris from 1895 to 1900, who best exemplified "le modern style" of Art Nouveau. Beginning with his posters that promoted the actress Sarah Bernhardt, Mucha's dominant theme was a sensuous female figure with flowing sensuous hair, surrounded by swirling stylized plants and flowers, mosaics, and folk art, and characterized by a sense of the unreal (Figure 2.21).

Figure 2.20   In the 1890s French artist Jules Cheret's boldly colored art posters advertised everything from cough drops to cigarettes to world expositions.

In England the native Arts and Crafts movement also inspired artists. English graphic designer Aubrey Beardsley utilized flat patterns, minimal lines, and the dynamic curves of Art Nouveau. And the Beggerstaffs, brothers-in-law James Pryde and William Nicholson, produced graphics whose powerful colored shapes and simple silhouettes went far beyond the prevailing floral Art Nouveau style.

Americans' first introduction to the sweeping Art Nouveau style most likely was through *Harper's* fashionable

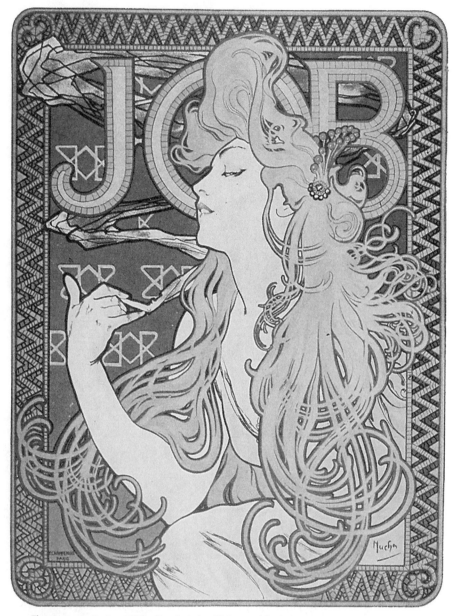

Figure 2.21 In the 1890s Czech artist Alphonse Mucha's art posters best exemplified the Art Nouveau style with their simplified designs, flowing curves, and floral art.

poster ads and cover illustrations. The magazine first commissioned Frenchmen Eugene Grasset in 1889, followed by Englishman Aubrey Beardsley and American William H. Bradley. Following *Harper's* lead, the publishing industry adopted the pictorial poster, and the art began to appear at newsstands announcing each new issue of major magazines such as *The Atlantic* and *Century*. In time Bradley and British-born Louis Rhead emerged as the two major artists of American Art Nouveau.

By the turn of the century, manufacturers had an ever-increasing variety of products to sell, the means to distribute their goods coast to coast, and a way to deliver their advertising message through newspapers, magazines, and direct mail. As these technologies became commonplace, businesses expanded the use and impact of advertising. The pioneers in early advertising had begun to develop sophisticated ideas in form, content, and campaign planning. With full responsibility for campaigns, the agencies evolved into their present-day form in the first decade of the twentieth century. In the next chapter we trace that evolutionary process.

Not only has the Pierce-Arrow turned the tide of imported cars so that there are to-day far less in proportion than some years ago—not only that, but the Pierce-Arrow in American hands has invaded Europe, giving greater satisfaction to its owners than a native car on its native heath.

The Pierce-Arrow Motor Car Company, Buffalo, N. Y.

1900

A wave of mergers consolidates 2653 independent firms to form 269 companies.
1898–1902

Elmo Calkins joins with Ralph Holden to form Calkins & Holden (C&H), the first full-service ad agency offering copy creation, ad design, space brokerage, and media planning.
1902

The United States starts digging the Panama Canal to cut travel between New York and San Francisco by 8000 miles.
1904

1900
The multimillion-dollar Uneeda biscuit campaign sets the standard for trademark advertising.

1903
The Wright brothers fly their airplane at Kittyhawk, North Carolina.

Chapter 3

1900–World War I The Rise of a Consumer Economy

Child labor laws prohibit employment of children under a certain age.

The Meat Inspection Act and the Pure Food and Drug Act pass to protect the consumer.
1906

Cecil DeMille releases the first full-scale Hollywood film, *The Squaw Man.*
1914

World War I ends.
1918

1908
Henry Ford sells the first four-cylinder Model T automobile.

1917
The United States enters World War I.

World War I

America emerged the world's leading industrial power in the 1890s, and over the next few decades economic output continued to increase. Businesses grew from little or nothing to multimillion-dollar ventures, selling brand-name products to customers through national advertising. A consumer society continued to emerge as a swelling number of Americans enjoyed increasing wealth and acquired goods.

The signs of a consumer economy had appeared everywhere by the time America entered World War I. Americans now spent hundreds of millions of dollars for wrapped soaps, packaged cereals, canned vegetables, bakery-baked bread, and ready-made clothes. The emergence of urban department stores, mail-order outlets, and chain stores provided new places to shop, while firms routinely introduced new products with a wave of advertising.

Order, efficiency, and scientific principles became the watchwords of progressive America in the early twentieth century. Public education enabled more people to learn their "reading, writing and 'rithmetic." Cities became cleaner and healthier. Electricity illuminated homes and streets and powered streetcars and appliances, while gasoline engines powered automobiles, trucks, and buses. Developments in steel making and architecture enabled construction of skyscrapers and large apartment buildings. Science and technology produced such wonders as elevators, escalators, telephones, gasoline engines, rayon fabric, and plastics. Advertising, too, responded to these influences, using science and health care as the basis for advertising campaigns. To Americans the possibilities of progress seemed limitless.

Yet many aspects of the previous century still lingered on. At the turn of the century, 20 percent of all Americans still lived in rural communities of 2500 people or less, most earning a living from agriculture.[1] Some still made their own clothes and used a horse and buggy for transportation. It was also a time when sugar cost 4 cents a pound, a restaurant dinner cost 20 cents, and a quality pair of women's shoes went for $1.50. Radios did not exist in 1900, nor did vacuum cleaners, electric irons, or traffic lights. And no one had to pay income tax.

The Emerging Consumer Economy

Millions of Americans' incomes steadily increased as industrialization expanded, stimulating the demand for consumer goods. American industry responded by shifting away from the manufacture of capital goods to the production of new consumer goods—everything from food and drink to home furnishings and automobiles. A flood of immigrants provided both a source of labor and a new class of consumer. And innovative packaging techniques and the development of chain stores helped keep the consumer goods moving.

Big Business Gets Bigger

The American business scene dramatically changed at the turn of the century. From 1898 to 1902 a wave of mergers consolidated 2653 independent firms to form 269 companies with $6.3 billion in capital.[2]

These large-scale corporations, called "trusts," controlled such basic industries as railroads, coal, iron, copper, oil, steel, sugar, and tobacco. When J. Pierpont Morgan purchased Andrew Carnegie's steel empire, his new U.S. Steel trust became the prime example of the trend toward mega-companies. Similarly National Biscuit Company (Nabisco) absorbed a number of independent bakers, while farm machinery manufacturer International Harvester incorporated. Gustavus Swift and J. D. Armour opened huge national meat packing plants in Chicago. And James Buchanan Duke reshaped the conglomerate of snuff, plug, and cigarette companies that he had purchased over the years to form the American Tobacco Company.

These firms quickly recognized the advantages of controlling production and centralizing management, as well as assuming marketing and purchasing activities. Although the newly consolidated companies offered fewer brands, they wielded much more capital and typically possessed large shares of the markets in which they operated. Here advertising played an important role in maintaining market power. Advertising proved beneficial to consumers as well, informing them of new products and establishing product differentiation.

Advertising also helped manufacturers move from selling fairly small quantities of goods to limited markets at high prices to mass-producing goods available at convenient locations and affordable prices. Scouring pads, toothpaste, and denim jeans, for example, found national markets. Packaging and promotion of soaps, crackers, and flour turned these essentially undifferentiated commodities into desirable products. Meanwhile, other manufacturers shifted their selling pitches to reach a wider audience. Coca-Cola's refreshing soft drink started as a medicinal tonic. Welch's substituted grape juice for wine. Postum Cereal food drink, a noncaffeine coffee substitute, made the claim "It makes red blood." And Edison's phonograph sold as a dictaphone machine.

Advertisements did more than merely inform customers. Now they relentlessly tried to persuade Americans to buy a particular manufacturer's brands and, above all, to accept no substitutes. The annual volume of advertising surged nearly six-fold in the twenty-year period following 1900, from $540 million to just less than $3 billion.[3]

The economic upswing that started around the turn of the century showed no signs of waning for the next three decades. As big business got bigger, industrial growth reached new heights.

Immigrants Flock to America

Fundamental to this early economic boom was electricity and the surplus of foreign-born labor. By 1920 more than one-third of the plants were fully electrified, as compared with one-twentieth in 1900.[4] These advances in production and advertising coincided with the country's explosive growth from 31 million people in 1860 to 105 million in 1920. This burgeoning population provided the huge number of workers that industry needed, as well as buyers for its products.

As it had done in colonial times, advertising attracted many new immigrants to America. Agents for railroads and western states ran newspaper ads, circulated posters, and handed out pamphlets in front of churches and other gathering places in European towns and cities. The development of ocean-going steamships made the Atlantic crossing faster and cheaper. In 1904 a drastic cut in steerage fares allowed Europeans to board a steamship with $10 in their pocket and arrive less than a month later at Ellis Island. With decent jobs awaiting them, many immigrants recouped their fare within a week. Some 9 million newcomers poured into the United States between 1900 and 1910 alone, helping to fuel the nation's rapid urban growth. By 1910 foreign-born residents and their children composed the majority of the population of large cities such as New York, Chicago, Detroit, Cleveland, and Boston.

In this era of economic prosperity, workers' incomes steadily increased, and many had money left over after they paid for basic necessities. This increased purchasing ability created a demand for still more consumer goods. American industry responded by shifting away from the production of capital goods used in making other products, such as steel, lumber, and machinery. New industries emerged to turn out new consumer goods, including ready-to-eat breakfast cereals, light bulbs, vacuums, irons, toasters, and washing machines. Other articles appeared entirely for the consumer's enjoyment, such as player pianos, phonographs, and board games. And two more inventions changed the way millions spent their leisure time—the automobile and the moving picture. Yet, perhaps more than anything else, marketing and packaging prodded the consumer economy and created a revolution in retailing.

Packaging Revolutionizes Mass Retailing

The soaring number of retail stores and mail-order catalogs took advantage of innovations in packaging. Improved transportation and distribution systems allowed canners and bakers to ship their goods beyond their established markets. Inevitably the need for improved forms of packaging arose. To fill the demand, marketers developed an array of sanitary and appealing containers. Some bakers packaged crackers in tins and in printed cardboard cartons. In 1889 a New York baker introduced a clear-fronted package to display the crackers inside. Later, wax-sealed cartons preserved the freshness of such foods as breakfast cereal grains, biscuits, cookies, and snack foods. Other innovative packaging included wood containers, sealed glass jars and bottles, cans, tins, boxes, wrappers, and metal tubes.

As the new retail outlets gained popularity, manufacturers designed their packages to stand out on store shelves. Packaging and brand names transformed generic products into unique ones, while advertising persuaded customers to demand now familiar brands. Colorful descriptive labels on packages further assisted shoppers in their selection. Packages also allowed price comparison as more stores affixed uniform, fixed prices to the merchandise. Inevitably this led to a new breed of customers, "smart shoppers," who felt free to shop at different markets to get the best products at the best prices.

In the cities shoppers flocked to local department stores, which provided luxury, comfort, and convenience. When they crossed the threshold of these magnificent emporiums, they entered a shoppers' wonderland. Sales floors displayed the latest fashions in dresses, kitchenware, home furnishings, and other amenities; eager clerks assisted them at every turn. At the same time, giant mail-order firms provided rural folks with everything from patent medicines and the latest gadgets for the home and workplace to livestock.

Chains Link Store After Store

The development of chain stores was the next step in mass retailing. Previously the typical shopkeeper had handled everything from purchasing and selling to display and advertising. General merchandisers and food retailers then began to apply the same economies of scale that had been used in manufacturing to sell their goods. That is, a centrally managed operation placed large orders at low prices, established low profit margins, and made money through volume sales. Consumers also came out ahead by being able to choose from a wider selection at affordable prices.

The chain store concept began with a few retailers who expanded the number of their outlets at first locally, then regionally, and eventually nationally. In time centrally managed chain stores replaced many small shopkeepers, who simply could not match the chains' variety and prices. For example, Woolworth's five-and-ten cent stores profitably operated almost 600 stores in 1913, and by 1920 J. C. Penney had opened almost 300 retail clothing outlets, which he called "chain stores."

A classic example of this phenomenon is the Great Atlantic and Pacific Tea Company (A&P), which evolved from a single store to become one of the most prominent chain retailers of the century. Founded in 1859, A&P started as a cut-price tea store in New York City; by 1912 it had expanded to a chain of four hundred food outlets. These small storefront groceries generally were about the same size as a typical urban corner store, and most had only one employee. A typical A&P grocer in New York City carried about twenty-five product categories, including one choice of many staple items—an enormous contrast to the thousands of items that fill today's supermarkets.

Prior to World War I, an era of rising food costs, many city dwellers spent up to half of their annual income on food. In this period A&P introduced a new strategy to provide quality food at low prices: the "Economy Store." To reduce costs, A&P pared down many services common to grocery stores of the time. A company officer explained: "In our so-called Economy Stores: we do not make any deliveries, we have no telephone communication, we close the store when the manager goes to lunch, we sell strictly for cash, we give no premiums, trading stamps, or other inducements."[5] With this approach, A&P emerged as the country's major grocer, using more efficient methods to process, warehouse, distribute, and sell food. The grocers, for example, applied their personal "Ann Page" brand to products supplied by other manufacturers. These "private brands" typically sold at lower prices than similar national brands. By 1929 A&P operated more than 15,000 stores and eventually became the largest retailer of any kind, a position it held until general merchandiser Sears surpassed it in 1965.[6]

Advertising Identifies Its Primary Audience

Over the decades spanning the nineteenth and twentieth centuries, the gap between advertisers and consumers based on both sex and class continued to widen. As the consumer society emerged, women became the nation's primary purchasers of consumer goods yet men primarily wrote the ads and created the images that they thought would influence women to purchase a variety of products.

Like their predecessors early twentieth-century admakers often assumed that their primary audience was female. The prevailing Victorian attitude provided an explanation. "From the philosopher's standpoint," James Collins wrote in 1901, "woman is an incidental helpmeet to man; from the standpoint of the wise advertiser she is queen of the nether world, mistress of the privy purse, keeper of the rolls, the hounds, and the exchequer."[7] Advertisers accepted that 85 percent of consumer purchases were made by women, though no one could cite an actual source for that number. Also, they believed that women's minds were "vats of frothy pink irrationality."[8] Professor W. I. Thomas further reinforced the accepted notion that the female mind was weak in his book *Sex and Society* (1907).

In many ways women found themselves increasingly marginalized or excluded. For example, they could not vote in national elections.

Also, women who once had worked as doctors and lawyers found themselves barred from attending the new medical and legal schools, obtaining professional licenses, and joining trade organization. Thus, as late as 1910, nearly 80 percent of working women still toiled at factory jobs or in domestic service, where pay was low and working conditions often poor. But the fact remained that earning wages allowed women to become more independent and even to participate in sports.

Around the turn of the century, adwomen also found themselves excluded from the advertising profession. As the industry gained prestige, men came to dominate the field, isolating females to work on products for the women's market (food, soap, cosmetics). Men filled the training programs and worked through the various departments in search of the right job for them. In contrast, women started lower, as secretaries or researchers, and struggled to get noticed as copywriters. Also, advertising clubs and organizations generally barred women, so they were forced to start their own groups. The Women's Publicity Club of Boston was one of the first; the League of Advertising Women of New York (now Advertising Women in New York) followed in 1912, as did similar groups in Philadelphia and Chicago.

Despite this conservative climate a few adwomen rose to prominence. On the agency side Helen Lansdowne Resor had a brilliant career as a copywriter and creative supervisor at J. Walter Thompson. Helen Rosen Woodward, one of the first prominent women account executives, worked for the Presbrey and Gardner agencies before turning author, publishing *Through Many Windows* (1926). And the Hoffman sisters of Chicago wrote and illustrated ads for Silver Leaf lard. Later, the manpower shortage during World War I and the postwar economic boom would reopen opportunities for women in advertising.

In this heady social and economic climate, advertising continued to mature as a business. The trademark continued to build brand images, but other, more sophisticated methods were used as well.

Turn-of-the-Century Advertising

The ability to capture the public's attention and to influence what people bought became the single largest determinant of success in business. Successful marketers recognized the importance of well-coordinated promotional planning that pushed the sale of particular brands and continually introduced new ones. By the turn of the century, manufacturers routinely introduced new brand-name products with a wave of advertising.

Advertisers also gradually began to turn their advertising entirely over to advertising agencies. With full responsibility for campaigns, the agencies evolved into their present-day form within the first decade of the century. Advertisements now were but one component of planned campaigns that had to be integrated into appropriate, sound marketing strategies.

Helen Rosen Woodward

In 1903 Helen Rosen Woodward began her copywriting career working for the Hampton Advertising Agency and then for the mail-order business J. A. Hill. Later she became a prominent account executive for Presbrey & Gardner (a position considered "undignified, unbusiness-like, and unfeminine" at the time). In her book *Through Many Windows* (1926) Woodward vividly described the days when advertising still had much to learn.

Woodward learned her craft writing about everything from elaborate sets of books, wall coverings, soups, and insurance to cigarettes. Believing that gloomy, negative ads would generate little response, she created cheerful, emotional, energetic spots that emphasized the rewards and pleasures associated with a given product. In explaining her philosophy, she noted: "Women seldom buy anything through logical reasoning, not even for their babies." She continued: "You must present even [a product's] facts so that they will reach the average mind, and that average has nothing to with reason. To sell articles to men, it is often wise to appear to reason with them, but you must be careful merely to do so—never actually be logical. Or you will sell no goods."[a]

Woodward retired in 1924 at the age of forty-three as one of the highest paid women in advertising and went to Paris to write her book. She followed it up with *Three Flights Up* (1935) and *It's an Art* (1938), critiques of the industry from within the business.

[a] Helen Rosen Woodward, *Through Many Windows* (New York: Harper, 1926), 205, 206.

Skilled copywriting, layout, and illustration became important in achieving continuity and strengthening selling appeals. In their early years the agency principals wrote the copy or, for important accounts, employed prominent freelance copywriters, who also assisted in trademarks, slogans, and other program needs. Although agencies began to hire full-time established writers to pen advertising copy, "art managers" typically sent an advertisement in its rough layout form to the printer. This changed, however, when designers and artists joined agency staffs and asserted that the "look" of an ad was just as important as the words.

The role of account executive expanded from simply bringing in new business to providing a needed liaison between the business-oriented client and the creative staff, while space brokers continued to shop around for the lowest bids for each media schedule. Market research, however, proved slower in getting started than skilled copywriting, layout, and account management.

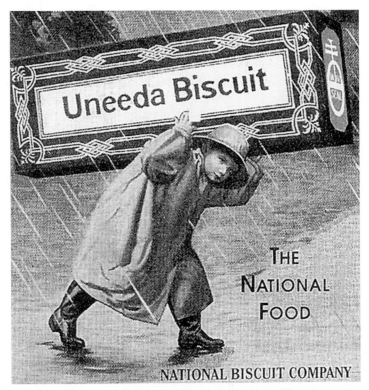

Figure 3.1 One of a series of 1890s ads from the National Biscuit Company (later Nabisco), featuring the trademark slicker-boy symbol for freshness.

The Golden Age of Trademark Advertising

Uneeda biscuit set the standard for the well-coordinated advertising plan that introduced a new product. The newly formed National Biscuit Company's first move was to create a brand-name cracker and to package it so as to preserve its freshness. Previously grocers had sold biscuits from open barrels, making no claims about their crispness or cleanliness. National Biscuit settled on a light, flaky soda cracker in a distinctive octagonal shape. To preserve the crackers' crispness, the firm packaged them in airtight, wax-paper-lined packages.

The biscuit company went to the N. W. Ayer & Son agency in New York City for advice on an appealing name and symbol for the new product that would appear both on the package and in advertisements. For the name the agency suggested "Uneeda" (pronounced "You-need-a"). Ayer also created the Uneeda biscuit slicker boy, a tyke posed in rain hat and a storm slicker, along with the catchy slogan "Lest you forget, we say it yet, Uneeda biscuit" (Figure 3.1). In 1899 the Ayer agency launched the first multimillion-dollar advertising campaign. A series of advertisements reached the public nationwide through newspapers, magazines, streetcar advertisements, posters, and painted signs.[9] After the success of Uneeda, National Biscuit quickly launched Oysterettes crackers, Zu Zu ginger snaps, Fig Newtons, Premium saltines, Nabisco sugar wafers, and Barnum's Animal Crackers.

Using Uneeda as an example, the N. K. Fairbank Company of Chicago made the Gold Dust twins a centerpiece for one of the most heavily advertised products after the turn of the century—Gold Dust washing powder. Fairbank first introduced the cleanser in the 1880s and sold the four-pound package for 25 cents, but soon a larger selection became available with prices as low as a nickel. The idea for the twins, Goldie and Dustie, came to Fairbank after seeing a cartoon in the English humor magazine *Punch*. It showed two black children washing each other; the caption read, "Warranted to wash clean and not fade."[10] In 1887 Fairbank commissioned famous cartoonist E. W. Kemble to draw the twins based on this image to decorate the yellowish-orange Gold Dust box. Also, Fairbank had a series of advertisements created that showed the Gold Dust twins doing various household chores for which the soap was recommended, along with the slogan "Let the Gold Dust twins do your work" (Figure 3.2). The campaign was an immediate success, and the slogan became one of the best-known phrases in America.

American women relied on Gold Dust washing powder to do their cleaning for the next fifty years. Over the years the two easily recognized little jet-black boys appeared naked except for tiny skirts on the package, in magazines, on billboards, and on other promotional items ranging from coloring books and trading cards to calendars, tin containers, hand-held mirrors, and thermometers. Over time the twins became more European-looking than African American with lighter skin and subtler, less caricatured facial features.

Other familiar personalities became the trademarks of the products they advertised and as famous as national heroes: Sir Thomas Lipton, Zu Zu ginger snap clown, the Old Dutch maid, the Campbell Kids, the Morton Salt girl, Buster Brown, the Fisk Tire boy, Planter's Mr. Peanut, and Cracker Jack's Sailor Jack, to name a few. And animals gained fame, too: Bull Durham's bull, Hartford's elk, the Our Pet cow logo, the Bon Ami yellow chick, MGM's Leo the Lion, Camel cigarette's "Joe" camel, and RCA's Nipper the smooth-haired terrier.

Printing innovations also encouraged creativity. The ability to reproduce gradations of light and dark tones, as well as the development of multiple-plate color printing, allowed printed pictures to look like opulent oil paintings, instead of hand-sketched black-and-white line drawings.

Figure 3.2 In the late 1880s the Gold Dust twins became a well-known symbol for the heavily advertised Gold Dust washing powder.

**MR.
PEANUT**
Ⓡ

When four-color front and back covers and one- or two-color interior ads became standard by 1900, magazines exploded with color. The look of the ad became increasingly important, so ad preparation fast became a key responsibility of the advertising agencies.

The Art of Advertising

Earnest Elmo Calkins, a native of Illinois, elevated the art of the advertisement, emphasizing the ad itself instead of the media selection or the size of the advertiser's budget. Already a skilled copywriter, Calkins went to work for Charles Austin Bates' New York agency in 1897. Later he started his own agency with Ralph Holden, an

Figure 3.3   In 1913 illustrator Joseph Leyendecker created the "Arrow Collar Man," who became a symbol for a generation of college men.

account man also from Bates. Calkins & Holden (C&H), based in New York City, promoted itself as "the first full-service agency," providing copy, design, space brokerage, and media planning.[11]

To Calkins the "look" of the ad meant "that combination of text with design which produces a complete advertisement."[12] If an ad had the "look," it would stop a reader from turning the page of the magazine or newspaper. Instead of highly detailed illustrations, Calkins preferred the simpler, modern format of the Arts and Crafts movement: simplified, sculpted forms; flat, unshaded planes of color; and silhouetted figures. This "look" built an image for the product and integrated branding, advertising, and other promotions. For example, Calkins hired artist Joseph Leyendecker to execute his creative vision for Arrow shirts. Leyendecker, known for his *Saturday Evening Post* covers, painted the "Arrow Collar Man," who became a symbol for a generation of college men. The models always appeared as more stylized than realistic in terms of the skin tones, folds of cloth, and so on (Figure 3.3). Other successful C&H soft-sell campaigns were done for Force cereal, Wesson oil, Sherwin Williams paint, Kelly Springfield tires, and Pierce-Arrow cars (Figure 3.4).

The Lackawanna railroad called Calkins for advice when they started to promote passenger rail service between New York and Buf-

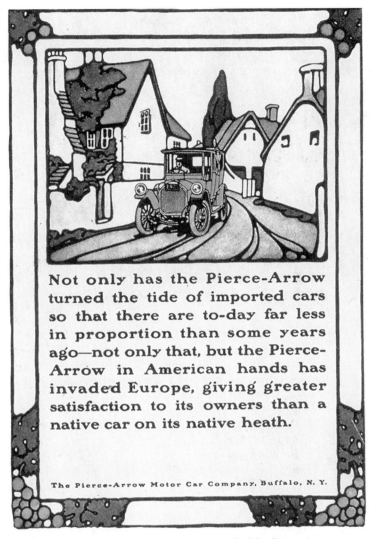

Figure 3.4 This 1913 Calkins & Holden soft-sell ad for Pierce-Arrow cars was but one of C&H's many successes.

falo. Author Mark Twain also helped develop the advertising theme when he traveled the line. Surprisingly Twain arrived with his suit still white, because the Lackawanna's locomotives burned hard-coal anthracite, which produced less soot than did soft coal. Thus the service gave passengers a cleaner trip and increased their comfort. With this in mind, the railroad coined the line "The Road of Anthracite."

Calkins developed a series of verses promoting a clean, comfortable trip on the Road of Anthracite. The admaker introduced the saga of the charming Phoebe Snow and hired artist Harry Stacy Benton to

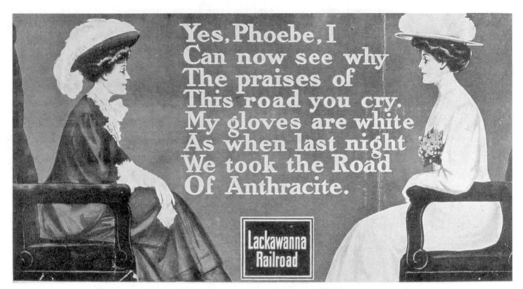

Figure 3.5   This 1900 streetcar ad by Calkins & Holden was one of a series describing "Phoebe Snow's" adventures riding the Lackawanna railroad.

create a spotless passenger who, like Mark Twain, traveled in immaculate white (Figure 3.5). One verse on that theme read:

> *Yes, Phoebe, I*
> *Can now see why*
> *The praises of*
> *This road you cry.*
> *My gloves are white*
> *As when last night*
> *We took the Road of Anthracite.*

Calkins' richly illustrated ads described Phoebe Snow's adventures riding the Lackawanna in a score of jingles. Over the course of the campaign, she met each member of the railroad's crew: "That day or night / They're all polite." She also admired "Each passing look / At nook or brook / a flying picture book / of landscape bright / Or mountain height." Along the way she also found romance with a white-clad young man, and eventually a white-frocked bishop married the couple en route. Lackawanna put her face on streetcars and railroad boxcars, on calendars, in vaudeville shows, and throughout a beautifully illustrated 128-page tour book. The guide described the "outdoor delights" and resorts along the Lackawanna route, along with "a fascinating love story entitled 'A Chance Courtship.'" The Phoebe Snow campaign lasted six years and made her a household name.

Other agencies followed C&H's pictorial style and hired gallery artists to create memorable advertising illustrations. For instance,

Figure 3.6   Famed illustrator N. C. Wyeth created this 1913 ad: "Where the mail goes Cream of Wheat goes."

Maxfield Parrish's meticulous painting style appeared in stunning Fisk tire and Community Silverplate advertisements. The artist achieved a full, detailed look by building up layers of glaze like the Renaissance masters. N. C. Wyeth painted ads for Cream of Wheat filled with cowboys and gold miners, creating a continuing environment for the product (similar to today's ongoing "Marlboro Country" cigarette campaign) (Figure 3.6). Norman Rockwell painted realistic figures with a humorous touch for everything from Heinz baked beans to Grape Nuts.

Memorable Slogans

His Master's Voice. (RCA Victrola)

Say Zu Zu to the grocer man. (Zu Zu ginger snaps)

When it rains, it pours. (Morton salt)

The ham what am. (Armour hams)

Say it with flowers.(American Florists Association)

The beer that made Milwaukee famous. (Schlitz)

Time to Re-tire. (Fisk tires)

Good to the last drop. (Maxwell House coffee)

The flavor that lasts. (Wrigley chewing gums)

Delicious and refreshing. (Coca-Cola)

The instrument of the immortals. (Steinway pianos)

The skin you love to touch. (Woodbury facial soap)

I'd walk a mile for a Camel. (Camel cigarettes)

Motorists wise Simoniz. (Simoniz car wax)

It beats as it sweeps as it cleans. (Hoover sweepers)

Ask the person who owns one. (Packard automobile)

Leave the driving to us. (Greyhound bus)

The more you eat, the more you want. (Cracker Jacks)

Drink an Orange. (Sunkist)

From World War I

Daddy, what did you do in the Great War?

Your country needs YOU!

While humor, jingles, and trademark characters kept the names of products in the public's mind, they didn't always sell them. For a familiar product like Sapolio soap, the devices effectively reminded customers of an already well-established brand. People may have found the characters and verses for a new product to be entertaining, but more often they failed to discover the benefits of using the product and the reasons the product was better than rival brands. Thus, as popular as Phoebe Snow was, Lackawanna eventually questioned her ability to sell, so the railroad brought in the J. Walter Thompson agency to shift to a harder sell that emphasized the line's equipment.

As the volume of advertising increased, so did an endless duplication of what appeared. As readers stopped responding, admakers shifted their pitch away from jingles, trademark characters, and pretty pictures to harder-selling copy with new appeals. In the process admakers would expand their theory and practice to embrace new techniques, approaches, and services.

Salesmanship in Print

A successful ad works because it creates a connection between the product being advertised and some need or desire that the audience feels. These links, called "appeals," fall into two categories: logical and emotional. Logical (or rational) appeals base selling pitches on either the product's performance features or its ability to solve a problem. In contrast, emotional appeals base selling pitches on the satisfaction that comes from purchasing the product and then owning it or making a gift of it. An extremely strong appeal tells the consumer: "This is *the* product that will meet your needs or fulfill your desires."

Although fundamental to advertising today, these ideas seemed novel and revolutionary in 1905—especially the idea that the skillful use of emotional appeals could move products faster than any other approach. But the emotional approach did not suddenly appear. Pioneering admakers first introduced the idea of the sales argument rather than brand identification as the basis of the sales campaign; the essential emotional appeal came later. Another new soft-sell strategy called "atmospheric advertising," took an even subtler approach, employing opulent art and suggestive sales pitches to convey a favorable impression of the product.

Print Ads Shift Gears

A new advertising approach, called "reason-why" copy, shifted the focus of ads to sales arguments designed to overcome any resistance. This hard-sell style was in sharp contrast to the simple brand-name identification campaign that sold the product name to the public. In the process reason-why practitioners John E. Kennedy, Claude Hopkins, Albert Lasker, and Helen Resor established the copywriter as crucial to ad agency operations.

John E. Kennedy, hired as Lord & Thomas' chief copywriter for the Chicago office in 1904, treated advertising as business news to be told in a detailed, straightforward style. "Advertising is salesmanship in print," Kennedy explained. Instead of jingles, soft-sell pictures, and general claims, an advertisement should state in print what the salesman would say in person to a customer. That is, it should offer a sensible argument with specific reasons the product was worth buying. Kennedy also wrote ads in a distinct style, using such devices as italics, underlining, and capital letters to grab the reader's attention.

In this classic 1903 pitch for the patent medicine Dr. Shoop's Restorative, Kennedy deliberately set out to overcome any consumer resistance. The ad carried a simple message: you have nothing to lose by trying our product. The mail-order ad opened:

> *My Book Is Free*
> *My treatment too—if that fails.*
> *But if it helps—if it succeeds,*
> *If health is yours again,*
> *I ask you to pay—$5.50 . . .*
> *And further, I will send the name of a druggist near*
> *you who will let you take six bottles of my remedy, on*
> *a month's trial. If it succeeds, the cost to you is $5.50.*
> *If it fails, the druggist will bill the cost to me.*

Not an entirely new idea, reason-why copy simply echoed the fundamentals of copywriters John Powers (let's try honesty) and Charles Austin Bates (advertising is business news). Kennedy's copy style also owed a debt to hard-selling patent medicine arguments—testimonials, samples, coupons, money-back guarantees, specific claims, and other attention-getting devices. In turn, Kennedy taught Lord & Thomas account executive Albert Lasker, who passed the reason-why gospel along to his apprentice copywriters at the agency. After Kennedy left Lord & Thomas, Lasker hired Claude Hopkins, who also wrote in the reason-why style.

Hopkins emerged one of the most influential copywriters in advertising, a pioneer in providing free samples and using coupons in his ads. Before starting at the Lord & Thomas agency, this skilled practitioner had already worked out his classic advertising strategy on a number of accounts to provide people with a logical "reason-why" to purchase a product. For example, his sales pamphlets for Bissell carpet sweepers were unlike anything dealers had used before. Instead of emphasizing the sweeper's mechanics and ability to pick up dirt, Hopkins gave women who bought the equipment numerous other reasons to buy the Bissell brand, like the special wood finishes, or to ask for it as a Christmas gift.

Hopkins' next triumph was Schlitz beer (Figure 3.7). To sell the Schlitz brand, Hopkins developed the "preemptive claim" technique that established a product's uniqueness. In touring the brewery for specific reasons to impress the public with the purity of the product, Hopkins discovered a number of selling points and countless numerical facts. For instance, the "mother yeast cell" had been selected after 1018 different experiments yielded unequaled flavor. Every drop of beer was filtered through special filters. And another procedure sterilized empty bottles. This last point inspired a powerful headline for Schlitz beer: "Washed with Live Steam!" In fact, other breweries could make this same claim, because the industry considered steam-cleaning

Poor Beer vs. Pure Beer

Both cost you alike, yet one costs the maker twice as much as the other. One is good, and good for you; the other is harmful. Let us tell you where the difference lies.

POOR BEER	PURE BEER
is easy to brew.	calls for the best materials—the best that money can buy.
The materials are cheap. The brewing may be done under any sort of surroundings.	The brewery must be as clean as your kitchen; the utensils as clean.
Cleanliness is not important, for the users never see it brewed.	The cooling must be done in filtered air, in a plate glass room.
Any water will do. No air is too impure for the cooling.	The product must be aged for months, until thoroughly fermented, else it causes biliousness.
No filtering, no sterilizing, almost no ageing, for ageing ties up money.	The beer must be filtered, then sterilized in the bottle.
What is the use of expense and care when there is no reputation to defend?—	You're always welcome to that brewery for the owners are proud of it.
When few people who drink it know even the name of the maker.	And the size of it proves the eventual success of worth.

Schlitz is a pure beer, famous for fifty years. To maintain its standard, we double the necessary cost of our brewing. Don't you prefer a pure beer, a good beer, a healthful beer, when it costs no more than the common?

Ask for the brewery bottling.

Schlitz

The Beer That Made Milwaukee Famous

Figure 3.7 In this turn-of-the-century spot Claude Hopkins used the "preemptive claim" technique to establish the product's supposed uniqueness.

bottles to be standard practice. Hopkins, however, theorized that if one took a product feature or quality that might be common to the industry and made the claim first, one owned it.

Other vintage Hopkins ads included spots for the patent medicine Dr. Shoop's Restorative (for which he took John Kennedy's place) and for a germicide called Liquozone. Here, Hopkins added the leverage of coupons for free samples and money-back offers.

Above all, Hopkins believed, an ad should be built around a single selling point, the preemptive claim. Hopkins then gave readers scores of reasons they should want the product, as his spot for Quaker Oats puffed-grain cereals showed (Figure 3.8). To move large quantities of a product, Hopkins argued, the copywriter had to talk to people, one at a time, with simplicity and force. In his book *Scientific Advertising,* Hopkins offered this advice: "The advertising man studies the consumer. He tries to place himself in the position of the buyer. His success largely depends on doing that to the exclusion of everything else."[13]

While working for the Lord & Thomas agency, Hopkins added the selling technique of mail-order advertising to his reason-why theories. These devices included free or inexpensive samples, premiums, coupons, hard-selling arguments, and functional illustrations with informative captions. For instance, ads for Pepsodent toothpaste pictured attractive people and explained how the dentrifice removed "the dingy film on teeth." An ad for Van Camps pork and beans positioned the "$100,000 Dish" against home-cooked beans: "Scientific cooks made 856 sauces before they attained this perfection." It forcefully closed with "Please order a trial meal." In the same way an ad for Palmolive shaving cream explained that the product was developed after testing "130 formulas." The ad also offered a free sample: "10 shaves free and a can of Palmolive After Shaving Talc."

The Feminine Point of View Finds a Voice

Helen J. Lansdowne Resor, a J. Walter Thompson copywriter, added the essential emotional appeal to the sales argument when her celebrated ad for Woodbury's facial soap first appeared in 1911 (Figure 3.9). The ad featured a painting of an attractive couple and a provocative headline that invited the audience to read further: "A skin you love to touch." The ad copy featured a skin-care regimen and closed with an offer for a week's supply of soap, plus the art from the advertisement. Instead of merely selling soap, the landmark ad also discussed the benefits of using the product, suggesting softness, sex appeal, and even romance. The advertisement shocked many *Ladies' Home Journal* readers and caused some to cancel their subscriptions.

Helen Resor was writing retail ads in Cincinnati, Ohio, when account executive Stanley Resor hired her as a copywriter for his small agency. When J. Walter Thompson in turn hired Stanley and his brother to establish a Cincinnati office, they brought Helen along as the sole copywriter, later moving to the New York office. A group headed by Stanley bought the retiring Thompson out in 1916, and the following year Stanley and Helen married. The husband-and-wife team ran the agency together; he managed client services, and she supervised ad creation. By 1922 the agency had tripled in size and boasted $10.7 million in annual billings.

In the early twentieth century J. Walter Thompson handled many products that were purchased by women. Helen Resor's understanding

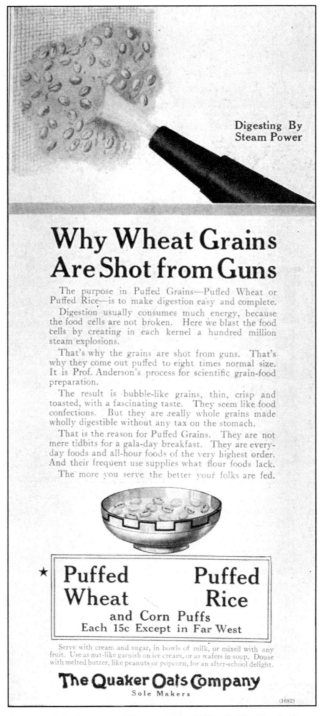

Figure 3.8 With this turn-of-the-century ad Claude Hopkins built a pitch around a single key selling point: Puffed Wheat grains were "shot from guns."

Figure 3.9   With this 1911 ad Helen Resor added the essential emotional appeal to the sales argument—sex could sell a lot of soap.

and insight made a tremendous difference in her work. "I added the feminine point of view," she explained. "I watch the advertising to see that the idea, the wording, and the illustrating were effective for women."[14] Her words and visuals embraced women's hopes, fears, desires, and dreams regardless of what they did for a living. She understood why women might prefer to buy soap over shortening, and so she presented provocative arguments for improving oneself and aspiring to the lifestyle of richer people.

Helen Resor's ads were characterized by an "editorial style" that resembled the adjacent reading material and that attracted readers' attention. A typical ad featured an arresting image followed by gentle selling copy that provided specific reasons to purchase the product;

the ad closed with a coupon offering free or inexpensive product samples by mail. Her powerful style thus blended Calkins' soft-sell with Hopkins' reason-why approach. Such human interest approaches also worked in promoting Crisco vegetable shortening, Maxwell House and Yuban coffee, Lux soap, and Cutex nail polish.

Image Builds the Emotional Appeal

The next new strategy represented a subtler approach than Claude Hopkins' and Helen Resor's reason-why, claim-and-coupon styles. With this soft-sell style, called "atmospheric advertising" or "impressionistic copy," the pitch revolved around suggestions or associations conveying the impression of integrity, quality, and prestige. The intent was to differentiate these products from those associated with hard-selling arguments, such as patent medicines and inexpensive mail-order products.

The atmospheric style recalled Calkins & Holden's lavish illustrations for Arrow shirts, Pierce-Arrow cars, and Community Silverplate. The opulent atmosphere lent an air of prestige in showcasing products in a unique selling environment. The theories of psychoanalyst Sigmund Freud, psychologist Carl Jung, and Professor Walter Dill Scott's influential book *The Psychology of Advertising* (1908) further justified this psychology of suggestion to make an impression. In particular, Scott called attention to a major weakness in reason-why copy: it described the product itself instead of extolling the pleasure it would provide the purchaser. Scott explained:

> How many advertisers describe a piano so vividly that the reader can hear it? How many food products are so described that the reader can taste the food? How many advertisements describe a perfume so that the reader can smell it? How many describe an undergarment so that the reader can feel the pleasant contact with his body?[15]

This idea was just beginning to take root. In the 1920s the advice offered by behavioral psychologist John B. Watson to the J. Walter Thompson agency would help popularize campaigns based on suggestion psychology aimed at the unconscious mind of the buying public.

The eloquent "Penalty of Leadership" essay for Cadillac established copywriter Theodore MacManus as the leader in the atmospheric soft-sell school (Figure 3.10). MacManus also kept other company names and trademarks like General Electric in the public eye. Another great "atmospheric" copywriter of the time, Raymond Rubicam, used suggestive sales pitches employing lavish art and layouts coupled with impressionistic copy that conveyed a sense of class. Rubicam's ads generated a positive response for Steinway pianos ("The Instrument of the Immortals"), E. R. Squibb pharmaceuticals ("The Priceless Ingredient of every product is the honor and integrity

Cadillac
Standard
of the World

The PENALTY OF LEADERSHIP

IN every field of human endeavor, he that is first must perpetually live in the white light of publicity. ¶Whether the leadership be vested in a man or in a manufactured product, emulation and envy are ever at work. ¶In art, in literature, in music, in industry, the reward and the punishment are always the same. ¶The reward is widespread recognition; the punishment, fierce denial and detraction. ¶When a man's work becomes a standard for the whole world, it also becomes a target for the shafts of the envious few. ¶If his work be merely mediocre, he will be left severely alone—if he achieve a masterpiece, it will set a million tongues a-wagging. ¶Jealousy does not protrude its forked tongue at the artist who produces a commonplace painting. ¶Whatsoever you write, or paint, or play, or sing, or build, no one will strive to surpass, or to slander you, unless your work be stamped with the seal of genius. ¶Long, long after a great work or a good work has been done, those who are disappointed or envious continue to cry out that it can not be done. ¶Spiteful little voices in the domain of art were raised against our own Whistler as a mountebank, long after the big world had acclaimed him its greatest artistic genius. ¶Multitudes flocked to Bayreuth to worship at the musical shrine of Wagner, while the little group of those whom he had dethroned and displaced argued angrily that he was no musician at all. ¶The little world continued to protest that Fulton could never build a steamboat, while the big world flocked to the river banks to see his boat steam by. ¶The leader is assailed because he is a leader, and the effort to equal him is merely added proof of that leadership. ¶Failing to equal or to excel, the follower seeks to depreciate and to destroy—but only confirms once more the superiority of that which he strives to supplant. ¶There is nothing new in this. ¶It is as old as the world and as old as the human passions—envy, fear, greed, ambition, and the desire to surpass. ¶And it all avails nothing. ¶If the leader truly leads, he remains—the leader. ¶Master-poet, master-painter, master-workman, each in his turn is assailed, and each holds his laurels through the ages. ¶That which is good or great makes itself known, no matter how loud the clamor of denial. ¶That which deserves to live—lives.

Cadillac Motor Car Co. Detroit, Mich.

Copyright 1914, Cadillac Motor Car Co.

Figure 3.10   In this 1915 car ad, one of the most celebrated in advertising history, Theodore MacManus used the atmospheric style to build prestige for Cadillac.

of its maker"), Rolls-Royce ("To A Man Who Is Afraid To Let His Dreams Come True"), and the International Correspondence School ("The University of the Night") (Figure 3.11).

The two schools of advertising theory, reason-why and atmospheric, coexisted for a period of time. The effectiveness of the style depended on the product being advertised. The Hopkins reason-why style worked best for small, inexpensive, frequently purchased items that could be cheaply offered as samples and sent through the mail, such as cigarettes, toothpaste, and soap. The MacManus soft-sell style, however, built prestige for large, expensive items bought infrequently and seldom on impulse, like automobiles and pianos.

Even as advertisers continued to flood the market with new products and experiment with different sales approaches, the advertising agencies continued to evolve. Now they were conducting market research and forming professional associations.

The Expansion of Agency Services

Agencies multiplied in terms of size, number, and services offered as the volume of advertising increased. New agencies began to offer the same services available today—planning, research, ad creation, and implementation of advertising campaigns. In particular, ad preparation, education in advertising practice, and market research marked key steps in the ad industry's development.

Beginning around 1900, correspondence schools offered courses in advertising technique, an indication of advertising's increased legitimation in the business world. For instance, the Alexander Hamilton Institute and the International Correspondence Schools included advertising among their subjects. A decade later, institutions of higher learning such as Harvard University, New York University, Boston University, Northwestern University, and the University of Missouri also began to take advertising seriously enough to include it in their business curricula.

The concept of marketing research, however, was slower to take hold. Advertisers had more questions—Who is the buying public? What are its tastes and desires? Which ads pull the best?—than answers. To understand their audience, some admakers went into the field to sell the product, observed it in use, or interviewed housewives in order to acquire a feel for consumer tastes and retail problems. Yet these early research efforts were primitive by today's standards.

J. Walter Thompson's study, combined with Curtis Publishing Company's own findings, provided a factual base on which future marketing researchers would build. In 1912 J. Walter Thompson's Stanley Resor commissioned a study entitled "Population and Its Distribution," which listed virtually every store by category and by state. The agency continued to update the research to describe more precisely

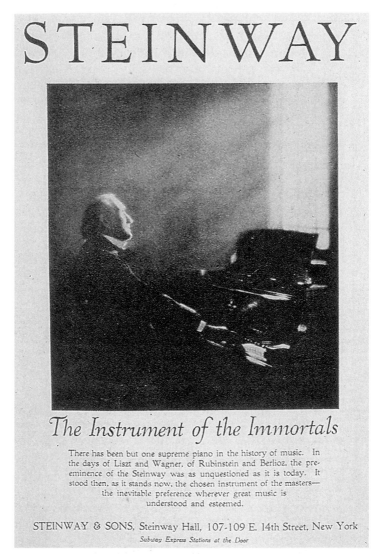

Figure 3.11 In this 1919 ad Raymond Rubicam used suggestive copy and lavish art to promote Steinway pianos.

the consumer population, to track the growth of wholesale and retail stores in large cities, and so on.

Mail-order response testing emerged as the major form of research that provided a rough idea of consumer preferences. For example, coded advertisements ran with coupons, which readers could cut out and return for information, product samples, booklets, or premiums. In test cities identical ads appeared in different magazines, and the results were compared. "Split runs" compared different versions of the same ads against each other in the same edition. From these studies agencies identified the best medium or media for the advertising of a given product. In addition, researchers sent crude surveys such as questionnaires to employees' friends, to women in the agency's own office, or to "typical" consumers (admen's spouses). Independent research firms also emerged, and departments began to form within agencies to obtain detailed data to assist in ad planning. This proved an important service.

Agencies were no longer primarily space brokers. The quality of the ads they prepared now became one of the agencies' prime methods of attracting clients. Agency representatives presented a portfolio of the agency's advertisements to make a favorable impression on prospective clients.

The first roster of advertising agencies appeared in 1917, listing N. W. Ayer as the largest agency in gross billings, followed by J. Walter Thompson. Meanwhile George Batten's agency went on to become Batten, Barton, Durstine & Osborne (BBDO), while H. K. McCann and the Erickson Company merged to become McCann-Erickson. And based on their soaring volume of sales, the media recognized the advertising agents' important role and agreed to pay them a commission, which was obtained from the advertiser.

Active organizations also brought together advertisers, agents, publishers, and others associated with advertising. Key professional organizations included the Association of National Advertisers (1915) and the American Association of Advertising Agencies (1917). Their efforts established standards for codes and ethics and simplified the mechanics of advertising. These groups also created a certified Audit Bureau of Circulation, which standardized rate cards with forms for placing media orders and established uniform page and column sizes in both magazines and newspapers. As a result, advertising activities became more effective and, as a whole, more reputable.

Even as advertising came of age in the early twentieth century, it was applied to a host of new products, services, and even social problems. This was the Progressive era, and advertising was one aspect of such "progress."

Advertising and Progress

During the Progressive Era (1901–1916) virtually every aspect of American society was revamped, reformed, or otherwise improved. For example, municipal governments and the nation's banking system both were streamlined; housing and health care standards were raised; public education was expanded; and the federal government addressed the child labor issue. There was also a host of new products and inventions for the home, as well as new ways of getting about.

Advertising, too, underwent scrutiny in this period. After years of exposure to unsubstantiated product claims, consumers eventually focused their growing resentment on ads for patent medicines, cure-alls,

A Taste of the Times

The Edwardian period (1901–1914) refers to the exuberant years after Queen Victoria's death in which many of the earlier era's genteel traditions were toppled. A group of journalists called "muckrakers" showed the need for reform through skillfully written articles and books about corruption in the nation's business and politics. Among the most influential books of the time were Ida Tarbell's 1904 *History of the Standard Oil Company* (which led to the breakup of one of the country's biggest monopolies), Lincoln Steffens' 1904 *The Shame of the Cities* (which attacked graft in local politics), and Upton Sinclair's 1906 *The Jungle* (which detailed the filthy conditions in the meat-packing industry).

Other artists tried to reform prevailing attitudes about art and design. In 1907 eight young painters, later called the "Ashcan School," organized an exhibition of their work. The artists painted realistic social scenes, ranging from slum alleys to smoke-spewing trains to gritty factories. Six years later, another show at the New York Armory highlighted European trends, from the older postimpressionists Gauguin, Cezanne, and van Gogh, to a new generation of artists including Duchamp, Picasso, and Matisse. The public ridiculed the Armory Show, seeing only deformed images, crude techniques, and unnatural colors. Fearful of revolutionary aesthetic ideas, many people felt reluctant to forsake their cherished clutter, ornate realism, and beloved knick-knacks for the newer simplicity. Thus they further delayed the broad

and health devices. The reform movement began when the *Ladies' Home Journal* refused to print medical advertising in 1892; other better-class magazines soon followed suit. A decade later the *Journal* shocked the public when it printed chemical analyses of advertised medicines showing that many contained such addictive substances as cocaine and morphine. Other magazines and leading newspapers joined the campaign to expose nostrums, quack doctors, and unscrupulous food manufacturers.

The resulting consumer movement led to government regulation—and to industry efforts at self-regulation. One outcome was strong federal laws such as the Meat Inspection Act and the 1906 Pure Food and Drugs Act, as well as laws requiring lists of ingredients on food containers, medicine bottles, and pill boxes. Also, the activities of long-time promoters of worthless stock certificates, deceptive retail announcements, and other advertising inaccuracies led to the "truth in advertising movement" and the formation of the National Better Business Bureau. This agency, supported by dues from member com-

acceptance of modern art and design in America until after World War I.

Architects also attempted to break away from outdated European traditions. The Arts and Crafts movement reached its height early in the century, and the design of the cozy bungalow summed up the movement's ideas—a cheap-to-build, one-story house with a verandah running the width of the square building. It especially caught on in the West. Architect Frank Lloyd Wright broke with tradition with his "prairie house," a long, low structure that proved both liveable and beautiful. Although the prairie house did not sell well at first, it set the style for the mass-produced "ranch-style" homes that would appear after World War II.

People also found new ways to amuse themselves. Collecting postcards became a national pastime, and fans displayed their card collections on parlor tables or in bulging albums. Parker Brothers mass-produced card games, board games, and jigsaw puzzles that provided entertainment, but the rage was their Ping-Pong table tennis game. Some even credit the game with having a lasting effect on women's fashions. Female players tossed away their corsets, shortened their skirts, and loosened their clothes to better play the game.

As for music, the uniquely American rhythms of jazz, based on the songs and dances of African Americans, emerged from the bordellos and cabarets of New Orleans. And the nickelodeon offered a night out at the movies, after which moviegoers gathered at the corner drugstore or at palace-sized establishments for syrup-flavored sodas, malts, and floats.

panies, primarily operated at the local level to protect consumers against fraudulent and deceptive advertising.

America Cleans Up Its Act

America's pursuit of cleanliness began in earnest during the mid-1800s and reached a peak in the post–World War II years. The nineteenth-century urban population explosion was a key factor in the health problems that followed. In the overcrowded cities housing was inadequate and public utilities and health care facilities could not meet the demands. And in this preantibiotics, presulpha age, diseases like tuberculosis, diphtheria, typhoid, and polio were a constant threat. In the eyes of upper- and middle-class Americans, the "unwashed" were immigrants from Southern Europe (who recently arrived in the country's new cities, and later, those from the rural South). The burden of cleanliness primarily fell on wives and mothers, but cleanliness meant more than keeping home and clothing clean. It also included personal hygiene and bathing. This posed special problems, however. Many immigrants considered the practice useless and only on occasion bathed during the summer months in local rivers or streams. People who recognized the importance of taking frequent baths usually bathed only on Saturday evening or before holidays. They also lacked plumbing and privacy as they waited their turn for the hot shower at a public bath or a large washtub at home until improved housing could offer bathtubs and toilets.[16]

The collective efforts of individuals, citizen groups, and government agencies improved public health and cleanliness standards over the first two decades of the century. Civic-minded women and sanitarians took on the challenge of persuading elected officials to improve inefficient municipal practices, while others worked to increase community awareness. Public health and cleanliness reformers focused their attention on education beginning in the 1910s. Schools, organized groups, boards of health, and businesses promoted cleanliness both in the workplace and through advertising. Cleanliness standards rose quickly as the result of explicit warnings from home economists, health practitioners, and manufacturers of sanitary and cleaning products, who ran lurid ads describing infectious germs.

Metropolitan Insurance joined the corps of activists and reinforced the popular idea of cleanliness with some successful advertising. Large numbers of immigrants invested in insurance premiums, so Metropolitan sent its agents out to befriend these families, encouraging "long life" and "great living." "Cleanliness" and "health" formed the foundation for Metropolitan's "Health Campaign." The firm's agents handed out pamphlets that explained the causes of tuberculosis and ways to avoid the disease. In the last panel of the booklet, families were told that "a bath a day keeps sickness away." Metropolitan also put disposable drinking cups on several railroad lines and as a promotion gave away thousands of flyswatters imprinted with this message: "Clean Homes, Pure Food, Clean Milk, No Flies, and No Mosquitoes."

Other entrepreneurs found opportunities in this climate of rising health consciousness, creating disposable sanitary products. In fact, entrepreneurs early on had recognized the value of manufacturing "throwaways": items like pins, needles, and straws that were used once and then tossed out, so that customers kept buying them again and again. And throwaways like paper cups, toilet paper, and paper towels all owed their initial acceptance to this rising health conscious.

One entrepreneur, Hugh Moore, attempted to sell drinks of clean water to thirsty customers, who filled a paper cup from his porcelain dispenser, satisfied their thirst, and tossed the cup away. Although it was a great idea, no one wanted to pay for a drink of water in 1908. But when health crusaders published the shocking results of a study about germs found on publicly shared drinking vessels, Moore shrewdly recognized that his disposable paper cups provided a reasonable solution to the sanitation problem. Thus he set out to promote his disposable paper cups with lurid ads and promotional material. One spot included the headline "Spare the Children" and showed a clearly diseased man drinking from a dipper—while an innocent young girl waited her turn. Another advertisement warned, "Avoid the common drinking cup as if it were the plague itself . . . Influenza sits on the brim." Moore first marketed his disposable hygienic cups as the clinical "Health Kups" but later switched to the friendlier-sounding "Dixie Cups." By 1912 states had outlawed public dippers for health reasons, and disposable cups quickly found their way into schools, offices, stores, and other public areas.

From the beginning toilet paper also had been a hard sell. Few people wanted to spend money for yellow pads of "medicated paper," as it was called then, when the pages of mail-order catalogs filled the need. When indoor toilets appeared, Philadelphia paper sellers Irvin and Clarence Scott bought sheets of tissue wrapping paper, cut them into a convenient size, and repackaged them for the home bathroom. Even after indoor plumbing became standard, however, people were embarrassed to ask grocers for toilet paper. One early Scott tissue ad noted the concern and advised, "Don't ask for toilet paper—ask for ScotTissue."

Scott Paper also introduced disposable paper towels and warned the public that one could not be too careful about sharing towels in public places. By accident the company had received a shipment of absorbent paper far too coarse for toilet paper. It promptly resold the paper as a throwaway hand towel—ScotTowels for the home and Sani-Towels for business. One 1912 ad suggested a number of uses in the kitchen: "They can be used for polishing cut glass; for absorbing bacon grease from fried foods; for wiping windows. . . . after shaving they dry the skin without friction." A more radical version appeared for Sani-Towels. One 1915 ad warns: "Next Time You Visit Any Wash Room HESITATE." The text goes on:

> You will find there some kind of a towel. If it is a fabric towel-roller or individual—pause and ask yourself these questions: Is it safe to use? Who used it last? How was their health? Did a mere laundering make the towel contagion proof? Think hard over these questions.

Scott Paper then invented a wall unit that dispensed the paper towels one at a time—a common sight in public facilities today.

Advertising Revolutionizes the Breakfast Menu

Science and health also formed the foundation for advertising campaigns that introduced two new breakfast ideas—orange juice and ready-to-eat breakfast cereals.

Today breakfast would seem incomplete without a glass of orange juice, but this was a new idea at the turn of the century. People prepared oranges in one way: they peeled, sectioned, and ate them. In an effort to sell more oranges, the Southern California Fruit Growers Exchange (a cooperative of citrus growers) hired the Lord & Thomas agency in 1908. Their first spot accentuated the healthful qualities of the fruit in an "Orange Week in Iowa" newspaper ad, which coined the name "Sunkissed" (later changed to "Sunkist").

Early on the fruit growers realized that they had to find new uses for the product, because oranges did not appear to lend themselves to being baked or in other dishes, as did apples. One strategy resulted in the design and marketing of a glass hand-held reamer that enabled people to squeeze their own fresh orange juice. In 1916 Claude Hopkins wrote one of the most famous Sunkist ads; it headlined, "Drink an Orange." The copy explained that orange juice was "a delicious beverage—healthfulness itself" and that "thousands of physicians" recommended the "live juice" for its food value, "which comes to you in Nature's germ-proof package, [and] is a natural regulator." The ad closed with an offer for a specially designed "Juice Extractor" for only 10 cents and a free booklet of tested recipes (Figure 3.12). Subsequent ads claimed that someone who drank orange juice enjoyed renewed vigor and performance and avoided what Sunkist called "the increasing common human habit of 'slipping,' mentally and physically." Such campaigns greatly increased the consumption of oranges.

Like orange juice, breakfast cereals also started out as part of a health regime. Before these grains came on the scene, a heavy meat-and-potatoes breakfast got workers going. However, the demand for lighter breakfasts grew as more people left the farm and worked at less strenuous office jobs. By this time oats advertisers had already conditioned the public to eating grain. Using Quaker Oats as an example, early cereal makers did not push their product as tasting good. Instead, familiar brands such as Kellogg's Corn Flakes, Grape Nuts, Post Toasties, and Shredded Wheat pitched health benefits and made serious scientific claims.

Dr. John Harvey Kellogg, of the Battle Creek Sanitarium in Battle Creek, Michigan, was the first to market a cold, ready-to-eat breakfast food. The Adventist church sponsored the sanitarium, so Dr. Kellogg had to conform to its vegetarian, no-stimulants diet regimen. In 1878 Dr. Kellogg introduced "Granola," a mixture of baked wheat, oatmeal, and cornmeal—the first cold cereal boxed and sold by a brand name. He next boiled, mashed, chilled, dried, and baked blobs of corn into crispy flakes. However, the product, marketed as "Sanitas Toasted Corn Flakes," did not find success. The cereal quickly turned rancid, and it didn't taste very good either.

At this point Dr. Kellogg's younger brother William, an accountant, stepped in and made changes. William Kellogg improved the taste of the flakes, wrapped the box with wax paper, dropped the "Sanitas"

Figure 3.12 In this 1916 ad Claude Hopkins sought to boost sales of oranges by promoting a new idea—orange juice.

name, acquired the product rights, and put his signature, "W. K. Kellogg," on the box. He distributed thousands of small trial boxes and made far simpler and more pleasant claims than lurid medical exaggerations advanced by his early rivals. Also, he invented a test market system for all advertising, promotion, and package designs: try them out in Dayton, Ohio; if sales shoot up, take the idea national.

William Kellogg's constantly changing, imaginative campaigns described the flakes as fresh, delicious, and nourishing. The "sweetheart of the corn" maiden pictured clutching a shock of corn further embraced this theme (Figure 3.13). Kellogg later put the wax wrapper inside the package, and a 1914 ad explained the benefits: flakes "so perfectly sealed that wherever and whenever you buy them, they will be as fresh and crisp as they are when they come from our ovens."

Figure 3.13   In this 1907 ad the "sweetheart of the corn" maiden
embraced the theme of Corn Flakes as fresh, delicious, and nutritious.

Another intriguing ad ran in New York City; it suggested: "Give the
grocer a wink and see what you'll get K-T-C." What they got were free
samples. These efforts paid off. The brand name "Corn Flakes" was so
successful that it became one of the first trademarks to go generic. In
Battle Creek, Michigan, alone, over one hundred brands appeared.

Of the many imitators, C. W. Post, a Texas real estate developer,
created a rival brand that proved extremely popular. After a stay at Dr.
Kellogg's Battle Creek Sanitarium in 1891, Post remained in the area
and opened a small convalescent home where he endlessly experimented to create edible, nutritious foods. Post created his first breakfast cereal in 1898, called it Grape Nuts, and promoted the nutlike

Figure 3.14   In the early twentieth century, Force cereal became very popular due mainly to the "Jim Dumps" character.

cereal as "Made of Wheat and Barley . . . A Food." Post's vivid ads insisted that the health food "made red blood or it made red blood redder" and "Makes Sturdy Legs!" In 1906 Post followed up with his own version of corn flakes, claiming that the easy-to-digest, "double-thick" Post Toasties stayed crisp longer in milk.

Post, an instinctive copywriter, wrote his own copy for his ads and promotions. For many years Post also inserted an eleven-page pamphlet in his cereal boxes, entitled "The Road to Wellville," which explained the keys to well-being: a positive mental attitude, moderate diet, exercise, and adequate sleep. Post's ads also presented images of health for everyone who followed the road to Wellville. From 1908 to 1909, Post reported profits of more than $5 million.

Entrepreneur Edward Ellsworth managed to achieve similar success with Force, a wheat-flake cereal made in Buffalo, New York. Introduced in 1901, the cereal owed its success largely to advertising jingles and a peculiar cartoon character, created by two schoolgirls, called Jim Dumps (Figure 3.14). Each ad opened with grumpy Jim Dumps and then described his transformation into smiling Sunny Jim after eating a bowl of Force cereal. After a successful test run, Ellsworth moved the account to Calkins & Holden, which made the campaign one of its most celebrated efforts. The enthusiastic public quickly popularized the product. People memorized the verses; fans mailed thousands of unsolicited jingles to the agency; and Sunny Jim appeared in numerous songs, marches, and comedies. Ironically the very fame that made Force a success also led to its demise. The campaign ended after running one year because Ellsworth's company encountered financial problems. In part, the firm simply couldn't keep up with the huge product demand.

After the company reorganized, Sunny Jim reappeared, but in a much reduced role. Ellsworth also called on the Lord & Thomas agency to shift the selling pitch to conventionally push the "Brain-Food" nutritional benefits: "FORCE is appropriate as soon as a few good teeth appear—and it starts right in the first day to make quick, elastic muscle and sturdy, solid bone." Force eventually disappeared from the shelves in the 1940s.

The other key breakfast cereal maker was a one-time store-keeper, schoolteacher, and lawyer named Henry D. Perky, who created Shredded Wheat in Denver in the early 1890s. Perky thought he had actually created a kind of wholesome "wheat pudding"—that is, steamed or boiled shredded wheat topped with vegetables and gravy. As Dr. Kellogg considered buying this new food idea, he suggested that Perky bake the biscuits dry after production so that they would stay fresh longer. Instead of selling out, however, Perky set out to persuade the nation to eat Shredded Wheat.

Perky moved East, built a factory at Niagara Falls, and eventually abandoned wheat pudding for breakfast food. He gave out thousands of samples and advertised heavily. One 1904 ad headlined: "You never tire of Shredded Wheat . . . Because it can be prepared in over 250 different ways . . . The New Toast is used as bread, toast, crackers, or wafers; as a crouton, or with butter, cheese, or preserves." Several years later another ad recommended such delights as spooning creamed oysters over the biscuit. Perky's copy boasted the health benefits of eating wheat instead of meat. "Stomach comfort in every shred," claimed one ad. "These delicate shreds are retained and assimilated when the stomach rejects all other foods." Perky shrewdly incorporated illustrations on his package and in his advertisements of Niagara Falls' pure water as the site for his natural food company.

Getting "Wired" Catches On

New consumer utilities and electrical appliances miraculously transformed the American home during this era. One of the first of such devices was the telephone. An exhibit at the 1876 Philadelphia Centennial Exhibition first introduced the American public to this ingenious toy. In the following year a resident installed the country's first private home phone line, connecting his home to his office—in order

New Brand Names

1900 Kodak's new Brownie camera sells for only $1, while film retails for 10–15 cents for a six-photo roll.

1902 Barnum's Animal Crackers adds a string handle to its circus-cage box to make it easy to hang on a Christmas tree.

1903 Crayola colored wax crayons expand Binney & Smith's line of paints and chalk.

1904 R. T. French perfects a golden yellow mustard that quickly becomes a national favorite.

1905 King C. Gillette puts his name and signature on his safety razor wrapper.

1908 Dixie Cup's waxed paper cup is sanitary and cheap enough to toss away after drinking.

1909 Bakelite, a new plastic material developed as a substitute for shellac, finds more uses as a substitute for glass and wood in many products.

1912 Life Savers peppermint candy, the candy with a hole in the middle, appears.

1912 Oreo Biscuit, with creme filling between two chocolate wafers, is a national best-seller.

1912 Ocean Spray markets its cranberry sauce as a sweetened, jellied condiment.

1912 Hellman's Blue Ribbon mayonnaise is sealed in glass jars to hold its freshness and texture indefinitely.

1913 Brillo's soaped scouring pads are called "S.O.S.," short for "Save Our Saucepans."

1914 Wrigley introduces Doublemint chewing gum and the next year follows up with Spearmint and Juicy Fruit.

1914 Morton Salt adopts the umbrella girl for its package.

1916 Keds introduces its canvas and rubber shoes, originally intended to be called Peds, from the Latin word for "foot."

1917 Converse invents the high-topped canvas athletic shoe.

The Morton Salt Girl in 1914.

to have someplace to call. Suddenly the public discovered the joys of instantaneous telephone communication, and phones were in demand. Throughout the nation soft-spoken switchboard operators, called "hello girls," fielded phone calls. By the turn of the century, some 1.3 million telephones were in service, and by 1907, the number had increased five-fold.

Electricity had begun to power more than factories and streetcars; it also lit up city streets and homes. But the utility needed some artful assistance from advertising professionals to sell the service to the public. By 1917 over half of all urban homes were "wired" for electricity; that is, a single wire hung down from the ceiling in the center of the room, because wall plugs did not appear until the 1920s.

Illumination initially proved the sole reason to add the power service, and the light bulb proved an easy sell. An early 1910 image ad for General Electric's Mazda Lamp featured a painting of the earth, the moon, and a GE bulb with these words: "His Only Rival" (Figure 3.15). Even as more and more people wired their homes, however, many people also feared not being able to pay their electricity bills. To overcome this obstacle, rival light bulb manufacturers pitched price, safety, and convenience and offered advice on how to economize on lighting bills—but not on light bulbs. As one Economical Electric Lamp ad from 1918 suggested:

> "A Little Light All Night is Right" for Halls, Bath Room, Sick Room, and that dangerous turn in the Stair. It is protection and comfort combined—infinitely better than stark darkness in these times.

Advertising also did a remarkable job of selling Americans on new electrical appliances. But manufacturers first faced the difficult task of explaining to people that the copper wires did more than provide illumination; they also supplied power to run small machines that could make their lives easier. For example, one ad explained that electricity "is right at hand—in your electric sockets" and "cost only pennies." Another ad in 1917 addressed this concern: "Drudgery has Vanished Since Electricity came into the Home," declared General Electric. The persuasive copy went on:

> The four walls of a kitchen no longer hold the American housewife in solitary confinement. . . . The modern servant, Electricity, washes the dishes and clothes, cleans the house thoroughly, grinds meat, turns the ice cream freezer, runs the sewing machine and cools the house in summer. It makes coffee and toast at the dining table, does the cooking by "wire" in a clean, comfortable kitchen and relieves ironing day of its toil.

Figure 3.15   This 1910 ad promoted the wonders of the light bulb, and indeed illumination initially was the sole reason for homes to be "wired" for electricity.

Still another 1917 ad from Western Electric directly appealed to the man of the house to modernize with this headline: "Why Have Two Standards of Efficiency?" The ad answered:

> *Your wife—your* home *manager is entitled to labor-saving equipment just as the manager of a business office, store, or factory.*

Take efficiency home with you. You are accustomed to every modern time and labor saver in your work. Your wife needs modern equipment, too. It will reduce housekeeping expense just as it cuts business costs. It will eliminate drudgery and tedious tasks in the home just as it does in business.

Demand for such appliances increased as electricity became common in homes. When electric irons first appeared in 1908, housewives no longer had to labor over old-fashioned oven-heated irons, because the electric iron let them work in comfort "inside or outside on the verandah." The following year the light, portable vacuum cleaner replaced previous models so large (80 pounds and more) that many women could not even move them around the room. The new appliance was called the Hoover Suction Sweeper: "it sweeps and dusts at the same time." Another ad offered "Your Washing Done for 2 Cents a Week" with the new power washing machine. Nor did the homemaker have to fuss over a hot, coal-burning stove any longer. Manufacturers such as Hughes Electric Ranges were "Making a Nation of Better Cooks . . . replacing guesswork with an almost scientific exactness." A host of other electrical "servants" soon followed: dishwashers, toasters, coffee percolators, hot plates, heaters, and hair dryers, to name but a few. Yet no invention would change the American way of life more than the automobile.

America Hits the Road

The Duryea brothers of Springfield, Massachusetts, built the first American automobile in 1893. The following year, the first auto ad appeared. These machines evolved from essentially adult toys into devices "rich folks" drove around town. For some years, however, most people doubted whether the "devil wagon" could prove practical for the average man. One required almost an engineer's knowledge to keep the early vehicles in working order, and the engines even blew up on occasion. Door-to-door salesmen proved important in getting potential customers into the car, taking a test drive, and experiencing the freedom that automobiles provided. Manufacturers also staged auto races, parades, and other events to reach mass audiences.

It was Henry Ford who brought the automobile to the "common man." Before Ford introduced his Model T, the average car priced out at about $2800, stripped, while prestige models ranged from $8000 to $10,000. In 1903 Ford founded his Detroit company; five years later he sold the first of many four-cylinder, four-passenger Model T vehicles without a top (Figure 3.16). The "family horse," as he called it, reflected Ford's goal to mass produce "more cars, better and cheaper." Mass production methods cut costs dramatically—Ford lowered prices from $950 in 1909 to an astonishing $360 eight years later. The

Figure 3.16 Beginning in 1908 Henry Ford used mass production to cut manufacturing costs dramatically and put his cars within the financial reach of the average American.

Model T, he boasted, was available in any color, so long as it was black. The Model T, however, had initially sold in a variety of vibrant colors until Ford reached higher levels of sales. The automaker then made a practical decision on one way to keep production costs down—in 1910 nothing but green cars, in 1911 nothing but blue cars, and from 1914 until 1925 nothing but black cars. Ford also paid workers in his automobile plant $5 a day, more than double the average man's daily wage. This enabled his employees to purchase a car and also forced other employers to raise salaries. The Model T proved so popular that by 1920 it accounted for more than half of all the cars on the road.[17]

Whereas Henry Ford leaned toward producing one versatile, low-priced car, William C. Durant of the Buick Motor Company had plans to offer a wide range of automobiles. Between 1908 and 1911 Durant merged a number of companies to form General Motors, including the well-known manufacturer Oldsmobile and Oakland, a company in Pontiac, Michigan, that produced the prestigious Model K and Cadillac. However, Durant found that his mergers overextended his capital, and in 1911 a banking syndicate took over General Motors.

In the same year, Durant moved on to a new venture with mechanic and race car driver Louis Chevrolet, forming the Chevrolet Motor Car Company to produce a low-priced car to compete with Ford's Model T. To lend an air of prestige, he gave the Chevrolets French names—the first was a two-door model called the "Coupe" (later, the Caprice, Cavalier, Chevette, and so on). Supposedly Durant based the Chevrolet's bow-tie-shaped logo on wallpaper that he had seen in France. Campbell-Ewald, the agency of record, then promoted Chevrolet "for economical transportation." However, in the 1920s the company joined forces with the General Motors' conglomerate, and by decade's end it overtook Ford as the nation's choice for a basic car.

Automobile advertising grew slowly in volume. The first car ads pictured silhouettes of the vehicle, while copy stressed mechanical features: horsepower, number of cylinders, kind of transmission, performance claims, and so on. Considerable effort went into persuading the public that they could expect a safe ride, so manufacturers also stressed reliability. One ad heralded, "The Packard gets you there and gets you back." Oldsmobile repeated, "The Oldsmobile Goes." And in the Winton Six, you could go "Four Times Around the Earth . . . on repair expenses of $127.30."

By 1910 the sales approach had become less technical. In addition to detailed copy, the ads included illustrations of people in the cars and promoted the pleasures of the open road. Five years later, auto advertising adopted a powerful new tactic. Instead of persuading potential customers by talking about the manufacturing process, admakers projected a look and an attitude to define the car's special personality—the all-important image of the product. Advertisements artfully suggested that an automobile should be valued for its quiet elegance and fashionable style, as well as for the pleasures of owning it. This concept of "added value" had far-reaching consequences for advertising. Admakers would begin to promote the fashion angle for everything from automobiles to bath towels.

Originally people had purchased autos for transportation. Now, however, they increasingly bought a car to reward themselves or to impress their neighbors. Thus the illustrations in the ads increasingly communicated appeals to status. For example, images of sophisticated persons of obvious refinement occupying a limousine driven by a chauffeur suggested a sense of power. A family in a closed sedan taking a leisurely turn in the park or touring on a happy vacation conveyed a sense of social achievement. Or a dashing roadster containing a spirited young couple offered the promise of romance.

Many people consider an image ad for the Cadillac to be one of the all-time greats. Star copywriter Theodore MacManus wrote the famous piece, headlined "The Penalty of Leadership" (see Figure 3.9). Astonishingly the ad ran only once, in the *Saturday Evening Post* of January 2, 1915. It had no illustrations and offered no mechanical details; in fact, it did not even mention automobiles.

Cadillac had built its reputation on its reliable, four-cylinder prestige cars. The automaker faced a new challenge when its main rival, Packard, came out with a six-cylinder engine. Not to be outdone, Cadillac introduced a high-speed, eight-cylinder model. However, when the new model proved to be prone to short circuits and fires, Packard seized the opportunity to publicize the V-8's shortcomings. In response MacManus set out to reclaim Cadillac's aura of reliability and high quality.

MacManus knew that the Cadillac owner purchased the expensive automobile only after careful thought, so he aimed to build a long-lasting image of quality and reliability for the brand, rather than simply seek fast sales. His "Penalty of Leadership" announcement carried the message that Cadillac had overcome its problems by virtue of its incomparable superiority to all other motor cars:

> *In every field of human endeavor, he that is first must perpetually live in the white light of publicity. Whether the leadership be vested in a man, or in a manufactured product, emulation and envy are ever at work. . . . When a man's work becomes a standard for the whole world, it also becomes a target for the shafts of the envious few. . . . That which deserve to live—lives.*

Readers admired the prose and identified with the message. For many years thereafter, Cadillac and its agency filled many requests for reprints.

Patterns of living changed once car ownership began to spread. For example, roads improved, traffic lights appeared, painted lines marked parking spaces, and gasoline service stations popped up. Owners built heated garages to store their cars, since the early models did not function well in the cold. With this new mobility automobile owners could now live in one town and work in another or travel to nearby cities for shopping and events. Cities began to promote themselves as tourist destinations. Other urban rapid-transit systems such as trains, buses, and subways also kept America on the move.

As road travel increased, the billboard industry developed as a means of addressing the newly mobile public. Billboards initially had found a ready market catering to bicyclists, who viewed the posters while pedaling by on their outings. Advertisers for automobiles and auto-related products took their cues from these popular ads, and the billboards continued to crop up. By 1915 roadsides were important advertising locales for companies such as U.S. Rubber, Firestone, and Goodyear, which knew that drivers going a distance would need to change tires. Other billboards also went up for Ford, Chevrolet, Carnation milk, Wrigley's chewing gum, and Coca-Cola, to name but a few. Advertisers also used large barns and walls along country roads and railroad tracks to promote miracle cures or chewing tobacco to passing travelers.

The emergence of advertising as a legitimate enterprise was perhaps best evidenced following the outbreak of World War I. Where once advertising had been the domain primarily of mail-order outlets, patent medicine bottlers, and the like, now "patriotic" businesses, citizen groups, and even the government got in on the act.

Advertising and World War I

When the United States entered World War I in 1917, the event boosted advertising. While many manufacturers converted from consumer goods to war production, others felt constrained from promoting nonessential consumer products during this time of national crisis.

Yet the shortages increased "institutional" advertising that kept company names and trademarks in the public eye. Following the Theodore MacManus approach, eloquent essays sang the praises of the firm's commitment to noble ideals, developed themes of how their product assisted in the war effort, and made appeals to buy bonds. One ad for Elgin Watch Company did so brilliantly. Under the headline "Guiding Star of the Service," the copy read, "hundreds of thousands of Elgins are in hourly use by the fighting men of America and her gallant Allies." Other ads carried the message that their products helped the fighting men hang on. The classic "Ivory Soap follows the flag" informed readers that the product was "in fact, the very joy of living to Our Boys when they are relieved from the front lines for rest, recreation, clean clothes, and a bath."

The government also created national advertising programs to gain public support. The newly created Federal Committee of Public Information helped shape public opinion, fostered wartime patriotism, and informed citizens of what they could do to help win the war. Within the committee artist Charles Dana Gibson formed a "Division of Pictorial Publicity" that contracted with professional designers and leading illustrators to contribute artwork to the war effort. Printers

The GREATEST MOTHER *in the* WORLD

Stretching forth her hands to all in need; to Jew or Gentile, black or white; knowing no favorite, yet favoring all.

Ready and eager to comfort at a time when comfort is most needed. Helping the little home that's crushed beneath an iron hand by showing mercy in a healthy, human way; rebuilding it, in fact, with stone on stone; replenishing empty bins and empty cupboards; bringing warmth to hearts and hearths too long neglected.

Seeing all things with a mother's sixth sense that's blind to jealousy and meanness; seeing men in their true light, as naughty children — snatching, biting, bitter—but with a hidden side that's quickest touched by mercy.

Reaching out her hands across the sea to No Man's land; to cheer with warmer comforts thousands who must stand and wait in stenched and crawling holes and water-soaked entrenchments where cold and wet bite deeper, so they write, than Boche steel or lead.

She's warming thousands, feeding thousands, healing thousands from her store; the Greatest Mother in the World—the RED CROSS.

Every Dollar of a Red Cross War Fund goes to War Relief

Figure 3.17   With this 1918 ad the Red Cross solicited contributions to its War Fund.

donated their services as well, turning out millions of dramatic posters at no charge. The advertising division also supervised the placement of donated ad space and copy. After the war the tradition of making free space available for public causes continued.

Hundreds of images developed by the committee became part of the national consciousness. These ads recruited men for the armed forces, encouraged women to volunteer in the domestic effort, sold bonds, and promoted conservation of war materials in the home. The

Figure 3.18 Illustrator James Flagg's image of Uncle Sam, created in 1918 to attract military recruits, has become part of the national consciousness.

Red Cross ran one of the most omnipresent advertisements: "The Greatest Mother in the World" pictured a saintly woman in a nurse's uniform cradling a wounded soldier, an image that embodied the organization's ideals (Figure 3.17). The Liberty Bond drive urged: "Buy til it Hurts." Other images sold the war to youths. Notably James Flagg's Uncle Sam pointed a finger at the viewer, declaring: "I Want YOU for U.S. Army" (Figure 3.18). And Howard Chandler Christy painted the lovely young "Christy Girl," an imagined soldier's sweetheart, in a series of successful recruitment posters.

After the 1918 armistice ended the war, manufacturers increased their advertising budgets and spurred the return to a consumer economy. In the following decade new consumer patterns would emerge and far-reaching social changes would occur. The war had created an entirely new market of young men and women who knew how to drive and wanted their own automobiles, and the automobile industry would respond with appealing new models. The war had changed another social habit by causing large numbers of men to switch from cigars, pipes, and chewing tobacco to cigarettes. And the war also greatly increased the number of working women and filled their purses with wartime earnings. New ads targeted women, tempting them with cosmetics, silk stockings, and dozens of other new products, as well as promoting daring new fashions. In the next chapter we examine advertising in the Roaring Twenties.

Modern American Advertising

The Eighteenth Amendment to the
U.S. Constitution forbids the sale
of liquor during Prohibition
(1920–1933).

The Nineteenth Amendment grants
women the right to vote.

Pittsburgh station KDKA airs the
first commercial radio broadcast.

1920

The first nonstop flight is made
across America.

1923

1920

1922
J. Walter Thompson reaches $10.7
million in billings, a number-one
ranking that it would maintain for
the next fifty years.

New York station WEAF airs the
first radio commercial, promoting a
Long Island real estate firm.

Chapter 4

1920–1929 The Roaring Twenties

Blackman hires Nedda McGrath,
the first female art director at a
major ad agency.
1926

George Batten Company merges
with Barton, Durstine & Osborne
to form BBDO.

Walt Disney makes the first Mickey
Mouse cartoon.
1928

1927
The Jazz Singer is the first "talkie"
feature movie.

The American public views a
demonstration of modern television
for the first time.

Charles Lindbergh flies nonstop
from New York to Paris.

1929
The stock market crashes.

1929

America emerged from World War I confident of its ability to address foreign policy issues, wipe out the war debt, and strengthen the economy. Following a brief depression in 1921, the economy took off on a period of rising prosperity. Factory assembly lines multiplied, the stock market soared, and industrial production nearly doubled between 1921 and 1929.

Americans also enjoyed a new prosperity. The consumer society, which had begun to develop around the turn of the century, now flourished. Wages increased, and more married women entered the workplace, so that families had extra money to spend on "wants" rather than needs, as well as more time to spend it. By 1925 about 40 percent of the population earned $2000 or more. The normal six-day work week was collapsed into five days, and more businesses granted paid vacations.

People's newly acquired affluence provided manufacturers with a ready-made mass market. For the first time more than half of the nation lived in urban areas (51 percent according to the 1920 census). Suburbs sprang up outside city limits as the sales of automobiles increased and roads improved. The price of electricity went down, and more families began enjoying its conveniences as power lines stretched across America. Light bulbs replaced smoky kerosene lamps; telephones kept people in touch; radios brought news and entertainment; and refrigerators took the place of iceboxes.

This newly affluent population also represented a new breed of consumer. Now basic necessities no longer had to be made at home, because everything from bread to dresses came premade and prepackaged. Large food, drug, and apparel chain stores provided new places to shop and offered consumers a cornucopia of products and services. The consumer economy even touched on the most intimate details of everyday life, as products like mouthwash, deodorant, vitamins, and disposable tissues became household staples.

Faced with an accepting society, a robust economy, and relaxed regulations, advertising would never again have so positive a climate in which to operate. The total volume of advertising expenditures skyrocketed from $2.2 billion in 1919 to $3.4 billion in 1929[1]; the food and beverage, drug and toilet goods, and automobile industries led the way.[2]

The Prosperous New Era

A number of factors accounted for the prosperity of the era, including advances in science and technology, the growth of certain industries, the development of new consumer products and markets, and new ways of marketing goods. Advertising, higher wages, and the availability of credit also prodded the economy. But perhaps the key factor was the attitude of an ascendant nation that "the business of America is business."

The Business of America Is Business

As America emerged triumphant from World War I, its citizens sensed that this was the best of times—and they were ready to enjoy them. New industries developed to satisfy the demand for consumer products. Electrical appliances such as fans, vacuum cleaners, refrigerators, dishwashers, and washing machines appeared on the market. The construction, the chemical, and especially the automotive industries also played a major role in America's growth.

The automobile industry impacted the whole economy. Auto manufacture stimulated the production of basic goods such as steel, glass, paint, rubber, and oil. Gas stations, garages, tourist cabins, and new roads were built. Overall the automobile, directly and indirectly, created millions of jobs in the first thirty years of the century. In fact, by 1925 the industry ranked third in the number of workers employed.[3] And by 1929 the total number of cars in the United States soared to nearly 30 million, or almost one per family, triple the total when the decade began.

As Americans took to the roads in record numbers, advertisers prodded this lifestyle change by promoting everything from new auto models to tires, batteries, and fire extinguishers. As auto accessory advertising grew in volume, so did the quality of the ads. For example, most battery makers initially took a dry, mechanical approach, with cutaway pictures showing the battery's interior. Other manufacturers used fear tactics to sell gasoline, motor oil, spark plugs, and the like; typical ads showed motorists who were stranded or who had been in violent auto accidents. One exception, the campaign for Kelly Springfield tires that ran from 1918 to 1931, emerged as one of the outstanding tire campaigns ever to appear in the print media. The ads featured the wash drawings of Laurence Fellowes accompanied by short captions; the soft sell, smart character, and sporty images moved a lot of tires (Figure 4.1).

Advances in technology and more efficient manufacturing methods were fundamental to the economic boom and dramatically increased factory output. In manufacturing, electricity powered moving assembly lines, which helped to boost productivity. As a result, the same number of workers put in fewer hours a week yet turned out more goods. Also, industries applied new scientific management principles and conducted studies that recommended ways to efficiently divide production into simple tasks and to eliminate wasted motion.

"Forty miles before we hit even a service station! We'll be in a nice fix if we have a blowout, with no spare!"
"I'm not worrying about blowouts; we've got Kelly-Springfields on all around. It's the gas I'm thinking about."

Figure 4.1   Laurence Fellows illustrated this ad as part of Kelly Springfield's classic campaign, which ran from 1918 to 1931.

Henry Ford's Highland Park plant, just outside Detroit, first used the moving assembly line in 1914. The line enabled workers to produce a new car in 93 minutes, as opposed to the 14 hours it took prior to the innovation. By 1925 a new car now rolled off of Ford's assembly line factories every 10 seconds! Hundreds of companies began to emulate Ford's profitable combination of high wages ($6 a day), low prices, and assembly line production methods.[4]

The turn-of-the-century trend in business consolidations also continued, as thousands of individually owned banks, manufacturers, and utility companies were absorbed by the bigger corporations. For instance, a single company now dominated the telephone industry; four meat-packing companies controlled that industry; Ford, General Motors, and Chrysler produced the majority of automobiles; and General Electric and Westinghouse commanded the electrical equipment sector. In fact, by 1929 a mere two hundred corporations controlled nearly half of the country's business wealth. And as the size of the business organizations increased, so did the volume of corporate advertising.[5]

Retailing Hits Its Stride

The retail chain store business thrived in the 1920s in a retailing revolution that encompassed groceries, general merchandise, apparel, and drugs. Several factors accounted for the immense success of the chain store. Retail managers quickly recognized the advantages of applying scientific management principles to their multiple-store operations. They located sites for their stores; standardized store operations, layout, and design; and managed consumer research, advertising, and human resources. Chain stores also changed the scale of doing business. High volume, high turnover, and low prices became the norm. In this way the Great Atlantic and Pacific Tea Company (A&P), J. C. Penney, Rexall Drugs, Montgomery Ward, and Sears, Roebuck & Co. became retailing giants.

A new type of self-service grocery store pushed A&P's economy food store format one step further. To cut costs, food retailers often relocated outside of high-rent inner-city shopping districts, adjacent to vacant lots to provide space for parking. Inside the one-level stores grocers stocked shelves with packaged merchandise placed easily within customers' reach—all with prices clearly marked to allow price comparisons. No longer did customers have to wait for sales clerks to search shelves, portion out goods from open containers, or tell them the cost of an item.

Piggly Wiggly, the first major self-service grocery chain, opened its first store in Memphis, Tennessee, in 1916. Shoppers selected items from the shelves, put them in hand-held baskets, carried them to the checkout counter, paid for them, and took them home. These self-service groceries enabled consumers to pick from a wider selection of foodstuffs and to pay less for their purchases (Figure 4.2). A 1928 store ad explained the advantages of the self-service format:

> *Take what you please from the shelves at Piggly Wiggly. Just read the price tags and help yourself. . . .*
> *Spread on the open shelves, the choice foods of the*

Through the turnstile
to a land of ADVENTURE!

A unique plan of shopping that 2,500,000 women are using today

Just walk through the turnstile and help yourself! Take what you please from the shelves, examine it, arrive at your own decision—at Piggly Wiggly

Choose for yourself, help yourself —at Piggly Wiggly

WOMEN like to tell their friends about this unique method of shopping. They enjoy discussing its advantages. Old customers send us thousands of new ones every week.

In a few swift years women have made this plan of household buying a nation-wide vogue.

With their new, wide knowledge of real values, the women of today want to *choose for themselves*. When they shop for foods, they want no clerks trying to urge and persuade them. To them, this special plan is an easy way to give their families more delicious meals at less expense.

Make your own decisions

Within easy reach, on open shelves and stands, the choice foods of the world are

A few years ago only one Piggly Wiggly store —today over 3,000, used daily by 2,500,000 women!

waiting to be looked over at Piggly Wiggly. Beyond the turnstile, a land of adventure!

Famous packages, familiar jars and cans, fresh inviting fruits and vegetables —each item with its big square price tag, at Piggly Wiggly. And no clerks—just help yourself.

Finer foods—lower cost

You linger or hurry as you please. Take what you like in your hands, examine it at leisure. You compare prices—make your *own decision*, uninfluenced by salesmen.

PIGGLY WIGGLY
STORES

The finest kinds of each food selected for you to choose from

A SERVICE NOW OFFERED IN OVER 800 CITIES AND TOWNS

An easy way to serve more tempting meals—and spend less: Piggly Wiggly

And ideas for your menus come flocking, while you shop at Piggly Wiggly!

Most important of all, you save money week in and week out at Piggly Wiggly. Consistently lower prices are assured by our unusual and economical plan of operation.

To serve finer food, to cut grocery costs —this is why 2,500,000 women are using this method of buying every day. To surprise your husband both at the table and with your monthly expenses try this plan. Visit the Piggly Wiggly store in your neighborhood and choose for yourself!

1929

Figure 4.2   As this 1929 ad shows, the new self-service grocery stores offered consumers wider selections and lower prices.

world are waiting for you to look over at Piggly Wiggly.
There are no salesmen to urge you. Slowly or quickly,
just as you please. . . . Best of all, you save money.

Manufacturers recognized the growing popularity of self-service grocery stores and designed their packaged goods to be sold directly off the shelf. They used shape, color, size, and even texture to deliver marketing messages, give product information, or demonstrate uses of products. Nationwide advertising sold shoppers on what brands to buy long before they entered the store.

The candy industry was comparatively slow to join the general shift to packaged merchandise. Stores traditionally sold small, inexpensive, unwrapped candies by the pound or piece and boxed or bagged it for the customer. The now familiar wrapped candy bars did not appear widely until the 1920s. Merchants then found an ever-growing number of customers by putting the packaged candy adjacent to cash registers in grocery stores, drugstores, newsstands, and cigar stores.

The Hershey milk chocolate bar provides a classic example of the packaged product that sold itself—largely without advertising. In 1905 Pennsylvania confectioner Milton Hershey began to produce America's first mass-distributed chocolate bar. Hershey priced the individually wrapped bars at 5 cents, printed his name on each wrapper, and sold the bars nationwide. In fact, Hershey's chocolate products sold so well by word-of-mouth advertising that Hershey did not run its first print ad until 1970.

Although Hershey became synonymous with chocolate, the confectioner did have competitors, some of whom relied on advertising for their sweet success. In particular, Otto Schnering of the Chicago-based Curtis Candy Company loved a good advertising gimmick. Schnering hired planes to drop scores of Baby Ruth candy bars fitted with little parachutes over forty cities. The campaign helped make Baby Ruth America's best-selling candy bar in 1926, selling at a rate of 5 million a day.[6] And many of that era's favorites are still today's bestsellers, including Wrigley chewing gum, Whitman's chocolates, Life Savers candies, and Oh Henry! candy bars.

Other chain stores began to change the way America shopped. The success of J. C. Penney's apparel and shoe outlets in large towns and small cities demonstrated that the chain store system could work for other types of merchandise. The J. C. Penney chain expanded from almost 300 stores in 1920 to more than 1000 outlets by 1928.

Mail-order houses also quickly grasped this opportunity to invest in retail stores. Rather than compete directly against the large urban department stores, Sears, Roebuck & Co. and Montgomery Ward opted to build outlets near highways outside the cities to capitalize on the new mobility. The suburban customer traveled to a Sears store by car instead of by foot or horse and buggy, so the chain shrewdly added automotive products. In time Sears became a leading supplier of do-it-yourself tools, sporting goods, and home appliances. Sears also did big business in shoes, apparel, and other merchandise. Montgomery Ward soon followed suit. That company, however, first targeted small to medium-size metropolitan towns rather than the outlying districts or large urban centers. By the early 1930s, for both Sears and Montgomery Ward, retail sales exceeded mail-order sales.

Enjoy Now, Pay Later

Advertising created markets for hundreds of goods from soup and soap to refrigerators and automobiles. Advertisements filled radio airtime around the clock, cluttered magazines, and lined roadsides, persuading consumers to want more "material" things. Ads promoted cosmetics and fashions to improve people's appearance, bicycles and automobiles to increase mobility, and canned foods and snacks to lend variety to the daily diet. Ads also demonstrated appliances and gadgets designed to speed people through their daily chores. By 1925 advertisers spent a billion dollars a year persuading Americans to buy the latest deodorant, freshest mouthwash, foamiest soap, or trendiest cigarette.

Even as advertising stimulated people's willingness to buy, higher wages and the availability of credit increased their ability to purchase new goods. Initially only a few items could be bought by installment payments, but that quickly changed. By the end of the 1920s, vendors of automobiles, home appliances, powerboats, fur coats, and furniture all trumpeted, "Enjoy now, pay later." As a result, Americans now bought over 60 percent of their cars, radios, and furniture on some form of credit.[7]

As new industries and products emerged, advertisers became strategic educators and promoters of habits of hygiene, dress, lifestyle, and new technology. Ad creators explored strategies to encourage the public to buy more, not because they needed things, but because they wanted to own certain items, use certain products, and adopt certain lifestyles.

Advertising's Role in Shaping Lifestyles

Agencies seeking to gain a professional standing for their work eagerly supported the trend toward scientific advertising. National advertisers with multimillion-dollar budgets sponsored market and psychological research to ensure that their advertising proved an effective marketing tool. Although some agencies expressed no interest in the new ideas, others, like J. Walter Thompson, seemed obsessed with discovering—and then exploiting—the secrets of human nature.

Dr. John B. Watson

In 1920 behavioral psychologist Dr. John Watson resigned from Johns Hopkins University and went to work for the J. Walter Thompson agency to help place advertising on a more scientific basis. Watson claimed to have discovered basic techniques for predicting and manipulating human behavior. According to Watson advertisers needed to tap into fundamental human drives (such as love, fear, and rage) and repeatedly associate the given stimulus with their products. That is why advertisers today often incorporate popular songs in commercials to evoke the same response as the songs themselves.

In one of his early successes, Watson conducted a controlled blindfold test which revealed that people could not recognize their favorite brand of cigarettes. Based on this finding, Watson concluded that cigarettes and other products could not be advertised by logical appeals. Watson also conducted employment, intelligence, and performance tests for the agency and gave speeches about the practical applications of behaviorism. Although the use of psychology in advertising was oversold at this time, the psychological sell that tapped into hidden motives and desires would later impact agencies in the 1950s.

J. Walter Thompson led the ad industry in both innovative copy styles and the variety of services offered to clients. The agency's president, Stanley Resor, the first major advertising executive with a college background, set out to make advertising a respectable profession. Resor hired behavioral psychologist Dr. John B. Watson and other experts in the social sciences who advanced the field of marketing research. The agency's billing more than tripled, from $10.7 million in 1922 to $37.5 million by the end of the decade, making it the industry leader in total billings, a position it maintained for the next fifty years. Barton, Durstine & Osborne (later BBDO), under the leadership of Bruce Barton, became another hot agency. Barton carried forward the "image" school of Theodore MacManus for such clients as General Electric, General Motors, and Alexander Hamilton Institute.

A common theme in advertising in this era revolved around issues of lifestyle and image. Consumers were encouraged to buy the "right" bread, the "right" vacuum, and the "right" car. But the ads didn't stop there. Consumers also discovered that, to be socially acceptable, they had to look and smell a certain way, had to maintain spotless modern bathrooms, and even had to smoke cigarettes. And the prime target of all this promotion was women.

Woman's Suffrage Timeline

1848

Reformers Lucretia Mott and
Elizabeth Cady Stanton hold the
first women's rights convention in
Seneca Falls, New York, to gain the
vote and other rights.
1848

After African American men gain
the vote, the suffrage movement
works for the right to vote state by
state.
1869

1851
Susan B. Anthony and Elizabeth
Cady Stanton begin a fifty-year
partnership for women's rights.

1872
Susan B. Anthony and fifteen other
women are arrested for attempting
to vote in the presidential election;
the trial gets national attention.

Targeting Women

From the very start many admakers recognized that their most important customer was the woman, who controlled the major share of
household spending. "The proper study of mankind is man" declared
one agency, echoing Alexander Pope, "but the proper study of markets is woman."[8]

Women overall enjoyed a role far different from their grandmothers a half century before. Ready-made clothing, bakery-baked bread,
packaged foods, and labor-saving appliances eased or eliminated many
time-consuming tasks. After women won the constitutional right to
vote in 1920, the woman's suffrage movement split. Most women felt
that they had achieved what they set out to and were satisfied with
the victory. For these women life remained essentially the same: they
cooked, cleaned, raised families, and managed households. Other
women, however, believed strongly that they should now strive for
other feminist goals such as economic independence. By 1925 the
number of women working outside the home had reached 25 percent.
Women made up half the financial community's employees and 90 percent of all clerks and typists. Their wages amounted to considerably
more than "pin money" or pocket change, although considerably less
than their male counterparts earned.

Admakers directed their advertising at these women who lived
and worked in the cities and who had money to spend. Economic prosperity had extended to a large segment of the population, but this
newly acquired affluence was accompanied by an anxious concern for
social acceptance and approval. With this in mind admakers, who considered women more emotionally vulnerable than men, often planted
the idea of one of women's worst fear—that of giving offense—and

A woman's suffrage amendment is
first introduced in the Senate; it is
reintroduced every session for the
next forty years.
1878

Parades, speeches, picket lines,
arrests, and hunger strikes call
attention to the cause.
1910–1920

1910
The first suffrage parade in New
York City attracts youth, radicals,
and working-class people.

1920
The Nineteenth Amendment is
ratified, giving women the right
to vote.

1920

then exploited it. Such ads manipulated women's hidden desires to be
sought after and well liked and to join the successful middle class.

The J. Walter Thompson agency pioneered this dramatic shift
away from selling goods and services to using well-known psychological devices to lure customers. The agency's advertisements of such
products as Woodbury's facial soap, Fleischmann's Yeast, Odorono deodorant, Lux soap, and Pond's cold cream successfully incorporated
fear, sex, and emulation appeals to condition consumers to want the
products (Figure 4.3). Other admakers quickly copied this fear-sex-
emulation formula to sell everything from books to scouring pads.

The Ruthrauff & Ryan agency, formed in 1921, developed a memorable series of ads designed to discreetly sell a two-volume *Book of
Etiquette* through mail order. These books proved to be a popular
source of information on how to avoid the horror of not knowing exactly what to do at all times. The agency triumphed with ads that
asked, "Has This Ever Happened to You?" showing a panicky guest
spilling coffee over the table. Others simply started out: "Are You Ever
Tongue-Tied at a Party?" or "Are You Ever 'Alone' in a Crowd?" Another classic ad portrayed an anguished girl seated at a restaurant
table: "Again She Orders—'A Chicken Salad, Please'"—for the third
time. She couldn't brave the humiliation of not knowing how to pro-
nounce the French names on the menu or use the elaborate table setting. Claude Caples wrote one of the most memorable ads among this
genre: "They Laughed When I Sat Down At the Piano But When I
Started to Play!" (Figure 4.4).

Two phenomena of popular culture provided admakers with new
insights into the female market—tabloid newspapers and confession
magazines. The tabloid newspaper's sensational style, first introduced

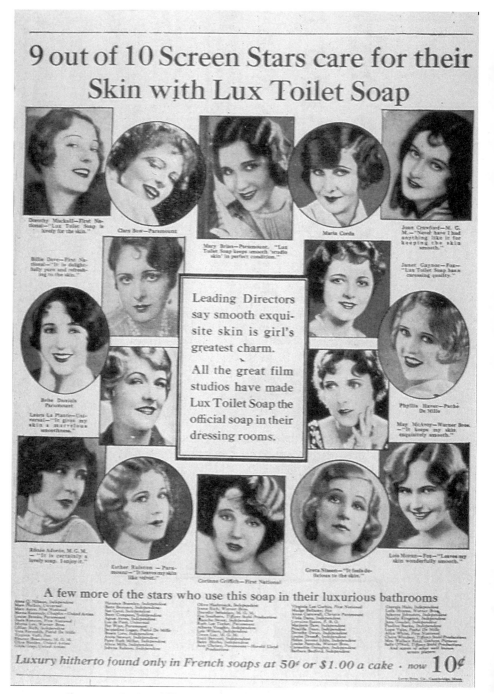

Figure 4.3 In this 1927 testimonial from J. Walter Thompson, the actresses did not actually speak the words attributed to them; nevertheless such testimonials proved highly successful.

"Can he really play?" a girl whispered.
"Heavens no!" Arthur exclaimed. "He never played a note in his life."

They Laughed When I Sat Down
At the Piano
But When I Started to Play!~

ARTHUR had just played "The Rosary." The room rang with applause. I decided that this would be a dramatic moment for me to make my debut. To the amazement of all my friends, I strode confidently over to the piano and sat down.

"Jack is up to his old tricks," somebody chuckled. The crowd laughed. They were all certain that I couldn't play a single note.

"Can he really play?" I heard a girl whisper to Arthur.

"Heavens, no!" Arthur exclaimed. "He never played a note in all his life. . . But just you watch him. This is going to be good."

I decided to make the most of the situation. With mock dignity I drew out a silk handkerchief and lightly dusted off the piano keys. Then I rose and gave the revolving piano stool a quarter of a turn, just as I had seen an imitator of Paderewski do in a vaudeville sketch.

"What do you think of his execution?" called a voice from the rear.

"We're in favor of it!" came back the answer, and the crowd rocked with laughter.

Then I Started to Play

Instantly a tense silence fell on the guests. The laughter died on their lips as if by magic. I played through the first few bars of Beethoven's immortal Moonlight Sonata. I heard gasps of amazement. My friends sat breathless — spellbound!

I played on and as I played I forgot the people around me. I forgot the hour, the place, the breathless listeners. The little world I lived in seemed to fade — seemed to grow dim — unreal. Only the music was real. Only the music and visions it brought me. Visions as beautiful and as changing as the wind blown clouds and drifting moonlight that long ago inspired the master composer. It seemed as if the master

musician himself were speaking to me—speaking through the medium of music—not in words but in chords. Not in sentences but in exquisite melodies!

A Complete Triumph!

As the last notes of the Moonlight Sonata died away, the room resounded with a sudden roar of applause. I found myself surrounded by excited faces. How my friends carried on! Men shook my hand — wildly congratulated me— pounded me on the back in their enthusiasm! Everybody was exclaiming with delight—plying me with rapid questions. . . "Jack! Why didn't you tell us you could play like that?". . . "Where did you learn?"—"How long have you studied?"— "Who was your teacher?"

"I have never even seen my teacher," I replied. "And just a short while ago I couldn't play a note.',

"Quit your kidding," laughed Arthur, himself an accomplished pianist. "You've been studying for years. I can tell."

"I have been studying only a short while," I insisted. "I decided to keep it a secret so that I could surprise all you folks."

Then I told them the whole story.

"Have you ever heard of the U. S. School of Music?" I asked.

A few of my friends nodded. "That's a correspondence school, isn't it?" they exclaimed.

"Exactly," I replied. "They have a new simplified method that can teach you to play any instrument by mail in just a few months."

How I Learned to Play Without a Teacher

And then I explained how for years I had longed to play the piano.

"A few months ago," I continued, "I saw an interesting ad for the U. S. School of Music—a new method of learning to play which only cost a few cents a day! The ad told how a woman had mastered the piano in her spare time at home—and without a teacher! Best of all, the wonderful new method she used, required no laborious scales— no heartless exercises — no tiresome practising. It sounded so convincing that I filled out the coupon requesting the Free Demonstration Lesson.

"The free book arrived promptly and I started in that very night to study the Demonstration Lesson. I was amazed to see how easy it was to play this new way. Then I sent for the course.

"When the course arrived I found it was just as the ad said — as easy as A.B.C.! And, as

the lessons continued they got easier and easier. Before I knew it I was playing all the pieces I liked best. Nothing stopped me. I could play ballads or classical numbers or jazz, all with equal ease! And I never did have any special talent for music!"

* * *

Play Any Instrument

You too, can now teach yourself to be an accomplished musician—right at home—in half the usual time. You can't go wrong with this simple new method which has already shown 350,000 people how to play their favorite instruments. Forget that old-fashioned idea that you need special "talent." Just read the list of instruments in the panel, decide which one you want to play and the U. S. School will do the rest. And bear in mind no matter which instrument you choose, the cost in each case will be the same—just a few cents a day. No matter whether you are a mere beginner or already a good performer, you will be interested in learning about this new and wonderful method.

Send for Our Free Booklet and Demonstration Lesson

Thousands of successful students never dreamed they possessed musical ability until it was revealed to them by a remarkable "Musical Ability Test" which we send entirely without cost with our interesting free booklet.

If you are in earnest about wanting to play your favorite instrument—if you really want to gain happiness and increase your popularity—send at once for the free booklet and Demonstration Lesson. No cost — no obligation. Right now we are making a Special offer for a limited number of new students. Sign and send the convenient coupon now — before it's too late to gain the benefits of this offer. Instruments supplied when needed, cash or credit. **U. S. School of Music, 1831 Brunswick Bldg., New York City.**

Pick Your Instrument

Piano	'Cello
Organ	Harmony and
Violin	Composition
Drums and	Sight Singing
Traps	Ukulele
Banjo	Guitar
Tenor	Hawaiian
Banjo	Steel Guitar
Mandolin	Harp
Clarinet	Cornet
Flute	Piccolo
Saxophone	Trombone
Voice and Speech Culture	
Automatic Finger Control	
Piano Accordion	

U. S. School of Music,
1831 Brunswick Bldg., New York City.

Please send me your free book, "Music Lessons in Your Own Home," with introduction by Dr. Frank Crane, Demonstration Lesson and particulars of your Special Offer. I am interested in the following course:

....

....

Have you above instrument?...................

Name..
 (Please write plainly)

Address..

City...................................State...........

Figure 4.4 This memorable 1925 ad sold mail-order piano lessons in particular and social status and approval in general.

in 1919, quickly generated enormous circulations. Although smaller in size than normal newspapers, the lively tabloids had something for everyone—outrageous scandals, gruesome murders, fantastic stories. Photographs dominated the news presentation and left little to the imagination, and the accompanying text provided fast-paced titillation.

The *True Story* magazine's first-person, confessional stories also attracted a vast audience and gave insight into the woman's viewpoint. The magazine aimed its stories at the young working woman, featuring dramatic personal accounts of tragic adventures, romantic temptations, and love triangles. Madison Avenue began to recognize that these readers had plenty of money to spend on automobiles, radios, appliances, cosmetics, and breakfast food. Once admen grasped the magazine's appeal, they advised copywriters to keep the copy short, personalized, and intimate, emphasizing romance rather than reality.

In order to reach the *True Story* audience, advertisers experimented with "True Story formula" ad formats. The women who starred in the ads faced dramatic real-life challenges—did their breath, teeth, or laundry measure up? Other dramatic "scare" or "whisper" copy went to new lengths to grab the readers' attention and often left them filled with feelings of guilt and anxiety: she could lose her job, germs threatened her health, a romance might end any moment, and so on. Yet every one of the domestic disasters could be averted simply by using the friendly advertiser's product. These ads often featured a caring "friend" such as Betty Crocker or Dorothy Dix, who invited readers to write for advice and encouragement.

And readers did respond. They wrote for advice, returned coupons, and purchased the promoted product. Advertisers measured consumer response through sales, personal letters, and coupons. The enormous returns convinced admakers that readers wanted a more intimate connection, so ads for Kotex, Lux, and dozens of other products featured chatty confidantes offering helpful advice. This friendly adviser might also be a society figure or movie star to heighten the sense of real people offering support.

In this 1927 scenario for S.O.S. scouring pads, Mary Dale Anthony, adviser on kitchen and household cleaning problems, responded to a "modern girl" who confronted her disapproving fiance with the headline "You think I'm a flapper but I *can* keep house" (Figure 4.5). The text went on:

> *"If we get married, I'll keep my house better than mother does hers. But I'm not going to turn into a slave. You men! You think drudgery is a sign of good housekeeping."*

Friendly Mary Dale Anthony commented on the tableaux and explained why S.O.S. handy scouring pads were so popular with this generation:

"You think I'm a flapper but I *can* keep house"

Mary Dale Anthony
Adviser on kitchen and household cleaning problems to thousands of women.

"If we get married, I'll keep my house better than mother does hers. But I'm not going to turn into a slave. You *men!* You think drudgery is a sign of good housekeeping."

By MARY DALE ANTHONY

Leave it to the modern girl to speak her mind. She's painfully frank, sometimes, but I've found that she's usually mighty capable, too .... alert and eager to learn .... looking for new time-savers. Girls today want more leisure, and they get it by using short-cuts.

And that is why S. O. S. is so popular with the younger generation. It is quick and easy to use. In almost no time it keeps kitchenware looking bright and new—even hard-to-clean aluminum. Vegetable stains, burned-on food, and smoke black come off in a twinkling with S. O. S.

No cloth, no soap, no powder is necessary. S. O. S. cleans and polishes in one swift operation. There's nothing else like these handy scouring pads, as you will find if you send me the coupon below.

S.O.S

Pat. Jan. 15, 1918—Reg. U. S. Pat. Off.

The Magic Cleaner of Pots and Pans

Figure 4.5 In this 1927 ad Mary Dale Anthony, adviser and confidante to thousands of women, offered advice while promoting S.O.S. scouring pads.

Leave it to the modern girl to speak her mind. She's painfully frank, sometimes, but I've found that she's usually mighty capable too . . . alert and eager to learn . . . looking for new time-savers. Girls today want more leisure, and they get it by using short-cuts.

In contrast to the many anxious and confused women who starred in these scenes, only a few men appeared. Occasionally an ad focusing on body odor might target men. When men appeared, however, admakers typically portrayed them as well-groomed, clean-cut businessmen—as agents of authority sitting behind desks—and not as blue-collar workers. And when men were pictured with women, the males either admired them or disapproved of them because they had the misfortune to suffer from bad breath or to serve the wrong coffee.

Who actually wrote these ads? And did they accurately depict women of the time? In his study *Advertising the American Dream,* Roland Marchand noted that men primarily created these images of the American woman, because few women were employed above the secretarial level in advertising and 99 percent of the ad writers were men.[9] Furthermore, in the 1931 *Who's Who in Advertising,* Daniel Pope identified only 3 percent of the men listed as Jews and found almost no Italian or Polish names. Also, staff pictures in trade journals and annual reports showed no African Americans.[10] Limiting his study to the period before World War II, Marchand concluded that the predominantly male admakers were suggesting to women that they could become better wives and mothers. Apparently the majority of women either bought into or at least accepted this image of the woman as mother and homemaker and the man as family breadwinner until World War II. In the 1950s minorities began to criticize agency norms, and in the 1960s feminists likewise challenged advertising.

Between the two world wars various agencies occasionally hired women to provide a woman's point of view. However, few women reached executive status, and they generally had limited influence in producing advertising; ethnic and racial groups had even less. In fact, it wasn't until 1926 that Nedda McGrath became the first female art director for a major agency, hired by Blackman in New York. The J. Walter Thompson agency provided the best opportunities for women, with its Women's Copy Group handling the majority of the agencies' soap, food, drugs, and toiletries accounts. Local retail work, especially in New York, provided more jobs for women in advertising. For instance, Mary Lewis managed the advertising for Best & Company, as did Jane J. Martin for Sperry & Hutchinson, the sellers of S&H Green Stamps. And Bernice Fitz-Gibbon wrote copy for Macy's (penning "It's smart to be thrifty"), Wanamaker's, and Gimbel's ("Nobody, but nobody, undersells Gimbel's").

New Brand Names

1920 Baby Ruth candy bars are named for daughter of former President Grover Cleveland.

1920 Eskimo Pie invents the ice cream bar, individually wrapped in aluminum foil.

1920 Wonder bread's red, yellow, and blue polka-dotted package is inspired by a sky filled with colorful balloons.

1921 Betty Crocker is invented to answer questions from Gold Medal flour customers.

1921 Wise packages "potato chips" as a way to get rid of extra potatoes.

1923 ESSO is adopted by Standard Oil as its primary brand name, a word play on "S.O.," the initials of the company.

1925 Ho! Ho! Ho! The Green Giant is born as a trademark for green peas.

The Jolly Green Giant.

The Kool-Aid Man.

1925 Howard Johnson buys a drugstore in Quincy, Massachusetts, and sells ice cream, hot dogs, hamburgers, and other quick-to-cook foods.

1927 Kool-Aid packs a powdered beverage mix in envelopes.

1928 Ding! Dong! Avon calling.

1928 Gerber baby food's first packages are tins with pictures of alphabet blocks on the label.

1928 Double Bubble is the perfect chewing gum to blow bubbles.

Discovering Odors

Advertising helped make America a cleaner nation. For instance, soap manufacturers, concerned that the nation still did not bathe enough, set out to change the American way.[11] In response, soapmakers strategically turned to advertising to improve the hygiene habits of Americans and to sell more soap. Their advertising campaigns and others became a forceful agent of change, instilling in many Americans the middle-class habits of cleanliness.

Whereas the Victorians had considered many bodily functions to be unmentionable, in this era social standards of modesty were relaxed. Advertising reflected the new urban attention to cleanliness. The newly liberated public was far more receptive to ads for mouthwash, toothbrushes and toothpaste, athlete's foot remedies, deodorant, laxatives, sanitary napkins, and toilet paper. Admakers offered more than cleaner bodies, clothes, and homes; they also promised popularity and self-esteem—now every woman could be a lovelier, happier, more likeable person simply by using the advertised product.

Ads for Odorono, Listerine, Lifebuoy, Lux, and Kotex reflected the hygienic spirit of the decade. Another J. Walter Thompson agency success, copywriter Jim Young's daring Odorono campaign, approached a delicate subject, underarm odor. A Cincinnati surgeon had invented the deodorant Odorono (pronounced "odor-oh-no"), and his daughter had first sold the product to women, because men kept their coats on and were expected to smell. Young's 1919 Odorono ad became an advertising classic; the headline ("Within the Curve of a Woman's Arm") artfully managed to avoid mentioning the armpit (Figure 4.6). The copy went on to present "A frank discussion of a subject too often avoided":

> A woman's arm! Poets have sung of it, great artists have painted its beauty.
>
> It should be the daintiest, sweetest thing in the world. And yet, unfortunately, it isn't, always.
>
> There's an old offender in this quest for perfect daintiness—an offender of which we ourselves may be ever so unconscious, but which is just as truly present. . . . For it is a physiological fact that persons troubled with perspiration odor seldom can detect it themselves.

This Odorono ad so insulted some two hundred *Ladies' Home Journal* readers that they canceled their subscriptions; nevertheless, Odorono's sales rose 112 percent in a year.[12]

What we know as mouthwash first sold as a "breath deodorant." Sales for the general antiseptic Listerine, invented by a St. Louis druggist named J. W. Lambert, moved slowly until Milton Feasley and Gordon Seagrove of the firm's Chicago ad agency, Williams & Cunnyngham, promoted the product as a remedy for bad breath. One simply did not talk about such personal matters in polite company, so the agency used the medical-sounding "halitosis" instead. Copywriter Milton Feasley created the halitosis idea in 1922. One expression of

There isn't a girl who can't have the irresistible, appealing loveliness of perfect daintiness

Within the Curve of a Woman's Arm
A frank discussion of a subject too often avoided

A woman's arm! Poets have sung of its grace; artists have painted its beauty.

It should be the daintiest, sweetest thing in the world. And yet, unfortunately, it isn't, always.

There's an old offender in this quest for perfect daintiness—an offender of which we ourselves may be ever so unconscious, but which is just as truly present.

Shall we discuss it frankly?

Many a woman who says, "No, I am never annoyed by perspiration," does not know the facts—does not realize how much sweeter and daintier she would be if she were *entirely* free from it.

Of course, we aren't to blame because nature has so made us that the perspiration glands under the arms are more active than anywhere else. Nor are we to blame because the perspiration which occurs under the arm does not evaporate as readily as from other parts of the body. The curve of the arm and the constant wearing of clothing have made normal evaporation there impossible.

Would you be absolutely sure of your daintiness?

It is the chemicals of the body, not uncleanliness, that cause odor. And even though there is no active perspiration—no apparent moisture—there may be under the arms an odor unnoticed by ourselves, but distinctly noticeable to

others. For it is a physiological fact that persons troubled with perspiration odor seldom can detect it themselves.

Fastidious women who want to be absolutely sure of their daintiness have found that they could not trust to their own consciousness; they have felt the need of a toilet water which would insure them against any of this kind of underarm unpleasantness, either moisture or odor.

To meet this need, a physician formulated Odorono—a perfectly harmless and delightful toilet water. With particular women Odorono has become a toilet necessity which they use regularly two or three times a week.

So simple, so easy, so sure

No matter how much the perspiration glands may be excited by exertion, nervousness, or weather conditions, Odorono will keep your underarms always sweet and naturally dry. You then can dismiss all anxiety as to your freshness, your perfect daintiness.

The right time to use Odorono is at night before retiring. Pat it on the underarms with a bit of absorbent cotton, only two or three times a

> Dr. Lewis B. Allyn, head of the famous Westfield Laboratories, Westfield, Massachusetts, says:
>
> "*Experimental and practical tests show that Odorono is harmless, economical and effective when employed as directed, and will injure neither the skin nor the health.*"

week. Then a little talcum dusted on and you can forget all about that worst of all embarrassments—perspiration odor or moisture. Daily baths do not lessen the effect of Odorono at all.

Does excessive perspiration ruin your prettiest dresses?

Are you one of the many women who are troubled with excessive perspiration, which ruins all your prettiest blouses and dresses? To endure this condition is so unnecessary! Why, you need *never* spoil a dress with perspiration! For this severer trouble Odorono is just as effective as it is for the more subtle form of perspiration annoyance. Try it tonight and notice how exquisitely fresh and sweet you will feel.

If you are troubled in any unusual way or have had any difficulty in finding relief, let us help you solve your problem. We shall be so glad to do so. Address Ruth Miller, The Odorono Co., 719 Blair Avenue, Cincinnati, Ohio.

At all toilet counters in the United States and Canada, 60c and $1.00. Trial size, 30c. By mail postpaid if your dealer hasn't it.

Address mail orders or requests as follows:
For Canada to The Arthur Sales Co., 61 Adelaide St., East, Toronto, Ont. For France to The Agencie Américaine, 38 Avenue de l'Opéra, Paris. For Switzerland to The Agencie Américaine, 17 Boulevard Helvetique, Geneve. For England to The American Drug Supply Co., 6 Northumberland Ave., London, W. C. 2. For Mexico to H. E. Gerber & Cia, 2a Gante, 19, Mexico City; For U. S. A. to The Odorono Co., 719 Blair Avenue, Cincinnati, Ohio.

Figure 4.6 This daring 1919 ad by the J. Walter Thompson agency addressed a delicate subject—body odor.

the concept became on of the best-known advertising headlines: "Often a bridesmaid but never a bride." The headline continued with different copy and illustrations for three decades. For example, this classic 1925 ad created new anxieties:

> *Edna's case was really a pathetic one. Like every woman, her primary ambition was to marry. Most of the girls of her set were married—or about to be. Yet not one possessed more grace or charm or loveliness than she. And as her birthdays crept gradually toward that tragic thirty-mark, marriage seemed farther from her life than ever. She was often a bridesmaid but never a bride.*
>
> *That's the insidious thing about halitosis (unpleasant breath). You, yourself, rarely know when you have it. And even your closest friends won't tell you.*

But the friendly Listerine adviser could. Listerine worked as a "breath deodorant" and halted "food fermentation in the mouth and [left] the breath sweet, fresh, and clean" (Figure 4.7).

Further installments of the dramatic Listerine campaign presented other social disasters, from missed invitations to ruined marriages, that supposedly could happen to anybody. One 1926 ad asked: "Was this a hint? This was the third time it had happened in a month: he the head of the concern, finding one of these advertisements on his desk, marked for his attention, no signature."

The campaign proved so successful that people's behavior changed. The morning mouthwash soon became as popular as the morning shower. To further boost sales, Listerine creatively introduced other uses for the product: a dandruff cure, an after-shave tonic, a cold and sore throat remedy, an astringent, and a deodorant; Listerine even developed its own brand of cigarettes. Annual ad expenditures for Listerine products rose from $100,000 in 1922 to $5 million in 1928, with Listerine generating a net $4 million profit over the same period.[13]

With Listerine as a model, ad campaigns revolving around "advertising by fear" or "whisper copy" fostered new anxieties and contributed solutions every day. Yet all the ads carefully masked the "unmentionable" in sober, medical-sounding terms (Figure 4.8). For example, Absorbine Jr. effectively treated the fungus "Tinea Trichophyton" (athlete's foot), Pompeiian massage cream eliminated "comedones" (blackheads), and Spencer corsets corrected "lordosis" (faulty posture).

Lever Brothers, the makers of Lifebuoy and Lux soap in Cambridge, Massachusetts, also were inspired by Listerine's ploy of creating a problem (halitosis) and then providing a solution. The company revised its advertising copy to reflect this stronger selling approach.

Often a bridesmaid but never a bride

EDNA'S case was really a pathetic one. Like every woman, her primary ambition was to marry. Most of the girls of her set were married—or about to be. Yet not one possessed more grace or charm or loveliness than she.

And as her birthdays crept gradually toward that tragic thirty-mark, marriage seemed farther from her life than ever.

She was often a bridesmaid but never a bride.

That's the insidious thing about halitosis (unpleasant breath). You, yourself, rarely know when you have it. And even your closest friends won't tell you.

Sometimes, of course, halitosis comes from some deep-seated organic disorder that requires professional advice. But usually—and fortunately—halitosis is only a local condition that yields to the regular use of Listerine as a mouth wash and gargle. It is an interesting thing that this well-known antiseptic that has been in use for years for surgical dressings, possesses these unusual properties as a breath deodorant.

It halts food fermentation in the mouth and leaves the breath sweet, fresh and clean. Not by substituting some other odor but by really removing the old one. The Listerine odor itself quickly disappears. So the systematic use of Listerine puts you on the safe and polite side.

Your druggist will supply you with Listerine. He sells lots of it. It has dozens of different uses as a safe antiseptic and has been trusted as such for a half a century. Read the interesting little booklet that comes with every bottle.
—Lambert Pharmacal Company, Saint Louis, U. S. A.

For HALITOSIS use LISTERINE

Figure 4.7 This 1925 ad for Listerine "breath deodorant" introduced a catchphrase that has endured to this day: "Often a bridesmaid but never a bride."

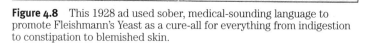

Figure 4.8   This 1928 ad used sober, medical-sounding language to promote Fleishmann's Yeast as a cure-all for everything from indigestion to constipation to blemished skin.

Since 1902 Lifebuoy had been advertised as "the soap that cleans and disinfects, purifies—at one operation." In 1928, however, a Lifebuoy soap ad assured consumers that the product would "protect" them from an even greater social disgrace: "B.O."—short for "Body Odor." Similarly, Lux originally had been promoted as a wonderful new product for "laundering fine fabrics"; and by the mid-1920s it could also preserve "soft, youthful, lovely feminine hands." In the early 1930s, however, Lever Brothers dramatically shifted gears and adopted a stronger sell. Lux could now prevent "undie odor": "She never omits her Daily Bath, yet wears underthings a SECOND DAY." As these stop-smelling pitches ran, business boomed for Lever Brothers.

Advertising the new product Kotex, made by Cellucotton Products Co. in Chicago, proved yet another delicate task. How did one mention the truly unmentionable? With the topic of menstruation a taboo, the early ads succeeded without using any descriptive words in the headline. A 1921 Kotex ad read: "Simplify the laundress problem," referring to the unwelcome chore of laundering soiled cloths or rags. "Kotex are good enough to form a habit, cheap enough to throw away, and easy to dispose of," explained the copy. In 1927 the Lord & Thomas agency claimed: "The Safe Solution of Women's Greatest Hygienic Problem, over 80 percent of the better class of women in America today employ Kotex" a product that "thoroughly deodorizes." Through friendly chatter the Kotex ads assured modern women of the value and convenience of the product while delicately avoiding an intimate discussion of feminine hygiene (Figure 4.9). Yet Kotex faced still another problem: women were too embarrassed to ask for the product by name. To address this issue, later Kotex ads included a new marketing device. Plain brown wrappers camouflaged the name Kotex on the packages; merchants displayed the product on the counter so a woman simply picked it up and left the money. Once women did not have to ask for the product by name, sales rose.

Creating Shrines of Cleanliness

As part of the 1920s trend toward personal hygiene and image projection, bathrooms modernized and became showplaces of style. Kohler Manufacturing Company in Sheboygan, Wisconsin, and Crane Co. in Chicago, both leading makers of plumbing fixtures, initially promoted the small and simple modern bathroom with its three standard "immaculately white enamel" fixtures—sink, tub, and toilet.

Subsequently new product designs and colors dramatically altered the look of bathroom fixtures and accessories. A 1925 ad for Crane bathroom equipment made this statement: "From a mere utility, the modern bathroom has developed into a spacious shrine of cleanliness and health." Striking four-color ads brought the reader to a full stop. Vivid illustrations demonstrated "the possibilities of bathroom beauty"—both simple and elaborate. In one Crane bathroom "the tiled floor and warm plaster walls have borders of spanish majolica in primrose, brown and green." New design and fixtures magically transformed another bathroom into an English cottage–style facility. Yet another ad portrayed an exotic bathroom with "Satara marble slab brought from Africa and design inspired by Italian art" (Figure 4.10). Kohler also ran four-color ads, and in 1927 the company illustrated the inconvenience of not having enough bathrooms to go around.

To harmonize with modern bathroom decoration, the plain white bath towel gave way to a palette of colors and decorative designs.

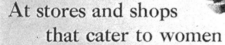

Figure 4.9   This 1920s ad for Kotex successfully avoided mentioning the "unmentionable" and instead linked women's use of this "sanitary absorbent" to its medical applications in World War I.

North Carolina's Cannon Mills backed its new line of towels with heavy advertising and charged four times more than for plain white ones! The company found that consumers would pay for the "class" towels' added value. Also, Cannon supported the "bath-a-day" habit, not for

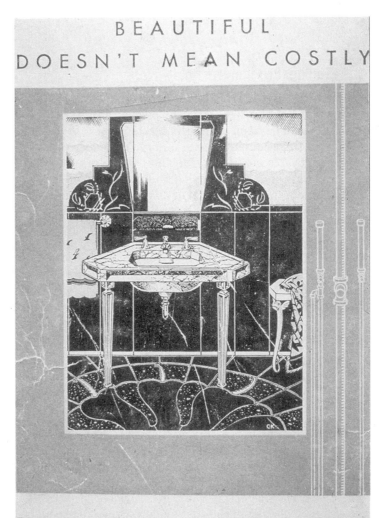

BEAUTIFUL
DOESN'T MEAN COSTLY

Because Crane Co. combs the world for new ideas for American homes
does not mean that Crane materials cost more. One result of this un-
arch is lavatories like the one above, with Safara marble slab bro
Africa and design inspired by Italian art. Another is new beauty an
sive fixtures for small homes and modest apartments. You owe i

Figure 4.10   As this ad suggests, Crane fixtures transformed ordinary
bathrooms into exotic "shrines of cleanliness."

reasons of comfort and hygiene, but because it increased the number
of towels needed and stimulated sales. One ad made this point: "Because the first towel absorbs impurities from the skin, it must never
(under any circumstance) be used again before washing." Competitor
Martex also introduced a line of towels designed by famous artists that
"cost no more than quite undistinguished towels." The line included

special designs from modernists famous for their posters and paintings, such as Rene Clark, Erte, and Leonard.

Selling the Cigarette Habit

The selling of cigarettes proved to be advertising's ultimate triumph of the decade. At that time many people considered cigarette smoking an undesirable habit. Moralists blasted cigarettes, referring to them as "coffin nails" and "gaspers." Henry Ford deemed cigarette smokers unemployable in a 1914 pamphlet. Others held that the cigarette smokers were most likely criminals, neurotics, or possibly drug addicts. The war and multimillion-dollar advertising campaigns changed all that. During and after World War I, cigarettes gained wider acceptance when both soldiers and civilians found smoking cigarettes to be more convenient, cheaper, and more sanitary than chewing tobacco.

To this audience R. J. Reynolds in Winston-Salem, North Carolina, directed its first nationally marketed cigarette, called Camel. The brand quickly achieved market dominance with an upscale-priced smoke that delivered a new tobacco taste. In no time George Washington Hill's American Tobacco Company in North Carolina created a richer, sweeter tobacco product, Lucky Strike cigarettes. The three major brands (Chesterfield was the third) then slugged it out for the market lead from 1917 until after World War II.

Hill hired hard-sell expert Albert J. Lasker of the Lord & Thomas agency and told him to do whatever was necessary to win the cigarette war. As a result, Lucky Strike advertising broke all previous records. Hill's enormous ad expenditures also brought the Lord & Thomas agency back into the ranks of the·major agencies. In 1929 alone the American Tobacco Company accounted for over one-fourth of the agency's $40 million in billings.

Lasker, a reason-why copy advocate, insisted that the headline was 90 percent of the ad: "You must write the headline first, and then having done that, the art must be the cartoon that illustrates the headline."[14] In his aggressive selling style a key phrase or slogan could be repeated as many as six times in a single ad. On the new medium of radio, for example, listeners heard these slogans blatantly iterated during the Lucky Strike radio shows and at other intervals during the day. This approach worked up to a point, but it quite naturally rankled many listeners. The Lucky Strike campaigns would hammer away with slogans like the following and then start up with a new one:

Nature in the Raw is Seldom Mild.
Reach for a Lucky Instead of a Sweet.
Be Happy, Go Lucky/Be Happy, Go Lucky Strike Today.
So Round, So Firm, So Fully Packed, So Free and Easy
    on the Draw.
Lucky Strike Means Fine Tobacco (simply "LS/MFT").
No Throat Irritation—No Cough.

Hill, urged on by Lasker, jumped at the chance to reach an untapped audience—women—who would double the potential market. Until now advertising had supported the notion that the pleasures of smoking were for men only. But a number of women took up smoking during World War I as cigarette tobacco became milder and easier to use than the roll-your-own varieties (although the filter had not yet been invented). Still, society did not consider smoking an acceptable social practice for women.

Throughout the decade women smokers remained a controversial issue. For example, many colleges prohibited women from smoking on campus. Women also found themselves unable to smoke in railroad diners, in many smoking rooms in train stations, and on board ships. By the mid-1920s, however, some colleges had established smoking rooms, while streetcars, railroads, and shipping lines liberalized their regulations. Some railroads opened their smoking cars to women despite men's complaints that women occupied their seats; others installed separate smoking compartments for men and for women or allowed women to smoke in the dining car.

Advertising further fueled this cultural revolution. One 1912 ad for Velvet Tobacco showed a "respectable" woman sitting with a man who was smoking; "I wish I were a man," she mused, suggesting that she might like to smoke. Some ads hinted at this daring idea, while others took a more direct approach. In 1926 the Newell-Emmett agency daringly presented a poster showing a romantic moonlit seaside scene and a man lighting his Chesterfield with a woman perched beside him saying, "Blow some my way." These four words shocked many people. Yet Chesterfield resolutely carried on with its campaign, paving the way to the vast women's market. Hill and Lasker quickly sensed an opportunity for the Lucky Strike brand and pitched the female audience, appealing to women's growing sense of independence.

The Lucky Strike advertising campaign incorporated several major innovations. First, Hill was concerned that women were resisting the green packaging because it clashed with their clothes (the original pack had a red bull's-eye on a dark green background until 1942, when it changed to red on white). To solve the problem, he hired Edward L. Bernays, a public relations pioneer, who promoted the color green as fashionable in fashion shows so that the dark green Luckies packages would complement women's ensembles. Hill also used celebrities from the entertainment world, such film stars, crooners, and jazz musicians, to promote his cigarettes. And for the first time women endorsed the product and popularized the image of the fashionable lady who, while she indeed smoked, still appeared stylish and respectable. Lucky Strike campaigns particularly favored testimonials from operatic sopranos, actresses, and society matrons, who attested to the positive effect Luckies had on their voices. One slogan ("Reach for a Lucky instead of a sweet") even drew protests from the candy industry (Figure 4.11). Nor was this a novel approach; a late-nineteenth-century

Figure 4.11 In this 1925 ad Lucky Strike's "sweetness" appealed especially to the newly liberated woman.

advertisement for Lydia Pinkham's remedy had promoted a similar idea: "Reach for a vegetable, instead of a sweet." Many marketers believe that this "sweet" campaign created more women smokers than any other single advertising effort.

The Federal Trade Commission (FTC) viewed Lucky Strike advertising in a different light. In 1930 the FTC ruled that American Tobacco's Lucky Strike brand must take a three-fold action: cease running testimonials by endorsers who had not actually used the product, indicate when testimonials had been paid for, and stop claiming that smoking cigarettes could control people's weight. After some modifications to his campaign, Hill forged on and emerged as the winner of the cigarette wars. Lucky Strike overtook Camel and remained the market leader until the 1950s.

Although advertisers focused on women as the primary purchasers of many consumer goods, their larger target was the increasingly affluent middle class. In response to that group's desire to enjoy the fruits of their new status, advertisers both introduced countless variations on familiar products and tapped new advertising media.

Selling Color, Style, and Time

The admakers' increasing sophistication about the basic sociological variables of gender and class strongly influenced advertising. Agencies primarily addressed their ads for everything from shaving cream to scouring pads to a middle-class, largely female readership that enjoyed growing affluence during this period. They reasoned that this audience had the means to buy the products advertised, whereas working-class people could afford to purchase only a limited range of products.

Advertisers also had a new marketing research tool to help them understand the middle-class market. Robert and Helen Lynd's *Middletown,* a report on their celebrated 1929 sociological study of the people of Muncie, Indiana, provided agencies with information on social attitudes for various classes of people. Previously most agencies had focused on quantitative market research, which factually described markets in terms of population statistics, numbers of outlets, buying power indices, amount of media coverage, brand preference rankings, and audience profiles by occupation and class. However, advertising that targeted various lifestyles would not become the norm until the 1950s. Here, the focus was clearly on the middle class. Advertisers sought to dress these people up, modernize their homes, and get them out on the road.

Fashion Takes a Bow

Ads encouraged the burgeoning middle class and nouveau riche to buy—not because they "needed" the material goods, but they "wanted" them to enhance their status. Admakers tapped ostentatious symbols of the upper class to flatter prospective purchasers with appeals to a "better class of woman." These portrayals included women wearing pretentious high fashions, domestic servants serving the well-

A Taste of the Times

The spirit of the "Roaring Twenties" represented a liberation from Victorian constraints. The era was a source of delight to some and of horror to others. Young women made it clear in many ways that, in addition to working outside the home, they wanted the same freedoms that men enjoyed. Who was this woman who threw away her corset, bound her breasts for a flat-chested look, replaced her cotton underwear with rayon and silk, raised her skirts to the knee, bobbed her hair, plucked her eyebrows, painted her lips in a Cupid's bow, used shocking words, drank, and smoked? In 1922 *Vanity Fair* called her a "flapper." In the same year, the *Pittsburgh Observer* reported "a change for the worse during the past year in feminine dress, dancing, manners, and general moral standards."[a]

Signs of the nation's pleasure-seeking mood appeared everywhere. Old restraints relaxed. Thriftiness gave way to installment buying. Church attendance declined. Speakeasies flourished despite Prohibition, which banned the sale of liquor. Magazines, books, and motion pictures reflected the national preoccupation with sheiks, vamps, and sex. The young and wild welcomed Sigmund Freud as a scientific excuse for pursuing boundless pleasure. Mass-market books such as *Ten Thousand Dreams Interpreted* and *Sex Problems Solved* sold well.

Americans got better and better at amusing themselves—whether it was playing contract bridge, roller-skating, yo-yoing, playing miniature golf, or enjoying the latest fads. Jazz, flagpole sitting, marathon dance contests, mah-jongg, crossword puzzles, and Ouija boards all became the

to-do, and "beautiful people" lounging in elegant settings; elaborate lettering and borders transformed the showcased products from the mundane into the luxurious.

Advertising also used the old idea of introducing "fashion" to enhance a product's value and thus to inflate its price. A splash of color or a minor design alteration enormously expanded the range of available products, as well as invigorated sales. Everything from bathroom towels to automobiles could be touted in terms of color, style, and fashion. And a color image of a product against the black-and-white magazine page demanded attention, given that color reproduction in the early 1920s was a relatively new technology.

For many products color and design breakthroughs first occurred between 1924 and 1928. For example, Willy's Overland introduced the Red Bird Car in 1924, and General Motors followed with new car models in a range of hues. Parker Pen merchandised a color-barreled foun-

Coles Phillips illustrated this risqué 1927 ad that pushed the limits of prevailing standards of public decency.

rage. The Charleston, the shimmy shake, and the lindy hop replaced the waltz and fox-trot. Many Americans spent Saturday afternoons watching "America's Sweetheart," Mary Pickford, act in films, Babe Ruth hit home runs, Jack Dempsey box, or college football teams battle.

Yet beyond the glitter of the big cities, the atmosphere in small towns and rural areas seemed closer to the nineteenth century than the Jazz Age. The church served as a community center. Doctors made housecalls. Band concerts, county fairs, hometown ballgames, and sing-a-longs remained the main entertainment. In many places the event of the year was when the circus came to town. Some things stay reassuringly the same even today.

[a] Clifton Daniel, ed., *Chronicle of America* (Mount Kisco, NY: Chronicle Publications, 1989), 620.

tain pen, and Kodak cameras came in five fashion colors. Color also showed up on bathroom accessories, tiles, and plumbing fixtures; in the bedroom; and on kitchen cookware, utensils, appliances, and flooring materials.

The advertised ensemble also coaxed people to buy more and increased the average size of each consumer's purchase. For a woman the purchase of a new dress now involved acquiring color-coordinated hosiery, shoes, hat, handbag, jewelry, and compact, as well as new shades of makeup, lipstick, and fingernail polish. With the ensemble concept in mind, manufacturers introduced color schemes into automotive interiors, underwear, clocks, linoleum, and even silverware handles. A new appliance, bathroom rug, or piece of furniture often made everything else in the room seem out of style and thus encouraged new purchases. As color and ensembles transformed utilitarian staples into fashion goods, merchandise sales skyrocketed.

The American Home Goes Modern

Many products appeared on the market that had not existed prior to the twentieth century. People claimed that they could get along quite well without most of the new inventions, thereby saving the money, time, and energy needed to acquire them. But the reality was, they didn't. Rather, they purchased radios, hand irons, toasters, dishwashers, washing machines, fans, refrigerators, and so on just as fast as they could.

Ads for everything from labor-saving household machines to packaged foods and detergents all promised to simplify daily chores. Whether the ad was for a washing machine, canned soup, or laundry detergent, admakers made ease, comfort, and convenience a major selling point. They constantly expressed concern for the housewife's well-being and acknowledged just how difficult and boring housework could be. And they urged housewives to free themselves from household chores in order to pursue more enriching activities. A classic Libby's food ad from 1920, "The Woman Who Never Went Out," fully developed this theme:

> *What happened when she realized there was more in the world than the view from her kitchen window? . . . It hurt—that sudden flash of seeing herself as others must see her. A drudge—that's what she was. One of the army of women past whom the world whirls gaily, while they grow older and more faded and colorless. Til finally one morning they wake up and realize that their chance to play has slipped away forever. . . . She had allowed her housekeeping to absorb not only all her time but her interest and vivacity . . .*

In the ad's conclusion, Libby assured the reader that this situation could be avoided. Simply using Libby's canned meats would free a woman up to engage in all sorts of enriching activities.

Advertisements typically suggested that women spend the time saved playing with their children, attending club activities, reading, playing golf, or going to the theater. None of the ads mentioned a career outside the home. In a 1920s America devoted to female domesticity, a woman worked outside the home only when she had to— that is, when she was single or when her husband's salary could not cover the family's needs.

Ads for refrigerators, vacuum cleaners, and pop-up toasters reflected the difficult task of selling entirely new technology. What we know as

Reddy Kilowatt.

modern home appliances were actually new conveniences designed to upgrade existing machines. For example, in the early post–World War I years, a homemaker might bolt a wringer onto her washtub or add a motor to her sewing machine to modernize her home. Similarly the first electrical refrigerator was not the appliance we know today, but rather was a device to be inserted into an existing icebox. One 1925 ad demonstrated how Frigidaire skillfully sold its electric cooling system to upgrade an icebox, "Make your Ice Box a Frigidaire" (Figure 4.12):

> *It's easy. The cake of ice now in your refrigerator is re-placed by the Frigidaire "frost coil," which is colder than ice and never melts. You enjoy, immediately, the full convenience of electric refrigeration.*
>
> *Frigidaire maintains a constant,* dry *cold—keeps foods fresh and wholesome in any weather—makes dainty ice cubes and delicious desserts for your table—saves the possible annoyance of outside ice supply—adds greatly to the convenience of house-keeping. And Frigidaire is not expensive, in many lo-calities the operation costs less than ice.*

Frigidaire quickly became the generic term for refrigerator, but rival General Electric followed in 1927 with a $1 million promotion to sell its own new refrigerator. Called the Monitor Top, the GE refrigerator enclosed the cooling mechanism on top of the unit and solved the problem of toxic leaks in the refrigeration system. The refrigerator, however, remained a luxury item until the 1930s. The appliance sold, on average, for almost double the price of a Model T Ford in 1924.[15]

Other early ads drove home the point that housewives often found even the simplest household tasks exhausting. One 1924 Hoover vacuum sweeper ad described the machine's role in easing the pain of "the brave little woman" at home:

> *As cleaning days come and go, she struggles resolutely with the only "tools" she has in her "workshop," your home. And they are woefully inadequate, wasteful of time and strength. As she wields her broom foot by foot across the dusty, dirty rugs her arms rebel and her back seems near to breaking. . . . The Hoover will save her strength. The Hoover will speed her work.*

Above all, a successful new-technology ad explained what the invention was, how it worked, how to use it, and why one *had* to have one. Skilled copywriters got the message across through persuasive copy and how-to pictures. Toastmaster's 1927 advertisement, a model example, announced the first electric pop-up toaster for the home (Figure 4.13). With accompanying step-by-step illustrations the copy read:

Figure 4.12   This 1925 ad for the original Frigidaire actually promoted an electrical cooling system to upgrade a traditional icebox.

An amazing new way to make toast . . . You do not have to watch the bread after you put it into the toaster. You do not have to turn it. There is no danger of its burning. Yet every slice is done to perfection. . . . And all you have to do is: 1. Drop a slice of bread into the oven slot. 2. Press down the two levers. This automatically turns on the current and sets the time device. 3. Pop! Up comes the toast automatically when it's done, and the current is automatically turned off.

Electrical appliance sales boomed as prices dropped and household incomes grew. Getting "wired" also caught on. In 1920 one-third

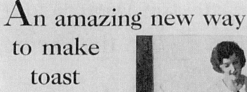

Figure 4.13 This 1927 ad combined persuasion and instruction to successfully promote the first pop-up toaster.

of American homes had electricity; by decade's end that number had doubled.

Automobile Advertising Shifts Gears

Automakers dominated this era of product styling. By mid-decade manufacturers had achieved an acceptable level of performance and reliability. At the same time, America's love affair with automobiles had intensified. The automobile had become a thing of beauty—a smart and elegant centerpiece of people's lives, promising mobility, excitement, adventure, and even romance.

One of the most celebrated car ads was a gem for the Jordan Playboy roadster headlined "Somewhere West of Laramie" (Figure 4.14).

Somewhere West of Laramie

SOMEWHERE west of Laramie there's a broncho-busting, steer-roping girl who knows what I'm talking about. She can tell what a sassy pony, that's a cross between greased lightning and the place where it hits, can do with eleven hundred pounds of steel and action when he's going high, wide and handsome.

The truth is—the Playboy was built for her.

Built for the lass whose face is brown with the sun when the day is done of revel and romp and race.

She loves the cross of the wild and the tame.

There's a savor of links about that car—of laughter and lilt and light—a hint of old loves—and saddle and quirt. It's a brawny thing—yet a graceful thing for the sweep o' the Avenue.

Step into the Playboy when the hour grows dull with things gone dead and stale.

Then start for the land of real living with the spirit of the lass who rides, lean and rangy, into the red horizon of a Wyoming twilight.

Figure 4.14   This 1923 ad for the Jordan Motor Car Company, one of the most celebrated in advertising history, employed vivid prose to capture the excitement of auto travel.

The giddy advertisement, which first appeared in a 1923 *Saturday Evening Post,* was written by founder Ned Jordan, who had a background in both advertising and auto sales. Never before had an automobile ad so captured the public's fancy, especially the newly emancipated women—"the lass whose face is brown with the sun when the day is done of revel and romp and race." The Jordan ads continued through the decade, but none of them equaled "Laramie." It had a wide-reaching influence on the advertising world. Instead of unadorned, reason-why copy, Jordan's copy was vivid and colorful—a style of copywriting that would also be used to sell fashion, furs, jewelry, perfumes, resorts, and liquor.

In this era American manufacturers also developed products for clearly defined groups of customers for the first time. This concept would later become known as a "marketing strategy." For example, Detroit-based General Motors, under chairman Alfred Sloane's leadership, advanced a three-point strategy to capture the mass marketplace, from farmboys to corporate executives. GM initially offered nine brand-name models—"A car for every purse and purpose"—to appeal to every income and lifestyle of the mass market, and all available on the "convenient GMAC payment plan." This strategy fostered the belief that one started with the Chevrolet and traded up through Pontiac, Oldsmobile, Buick, and so on to the Cadillac.

The idea that appearance might affect sales ripened into the "planned-obsolescence" styling strategy. Sloane wanted "a production automobile that was as beautiful as the custom cars of the period," so he hired automotive designer Harley Earl to execute the concept.[16] GM's newly created Art and Color Section, under Earl's direction, emphasized styling and deluxe interiors and introduced colored body styles in a palette of Duco lacquer finishes—French gray, royal oak green, and beige brown—for the 1927 Chevrolet (Figure 4.15). This division emerged the source of all the styling cliches that Americans came to take for granted: chrome, two-tone paint, tail fins, hardtops, wraparound windshields. To sell Americans on the necessity of owning an up-to-date car, admakers glorified each annual model change so that owners became dissatisfied with the model they owned and purchased the "superior" car.

Also, GM cultivated the rapidly growing used car market as millions of people discarded their current models to purchase new ones. GM used skillful advertising to explain that a new car need not be "new." The 1929 ad headlined "Marooned!" showed a wife and two children tearfully waving farewell as the husband and father stepped into his car:

> *Marooned! That was the fate of many a woman until I got an inexpensive car for my very own. . . . The second new car need not necessarily be a new car. Many used cars have thousands of miles of unused transportation in them.*

When Henry Ford's low-cost Model T ("It's available in any color you want, as long it is black") began to lose market shares to GM's more colorful models, the automaker countered with the Model A. Ford also felt compelled to restate his commitment to quality, reliability, and low prices. In 1927 he launched a $1.5-million campaign to

Brilliant in their modish new colors—alluring in their distinguished smartness, the new Chevrolet models disclose that individuality and perfection of silhouette you would expect to find only in the costliest of custom-built creations.

One of the most revolutionary advancements ever made in the development of the low-priced motor car, the Most Beautiful Chevrolet introduces marvelous new bodies by Fisher with their beauty emphasized by bullet-type lamps and one-piece full-crown fenders. In addition, longer life and better operation are assured by a host of mechanical improvements, including an oil filter and an air cleaner.

Thus, for the first time there are available at such low prices both that extraordinary ease of handling and that elusive something which women of discrimination have always demanded in a motor car.

Plan to visit the nearest Chevrolet dealer. There a single inspection will reveal how successfully the world's largest builder of gearshift automobiles is maintaining leadership with new models of delightful beauty and amazing value!

CHEVROLET MOTOR COMPANY, DETROIT, MICHIGAN
Division of General Motors Corporation

Figure 4.15 With ads like this 1928 spot, Chevrolet became America's choice for cars, emphasizing styling and colors.

promote the new car: "Everything you want or need in A Modern Automobile," declared a 1928 ad, "beauty of line and color—steel body—and speed to 55 to 65 miles an hour." Thousands flocked to see the car, which featured a speedometer, shock absorbers, and colored body styles (Figure 4.16). Yet the styled Chevrolet proved a hard act to follow; by 1928 it had become the nation's first choice for transportation. For the first time, a GM model outsold a Ford.

With GM as a successful example, other automakers also developed cars for clearly defined groups of consumers. From 1925 to 1930,

Figure 4.16 In this 1928 ad Ford promoted the colorful new Model A in an attempt to counter the popular, styled General Motors' models.

for instance, about 5 percent of American-built cars targeted the luxury market, offering grand automobiles with legendary names: Dusenberg, Cunningham, Packard, Pierce-Arrow, and the English Rolls-Royce (also built in Springfield, Massachusetts).

How could people afford to buy an automobile, let alone a new model, every few years? As early as 1912, dealers offered to sell cars on credit. An ad for the 1916 Maxwell declared: "Pay as you Ride." The idea sounded marvelous. It became commonplace to buy a new car, drive it for thousands of miles, and then trade it in for a newer model—without having fully paid for the old car. By 1925 three-fourths of all cars were sold on installment plans. Ever since, anxious shoppers have asked, "What's the monthly payment?" rather than "What does it cost?"

Advertising Hits the Road

The revolution in auto travel opened new avenues for outdoor advertising. Families gained mobility, roads became smoother, and tires

Memorable Slogans

Reach for a Lucky instead of a sweet. (Lucky Strike cigarettes)

L.S./M.F.T. Lucky Strike means fine tobacco.

The pause that refreshes. (Coca-Cola)

Drink a bite to eat at 10, 2, and 4 o'clock. (Dr. Pepper)

America's favorite candy. (Baby Ruth)

Ride the Greyhounds. (Greyhound bus)

Buy 'em by the sack. (White Castle 5-cent hamburgers)

You too can have a body like mine. (Charles Atlas)

That schoolgirl complexion. (Palmolive soap)

Colder than ice. (Frigidaire refrigerator)

lasted longer. Speed limits were raised to 35 miles per hour. The roadside cabin, which rented for $2 or $3 a night, increased in popularity, and camping became the new craze. Naturally outdoor ads also multiplied: billboards for automobiles, tires, soft drinks, chewing gum, and many other products increasingly dotted the landscape.

After World War I outdoor advertising also became more scientific as advertisers conducted market research and applied statistical analyses to identify target audiences and preferred locales. Agencies designed outdoor campaigns to meet a company's sales objectives by achieving a specified market "saturation" with a prescribed number of billboard "showings." The advertiser's message would appear on as many billboards as needed to reach a given percentage of potential customers. And a company called Outdoor Advertising Incorporated provided advertisers with a service that conveniently placed signs and billboards coast to coast or in a single city. Advertisers now could reach a specific audience with a custom-tailored message and careful placement.

One notable example, the unusual Burma-Shave billboard campaign, quickly captivated Americans' attention beginning in 1925. Although Clinton Odell invented the brushless shaving cream, his son Allan suggested the series of small roadside signs. Allan got the idea after seeing a series of signs advertising a gas station. A reluctant Clinton Odell put up $200 to finance his son's idea—one that admen insisted would not work. The Odells placed the first set of six tiny wooden signs at 100-foot intervals outside Minneapolis, Minnesota, extolling the wonders of Burma-Shave. Within several months repeat orders for the shaving cream were rolling in from druggists whose cus-

Figure 4.17 Beginning in 1925, following the example of Burma-Shave, road signs like these became familiar landmarks to travelers.

tomers traveled that road. Soon thereafter, serial signs for Burma-Shave and other products were popping up all over the country, and within a few years such signs had become familiar landmarks to the nation's motorists (Figure 4.17).

The roadside signs took approximately 18 seconds to read when a passing car traveled at a speed of 35 miles per hour. The spacing added an unhurried cadence to the reading that built up to a punch line. One series of signs read: THE BEARDED LADY / TRIED A JAR / SHE'S NOW / A FAMOUS / MOVIE STAR / BURMA SHAVE. Another read: HE HAD THE RING / HE HAD THE FLAT / BUT SHE FELT HIS CHIN / AND THAT / WAS THAT. And when the electric razor arrived, the Odells countered the competition with A SILKY CHEEK / SHAVED SMOOTH / AND CLEAN / IS NOT OBTAINED / WITH A MOWING MACHINE / BURMA SHAVE.

Figure 4.18 In the 1920s and 1930s wacky roadside attractions, or "programmatic advertising," became a popular advertising phenomenon.

Sales of Burma-Shave rose every year until 1947, at which time they leveled off and then began to decline. Increased travel on super-highways contributed to this decline, but even on country roads people drove too fast to read the amusing signs. Nevertheless the Odells had used more than five hundred jingles by the time the campaign ended in 1963.[17]

Another ingenious advertising idea, called "programmatic archi-tecture" or "architecture-as-advertising," catered to the newly mobile public and became an American phenomenon. These wacky roadside attractions made people stop, look twice, and pull off the road to buy food or beverages. Examples of programmatic architecture included walk-in coffee pots, gigantic cups and saucers, two-story milk bottles, pig-shaped rib joints, and igloos selling cold drinks. The attractions peaked in popularity from 1928 to 1934; regrettably, few remain standing (Figure 4.18).

Other enterprising advertisers looked to the sky as soon as hu-mans invented methods to fly. Advertisers experimented with gim-micks ranging from hanging signs from blimps, to shouting messages from low-flying planes, to bombarding cities with flyers and product samples. But it was skywriting that really caught on with the public. The technique was originally developed for military signals by Major John Savage of the Royal Air Force, who patented the invention in 1923. New York became the center of skywriting in the following decade, and residents received heavenly messages almost daily. Ever since, skywriting has been a standard feature at air shows, football games, and countless other outdoor events.

Another invention in this era would have a profound effect not just on advertising but on the American sociocultural environment. That invention was the radio.

The Voice of Radio

Newspapers and magazines dominated mass communications until the first commercial radio broadcast in 1920. Over the course of the decade, radio emerged a major industry through both the marketing of radio sets and the selling of airtime to advertisers.

When Pittsburgh station KDKA aired the first commercial radio broadcast in 1920, fewer than a thousand receivers were tuned in to the program. These listeners heard the Harding–Cox presidential election returns interspersed with music—but no advertising. Soon weekly programs featuring live orchestra music, baseball scores, and farm news were airing. Radio was an instant hit. Thousands of amateur set-builders formed this ready-made audience. In a six-month period, starting in fall of 1921, a half-million radio sets were sold (Figure 4.19). In fact, two of every five American families owned radio sets by 1929, and four out of five families did so by 1940.[18] The number of licensed stations also increased from 30 at the end of 1920 to 576 in early 1923.[19]

Radio transmitted the spoken word so powerfully that it could simultaneously reach into thousands, even millions, of homes. Radio brought news as it happened, often from the scene. Broadcasts carried the voices of the president and other political leaders into people's homes. Also, the technology opened up a new world of family entertainment with programs ranging from music to soap operas, dramas, and comedies. And Americans no longer had to wait for the morning newspaper to find out what had happened in the world of sports. Listeners simply turned on their radios to hear play-by-play accounts of baseball and football games or ringside descriptions of boxing matches.

Early stations, however, did not welcome commercial advertising messages. "The family circle is not a public place," warned the advertising trade journal *Printers' Ink* in 1922, "and advertising has no business intruding there unless it is invited."[20] Later that year, New York station WEAF took a risk and sold time to advertisers. The first radio commercial was for a Long Island real estate firm, which purchased 10 minutes of air time for $50; the announcement quickly led to the sale of several apartments. In less than a year, WEAF had twenty-five sponsors including Macy's, Colgate, and Metropolitan Life Insurance. Most station managers and many public officials feared that the dignity of radio would be compromised by the advertising chatter, and critics protested radio's commercialization. But broadcast

MODEL XI .

A gold trimmed KENNEDY set in a beautiful mahogany set adjusted, with built-in loud speaker for reception of local and distant stations. Simplified tuning—only one dial is used. Each station has its own dial setting and is always found at that point. Volume can be regulated. Non-radiating. Licensed under Armstrong U. S. Patent No. 1,113,149.

Without accessories $165.00   **West of the Rockies $190.00**

Listen to the best in radio

*R*IGHT in your own home, with a KENNEDY, you can hear the finest programs that have ever been offered to the public. Broadcasting attracts the headliners—and it is constantly improving in quality. The living voices of great speakers, the music of operas, bands, orchestras and soloists, can be heard with brilliant realism.

New heights have been attained in perfect reception on the KENNEDY, to equal the marvelous achievements in nationwide broadcasting. Every note and syllable comes in on the KENNEDY flawlessly clear, round, full and natural in tone. It is the instrument trained musicians approve.

KENNEDY prices—always moderate—are even lower this season.

Any KENNEDY dealer will gladly demonstrate the set you prefer in your home. Write for the nearest dealer's address, if you do not know where he is located.

THE COLIN B. KENNEDY COMPANY, *Saint Louis*

MODEL VI

This model receives distant stations on the loud speaker. Simplified, logged tuning. Non-radiating. Licensed under Armstrong U. S. Patent. Not a crystal set.

Without accessories $105.00
West of the Rockies $107.50

MODEL XV

Super-selective radio frequency model. Cuts through local broadcasting and brings in distant clearly. Simple, logged tuning. Non-radiating. Operates on a loop or indoor antenna. Ideal for log cabins.

Without accessories . . . $142.50
West of the Rockies $145.00

KENNEDY

The Royalty of *Radio*

Figure 4.19   In the 1920s the radio became a powerful mass communications technology, broadcasting news, sports, and entertainment—and advertising.

operating costs and pressure from potential advertisers forced the issue, and commercial messages on radio eventually became acceptable. Ever since, radio has accepted advertising's financial support.

However, advertisers did not know what to do with the new medium in the early years. Initially many broadcast advertisers simply filled entire segments of leased time with promotional messages. Others experimented with creating programs relevant to their product, such as Gillette, which hosted a talk show on fashions in beards to generate sales. Yet a mere 20 percent of radio programs had sponsors as of 1927.

The development of regular weekly programs, rather than one-time efforts, gradually convinced advertisers that the new medium deserved their backing. To fill program segments, radio picked up many popular vaudeville shows that featured song-and-dance teams, singers, and ethnic and black-face comics. Many early commercial programs were actually musical variety shows sponsored by advertisers of batteries, radios, soft drinks, bread, candy, and so on. Listeners enjoyed music and variety shows such as the "Cliquot Club Eskimos" for Cliquot soft drinks, "The Ever Ready Battery Hour" for Eveready batteries, and "The A&P Gypsies" for A&P grocery stores.

Most stations permitted only a single mention of the sponsor and product name during their programs. The agencies, however, artfully circumvented this limitation and managed to insert the sponsor's name at various intervals. For example, the writer for the Gold Dust washing powder program managed to refer to the sponsor's name six times in one opening spot:

> *Relax and smile, for* Goldy and Dusty, *the* Gold Dust Twins *are here to send their songs there, and brighten the corner where you are. The* Gold Dust Corporation, *manufacturer of* Gold Dust Powder, *engages the facilities of station WEAF, New York, WJAR, Providence, WCAE, Pittsburgh, WGR, Buffalo, WEEL, Boston, WFI, Philadelphia, and WEAR, Cleveland, so that listeners-in may have the opportunity to chuckle and laugh with* Goldy and Dusty. *Let those* Gold Dust Twins *into your hearts and homes tonight, and you'll never regret, for they do brighten the dull spots.*

Listeners familiar with Gold Dust washing powder could not miss the message that this "institutional" commercial referred to the brand name "Gold Dust."

Lord & Thomas and J. Walter Thompson emerged as the dominant advertising agencies in radio. Lord & Thomas handled the "Lucky Strike Show" and aggressively injected catchy cigarette slogans at the end of every song as well as throughout the show. The agency also produced radio's first runaway hit, the "Amos 'n' Andy Show,"

Early Radio Timeline

1840

The first transatlantic cable is laid.
1866

Samuel Morse transmits the first
telegraph message between two
cities.
1844

Reginald Fessenden broadcasts the
first known wireless transmission,
and Lee De Forest's improvements
make "practical" radio possible.

Thomas Edison records the first
commercial on his phonograph
record (for the Edison
phonograph).
1906

Guglielmo Marconi sends the first
wireless transmission.
1901

1876
Alexander Graham Bell's telephone
transmits speech, eliminating the
need for coding of messages.
1877
Thomas Edison's phonograph
record plays back a voice message.

sponsored by Pepsodent toothpaste. The comedy show, which debuted
in 1929, employed two white actors who spoke in an African American
dialect.

The 1930s saw radio mature and eventually pass magazines as the
number-one source of advertising revenue, a gap that kept widening
until the introduction of television. The look of advertising, too, kept
pace with the changing time.

The Look of Modern Advertising

Many admakers believed that vivid colors and modern art caught the
reader's attention. Advertisers, like modern artists, tried to see things
in a fresh way. Their advertising reflected a significant departure from
traditional layout and design formats. The admakers attempted to reflect the new world by means of association, distortion, abstraction, or
unexpected angles. Never before had the look of advertising changed
at such a rapid pace as admakers searched for new ways to express
the idea of "modern."

The Art Deco movement had a significant impact on advertising.
The style originated with the 1925 "Exposition des Arts Decoratifs" in
Paris, which sought to establish international standards in the decorative arts and in architecture. The resulting Art Deco ornamentation
encompassed a variety of exotic motifs: oriental, Egyptian, Aztec, and
other historical styles. The style also drew on numerous new design
ideas. For instance, cubism in painting contributed simplified geomet-

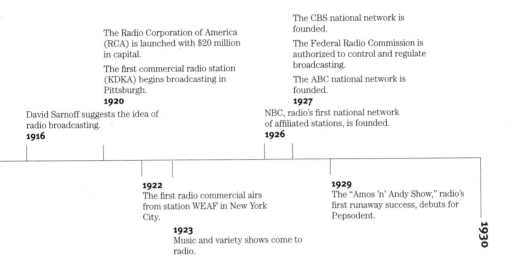

The Radio Corporation of America (RCA) is launched with $20 million in capital.

The first commercial radio station (KDKA) begins broadcasting in Pittsburgh.
1920

David Sarnoff suggests the idea of radio broadcasting.
1916

The CBS national network is founded.

The Federal Radio Commission is authorized to control and regulate broadcasting.

The ABC national network is founded.
1927

NBC, radio's first national network of affiliated stations, is founded.
1926

1922
The first radio commercial airs from station WEAF in New York City.

1923
Music and variety shows come to radio.

1929
The "Amos 'n' Andy Show," radio's first runaway success, debuts for Pepsodent.

1930

ric forms and "streamlined " the lines of furniture, clothing, and architecture. In addition, the arts of Africa brought highly stylized and colored fabrics. The effects of this movement lasted about twenty years, initially presenting us with luxurious, expensive furniture and interior decoration. Manufacturers brought consumers an affordable version of the Art Deco movement in the late 1920s and early 1930s, called "Art Moderne." The style's smooth lines and simplified forms lent itself to mass production. Taste for streamlined, exotic, "Moderne" products extended to virtually every object in daily use: furniture, silverware, cigarette lighters, jewelry, clocks, lamps, appliances, posters, clothing, textiles, and so on.

A diversity of advertising styles also became identified with the Art Deco movement. Inspired designers and illustrators created unique environments to showcase their products, and their ornate imagery conveyed a sense of impeccable taste and superior craftsmanship. The artists set advertising messages for smooth-lined Art Deco products amidst skillfully rendered pen lines of intricate ornamentation, rich naturalistic forms, and timeless images from antiquity. Interestingly the all-important ingredient—the product—was often absent from or secondary to the design. For example, Franklin Booth's 1926 pen-and-ink drawing surrounded copy for Willys Overland automobile with a medieval castle, a presentation aimed at "discriminating buyers of motor cars above the 'pony class'" (Figure 4.20). Thomas M. McCleland framed Locomobile's "fine coach work" with classic Pompeian decorations to appeal to a select audience. And Walter D. Teague's

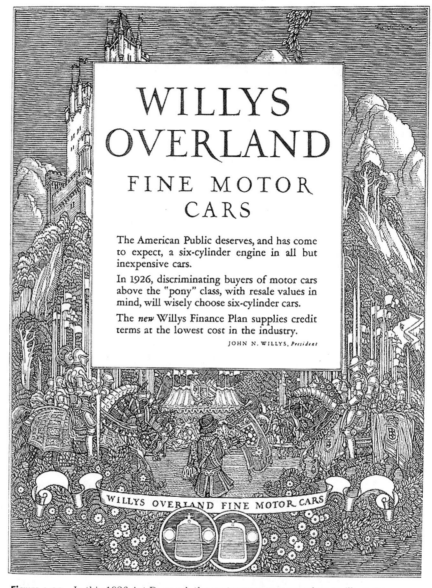

Figure 4.20 In this 1926 Art Deco ad, the motor car was secondary to illustrator Franklin Booth's ornate imagery, meant to convey a sense of impeccable taste and craftsmanship.

decorative art notably enhanced Community Silverplate tableware and Phoenix Hosiery.

New theories about color and design also emerged. Ad designers schooled in the modern movements of cubism, constructivism, futurism, abstraction, and surrealism experimented with a number of new concepts. Even the Dadaists, who completely disregarded accepted

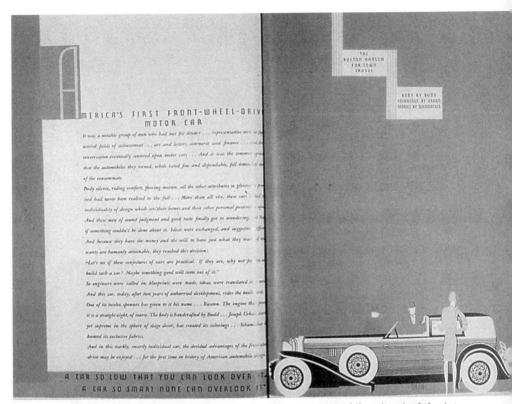

Figure 4.21   This 1920s ad for the Ruxton Hansom automobile epitomized the Art Deco emphasis on stylized figures, clean lines, simplified shapes, and flat colors—often to the exclusion of the product itself.

rules of design and typography, influenced ad designers. Dadaists mixed unrelated images in their collages, assembled from randomly selected magazine and catalog pictures. The resulting design revolution reflected a general movement away from traditional balanced layouts and toward more asymmetrical arrangements. Artists stylized, generalized, and symbolized. This simplified drawing style reached its height in the late 1920s as rendered forms simplified to a geometric view (Figure 4.21). Vignetted figures appeared against simplified backgrounds. Shapes, colors, and lines were repeated. Admakers placed copy blocks off-center, at an angle, or wrapped around an abstract shape. Warm colors were juxtaposed with cool ones. Designers also introduced a variety of sans-serif typefaces to complement the modern page design: Futura, Metro, Vogue, Tempo, and Spartan, to name a few (Figure 4.22).

Art Deco came and went in the twenties. As modernism swept through agency after agency, advertising designers produced some of the most beautiful ads ever drawn—and received an equal amount of criticism. At first glance, one senses too much emphasis on the art, as

Figure 4.22 This 1920s ad for Perrin gloves reflects the Art Deco use of asymmetrical layouts, startling imagery, and sans serif typefaces.

the product and the sales message became secondary to the design. In fact research confirmed that the public preferred sentimental realism to modernism. The compilation of "300 Effective Advertisements" concluded that the public liked Norman Rockwell's "homey" magazine cover art over striking, modern illustrations.[21]

Critics of these modern styles also suggest that advertising's creative leaders pursued their own nonrepresentative tastes. These educated, cultured admen often made the mistake of trying to uplift the public's taste and of using an artistic language that was too "toney" and abstract for their audience.

The end of the Roaring Twenties was signaled by the stock market collapse of October 29, 1929, a day known as "Black Tuesday." For the previous five years prices of shares in American corporations sold on the New York Stock Exchange had been rising. But when rampant stock market speculation sent the prices of stocks skyrocketing, the market collapsed, wiping out many stockholders and crippling or ruining many companies. For example, a share of U.S. Steel peaked at $297 in 1929; in 1932 it sold for $22. American Telephone and Telegraph hit $310 a share in 1929; it commanded only $72 in 1932. Even though few Americans had stock market holdings, all were affected by the Great Depression that followed.[22] In the next chapter we examine how the Depression not only altered the lives of all Americans but also dramatically changed advertising.

1930

The magazine *Ballyhoo* reflects the public's rising distrust of advertising.
1931

1932
The Blackett-Sample-Hummert agency introduces the soap opera—long-running sentimental stories in daily installments on daytime radio.

President Franklin Roosevelt addresses the nation over the radio with the first of his "fireside chats" to introduce his New Deal programs.

Prohibition is repealed.

The National Industrial Recovery Act is enacted to revive industry and employ millions of jobless Americans.
1933

1934
The Pure Food, Drug, and Cosmetic Act and the Truth in Advertising law are enacted.

Leo Burnett opens his creative shop, Leo Burnett Co., in Chicago.
1935

Chapter 5

1930–1945 The Depression and World War II

The first televised sports event is broadcast by NBC-TV's experimental station in New York.
1939

The Fair Labor Standards Act establishes minimum wages and maximum hours in industry and prohibits the hiring of children.
1938

America drops the atom bomb on Hiroshima and Nagasaki; the surrender of Japan ends the war.
1945

1936
Margaret Mitchell's *Gone with the Wind* sells a record one million copies in one month.

Consumer Reports magazine offers advice and ratings on products ranging from cereals to new cars.

1941
The first TV commercial, for Bulova watches, runs on New York–based WNBT during a baseball game.

Pearl Harbor is attacked; the United States enters World War II.

1945

The stock market crash marked the beginning of the worst economic depression in American history, as well as hard times for advertising. Within weeks of the October 1929 panic, billions of dollars in stock value evaporated as investors desperately sold shares at a huge loss or could not cover stock purchases made on margin. When the market finally hit bottom, almost all of the financial gains of the 1920s were gone. Investors lost nearly $70 billion in the stock market between the crash in 1929 and the low point in 1933, the value of all stocks having plummeted from a high of $87 billion to $18 billion.[1] The total volume of advertising revenue also plunged nearly 70 percent—from a 1929 high of $3.4 billion to a low of $1.3 billion in 1933.

The shock of the Great Depression was especially traumatic because many people believed that the nation had achieved a permanent level of prosperity in the previous decade. Businessmen operating under the assumption that markets would expand indefinitely had gone heavily into debt building factories and buying manufacturing equipment. Their expectation was that demand and prices would keep increasing, so that they could easily repay creditors. In the 1930s they found out they were wrong. Others turned to highly speculative investments hoping to reap quick windfall profits, but their assumptions proved unrealistic because the markets for many new products were saturated. Meanwhile, advertising kept repeating the old promises, but nothing seemed to work anymore.

Although the stock market crash directly affected relatively few citizens, the entire nation felt the reverberations. By the end of 1932, American industry was operating at less than half of its 1929 volume. American businessmen became uneasy about expanding their plants or inventories. The movement of capital and credit initially froze, because the market crash forced many investors into bankruptcy. In short, overproduction and underconsumption plagued the American economy.

American industry continued to turn out vast numbers of products, but few Americans could afford cars, houses, and other consumer goods. People with money to spend reduced their purchases, while factories cut production, lowered salaries, and laid off workers. Thousands of newly unemployed workers lost their homes because they were unable to make mortgage payments, while creditors repossessed goods purchased on so-called easy installment payments. Consequently the stockpiles of unsold American goods increased. There seemed no end to the vicious cycle of declining demand and declining income.

The Depression worsened as the purchasing power of businesses, workers, and farmers continued to erode. The unemployment rate increased to an unprecedented level, and the flood of consumer buying decreased to a mere trickle. Factories lay idle, businesses failed, and construction halted. By 1931 five thousand banks weakened by unpaid loans and ill-fated stock speculation went under, wiping out 9 million personal savings accounts. Agricultural prices tumbled, and banks repossessed thousands of farms. Instability developed in industry after industry. Advertising expenditures, too, withered with the cutback on production. Recovery seemed far away.

Brother, Can You Spare a Dime?

A staggering number of Americans remained unemployed throughout the Depression. No one knew exactly how many people were out of work during this era, but estimates suggest that the number of unemployed jumped from fewer than half a million people in October 1929 to 15 million in the spring of 1933—nearly one of every three workers.[2] Unemployment struck across the classes, from unskilled laborers to professionals. For some people life went on as though nothing had happened. Others felt the pinch when their hours and wages were reduced. But everyone shared the insecurity of knowing that their turn might come next. As an indication of how tough things got, in 1929 the typical family needed at least $2000 a year in order to buy basic necessities. During the Depression 40 percent of American families lived on less than $1000 a year, and a significant number of those lived on just half that sum during some years.[3]

The Effects of the Depression

The Depression was felt in a number of ways. For example, young people postponed marriage because they couldn't afford to start a new household, while newlyweds moved in with their families. With income limited and uncertain, married couples conceived fewer children, and the birthrate dropped sharply. Families also slashed expenses, eliminating "luxuries" like the daily newspaper and putting off repairs on the family car and the house, as well as trips to the dentist and doctor. With reduced food budgets, family diets became less nourishing. Education, too, felt the effects of the Depression. Even as hard-pressed schools dismissed teachers and shortened school terms, enrollment in high schools and colleges increased because many young people elected to remain in school rather than enter a depressed job market. College students shifted away from traditional liberal arts studies and into vocational courses that they believed might lead to employment.

The hardest hit, of course, were the unemployed. Half the nation's jobless clustered in large cities, so the urban centers displayed the most visible effects of the depression. Thousands of out-of-work and homeless people built makeshift shelters, and shantytowns sprang up on the outskirts of every major city. People spent their days scavenging garbage dumps for food and their nights trying to stay warm. Breadlines and soup kitchens sprang up in large cities, and men sold apples for a nickel on street corners. Serious poverty struck rural America as well. For example, in the South sharecroppers and migrant workers struggled on less than $300 a year.[4] Dust storms ravaged the Great Plains states and worsened the plight of farmers, many of whom headed for California in search of work. Other desperate Americans hitched rides, hopped freight trains, and wandered the country, looking for a job—any job.

While Americans had remained optimistic through seventy years of industrialization and tumultuous social change, the Depression threatened their belief in the future of America and the capitalist economic system. People contemplated the possibility that the societies of the Western world might break down. Economic recovery required expanded governmental power and a broad program to lead America out of its crisis and enable the nation to emerge more powerful than ever before.

A New Deal for the Forgotten Man

In the first of many weekly radio "fireside chats," President Franklin D. Roosevelt reassured the American public and proposed his bold program of action, a "new deal" for the "forgotten man." The plan overlooked no part of the national economy, impacting industry, agriculture, banking, and the stock market.

Roosevelt's presidency has been called the "alphabet soup" administration. By 1934 the language of the New Deal had become well known as new federal agencies were created: the NRA (National Recovery Administration), WPA (Works Progress Administration), FDIC (Federal Deposit Insurance Corporation), FHA (Federal Housing Authority), HOLC (Homeowners Loan Corporation), FERA (Federal Emergency Relief Administration), PWA (Public Works Administration), NLB (National Labor Board), SEC (Securities and Exchange Commission), and many others. These unprecedented programs gave financial aid to the unemployed, put millions of people back to work, supported farmers, provided loans to homeowners unable to pay their mortgages, promoted industry–government cooperation, created Social Security, insured savings accounts, and placed tighter regulations on Wall Street.

The National Industrial Recovery Act (NIRA) became the keystone of the New Deal's recovery program. Enacted in 1933, the legislation authorized businesses to draft industrywide agreements temporarily free from antitrust restrictions and supervised by the

Figure 5.1   The blue eagle symbol promoted the New Deal recovery program in the 1930s.

NRA. The agreements (called "codes") set prices, quotas, minimum wages, and maximum hours. The act abolished child labor, improved working conditions, guaranteed workers the right to collective bargaining, and set up the National Labor Board to hear grievances. The NIRA legislation encouraged industries to again hire workers and produce goods, setting the nation on the road to recovery.

The NRA created the blue eagle emblem to promote the campaign with the slogan "We Do Our Part" (Figure 5.1). The eagle symbol was based on the thunderbird, an ancient Native American ideogram. Advertising then urged the nation's women to purchase only merchandise produced under the codes to further support the campaign.

Within a year of the act's passage, the NRA organized almost all of American industry and commerce under codes that applied to the manufacture of everything from chewing gum to automobiles.

The second part of the NIRA created the Public Works Administration to put people back to work and give them an income with which to buy goods and services. The PWA employed one-third of the nation's 11 million jobless and spent billions on large-scale public works projects—roads, bridges, dams, power plants, hospitals, schools, and housing. The program also helped build Chicago's subway system, and it modernized the armed services with new facilities and equipment. By 1934 the nation had begun to emerge from the depths of the Depression.

The federal government also created the Works Progress Administration (WPA) in an effort to replace direct relief for the jobless with employment opportunities. From 1935 to 1941 the WPA pumped billions of dollars into the economy to pay workers $15–90 per month. The WPA found ingenious ways of putting people back to work. For example, workers built or improved roads, hospitals, schools, playgrounds, athletic fields, airports, and a vast number of public works. The WPA also gave creative people jobs in keeping with their talent. For instance, with WPA funds artists spruced up post offices, schools, and other public buildings by painting large murals. Sculptors and painters joined with unemployed illustrators and graphic designers to produce over 2 million copies of approximately 35,000 poster designs. Government-sponsored cultural events such as art exhibitions, theatrical productions, and musical performances became frequent poster subjects. The WPA also employed writers to collect oral histories, research guide books, and create useful resources such as the *Index of American Design*. Americans also learned about the arts and music from WPA workers, who gave instruction and demonstrations on everything from tap dancing to the use of shadow puppets.

These bold measures contributed significantly to economic recovery. In 1937, 6 million fewer citizens were unemployed than in 1932. Over the same period national income increased from $42.5 billion to $57.1 billion. In addition, the stock market climbed steadily, industrial production almost doubled, and corporate profits rose. And, the Rural Electrification Act extended power lines into isolated areas and changed rural life. In 1935 only one farm family in ten had electricity; by 1950 more than 90 percent of the nation's farms were wired.[5]

For the rest of the decade, until World War II broke out, the economy remained largely stagnant. Although millions of Americans still had no jobs and industrial production had not yet reached precrash levels, the nation had a renewed vitality and a guarded optimism.

In the general climate of the Great Depression, advertising suffered like any other sector of the economy. Admakers faced the difficult task of promoting products that Americans either could not afford or were hesitant to purchase. In response, admakers increasingly resorted to hard-sell and even sensationalist campaigns.

A "Hard Sell" for Hard Times

Advertising had helped spur the business boom in the 1920s, and some observers suggested that it could even prevent future economic downfalls. That is, advertising could best reverse the "depression state of mind" by hammering out messages of reassurance. But advertising had failed to stem the onset of the Depression, and agencies soon felt the tremors of the stock market crash.

Agencies and corporate advertising departments increasingly engaged in a desperate struggle for survival after the market crash. Although advertising linage and revenue dropped significantly between 1929 and 1930, most of the large, well-established agencies, such as J. Walter Thompson, Lord & Thomas, BBDO, and Young & Rubicam, maintained their leading positions in billings. The following three years, however, brought even steeper declines in advertising expenditures and revenues, which in turn led to deeper cuts into staff, salaries, and agency self-confidence. Virtually all the agencies felt the economic pinch by 1932. In response, some agencies eliminated paid vacations, forced staff members to take days off without pay, and slashed salaries and staffs. Not surprisingly, married women with apparently secure jobs were the first to be let go. Other agencies simply closed up shop.

The Depression placed enormous pressure on an already competitive advertising industry. Prior to the Depression most agencies had considered a speculative presentation to a prospective client to be a waste of time. Now, every account was "hot" all the time. J. Walter Thompson's Stanley Resor proposed that the major New York agencies agree to a voluntary moratorium on trying to steal one another's accounts, but the competing agencies relentlessly solicited manufacturers and bombarded them with alternative advertising campaigns. Many manufacturers responded by pressuring agencies for rebates, cut-rate deals, more effective ads for less money, and severe cutbacks on their in-house advertising departments. Agencies faced sharply reduced commissions as a result. Yet clients still expected the agencies to give more and more free services, to suggest new ideas even when campaigns were in progress, and to provide a greater variety of merchandising and collateral services. Gone were the days when clients approved campaigns for an entire year.

Advertising Again Goes for the Hard Sell

Economic and professional concerns eventually affected the look and content of advertising in the early 1930s. Cost-conscious advertisers used color and illustrations sparingly, substituting extensive text in a multitude of typefaces to grab attention. Louder headlines, strident hard-sell copy, and gross exaggerations appeared as pseudoscientific arguments and appeals to emotion. Ads especially capitalized on consumers' intensified economic and personal insecurities. BBDO leader Bruce Barton put it this way: "Under the lash of bad business, ideals have been abandoned, standards have sunk. . . . The silly advertisements, dishonest advertisements, disgusting advertisements," Barton added, "had cast discredit upon the business and put us on the defensive."[6]

Advertisers worked hard to show how their client's product was necessary or attractive in terms of price, function, or value. They also sought to empathize with the Depression-wracked public's concerns about economizing and employment. In the process admakers found two appeals of immense value. One obvious tactic was a blatant emphasis on price. Although hardly a new idea, these economy appeals intensified in the early 1930s, as evidenced by the emergence of supermarkets and ads featuring price as the attention-getting element. The other tactic tapped into consumers' economic insecurities.

In these tough times when American households sought bargains over quality and service, the new "food coliseums," or supermarkets, proved popular. In 1930 Henry Socoloff opened the nation's first modern supermarket in Queens, New York—King Cullen Grocery, "The World's Greatest Price Wrecker," which was ten times larger than the average grocery store. Hundreds of other giant food stores quickly sprang up all over the country. The modern supermarket featured plenty of parking, self-service, and low-price, nationally advertised merchandise. With their enormous volume these chain stores quickly outperformed independent merchants.

Supermarket operators hoped that customers would buy in quantity and supplied shoppers with hand-held wire baskets to carry their purchases. However, baskets loaded with bulky food products quickly overburdened shoppers. This problem led Sylvan N. Goldman, an Oklahoma grocer, to create the wheeled shopping cart. Goldman placed ads to announce the "No Basket Carrying Plan." The idea proved a complete flop until Goldman hired people to push carts filled with groceries around the front of his store to convince other shoppers that the carts actually made shopping easier.

A heavy emphasis on dollar figures gave some national advertisements the look of retail ads. Some automobile ads even employed the traditional bargain-offer format that featured a crossed-out price. Other ads emphasized the potential savings associated with purchasing a given product. For instance, an ad for Hoover vacuum cleaners boasted: "The richest woman in the world can have no finer electric cleaner than any woman can have and for as little as $4.50 down." A Fabray window shade ad argued that people should not throw away filthy window coverings, but instead should wash them: "Now, Window Shades That Are Really Washable . . . Yet Cost Only 45 Cents." Listerine toothpaste ads suggested another method to cope with tough times: "See what you can buy with the $3 you save" (that is, the money one saved after a year of buying a Listerine product at 25 cents a tube rather than other brands at 50 cents). Listerine ads listed potential uses of the money—purchases ranging from galoshes and underwear

Figure 5.2   In this early 1930s ad Listerine suggested that consumers could apply the savings from buying this product to purchases of necessities such as shoes, underwear, and milk.

to milk and other staples (Figure 5.2). The economic appeal also addressed the mushrooming demand for "something for nothing," as contests, premiums, prizes, and two-for-one promotions appeared everywhere.

At the same time, advertisers' attempts to sell more products reflected their growing desperation. Traditional slice-of-life stories tapped emotions such as guilt, fear, shame, and blame to reinforce advertising appeals. These ads conveyed a common message: "If you don't buy this product, you'll be sorry."

In particular, the makers of cigarettes, soaps, sanitary napkins, disinfectants, deodorants, and yeast violated previously accepted standards of decency. Ads in this era reflected an extraordinary preoccupation with bodily flaws, functions, and odors. Among the

Figure 5.3 This 1932 ad used scare tactics and sensationalized copy in a desperate attempt to sell more toilet tissue.

worst offenders was Scott tissue, which recounted melodramatic tales of "Toilet Tissue Illness"—rectal disease caused by the needless use of harsh toilet tissue. One 1932 ad in the Scot Tissue series made this frightening claim (Figure 5.3):

> *For two-thirds of the so-called "brands" of toilet tissue are unfit to use . . . and contain impurities which are an actual menace to health. Strong acids, mercury, sand, chlorine—and even arsenic were found.*

In a similar manner a 1936 ad for Absorbine Jr. described in lurid detail the gruesome symptoms associated with athlete's foot. The only remedy, of course, was cooling, soothing Absorbine Jr.:

Memorable Slogans

We do our part. (NRA member)

Call for Phil-lip Mor-ris. (Philip Morris cigarettes)

Guinness is good for you. (Guinness beer)

A diamond is forever.

For the smile of beauty. (Ipana toothpaste)

Mellowed a hundred million years. (Sinclair motor oil)

Duz . . . does everything. (Duz soap)

Look at all three. (Plymouth automobile)

Breakfast of champions. (Wheaties)

It's the real thing. (Coca-Cola)

Don't be a paleface. (Coppertone suntan cream)

From World War II

Loose lips sink ships.

Careless talk costs lives.

Walls have ears.

Is your journey really necessary?

. . . or else tiny, itching blisters may appear. Often there comes excessive moisture; white dead-looking skin; painful peeling; broken skin, raw distressing tissues. . . . So stubborn is the disease, your own socks may reinfect you unless they have been boiled for 20 minutes.

The outpouring of such sensational copy seemed to have no limits. Consider these examples. In a dramatically photographed ad a man sadly reflected: "She was a Beautiful Woman before her teeth . . . went bad"; her downfall had been her failure to use Fohran's toothpaste to safeguard her teeth and gums from pyorrhea. Another melodrama pictured a hospitalized man with his face bandaged, the result of an infection brought on by a nick of his razor; he could have avoided this situation had he only used Listerine Antiseptic as an after-shave. And Dentyne gum ran a startling ad in 1934 that headlined: "Let the Man

With the Withered Arm Warn You . . . chew delicious Dentyne often."
The copy read:

> *For ten years the Indian fakhir held his arm motion-*
> *less, pointing towards Mecca. Now, through lack of ex-*
> *ercise, his arm is withered. . . . The mouth, too, needs*
> *exercise—regular vigorous chewing to make it work*
> *normally . . . to help keep the mouth and gums*
> *healthy . . . to keep the teeth clean and sound. Den-*
> *tyne, a special gum with an extra firmness, supplies*
> *the vigorous chewing we need . . . in a pleasant way.*

Scare campaigns aimed at job insecurity surpassed even economy
appeals in capitalizing on Depression-era fears. The Ruthrauff & Ryan
agency modeled a series of slice-of-life ads for Gillette razor blades on
the successful Listerine social melodrama. The campaign warned
readers that when a man became careless about shaving, business associates turned away to whisper to their wives: "Don't worry . . . I
won't bring him again." Or bosses and prospective employers warned
him to "spruce up or get out." Admakers offered consolation, however:
one could achieve job security and thrive on new opportunities simply
by using their products.

Other advertisers also concluded that job insecurity might be a
strong selling appeal, so the messages continued. For example, Fleischmann's yeast blared: "Say, haven't you finished that *YET*? Only half on
the job!" Such shortcomings were "danger signs" of the run-down condition that only this product could correct. Kellogg's All Bran warned:
"A sick man had no place in business." A businessman's failure to eat
the breakfast cereal had made him unable to compete. Scott tissue recounted tales of careers cut short by the needless use of "harsh toilet
tissue." And Paris Garters drove home the point that even a man's
socks were a potential hazard. A 1936 ad declared: "HE talked himself
into an interview . . . but his SOX talked him out of a job! The word
"FAILURE" was boldly surprinted over the illustration; the text told
the sad story:

> *He made a great impression until he sat down . . .*
> *then all that could be heard or seen were his sox . . .*
> *they not only hung over his shoe-tops, they also hung*
> *over the entire interview . . . every time he said any-*
> *thing, his sox interrupted him . . . he never even had*
> *a chance . . . yet a pair of Paris Garters would have*
> *saved him.*

The ad ended with a final thought: "It seems there's no place for a man
who can't keep his sox in place."

Depression-Era Advertising Adopts a New Look

The ads that appeared during the Depression even managed to look depressed compared to the lavish, colorful, imaginative ads of previous decades. Agencies hired fewer prominent artists and set up in-house art departments, many staffed by inexperienced, inexpensive commercial artists.

Remarkably both the Getchell agency and Ruthrauff & Ryan dynamically expanded and became Depression-era sensations even as hard times and economic upheavals weeded out many smaller firms. New Yorker J. Stirling Getchell had an enormous impact on the look of advertising. After working for leading agencies Lord & Thomas, Barton, Durstine & Osborne (later BBDO), and J. Walter Thompson, Getchell started his own agency in 1931, two years into the Depression.

Getchell took on the challenge of introducing the new 1932 Plymouth and changing the popular perception of the Plymouth as the bottom of the Chrysler line. Fortunately for Getchell, Chrysler's main rivals, Ford and Chevrolet, did not take the car or the campaign seriously. Getchell's ad carried the headline "Look at All Three!" in big bold type above a stark photograph of Walter Chrysler leaning over the hood of a Plymouth. The copy provided a technical explanation of why the car was superior to the unnamed competition (Figure 5.4). The ad immediately drew attention because the advertising industry at that time had an informal ban on competitive or comparative pitches. Getchell skirted this restriction by not naming Ford or Chevrolet, but the reference was obvious. The campaign extended the theme with "Plymouth sets the pace for All Three." In 1932 Plymouth had 16 percent of the low-priced car market; in 1933 its share jumped to 24 percent.[7]

As Getchell attracted new accounts, he developed and refined a distinctive photojournalistic style. For models Getchell went back to "news-minded salesmen" John E. Kennedy and Claude Hopkins. Like those copywriters Getchell visited production facilities and studied products to uncover unusual features. He then presented his ads in tabloid format, with rectilinear layouts, sensational headlines, and punchy copy built around realistic, attention-getting photographs. His ads for everything from cars to Ritz crackers clamored for the reader's attention and soon became the latest fashion (Figure 5.5).

Indeed the beautifully painted and drawn illustrations of the previous decade had fallen out of favor, yielding to the cheaper alternative of photographs. "It's the same thing we used in our early days before beauty got to be in fashion," commented copywriter Helen Woodward. "The sales appeal is the same. What is new in the Getchell idea is his able use of modern action photographs. . . . This screaming, direct, ugly stuff hits the public as hard as ever."[8] But the style

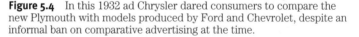

Figure 5.4 In this 1932 ad Chrysler dared consumers to compare the new Plymouth with models produced by Ford and Chevrolet, despite an informal ban on comparative advertising at the time.

worked. In less than a decade Getchell boosted his agency's annual billings to the $10-million range.

The Ruthrauff & Ryan agency, another Depression-era sensation, applied proven mail-order advertising formulas to non-mail-order products. Experienced in patent medicine "symptom-and-cure" copy, Ruthrauff & Ryan combined cartoons and testimonials to successfully promote Rinso soap. The agency also dramatically shifted Lifebuoy's sales pitch from skin care to the social disgrace of "B.O." (body odor). Print ads using scare tactics appeared in the popular comic strip story format, and on the radio shows a foghorn boomed, "Beeeeeeee . . . Ohhhhhhhhhhh." After all, Lifebuoy deodorant soap would protect its customers.

Figure 5.5 This 1930s ad epitomized the hard-sell photojournalistic approach with its attention-grabbing photographs and blaring headlines.

Two campaigns in particular demonstrated Ruthrauff & Ryan's influence on Depression-era copy trends. The first campaign was for Dodge automobiles. The agency adopted the tabloid format, using numerous photographs and bold, black headlines, a "news-appeal" technique that dramatically boosted sales of the Dodge (Figure 5.6). The second campaign was for Cocomalt milk additive. Here Ruthrauff & Ryan transformed the advertising style of Cocomalt from "pretty art" to photographic melodrama with cartoon dialog balloons. The early 1930s campaign evoked the guilt and shame of mothers by presenting dramatic scenarios of undernourished children who refused to drink their milk. Glaring headlines drove home the point: "Whose fault when children are frail?" and "People pitied my boy he was so thin" (Figure

Figure 5.6   This 1930s ad used the "news-appeal" technique and tabloid format to dramatically boost sales for Dodge.

5.7). The ads' theme was a potential source of torment to mothers who committed the grievous sin of allowing their children to become skinny even when times were tough. Thinness suggested impoverishment, while a "husky" child connoted not only robust health but also financial well-being.

Ruthrauff & Ryan's dramatizations inspired other advertisers to elaborate on themes targeted at anxious Depression-era parents. A wide range of advertisements showed tired, dejected children who failed exams and brought home distressing report cards. The explanation: parents had denied their children the advantages of everything from Quaker Oats, Corona typewriters, and Eagle pencils to General Electric light bulbs and Metropolitan Life Insurance, to name a few. As one ad for General Foods' Postum cereal drink sadly related: "Held back by Coffee . . . this boy never had a fair chance." The failing child

Figure 5.7   This 1930s ad presented melodramatic tales of undernourished children who refused to drink milk to evoke guilt and shame in mothers.

kept after school could not be blamed: "A Dunce they called him . . . a sluggard" (Figure 5.8).

Scott tissue used the same approach and drove home the point that even the wrong toilet tissue might be holding one's child back in school. One 1933 ad headlined: "Mary was so fidgety she couldn't concentrate . . ." The reason? "Harsh toilet tissue was the cause":

> *"I was worried when Mary's teacher told me she was restless in school and couldn't seem to concentrate.*
>
> *When I asked Mary what was the matter she complained of an itching . . ."*
>
> *Experiences like this are common. Harsh tissue can cause serious inflammation. Women and girls*

Figure 5.8   This 1933 ad targeted anxious Depression-era parents who would doom their children to failure unless they purchased Postum cereal drink.

> *especially, because of their peculiar requirements need a soft, highly absorbent tissue—such as ScotTissue or Waldorf.*

Most admakers believed that this grim, hard-sell approach moved products off the shelves during these hard economic times, but the style did not enhance the ad industry's reputation.

The Best and Worst Collide

The work of the Young & Rubicam agency (Y&R) stood out amidst the proliferation of sensationalized advertising. While other agencies failed or cut back staff, Raymond Rubicam drove the agency to second place in annual billings, trailing only J. Walter Thompson. In 1934 John Orr Young, one of the founders, departed Y&R, leaving Rubicam with a controlling interest in the business.

Rubicam made an unusual move for an agency. He gave creative control to his copywriters and artists at a time when the administrators or account executives who made contact with the client often tinkered with an ad to suit themselves or the client. Moreover, Rubicam pushed his creative department to develop fresh approaches, rather than use the prevailing hard-sell, sensationalized style. "Advertising has a responsibility to behave properly," said Rubicam. "I proved that you can sell products without bamboozling the American public."[9] In this arena two prominent women emerged: Louise Taylor, who wrote campaigns for Eagle Brand condensed milk before becoming the agency's first woman copy supervisor and vice president; and copywriter Ophelia Fiore, who warned about "Tattle-Tale Gray" for Fels-Naptha soap.

Young & Rubicam promoted the agency's scientific approach, which included "reading and noting" newspapers and periodicals, as well as accurately measuring radio listenership. The agency also was among the first to make research part of the creative process by bringing in George Gallup, a professor of advertising and journalism. According to Gallup's research readers preferred that lengthy blocks of copy be broken into short paragraphs and that type devices such as italics, boldface, and subheads be employed. Another finding by Gallup—the popularity of comic strips—led agencies to create advertising for the comics section of Sunday newspapers. Early in the 1930s Ruthrauff & Ryan experimented with cartoon strip ads for Rinso and Lifebouy soaps (Figure 5.9). As the results of Gallup's survey became well known, the comic strip style of advertising spilled over from the funny papers to other print media. The speech balloons superimposed over a sequence of panels created minidramas with an aura of realism that promoted everything from soap, food, and drugs to razors, fountain pens, and typewriters (Figure 5.10).

Advertisements from Young & Rubicam set a new standard of taste. Y&R favored stylish, well-crafted, and visually attractive ads that often used humor to make the pitch. Notable Y&R campaigns of the decade included a series of humorous advertisements for Arrow shirts. One classic ad pictured a man talking to a horse hitched to a milk wagon. The curious headline read, "My friend, Joe Holmes, is now a horse," and the copy explained that one day Joe died from a shirt collar that choked him to death (Figure 5.11). For the Borden Company the agency devised friendly Elsie the Cow as the symbol for all its varied dairy products (Figure 5.12). The first of a series of ads for Four Roses whiskey is often mentioned as one of the most distinctive liquor advertisements ever created. It pictured four roses frozen in a block of ice with the line "Cooling Idea" (Figure 5.13). The ad ran every summer, year after year. Y&R also produced an inspired

George Gallup

In the 1920s George Gallup, a Northwestern University professor of advertising and journalism, began to poll readers about what they noticed most in newspapers and magazines. Gallup's newspaper studies covered some fourteen newspapers and 40,000 readers. The results showed that 85 percent of the respondents noticed the picture pages, 70 percent the comics, and 40–50 percent the editorial cartoons—a far greater share than the front-page story and the lead editorial. Predictably women read the society and cooking sections, men the sports.[a]

Gallup's 1931 survey of magazine readership yielded a few surprises. The researcher first ranked appeals by the number of times they appeared in advertisements. Economy and efficiency ranked first and quality fifth, while sex and vanity tied for ninth. Interviewers then rang doorbells, asking some 15,000 people which ads they remembered reading. It turned out that men noticed those ads with quality appeals first, and then sex; women responded most to ads featuring sex, vanity, and quality. Interestingly the advertisers preferred appeals that drew the least attention from the public.[b] After Gallup published his results, Raymond Rubicam persuaded him to join the Young & Rubicam agency full time.

[a] *Advertising & Selling* (March 31, 1932).
[b] *Printers' Ink* (March 24, 1932).

advertisement for Rolls-Royce entitled "To the Man Who Is Afraid to Let His Dream Come True" (Figure 5.14). The advertisement appeared only once, yet it "actually sold more automobiles off the floor than any other Rolls-Royce ad of record."[10]

Gallup's influence extended beyond Young & Rubicam. Advertisers short of money wanted to know if advertising brought in sales—and if so, how, when, and why. A. C. Nielsen Company, a New York research and marketing service, sold the syndicated *Food Index and Drug Index,* a report measuring consumer product purchases in specific categories in food, drug, and mass merchandiser outlets. Daniel Starch and Associates, another New York research firm, measured consumer response to and recognition of periodical advertising. Motivational psychology, eye-tracking, store interviews, and test cities also became common agency tools. Gallup's findings and other studies confirmed the advertisers' image of the public as a "tabloid audience" that responded to unsophisticated, sensationalized, and frivolous entertainment. These findings resulted in the greater use of nudity, sex, and comic strip formats, as well as the appearance of other readership services.

Figure 5.9 These ads for Lifebuoy and Rinso soaps, featuring cartoon panels superimposed with speech balloons, created a minidrama with an aura of realism.

Although sex had been used in copy before, illustrations had barely hinted at it. Now scantily clad women, formerly encountered mostly in lingerie ads, sold bathroom, household, and even industrial products. Full female nudity is thought to have been first introduced in a photograph in a 1936 Woodbury soap ad, "The Sun Bath." In a different way Simoniz car polish used sex to lure male customers to purchase "male products" in a 1937 ad that featured an unclad woman under the headline "Your Car's No Nudist." Indeed, these ads went far beyond the standards of acceptability established by the previous decade, when most people still considered showing the backs of the knees a taboo.

Consumers Organize

The Great Depression helped spur increased consumer concern for prudent spending. Fueled by a series of publications that questioned product claims, the public demanded that the advertising industry be brought under government scrutiny. The overnight smash success of a new 1931 periodical entitled *Ballyhoo,* which lampooned notorious advertisements, evidenced the rising public distrust of advertising. For instance, *Ballyhoo* parodied Listerine toothpaste's suggested uses by describing the wonders of "Blisterine": "Buy yourself some false teeth with the money you save on toothpaste." Another spot lampooned Lux toilet soap's starlet campaign: "Nine out of ten stars," *Ballyhoo* proclaimed, really "clean up" with paid "Lox Toilet Soap testimonials." Still another parody zeroed in on the melodramatic new Cocomalt style: "How Georgie Cursed When Milktime Came."

Another sign of the rising public distrust was the new consumer movement. Former copywriter Helen Woodward's *Through Many Windows* (1926) presented an informed critique of the business and took readers inside an agency. Economist Stuart Chase and former National Bureau of Standards engineer Frederick Schlink took a broader view of the industry in their muckraking *Your Money's Worth* (1927), which attacked shoddy merchandise and sleazy sales

Figure 5.10 In this 1940s ad the cartoon strip format evolved to include sequences of photos featuring real people.

Figure 5.11   This 1936 Young & Rubicam ad used humor to sell Arrow shirts.

techniques. Chase and Schlink also suggested that the federal government subject consumer goods to standardized tests and publish the results so consumers could make informed decisions.

In a follow-up best-seller Schlink and co-author Arthur Kallett published *100,000,000 Guinea Pigs* (1933), a more radical version of *Your Money's Worth.* They warned readers of hazardous foods, drugs, and cosmetics on store shelves, detailing cases of fatalities and disfigurements caused by mislabeled and impure goods. The public response encouraged Schlink to expand his basement "Consumers Club" in White Plains, New York, into a national product-testing organization, Consumers' Research Inc. The new organization employed technical experts, set up a research lab, and published a newsletter that later became a monthly magazine.

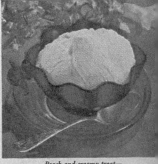

Figure 5.12 Young & Rubicam debuted Elsie the Borden Cow in 1936 to promote a variety of dairy products.

Cooling idea

REMEMBER this picture?

We first used it 6 years ago to remind you how gloriously cool and refreshing a Four-Roses-and-ice-and-soda can be on a warm midsummer afternoon.

We're certain you haven't forgotten, if you tried one. For the keen enjoyment of Four Roses' matchless flavor and mellow smoothness in a highball is something to be long remembered.

Today, as then, there's no other whiskey with quite the distinctive flavor of Four Roses. You'll see how right we are if you'll just make this cooling idea a memorable reality—now! Try a Four-Rose-and-soda—won't you?

• • •

Four Roses is a fine blended whiskey—93.5 proof, 40% straight whiskies 5 years or more old, 60% grain neutral spirits.

FOUR ROSES

A TRULY GREAT
BLENDED WHISKEY

Frankfort Distillers Corporation, N.Y.

Figure 5.13 This celebrated 1930s ad from Young & Rubicam was the first in a series conveying the appeal of a cool, refreshing drink on a hot summer day.

Other organizations with similar goals of consumer education appeared. In 1936 Consumers Union introduced its own magazine with a similar consumer-oriented mission to test, inform, and protect. From the outset *Consumer Reports* magazine offered advice on products ranging from cereals to new cars, attacked false advertising, reported on the labor conditions under which various products were made, and refused advertising to avoid even the hint of bias. The second issue cemented the publication's no-holds-barred approach when it dismissed the "Good Housekeeping Seal of Approval" as a reward to loyal

Figure 5.14 This 1930s Young & Rubicam ad actually appeared only once, but it helped build an image for Rolls-Royce.

advertisers. The magazine evolved into one of the nation's most popular publications, one that consumers still routinely consult before buying everything from hair dryers to automobiles.

When these powerful new consumer organizations brought their concerns to the attention of the federal government, Congress passed a flood of legislation to protect consumers. In 1934 the power of the Food and Drug Administration (FDA) was expanded to cover cosmetics and to regulate advertising as well as labeling. Four years later the Copeland bill gave the FDA new powers over the manufacture and sales of drugs, although the legislation did not call for a government grading system for food. That same year the Federal Trade Commission (FTC) declared "deceptive acts of commerce" to be unlawful. Over the next two years the FTC also issued a number of orders to Fleischmann's yeast, Lifebuoy and Lux soaps, and Ipana toothpaste to drop many claims and campaigns. These rulings chastened advertisers and advertising agencies. The industry eventually acknowledged it could no longer ignore the consumer movement's political clout and began a trend toward self-regulation.

By the end of the decade, the economy showed signs of recovery, and gradually the gross exaggerations and downright deceit went out of favor. Instead, new themes such as gracious living, and new techniques of promoting those themes, provided a welcome relief. And with its emergence as a dominant communications medium, radio became a key advertising vehicle.

The Maturing Voice of Radio

Radio had struck a chord with Americans of all classes. Although briefly shaken by the Depression, radio quickly rebounded, expanding its number of stations and attracting new listeners and advertisers. With the motion picture business slumping, the theater collapsing, and vaudeville dying, show business talent flocked to radio along with listeners and sponsors. Spurred by advertising revenue, radio matured in this era to become part of the fabric of American life.

The new national radio networks provided both new and affordable entertainment and a distraction from the problems of everyday living. People could buy a receiver for as little as $15, and by 1937 as many as three-fourths of all American homes had radios.[11] Listener loyalty became "almost irrational," according to broadcast historian Erik Barnouw: "Destitute families, forced to give up an icebox or furniture or bedding, clung to the radio as a last link to humanity."[12]

Broadcasters and advertisers remained sensitive to radio's privileged position as a guest in the home, so certain standards of propriety were maintained. Some stations even expected their announcers to wear dinner jackets during the evening broadcast. With its self-professed obligation to maintain proper standards of taste and propriety, radio maintained its ban on any mention of prices until 1932.

Early broadcast advertising was designed to sell a company name, not a specific product. Broadcasters simply read commercial announcements while advertisers and music publishers supplied broadcast material. To maneuver around the informal ban on advertising, copywriters had to learn new tricks to write for radio. Agencies slipped low-key references to their client's name or products into broadcasts through a number of gimmicks. Celebrity testimonials and constant repetition proved an effective sales tool; one example was the iteration of the famous line "L.S./M.F.T. Lucky Strike Means Fine

Tobacco." Or, to sell a specific product, announcers motivated listeners with lines like these:

> *Rush right down to your neighborhood drugstore and ask for . . .*
>
> *Get some . . . TODAY!*
>
> *Don't forget to put it on your shopping list.*

In a more difficult transition the ad agencies themselves assumed the production of theatrical radio shows. A single sponsor underwrote most of the popular shows, while its agency served as the producer. Lord & Thomas and J. Walter Thompson initially ranked as the most active agencies in radio. In time, Young & Rubicam and other newer agencies participated as well. The agencies created company-sponsored programs that proved the most potent vehicle for advertising during radio's Golden Era of the 1930s and 1940s. The agencies best achieved the underwriter's identification when they worked the advertiser's name into one particular program title or time slot over a long run.

Advertising agencies produced a number of hit shows for radio. For example, by 1933 J. Walter Thompson had nine shows on the air including the musical variety hits the "Fleischmann Yeast Hour" with crooner Rudy Vallee, the "Chase and Sanborn Hour," and the "Kraft Music Hall." Sponsor Jell-O gelatin entertained listeners and promoted the product with a gentle selling style for Young & Rubicam's first prime-time hit, a musical variety show. Instead of a straight sell, the agency sprinkled the sponsor's name throughout the show: "Jell-O again. This is Jack Benny." Y&R went on to produce other hits for such stars as Kate Smith (for Calumet baking powder and Swansdown cake flour) and Arthur Godfrey (for Lipton tea).

During the 1930s William Benton, co-founder of Benton & Bowles, also helped revolutionize commercial radio. To be effective on radio, advertising had to break away from the copywriting style of print media and somehow compensate for the lack of visuals. On the "Maxwell House Showboat" Benton subtly staged commercials so audiences heard clinking cups of coffee and smacking lips—while performers spent a lot of time drinking the beverage. But Benton did more than launch successful shows in this period; he also developed consumer research techniques, recorded audience reactions prompted by cue cards, and popularized the singing commercial.

Daytime radio initially attracted few sponsors because many advertisers thought that housewives had no time to listen to the radio. However, in 1932 the Blackett-Sample-Hummert agency in Chicago began producing "soap operas"—long-running, sentimental, human interest stories in daily installments with continuing characters—with this audience in mind. Frank Hummert dreamed up the storylines and

Favorite Radio Jingles

Pepsi-Cola
Pepsi-Cola hits the spot, / Twelve full ounces, that's a lot. / Twice as much for a nickel, too. / Pepsi-Cola is the drink for you. / Nickel, nickel, nickel, nickel. / Trickle, trickle, trickle, trickle . . .

Rinso Detergent
Sound Effect: *Bird call whistled twice.*
Girl Singer: *Rinso white! / Rinso bright! / Happy little washday song!*

Tide Detergent
Tide's in, dirt's out. / Tide's in, dirt's out. / Tide gets clothes cleaner than any soap. / T-I-D-E, Tide!

Halo Shampoo
Halo, everybody, Halo. / Halo is the shampoo that glorifies your hair. / Halo everybody, Halo. / So Halo Shampoo, Halo!

Lifebuoy Soap
Announcer: *Lifebuoy really stops . . .*
Foghorn Effect: *Beeeeeeee . . . Ohhhhhhhhhhh!*

Bulova Watches
Announcer: *The time is _____ o'clock, B-U-L-O-V-A, Bulova watch time.*

Pabst Blue Ribbon Beer
Bartender: *What'll you have?*
First Voice: *Pabst Blue Ribbon!*
Bartender: *What'll you have?*
Second Voice: *Pabst Blue Ribbon!*
Bartender: *What'll you have?*
Third Voice: *Pabst Blue Ribbon!*
Chorus: *Pabst Blue Ribbon Beer!*

Gillette Razor Blades
Announcer: *Look sharp!*
Sound: *Prizefight bell*
Announcer: *Feel sharp!*
Sound: *Prizefight bell*
Announcer: *Be sharp!*
Sound: *Prizefight bell*
Announcer: *Use Gillette Blue Blades . . . with the sharpest edges ever honed.*

(Continued)

Favorite Radio Jingles
(Continued)

Chiquita Bananas

*I'm Chiquita Banana and I've come to say /
Bananas have to ripen in a certain way. / When
they are fleck'd with brown and have a golden
hue, / Bananas taste the best and are the best for
you. / You can put them in a salad / You can put
them in a pie-aye / Any way you want to eat them
/ It's impossible to beat them / But bananas like
the climate of the very, very tropical equator. / So
you should never put bananas in the refrigerator. /
No no no no!*

Miss Chiquita Banana.

then turned them over to his assistant, Anne Ashenhurst, for production. Soap operas like "Just Plain Bill," sponsored by Kolynos toothpaste, and "Betty and Bob," sponsored by Gold Medal flour, kept housewives company from 10:00 A.M. to 4:30 P.M. The soap opera starring "Oxydol's own Ma Perkins" developed possibly the best sponsor identification, in part due to the show's twenty-seven-year association with Oxydol detergent.

Inevitably the roster of shows extended beyond scripts aimed at housewives. Adventure serials targeted children. For example, "Tom Mix and the Ralston Straight Shooters" pitched Ralston wheat cereal. Comic strip–based "Little Orphan Annie" sold Ovaltine. And "Jack Armstrong, the All-American Boy" promoted Wheaties, the "Breakfast of Champions." Also, sponsors offered premiums to listeners. By redeeming boxtops and cash, young fans could receive such prizes as a whistling ring, a hike-o-meter, a mug, or a secret decoder that deciphered the daily clues given at the end of the broadcast.

In the evening the radio filled homes with drama, comedy, musical variety, and quiz shows. Millions laughed at the quips between ventriloquist Edgar Bergen and his dummy Charlie McCarthy, sponsored by Chase and Sanborn coffee. The top-rated comedy, "Fibber McGee and Molly," carried messages for Johnson wax. And listeners easily learned who sponsored one show: "This is Bob 'Pepsodent' Hope saying that if you brush your teeth with Pepsodent you'll have a smile so fair that even Crosby will tip his hair."

Generally agencies and sponsors produced the most popular, best-rated shows, while the radio networks developed programs aimed at a higher cultural and economic class. But if a show drew substantial attention, then a sponsor usually would pick it up. The "American Mercury Theater," for example, made its own news when actor Orson Welles presented the sensational science fiction adventure "The War of the Worlds," a 1938 production adapted from H. G. Wells' book. The show dramatized an imaginary invasion from Mars in the form of a series of radio news reports. The broadcast caused widespread panic among listeners, many of whom began to flee from the imaginary Martians, even though the presentation had been clearly identified as a Halloween prank. As a result, the program gained popularity, and Campbell Soup offered to sponsor the show for an additional thirteen weeks.[13]

One of the Campbell Soup Kids.

People also listened avidly to the radio news coverage and the live and recorded music, both popular and classical, that filled the remaining air times. In the mid-1930s over half of all radio programming was music.[14] Regular broadcasts of the Metropolitan Opera began in 1931, and starting in 1940 Texaco underwrote the Met broadcasts; this was to become the longest-running continuous commercial sponsorship of a program in the history of radio. Among other sponsored music programs "The Fitch Bandwagon" encouraged listeners to "Laugh a while, let a song be your style, use Fitch shampoo." Lucky Strike's "Your Hit Parade" presented the top popular songs of the week. These programs and others created a huge new public appetite for all sorts of music, as well as popularized the phonograph.

In 1938 radio surpassed magazines as a source of advertising revenue for the first time.[15] But over the course of the decade, the print medium remained a key advertising vehicle. As in previous eras, the style and design of ads reflected the moral, cultural, and artistic tenor of the times.

Another New Wave of Design

Although modern art met with a storm of protest in America, the inventiveness of European design gradually gained acceptance, especially in the areas of editorial design, corporate graphics, and product design. A wave of cultural leaders migrating from Europe, including many graphic designers, spurred the design movement of the late 1930s and 1940s. Scientists, writers, architects, and artists fled the Nazi onslaught in Europe for safer shores in America. The artists included Piet Mondrian, Max Ernst, and Marcel Duchamp; architects and designers such as Walter Gropius and Marcel Breuer also brought their innovative ideas to America.

Design historian Philip P. Meggs credits three individuals in particular with bringing European modernism to American graphic design—Erté (born Romain de Tirtoff), Dr. Mehmad Agha, and Alexey Brodovitch. Interestingly these three Russian-born, French-educated immigrants all worked in editorial design for fashion magazines. Erté designed covers for *Harper's Bazaar* magazine, working in the stylized Art Deco pictorial manner. Dr. Agha revitalized Conde Nast's

Vogue, House & Garden, and *Vanity Fair* by using bleed photography, sans serif type, white space, and asymmetrical layouts. Not to be outdone, rival publisher Randolph Hearst hired Alexey Brodovitch to become art director of *Harper's Bazaar* in 1934. In that role Brodovitch combined dynamic and experimental photography with distinctive typography.

The Container Corporation of America proved to be a trendsetter by advocating design experimentation in its packaging, corporate graphics, and advertisements. In 1937 Container Corporation commissioned the N. W. Ayer agency to design a series of advertisements. The resulting work by European art director A. M. Cassandre set the firm's corporate identity apart from the general clutter. In contrast to the long-winded copy of the time, these ads typically contained strong graphics and limited copy (Figure 5.15). Nevertheless, another decade would pass before pioneers like American designer Paul Rand would apply these experimental graphic techniques to advertising layouts.

The American modern movement found a more accepting public when it applied advanced European design principles to product design. Prior to the 1920s the design industry had largely confined its efforts to the minor arts, including silverware, table china, textiles, and expensive art objects. However, the Depression had a marked influence on the evolution of product design. Manufacturers and industrial designers facing dwindling sales after the stock market collapse began to turn out more affordable, attractive objects targeted at the middle-class market. They hoped that these artistically designed, low-cost products could breathe new life into a lagging consumer market.

Product designers sought the "ideal form" that could be easily mass produced, packaged, transported, and used. They emphasized simple forms, quality materials, sound construction, and practicality, adding decoration only to satisfy prevailing tastes. In the process the applied arts progressed beyond a superficial appreciation of form to adapt commercial attitudes and technology.

The resulting period, which both followed and overlapped the Art Deco of the previous decades, has been called the "Streamlined Decade." "The concept of streamlining had a long and complex evolution stemming from 19th century studies in the natural sciences of the efficiency of fish-, animal- and bird-forms," notes design historian John Heskett, "though by the early twentieth century, visual concepts were abstracted from natural forms."[16] In practice the jagged geometry of Art Deco eventually gave way to the organic, streamlined shape that symbolized "modernity"—the raindrop.

Designers like Bel Geddes, Raymond Loewy, Henry Dreyfuss, Harold Van Doren, and Walter Dorwin Teague influenced the design of many objects, from locomotives to teapots. In the fashion world fringed flapper dresses gave way to curvilinear sweeps of cloth, while architects designed long, low, rounded modern buildings. Although overall tastes in architecture continued to be conservative, smaller artifacts acquired new beauty and efficiency as designers applied the

Figure 5.15   This 1937 ad for Container Corporation of America, with its strong graphics and limited text, was a design trendsetter

streamline principle to them. Streamlining smoothed the lines of a range of consumer products, including stoves, power lawn mowers, motorboats, aquariums, soft-drink bottles, vacuum cleaners, trailers, fountain pens, and staplers.

One notable home product, the Coldspot refrigerator, designed by the Raymond Loewy studio for Sears, Roebuck & Co., first appeared in 1935. The new design encased the working parts in a smooth housing, and the appliance was advertised as having "automotive styling."

A Taste of the Times

Artists in this troubled era not only recorded what they saw but also engaged their art in social causes. Social realism was the dominant theme of artist Fletcher Martin, who painted scenes of labor violence, and caricaturist William Gropper, who satirized politicians; artists like Reginald Marsh and Isaac Sayer also portrayed the problems of life in the big city.

The depression years also introduced a new type of novelist who reflected on the social problems of the age. John Steinbeck's *Grapes of Wrath* (1939) depicted the desperate plight of Oklahoma farmers who left the Dust Bowl for the promise of plenty in California, where only the grinding poverty of the immigrant farmer awaited them. Erskine Caldwell's *Tobacco Road* (1932) revealed the harsh life of the Southern backwoods farmer. Another writer, John Dos Passos, covered the troubled economic history of the first third of the twentieth century in his famous trilogy *U.S.A.*

Yet people could escape for as little as a dime. Movie theaters provided affordable entertainment for a few hours at a time and a place for the hordes of jobless to go. The added lure of double features, free dishes, and bingo contests bolstered sagging box office receipts. Many Americans forgot their troubles watching the western adventure *Stagecoach,* the fantasy *The Wizard of Oz,* the Civil War epic *Gone with the Wind,* the animated *Snow White,* the terrifying *Bride of Frankenstein,* the stylish song-and-dance team of Fred Astaire and Ginger Rogers, the antics of the Marx Brothers, or Busby Berkeley's extravagant musicals. By middecade some 60 percent of all Americans attended the movies weekly.

Hollywood symbolized wish fulfillment and a land of romance where success lurked around every corner. A "star system" evolved with a new aristocracy of movie people living in palaces as exotic as the theaters that showed their films. Millions followed their screen idols' careers with avid interest and read the latest gossip about the stars' private lives, which were reported in newspapers and fan magazines. Americans feasted on the exploits of the rich and carefree new royalty: swashbuckler Errol Flynn, heroic Ronald Colman, debonair Cary Grant, sexy Clark Gable, sultry Greta Garbo, passionate Bette Davis, glamorous Jean Harlow, and strong-minded Katherine Hepburn. Many of these stars appeared in magazine ads endorsing everything from cosmetics to cigarettes—Douglas Fairbanks Jr. for Lucky Strike, Humphrey Bogart

The Heinz Aristocrat.

for Camels, and Bing Crosby for Chesterfield.

Americans' reading habits also changed. Although people had little money for expensive, hardbound books, they usually had a few cents for a newspaper or magazine. Newspapers chains like Hearst, Scripps-Howard, and Munsey continued to expand, informing and influencing millions. New comic book characters and cartoons debuted, such as Little Orphan Annie, a flapper named Blondie, crime-stopper Dick Tracy, hillbilly Li'l Abner, and heroic Flash Gordon, Superman, and Batman. Magazines, too, became big business and also furnished escape, especially the new, inexpensive detective pulps. *Newsweek* and *Esquire* began publication in 1933. *Life* debuted in 1935 with its dramatic photo-graph on the cover and dozens of pictures inside chronicling current events and entertainment news; picture-filled *Look* followed two years later.

Lively music also brightened a drab era. Although Americans continued to dance the fox-trot and waltz, a loyal young following wildly gyrated to the big band sounds of Benny Goodman, Duke Ellington, and Tommy and Jimmy Dorsey. Radio also helped popularize the sound. The nation was "getting in the groove." Enthusiasts danced the swing, the rumba, the conga, the shag, and the "mad" dances, too—the jitterbug, Susie Q, lindy hop, and Big Apple.

Others looked for a fast buck by competing in endurance contests. How long could contestants dance? Talk nonstop? Kiss? Listen to the radio? Roller-skate? The era also bore witness to a flurry of tree sitting, marathon bicycle riding, teeter-tottering, gum chewing, peanut pushing, marathon eating, and goldfish gulping. Game fads such as Monopoly, Bingo! Keno! and Beano! revealed the escapist mood in the land as well. Yet it was the chain letter craze that seemed to offer the greatest promise of riches. Wild tales of fabulous wealth from participation in a chain letter sprang up. Many individuals gave it a try; some turned a profit, but more, many more got nothing back.

Interestingly the controlling interest in the firms producing refrigerators often was held by the major car manufacturers (for example, General Motors owned Frigidaire). The techniques for rolling sheet metal for auto bodies were transposed onto the making of fashionable iceboxes. In the same way that car models changed from year to year, so did refrigerators; minute styling differences made this year's model more desirable than last year's. In five years sales of refrigerators soared from around 15,000 per year to an estimated 275,000.[17]

Efficiency and speed also were characteristic of the new age. Industrial designers applied streamlining concepts to ships, trains, automobiles, and airplanes, reducing both wind resistance and operating costs. Passengers eagerly booked passage on the new ships, and ads promoted the traditional Grand Tour in Europe and cruises to other parts of the world. Likewise, trains radically changed in form, with new streamlined shapes, blunt rounded fronts, and tapering rears, as well as modern interiors. The new diesel-powered passenger trains offered speed and luxury. Notably the Super Chief traveled from Los Angeles to Chicago in less than forty hours, breaking the record set some three decades earlier by almost six hours. Magazines were filled with ads that promoted the romanticism of rail travel—comfort, the best in food and drink, and unsurpassed scenery.

Car designers, too, pursued a similar goal of streamlining form. A 1934 Chrysler ad heralded this achievement with the headline "A New Era of Transportation Brings Functional Design" (Figure 5.16). The copy explained how the automaker achieved this goal:

> *When nature forms her creatures for speed, she shapes them in smooth lines from a rounded head to a tapering tail in order to overcome the resistance of their environment, whether it be wind or water.*
>
> *Chrysler engineers have departed from the conventional and have designed the new Airflow Chrysler in accordance with this basic natural law. In these daring new models, the lines of the gracefully rounded front end sweep smoothly over the flowing curves of the body to the tapering rear.*
>
> *All of the air disturbing appendages, fenders, head lamps, horns—have been covered and the new Airflow Chrysler slips through the air . . .*

However, a new car was only a distant dream for most Americans during the Depression.

For those who could afford it, air travel best served their taste for speed. Airplanes rapidly evolved into sleek, streamlined machines. Domestic air travel became more accessible as prices dropped and as the growing airlines vied for business. Also, the rapid development of planes capable of transocean flight shrank time and distance yet again.

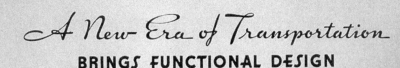

New era in railroad transportation—Streamlined passenger train

Automobile streamlining on the continent as featured at recent Berlin Auto Show

A new era of transportation has arrived—an era whose influence is revolutionizing transportation in every field, changing all precedent and obsoleting all the hide-bound traditions inherited from a horse-and-buggy age. It is an era that is fashioning all modes of transportation to a better performance of their functions. ☆ Exhaustive research has demonstrated the tremendous inefficiency and extravagant waste of power of conventionally shaped vehicles in battling wind resistance. Just put your hand out of a car window going at 30 miles per hour—then do the same at 60. Notice the tremendous difference in air pressure on your hand. From this simple test some idea is gained of the resistance encountered in propelling the conventional car over the highways. At 50 miles per hour the conventional car of the old horse-and-buggy design will waste approximately half its fuel overcoming wind resistance. ☆ When nature forms her creatures for speed, she shapes them in smooth lines from a rounded head to a tapering tail in order to overcome the resistance of their environment, whether it be air or water. ☆ Chrysler engineers have departed from the conventional and have designed the new Airflow Chrysler in accordance with this basic natural law. In these daring new models the lines of the gracefully rounded front end sweep smoothly over the flowing curves of the body to the sloping, tapering rear. ☆ All of the air disturbing appendages, fenders, head lamps, horns—have been covered and the new Airflow Chrysler slips through the air so perfectly that wind roar, present in conventional cars at high speed, is eliminated.

Ultra modern transportation and architecture—Graf Zeppelin over Chrysler Building

Figure 5.16 This 1934 ad for the Airflow Chrysler focused on the car's streamlined shape, which symbolized "modernity."

The streamlined era culminated with the New York World's Fair (1939–40), which featured a "World of Tomorrow" theme. Sixty nations and many corporations exhibited the latest technological wonders and provided a glimpse into the future. For example, General Motors' "Futurama" enabled visitors to view a future in which the automobile played a vital role. In the exhibition visitors sat on moving benches that wound through tunnels to view representations of the autos and highways of 1960. This is what they heard:

> *America in 1960 is full of a tanned and vigorous people who in twenty years have learned to have fun. . . . When Americans*

of 1960 take their two-month vacations, they drive to park-lands on giant express highways. A two-way skein consists of four 50-mph lanes on each of the outer edges; two pairs of 75-mph lanes, and in the center, two lanes for 100-mph express traffic. . . . The cars, built like raindrops, . . . cost as low as $200.[18]

Television Enters the Picture

Television had existed for decades before it became a mass medium. The pioneering work of the motion picture industry, which created the "talkies," planted the seeds for radio-with-pictures, or television. Early television broadcast systems worked, but the pictures were far too crude to be regarded as anything but a curiosity. In 1927 American Telephone & Telegraph first presented the new invention to the public and demonstrated its potential as both an entertainment medium and a political tool. In this demonstration, the first image to appear was that of Secretary of Commerce Herbert Hoover. The extraordinary invention attracted enormous interest.

But television technology took far longer to achieve commercial success than anticipated. In the 1930s RCA laboratories in Camden, New Jersey, established a group of research engineers. The team solved all the key problems and gradually progressed to higher and higher picture resolution from the 60-line standard of 1930 (as compared with the over 525-line resolution used today in the United States). RCA chose the 1939 New York World's Fair for a major public demonstration of its latest version. For the first time the public had a chance to see (and to be seen on) modern television.

An experimental NBC-TV station in New York City, W2XBS, aired the first broadcast in 1939, but only four hundred television sets could receive the sights and sounds of the baseball game broadcast by the station.[19] The Federal Communications Commission withheld permission for full-scale commercial operations until manufacturers reached an industrywide agreement on engineering operations two years later.

The first TV commercial, for Bulova watches, ran in 1941 during a baseball game on station WNBT in New York; the commercial cost $9 to air. At the time about four thousand American households had TV sets. That same year the United States went to war. Production of civilian consumer electronics came to a halt, and the widespread introduction of television had to be shelved until after the war.

The War Years

World War II brought profound changes to the American way of life and unprecedented prosperity to millions. The war speeded up industrialization, and production boomed at aircraft factories, shipyards,

New Brand Names

1930 Twinkies fills shortcakes with banana creme (later changed to a vanilla flavoring).

1930 Scotch Tape invents a clear adhesive to seal cellophane wrapping on bakery products.

1932 The Zippo lighter lights up a cigarette.

1932 The 3 Musketeers candy bar becomes a mouth-watering winner.

1932 Frito corn chips are a crunchy new treat.

1935 The board game Monopoly for wheeler-dealers is a runaway best-seller.

1937 Aqua Velva after-shave makes a splash with men.

1937 Spam, short for "spiced ham," becomes a slice of American life as a canned meat that requires no refrigeration.

1937 Alcoa aluminum foil becomes indispensable in the kitchen.

1937 Pepperidge Farm begins a mail-order business selling healthful whole-grain bread to doctors and patients.

1939 Colonel Sanders begins serving Kentucky Fried Chicken with eleven herbs and spices from a roadside cafe.

1940 M&M's hard-coated chocolate candies combine the initials of candymaker Forest E. Mars and his associate Bruce Murrie.

1941 Kellogg's Rice Krispies debut Snap, Crackle, and Pop, who give the puffed rice cereal a lively personality.

1941 Cheerios, initially called "Cheery Oats," shows up at the breakfast table.

1944 Miss Chiquita, the animated fruit, has come to say, "Bananas have to ripen in a certain way."

ammunitions plants, and other critical wartime industries. A country that had spent over a decade coping with unemployment suddenly faced an acute "manpower" shortage. Millions of people left their home towns to work mandatory forty-eight-hour weeks in factories and on assembly lines. And to replace the men who had joined the military, almost 18 million women entered the labor force working on factory assembly lines, running offices, and selling in stores while still managing the home.

As part of the war effort, the government urged citizens on the home front to "use it up, wear it out, make it do, or do without."

Americans conserved power, saved fat for explosives, and collected tin cans, paper, and rubber for recycling. Food staples such as butter, sugar, cheese, coffee, flour, and meat were rationed, and the limited supply of gasoline curtailed auto travel. The wartime demand for textiles also forced fashion changes at home. For men the fabric shortages resulted in the "victory suit," a single-breasted garment without vest, lapels, or cuffs. For women the fabric-saving trend raised hemlines and created more tailored fashions that eliminated ruffles, pleats, and patch pockets. With silk and nylon hosiery unavailable, women even drew lines to resemble seams on their bare legs. Wartime production also caused a sharp drop in the manufacture of automobiles and most appliances. The list of scarcities seemed endless: tires, cigarettes, liquor, many packaged foods, train seats, plane seats, and hotel rooms, to name a few. Instead of purchasing scarce consumer goods, people bought war bonds, paid off old debts, and did something extra for the war effort—serving on rationing boards, donating blood, and planting "victory" vegetable gardens.

Advertising contributed to the war effort as well. After the attack on Pearl Harbor, the U.S. government revived the poster and ad programs that had been so successful in World War I. The Office of War Information formed the War Advertising Council in 1942. The council snapped into action and produced the largest, most extensive advertising campaign in history, promoting war bond sales, internal security, rationing, housing solutions, and precautions against venereal disease.

Campaigns quickly communicated wartime themes of conservation, patience, and teamwork. War bond rallies became big events. Propaganda posters promoted production and boosted morale. The council also encouraged women to enter the labor force and take over jobs previously held by men with messages such as "We Can Do It" and "Do The Job He Left Behind" (Figure 5.17). Advertising manipulated powerful human emotions, frequently evoking fear and pushing patriotism as the war progressed. Explicit ad campaigns depicted soldiers dying or pointed out that they were "over there for you." More than a hundred public service themes were developed, and the advertising community donated virtually all the copy and artwork.

As defense production increased, many wartime advertisers found that the theme of patriotism fostered consumer loyalty and sold goods. Companies explained how their products were a vital part of the war effort. For example, Ford boasted that its development of innovative materials for automobile parts, such as plastic, freed strategic metals for wartime production. Each advertisement of the "Paperboard Goes to War" campaign featured a specific use of a Container Corporation product in the war effort. And the New Haven Railroad gained a lot of attention with its classic print ad "The Kid in Upper 4," which was reprinted, distributed by the government, read on the radio, and even set to music (Figure 5.18).

In addition, ads frequently encouraged conservation due to wartime shortages. For example, the Window Shade Institute advised

Figure 5.17   This 1942 poster of "Rosie the Riveter" symbolized the contributions of American women to the wartime effort.

citizens to pull down their window shades to save up to 10 percent on usage of heating fuel. Brer Rabbit molasses offered sugar-saving recipes. Swan soap suggested dissolving Swan slivers in boiling water to make a soap jelly for use as dish soap, shampoo, and so on. In a time of auto shortages and gasoline rationing, Roadmaster bicycles

Figure 5.18   This classic 1942 ad for the New Haven Railroad employed patriotism to foster consumer loyalty.

informed America that it was on duty for transportation. Stetson hats even warned people of the need to "conserve" information (Figure 5.19). But advertisers still managed to make the point that their product was somehow superior to the rest and able to outlast all other brands.

Idle words make busy subs!

1. IN MAINE A SHIPYARD WORKER SPOKE WITHOUT MUCH THOUGHT...(THE SHIP!).

2. IN FLORIDA A WAITER OVERHEARD SOME CARELESS TALK...(THE PORT!).

3. IN NEW YORK A SAILOR'S FRIEND GOT CONFIDENTIAL...(THE DATE!).

4. IN MICHIGAN AN OFFICE WORKER MADE A TOO-GOOD GUESS...(THE CARGO!).

5. AND A U-BOAT CAPTAIN EARNED AN IRON CROSS.

Remember, the enemy gathers most of its information in small quantities—little scraps of our careless talk—that can be pieced together into knowledge useful to them and dangerous to us. Help beat them with silence. Let our tanks do our talking.

Stetson "Whippet"...bound edge, medium brim and a fine, medium tapered shape to the crown. Rich felt made light and springy by the exclusive Stetson Vita-Felt® process...$10.

Keep it under your STETSON

Figure 5.19   In this 1943 ad Stetson reminded patriotic Americans of the dangers of loose talk in wartime.

Other familiar products followed the troops around the world. At the military's request Coca-Cola set up bottling plants close to the fighting fronts around the world, so American soldiers rarely lacked the familiar product from home. G. W. Hill switched the image on Lucky Strike's cigarette package from a red bull's-eye on a green background to red on basic white in 1942, supposedly because green dye contained precious metals that were vital to the war effort. A new slogan also appeared—"Lucky Strike Green has Gone to War"—and GIs found packs of Luckies in their weekly rations. Also, the government shipped abroad Zippo cigarette lighters and tens of millions of cans of Spam.

At the end of the War, the council established a private, nonprofit corporation supported by the advertising and communication industries. Its efforts sounded familiar themes like "Prevent Forest Fires," "Register and Vote," and "Buy U.S. Savings Bonds."

The New Deal did not end the Depression; World War II did. But the long-term impact of the war on the country would not be evident until the postwar boom of the 1950s. With the defeat of Germany and Japan and the return to a peacetime economy, the United States enjoyed another surge in prosperity. In the next chapter we will discuss these developments.

Gowns for mother and daughter created for Cadillac by Jean Derby

One of the special delights which ladies find in Cadillac ownership is the pleasure of being a passenger. First of all, there is the sheer physical luxury of riding in a new Cadillac. The car is wondrously spacious and comfortable—and perfectly proportioned for complete freedom of movement. Then there is its enchanting interior beauty . . . the marvelous convenience of its appointments . . . its great smoothness of ride . . . and its marvelous quietness of operation. We invite you to visit your dealer soon—with the man of the house—and spend an hour in the passenger seat of a 1959 Cadillac. We know you will agree that it is the world's nicest place to sit.

Cadillac

The 30-ton Electronic Numerical Integrator and Calculator (ENIAC) is the first electronic digital computer.
1946

David Ogilvy sets up shop on Madison Avenue in 1949 (later Ogilvy & Mather).

Ned Doyle, Maxwell Dane, and William Bernbach open their Doyle Dane Bernbach agency in New York.
1949

1948
Lloyd Warner's *Social Class in America* provides advertisers with a key to understanding the market.

Bell Labs physicists display the tiny transistor that will revolutionize electronics.

Television begins its explosive growth in America.

1951
The Universal Automatic Computer (UNIVAC) by Remington Rand is the first such machine to be put on the market.

Chapter 6

1945–1960 The Postwar Boom

Disneyland opens in Southern
California and is an almost
overnight success.
1955

The McCarthy hearings are
televised for a marathon
187 hours.
1954

The Soviet Union launches
Sputnik, an unmanned satellite.
1957

1956
Ground is broken for a 40,000-mile
interstate highway system.

Vince Cullers launches his agency
specializing in the African
American market.

1958
The United States enters the Space
Age with the successful launch of
Explorer, an unmanned satellite.

The first commercial jet plane
service linking America to Europe
is established.

The U.S. Supreme Court orders
school desegregation.

1960

The United States emerged from World War II not just as a victor, but as a global power. Far from slipping back into an economic downturn as some feared, the nation embarked on a remarkable period of economic growth powered by the massive war spending. The productive wartime economy transformed into an even stronger consumer economy, and people began to consume more goods than ever before. Advertising maneuvered events of this flush time—the cars and superhighways, the baby boom, the new patterns of suburban consumption, the explosive growth of television—and realized its greatest prosperity since the 1920s. Between 1945 and 1960 gross annual advertising expenditures quadrupled. Automobiles replaced packaged goods and cigarettes as the most heavily advertised product.

The war experience also moved America into a period that would become known as the "Atomic Age," the "Jet Age," and eventually the "Space Age." The new world held the promise of even better times to come—of technological breakthroughs, labor-saving devices, and dazzling inventions. With astonishing speed scientific developments and discoveries impacted every dimension of American life. Medical researchers created wonder drugs such as penicillin, cortisone, and antihistamines. Scientists synthesized nylon, dacron, plexiglass, silicone, and teflon. Inventors engineered push-button gadgetry to ease household chores and business tasks. Engineers developed nuclear power stations and nuclear submarines. Jet travel, electronic miniaturization, cybernetics and robotics, and space exploration all become reality in this era.

Large families, new suburban homes, televisions, and enormous chromed automobiles symbolized the hopes and possibilities of the era, and advertising helped shaped popular standards. Enticed by Madison Avenue pitchmen, young families headed for the suburbs. Their "dream" car was a convertible with whitewall tires, and TV situation comedies like "Ozzie and Harriet" seemed to mirror real life. It was a time when $10,000 bought a house, and 25 cents a gallon of gasoline. Advertising courted the newly affluent as never before, and Americans pushed mass consumption to new heights.

The Fabulous Fifties

The postwar era consisted of two distinct phases. The first period, which lasted until 1953, was about "catching up." The wartime rationing of shoes, tires, foodstuffs, and so on had come to an end, and returning servicemen clamored for housing and jobs. People quickly made up for lost time purchasing the automobiles, houses, and appliances that they had denied themselves or had put off buying in the preceding Depression and war years. Corporate fears prompted the next phase, which lasted from 1954 to the mid-1960s. Once everyone had caught up on consumption, many businesses feared that the shopping spree would end, plunging the nation into a new depression, so they explored new ways to ensure a constant demand for their flood of new products.

Realizing the American Dream

The restoration of peace gave people a chance to pick up the pieces of their former lives, to revive their dreams, and to again enjoy the finer things in life. "Demobilization" and "reconversion" became the new buzzwords. Despite concerns that if too many troops were returned home immediately there might not be enough jobs for them, pressure to "bring the boys home" resulted in servicemen and servicewomen reentering the civilian world at a rate of thousands a day. The GI bill assisted veterans to adjust to civilian life, helping them buy homes and farms, start businesses, get medical care, and continue their education.

Reconversion of the economy from a wartime to a peacetime footing went much more quickly than anyone expected. Virtually overnight manufacturers switched from the production of jeeps, tanks, aircraft, uniforms, and so on to production of consumer goods for the free market. Within days newspapers and magazines began carrying advertisements heralding new products. Instead of producing a glut of consumer goods as some feared, industry found it could not crank out enough to keep up with the demand. Until 1948 there were chronic shortages of goods such as clothing, refrigerators, cars, and stoves.

With a reborn sense of economic security, millions of Americans also turned their attention to home and family. The postwar "baby boom" was a worldwide phenomenon, but it was more pronounced in the United States than elsewhere. The birthrate, which had fallen in the mid-1930s, soared by 25 percent following the end of the war and remained there through the 1950s. In 1965 *Time* magazine named the baby boom generation, those born between 1946 and 1964, its man of the year. As *Time* observed, "cushioned by unprecedented affluence in the welfare state, [the typical baby boomer] has a sense of economic security unmatched in history."[1]

Indeed, the combination of an expanding economy and better-paying jobs made the American dream of social and economic advancement much easier to realize. GIs came home from the war to enjoy the fruits of government loans, subsidized education, higher-paying jobs, and wives with accumulated savings from wartime jobs. In 1950 the average weekly wage hit a new high of $60.53, double pre-Depression levels. Even "blue-collar" factory workers were rapidly attaining middle-class incomes. Many Americans now could afford luxuries that they had previously only dreamed of acquiring. Homes sold fast, and automobile ownership became a reality.

The baby boom also spurred the demand for affordable single-family, free-standing homes in suburban developments. In the immediate postwar years housing was both inadequate and out of date. Virtually no home construction had taken place since the 1920s, and prior to the war the suburbs had been the exclusive province of the well-off. Working Americans lived in apartments or cramped row houses near their workplaces, and except in the Midwest, most workers rented. After all, purchasing a house required as much as a 50 percent down payment on a ten- or fifteen-year mortgage.[2]

To fill this need, contractor William J. Levitt applied his wartime experience constructing family quarters on a navy base to building affordable family housing. In 1949, in the New York development called Levittown, Levitt used automobile assembly line production methods to transform acres of potato fields into a prefabricated suburban housing community. Hundreds of modest Cape Cod–style homes with green lawns, well-equipped kitchens, outdoor barbecues, and washing machines sprang up, all looking much the same. The price was right: the smallest homes sold for $6990 each, and the government helped finance purchases with low-interest loans. Thus the move to the suburbs began.

Advertisements for these new housing tracts promised, "Your happiness is a 'sure thing' at beautiful Haywood Park" and evoked picturesque images. An ad for the Presidential Lakes development claimed: "A vacation that lasts a lifetime begins here." In the midfifties nearly all realtors lured potential homeowners with offers of "no money down for veterans!" Instead of finding their dream home, however, the first suburban home buyers typically discovered developments in patches of what used to be countryside. In place of green lawns, buyers found muddy lots with only a few mature trees. Nevertheless, new highways and shopping centers made these outlying tracts feasible sites for development. Yet it was the reasonable prices, perhaps more than anything else, that attracted buyers. By 1960 home ownership had become the norm, with three out of five families owning their dwelling.[3]

The postwar economic boom also uprooted many families, in part to meet the demands of ever-expanding industries and corporations. Approximately one in five American families changed its home each year, giving many people an opportunity to adopt a new lifestyle.[4] Millions of former farmers and farm workers continued to pour into cities and their sprawling suburbs to work in factories, offices, and stores. The 1940 census showed that nearly 25 percent of Americans lived on farms; by 1964 the number of farm residents had dropped to below 7 percent. At the same time, millions of younger Americans migrated to the West and Southwest to seek employment, while many older people found that the regions offered a pleasant climate for retirement. Between 1940 and 1964, the population of the Pacific Coast states grew by 140 percent, and by 1964 California was the nation's most populous state.

This growing suburban population assured automobile, furniture, and appliance manufacturers of a market for their mass-produced goods. To meet the pent-up demand for affordable consumer goods, manufacturers shifted their emphasis from selling people what they happened to make to producing what people would buy. This change came as the new materials, improved technologies, and efficient manufacturing systems developed for wartime production were adapted for civilian uses. For example, nylon, which had been created to make parachutes, replaced costly silk in women's stockings. The aerosol container first appeared as a "bug bomb" in the South Pacific. With the addition of a simple spray top, the new cans dispensed everything from furniture polish, cheese, whipped cream, antiseptics, hairspray, and perfume to deodorant. The new lightweight plastics also found new applications, offering convenience and adding affordable glamour to everything from squeeze bottles to furniture. Styrofoam, initially used as a military flotation device, found a commercial use first as a floral or craft decoration and later as an insulation element. Other wartime innovations such as adding machines, electric typewriters, and computers streamlined office operations.

Ads for "electric servants" promised to ease or to eliminate virtually every manual household task imaginable. Americans bought refrigerators, freezers, washing machines, clothes dryers, dishwashers, electric can openers, food mixers, and juicers in unprecedented numbers. Early postwar advertisements made a convincing sales pitch for these appliances. For example, this 1948 ad tackled the initial problem of selling an automatic dishwasher: "Are you sentenced for life to the messy, monstrous job of washing dishes?" asked one appliance manufacturer. The persuasive copy went on:

> *Dishes for breakfast . . . dishes for lunch . . . dishes for dinner. Dishes . . . dishes . . . dishes . . . dishes! They pile up in the sink . . . they "eat up" your evenings . . . they ruin your hands . . . get rid of all the mess and misery of "dishwashing"—right now.*
> *Get yourself the new Thor Automatic Dishwasher. A postwar wonder if ever there was one!*

Advertisers took a similar approach to the problem of selling electric clothes dryers and drove home the point that hazards accompanied even the simplest laundry tasks. This 1953 ad explained how the new appliance could ease the homemaker's burden of laundering an average of 65 pounds of clothes a week: "Throw away your clothesline,

New Brand Names

1948 The Polaroid Land Camera produces an instant black-and-white snapshot.

1948 The McDonald brothers open their first "fast food" restaurant; hamburgers cost 15 cents, french fries 10 cents, and shakes 25 cents.

1948 Nestlé's Quik turns milk into a delicious chocolaty drink.

1949 Silly Putty is packed into plastic eggs and first sells as an adult toy.

1950 Sugar Pops breakfast cereal is tops with kids.

1951 Holiday Inn gives travelers clean, secure, and inviting accommodations from coast to coast.

1952 Bic gets rolling when Frenchman Marcel Bich creates a dependable, low-cost ballpoint pen.

1952 Swanson's frozen dinners are perfect for eating while watching television.

1956 Raid kills bugs dead.

1956 Comet cleanser bleaches out tough stains.

1957 The Ford Edsel carries auto styling to excess.

1958 Sweet-n-Low appears as the first low-calorie sweetener in powdered form.

1958 The Hoola Hoop twirling fad creates a lot of hoopla.

1959 The Barbie doll and her up-to-date wardrobe create a sensation.

clothespins, clothes baskets!" declared Kelvinator. The accompanying copy read:

> *Is this you—hauling out, hanging up, taking down wet wash every week . . . in all kinds of weather? Do you risk clothesline breaks, rain, smoke, soot, and dust? Do you hang clothes in the basement when storm clouds gather? . . . Or is this you? Having clothes dried automatically with your new Kelvinator dryer.*

Manufacturers also formulated other new products to be used in conjunction with the specialized appliances. Tide heavy-duty laundry detergent, for example, came out the same year as the automatic washing machine; and Cascade dishwashing detergent was packaged with new dishwashers. In another marketing effort advertisers prom-

ised free samples of the cleaners for attending a
demonstration of the appliance. Countless other
specialized cleaning products such as sham-
poos, liquid dishwashing soap, and household
cleansers soon filled whole supermarket aisles,
where once simple soap had been the sole
option.

Mr. Clean.

    This spending spree could not go on for-
ever, and by the early 1950s businesses had
become concerned. How could they assure themselves of a continued demand for their flood of new
products when Americans finally caught up on their long-postponed
purchases?

Keeping Up with the Joneses

Postwar manufactures recognized one promising characteristic of this
new generation: it had more money to spend and was willing to spend
it. This was a time when consumers could be persuaded that a lifestyle might be bought on credit, and they were encouraged to own two
cars and several television sets and to shop excessively. Thus manufacturers implemented the first part of their marketing strategy: satu-
rate the marketplace with advertising. To lure people into stores and
to convince the public that happiness depended on using their products, manufacturers invested in a blizzard of serious, humorous, and
sexy ads.

    The availability of credit cards made it that much easier to buy
goods and services. The first credit card, the Diners' Club card, appeared in 1950. The cardboard card allowed bearers to charge food
and entertainment at twenty-eight participating establishments listed
on the back. Eight years later American Express introduced a credit
service, and by the end of the year, half a million people were using
the card. Furthermore, with liberal "10 percent down and $10 a
month" installment purchase policies, consumers could become the
proud owner of almost any item. People no longer had to delay a purchase because of a lack of funds.

    Manufacturers also promoted a two-part concept of "newness."
Whether it was a two-year-old car, a five-year-old house, or whatever,
it was "used," and therefore second-best. Thus the newness had to be
visible. Market research tested ideas, and new products such as convenience foods, garbage disposals, and push-button gadgetry began to
appear. But manufacturers had to do more than make a good product;
they also had to make it look attractive to the shopper.

    The second part of the newness strategy applied "planned obso-
lescence" to encourage more frequent purchases. Although General
Motors' chairman Alfred Sloane had outlined this concept back in the
1920s, it was fully realized in the 1950s. "It was design intended to

solely sell a new product," explains Thomas Hine, author of *Populuxe* (his term for the look and life of America in the 1950s and 1960s). "By giving new looks and features to familiar products, manufacturers gave products the same limited lifespan as a fashionable dress."[5]

In the process the modern kitchen emerged as a status symbol. Because consumer items were concentrated in this room, this was where the products of marketing inevitably began to appear. Manufacturers applied the same styling philosophies that characterized automobiles to consumer mass-produced items. For the first time a range of colors introduced a new fashion element to kitchens and appliances that made them appear dated in a briefer time. In the United States the refrigerator became second only to the automobile as an exercise in planned obsolescence. Each new year's model had extra features, different styling, and even color changes. For example, one appliance manufacturer claimed, "Only Westinghouse Refrigerators give you 50 color combinations!" and promised to "transform your kitchen without remodeling." Style consultant Christopher Pearce explains:

> [Consumers] were prepared to discard a perfectly good two-year-old Frigidaire in favour of the latest two-tone model, not only because they could afford to do so but also because it was the tempo of the age—with its latest deluxe features, it just had to be better.[6]

Consumers soon became conditioned to accept the premise of planned obsolescence. Magazine articles, newspaper "women's sections," television programs, and advertisements dispensed advice on maintaining the good life through constant product "upgrades." Decorating magazines launched annual features on "this year's colors," including complicated color charts for readers. New colors meant that everything had to change more often. Glossy advertisements sold the ever-changing "new" ideal. One 1955 ad heralded: "And Now! Fabulous 'Foodarama' by Kelvinator! 8 Glamorous Exterior Colors to Choose From! . . . Select the decorator color that harmonizes with your kitchen decor . . . Bermuda Pink, Spring Green, Fern Green, Dawn Grey, Sand Beige, Buttercup Yellow, Harvest Yellow, Lagoon Blue." The same year General Electric offered Spacemaker ranges in one of the new "GE Mix-or-Match colors." And Royal standard typewriters came in "your choice of 6 exciting colors."

Manufacturers next shifted from promoting the obvious labor-saving benefits of appliances to incorporating sophisticated new push-button gadgetry designed to activate unseen machinery. The advertisements made their operation sound simple and promised to liberate homemakers from the drudgery of household chores. "With ordinary automatics," a 1957 sewing machine ad explained, "you have to flip levers, twist dials, practically be a mechanic. With a Necchi, you just press a button."

While many innovations proved an instant hit, others presented marketers with new challenges. The slow acceptance of frozen foods

Figure 6.1   This 1952 ad introduced an American Classic—the frozen TV dinner.

is a classic example. In 1929 General Foods purchased Clarence Birdseye's frozen food operation, extensively tested the product, hired the Young & Rubicam ad agency, launched a major marketing effort, and anticipated a runaway success. But frozen foods came out before most Americans had refrigerators, let alone freezer compartments or deep-freezes. Yet the agency identified an even bigger problem: housewives resisted the long preparation time ("thaw before using") because it was simpler to open a can.

Frozen food did not begin to play an important role in the American diet until the introduction of the Swanson TV dinner in 1952 (Figure 6.1). Inspired by the segmented metal plates used in diners, the Swanson Company made similar trays out of aluminum and put turkey dinner courses on them. The food trays seemed perfect for eating

while watching TV, so Swanson tied the meal into the TV craze, rounding the tray corners to look like a TV screen and calling them TV Dinners.[7] Other frozen, canned, dehydrated, and pre-cooked dinners quickly appeared to help the busy homemaker prepare daily meals. Americans today wonder how they ever did without heat-and-serve dinners and entrees, prepared cake mixes, frozen pizzas, and desserts.

What previously had been luxuries now became necessities for the suburban home. "People wanted to be known for their good taste," explains author Thomas Hine, "but they also wanted to have great showy things that demonstrate they have arrived."[8] Nearly every home had at least one radio or television set. Stereos, electric vacuum cleaners, food mixers, refrigerators, freezers, air conditioners, washers, and dryers became the norm. The growing number of second cars in driveways, the barbecue equipment on patios, the pools in backyards—all reflected a trend toward luxury purchases that would have been unthinkable to many middle- and lower-class Americans prior to World War II.

Dressing Up the Automobile

Nothing symbolized the postwar boom period better than the new, chromed automobile. Production of civilian motor vehicles had halted during World War II, and for nearly a decade afterward car-starved Americans bought nearly everything that Detroit turned out. In 1949 alone 5 million cars were sold, surpassing the record set way back in 1929. In subsequent years auto production rarely slowed.

Auto manufacturing also represented the height of postwar technology, as well as secure, high-wage employment. The industry also spurred both the growth of suburbs and the development of a booming car culture, as reflected in the emergence of drive-in movies and restaurants. The spectacular success of the automobile became possible only because average family income almost doubled between 1941 and 1969, enabling many Americans to realize their dream of automobile ownership.

Automakers now turned their attention to producing stylish cars. Since the 1920s General Motors had stressed the idea of market segmentation and created separate identities for each of its auto divisions. Under the direction of Harley Earl, head of GM's styling division, the firm realized this strategy. "It was Harley Earl's job to differentiate between each product level," explains his biographer, Stephen Bayley, "so that the fantasies this practical dreamer offered the Chevrolet customer were visibly and spiritually different from the highest dollar dreams offered to the more plutocratic owner of the Cadillac."[9] New models therefore offered more than a means of transport; they also

Memorable Slogans

Timex takes a licking and keeps on ticking. (Timex watches)

M&M's melt in your mouth, not in your hands.

Wonder Bread builds strong bodies eight ways.

Cleans your breath while it cleans your teeth. (Colgate)

You'll wonder where the yellow went. (Pepsodent toothpaste)

Does she . . . or doesn't she? (Clairol hair color)

Thirty-one flavors. (Baskin-Robbins ice cream)

When you care enough to send the very best. (Hallmark cards)

They're GR-R-R-EAT! (Tony the Tiger for Frosted Flakes)

Pepsi, for those who think young.

See the U.S.A. in your Chevrolet.

Aren't you glad you use Dial? Don't you wish everybody did! (Dial soap)

Remember only you can prevent forest fires. (Forest Service)

Smokey the Bear.

suggested a lifestyle. In this era the basic message was "You are what you drive."

"Go all the way and then back off" was Earl's general advice. "Our job is to hasten obsolescence. In 1934, the average ownership span was five years; now it is two years. When it is one year we will have a perfect score."[10] These ideas became embodied in GM's postwar automobiles. Initially automobiles carried over the look of the 1930s, because design had stagnated during the war. But for Earl the war provided an inspiration for the form that would become the aesthetic of the fifties. It was a warplane that did it—the 30-foot-long "twin tail booms" of the P-38 became the celebrated tail fins. The 1948 Cadillac became the first to receive this new styling.

The form proved so successful that it spread to the entire GM line. To the marketing people the prestige associated with new motifs like the tail fin emerged as the crucial "nonprice" factor that made a given year's model a success. "They'll take the Cadillac tonight," headlined a 1955 advertisement. "How proud they'll be, for instance, when they drive in the 'car of cars' and find themselves the subject of admiring glances on every hand." What had started as little more than a taillight had reached its ultimate form by the end of the decade (Figure 6.2).

Figure 6.2 This 1959 ad for Cadillac combined appeals to women with design features like tail fins and a chic pink color.

The tail fins were only one of the first of many ideas that Earl applied in his constant search for visual novelties to offer customers. Other styling innovations that characterized the 1950s included panoramic windshields, chrome trim, heraldic badges, and gun ports. In his 1959 collection Earl offered designs to meet the needs of the newly emerged "fashionable woman," such as slipcovers to change with the seasons, chic color combinations to match with dresses, luggage to match the interior, and removable cosmetic cases. And styling took yet another direction when Detroit introduced compact cars.

"Dynamic obsolescence," as Earl called it, also served a social purpose. The concept made good design available to people who could not otherwise afford it and led to an increase in consumer choices. These same styling philosophies were embodied in the work of the great designers of the age, who gave new shapes and trendy colors to objects that filled highways, homes, and businesses. Popular magazines further publicized the role of designers, and public exhibitions made noted designers like Marcel Breuer, Charles Eames, and Raymond Loewy into emblems of contemporary taste. The professional designer replaced the individual craftsman, who was fast becoming a vanishing breed in the new era of automated mass production. Thus Earl's dream cars and other new designs helped condition the public to look forward to change.

Yet few cars could match the Edsel, possibly the biggest single product marketing flop of the century (Figure 6.3). Ford spent over nine years and $250 million to design, engineer, and build 110,000 Edsels, named after one of Henry Ford's sons. The car, which sold from 1957 to 1960, offered a host of new features such as an automatic transmission controlled by push buttons, self-adjusting brakes, and safety rim wheels. J. Walter Thompson, the agency of record, created ads that boasted: "Dramatic Edsel styling is here to stay." But the car failed miserably. Ford executives apparently weighed the data uncovered by marketing research and ignored the negative results. The styling was widely criticized, with derision focused especially on the vertical grille. Ford also mistakenly assumed that the young executive on the make would prefer a glittering, opulent family car to another Ford Thunderbird. Unfortunately top management felt confident that the Edsel's features and $30 million in consumer advertising would make the car a winner. Today, to call something an Edsel is to denounce it as a flop.

Gasoline suppliers, too, searched for new ways to court customers. With gasoline stations sprouting on every street corner, hard competition took forms other than price wars. Daniel Yergin, author of *The Prize: The Epic Quest for Oil, Money, and Power* (1992), explains that all gasoline was basically the same, so the goal in advertising gasoline to motorists became to create brand identification for an oil company's product. In the mid-1950s the companies began to sell new "premium" gasolines, outdoing one another with extravagant claims. For example, Shell claimed that its "TCP" (tricresyl phosphate) would counteract spark plug fouling. Sinclair's "Power X" contained additives that supposedly prevented engine rust. Mobil provided "high-energy gasoline." These ads proved effective in selling gasoline, because motorists were increasingly willing to pay a few cents more to put "high-performance" fuel—whether real or imagined—into their "high-performance" cars.[11]

Figure 6.3   Despite a blizzard of advertising, the late-1950s Edsel was perhaps the biggest marketing disaster in U.S. history.

The material affluence in the 1950s also helped mask rising tensions—fear of atomic war in the wake of Hiroshima and Nagasaki, the advent of the Cold War, rebellion against conformity, and the struggle for civil rights. Thus, even as the 1950s became a decade of relative tranquillity and prosperity, the seeds of the social and cultural upheaval of the 1960s were being planted. The "Atomic Age" would prove to be as volatile as its name implied.

The Atomic Age

The development of the hydrogen bomb, first by the United States and then by the former Soviet Union, brought the world into the era of nuclear power—and nuclear anxiety. "The Bomb" became part of the public consciousness, and many people prepared for the possibility of nuclear war. Meanwhile in 1957 the Soviets beat the United States into space with the *Sputnik* satellite; the following year America answered with its own satellite. Other developments contributed to the growing "Cold War" between America and Russia, including the witch-hunt for supposed communist subversives in America, the development of increasingly sophisticated weaponry and spying technology, and the struggle for global influence. Designers trivialized the molecular structure as a motif, and bomb shelters became fashionable accessories for the modern home. But it was the launch of *Sputnik* that woke America up to the "Space Age." Almost overnight Congress set up the National Aeronautics and Space Administration (NASA) to plan and execute space exploration. Congress also passed the National Defense Education Act, which shifted the focus of education to strengthen curricula with advanced programs in science, advanced mathematics, and languages. The massive expenditures for the defense and space programs also stimulated the economy, employed millions in higher-paying jobs, and fueled the growth of the aviation and electronics industries.

Don't Rock the Boat

Amidst the rapid technological progress and booming economy, the popular sentiment favored a return to supposedly traditional comforts of home and family life. The signs were everywhere: the baby boom, the record number of housing starts, the rise in churchgoing, and stricter standards of accepted dress and behavior.

Advertisers, too, reinforced traditional family values. The results mirrored what postwar American society regarded as the most appropriate life for its citizens. A profusion of ads pictured idealized versions of Mom, Dad, Junior, and Sis, and Americans struggled to fill these unrealistic roles. The ads usually portrayed Dad as the strong, decisive father and businessman, equally productive around the home and at the office. Yet Dad was also married to his employer, taking off to distant places at a moment's notice and uprooting his family to new locations. In contrast, society did not expect the woman to have a productive role in the economy. Instead, she was to find satisfaction in the narrow roles offered by conventional family life as homemaker, mother, and wife. Even as men continued to dominate the advertising industry, advertisements presented the woman's point of view as seen by men. Ads also constantly reminded the American woman of everything she ought to be.

Typically ads centered on the themes of helping the housewife to avoid drudgery and glorifying her everyday life. They presented glamorous female figures whom women would admire and listen to for advice. Elegantly attired models sometimes wore a glove to press the button of the latest appliance, showing how the new technology removed drudgery from household chores. The lady of the house even

Figure 6.4 This 1960 ad implied that the typical housewife—and her daughter sometime in the future—would feel like a queen for owning a Frigidaire.

wore a crown while striking a pose, a privilege previously reserved for royalty until the daytime television program "Queen for a Day" and advertisements popularized the theme (Figure 6.4).

Another wave of advertising portrayed the "little woman" in what the admakers promoted as middle-American, slice-of-life scenarios. Ads featured familiar stereotyped characters like the shy but lovely single girl, the triumphant bride, and the gossipy neighbor. Perhaps the most common stereotype, however, was the dedicated homemaker who sacrificed all personal aspirations to pamper her husband, chauffeur her children, scrub floors, and teach her daughters to do the same (Figure 6.5). These familiar themes are still being used today.

Despite the emphasis on "family values," the postwar era also gave birth to the materialistic and sexually permissive (at least for men) philosophy embodied in *Playboy* magazine, first published in 1953.

Figure 6.5 This 1945 ad portrayed the "little woman" as a happy homemaker who sacrificed all personal aspirations to dote on her family.

Admakers used sex to move merchandise more than ever before. Elliot Springs, owner of Springs Cotton Mills and seven other textile mills, has been called the "expert on tease." Springs created a new approach by combining the typical sexy image with a humorous sales pitch favoring double entendres and puns. But Springs insisted that the ad sell some Springmaid fabric and that the logo be prominent. For example, one 1949 ad showed an illustration of a Native American sleeping in a hammock with the headline "A buck well spent on a

Perfume and Parabolics

SPRINGMAID FABRICS

During the war, The Springs Cotton Mills was called upon to develop a special fabric for camouflage. It was used in the Pacific to conceal ammunition dumps and gun emplacements, but the Japanese learned to detect it because of its lack of jungle smells. To overcome this, when the fabric was dyed, it was also impregnated with a permanent odor of hibiscus, hydrangea, and old rubber boots. The deception was so successful that when Tokyo fell, the victorious invaders hung a piece of this fabric on a Japanese flagpole.

This process has been patented, and the fabric is now available to the false bottom and bust bucket business as SPRINGMAID PERKER, made of combed yarns, 37" wide, 152 x 68 approximate count, weight about 3.50, the white with gardenia, the pink with camellia, the blush with jasmine, and the nude dusty.

If you want to achieve that careless look and avoid skater's steam, kill two birds with one stone by getting a camouflaged callipygian camisole with the SPRINGMAID label on the bottom of your trademark.

Figure 6.6   This 1948 ad, like many for Springs Mills, used sex and double entendres to sell the product.

Springmaid sheet." And a 1948 ad, "Perfume and Parabolics," used a "girlie" illustration of a skater with her skirt billowing around her legs (Figure 6.6). The copy read:

> During the war, The Springs Cotton Mills was called
> upon to develop a special fabric for camouflage . . .
> but the Japanese learned to detect it because of its lack

of jungle smells. To overcome this, when the fabric
was dyed, it was also impregnated with a permanent
odor of hibiscus, hydrangea, and old rubber boots. . . .
    This process has been patented, and the fabric is
now available to the false bottom and bust bucket
business as SPRINGMAID PERKER. . . . If you want to
achieve that careless look and avoid skater's steam,
kill two birds with one stone by getting a camouflaged
callipygian camisole with the SPRINGMAID label on
the bottom of your trademark.

The Springmaid ads generated more than publicity. Surveys showed the ads resulted in far greater brand recall than any other campaign from 1947 to 1951.[12] In the process Springs conditioned the public to accept more explicit advertising. Or did he?

Women's objections to sex-based ads and to narrow social roles went largely unrecognized in the 1950s, but the seeds of discontent had been planted. The advertising image of women as happy home-makers had always worked, and traditionally few women had voiced the desire for more from life than this role could offer—at least until World War II. Between 1942 and 1945 millions of women had entered the work force to fill the manpower shortage, many in jobs previously held only by men. The advertising field was no exception, as women increasingly filled nonclerical positions. For example, in 1941 copywriter Bernice Fitzgibbon left Wanamaker's and joined Gimbels department store, earning over $90,000 per year as one of the highest-paid women in advertising at the time (Figure 6.7 on page 260). In 1944 Jane Wade Rindlaub became BBDO's first woman vice president, and that same year Ruth Waldo became the first woman vice president at J. Walter Thompson. However, women still mainly handled women's products and worked as copywriters and researchers; few served as art directors or account executives or worked on lucrative liquor, cigarette, and automobile campaigns. But for the first time, many women experienced meaningful work, enjoyed economic independence, and at the same time managed home life.

For some women the transition to peacetime had been smooth. As men returned home to waiting jobs or attended school on the GI bill, many women gladly abandoned the war plants to cook meals, raise babies, and take care of the home. Others saw themselves as temporary workers whose income was directed toward a specific goal like clothes for the children, a vacation, a larger house—or marriage. A 1952 ad for U.S. Savings Bonds mirrored this sentiment: "When a young girl goes to work, she is apt to look on her job pretty much as a fill-in between maturity and marriage."

For other women, however, signs of discontent were evident. In 1950 about 31 percent of all women were employed. Unlike women

A Taste of the Times

In the postwar era of planned obsolescence, styling was the design watchword. As advertising promoted the ever-changing new ideal, people no longer saved for furniture that would last a lifetime. Instead, the newly affluent eagerly bought the futuristic shapes of the age. Images of molecular atomic structures appeared on curtain fabrics, plastic wall ornaments, and neon motel signs. Other popular patterns included orbiting satellites, flying saucers, and rocket imagery. The boldly experimental drip canvases of painter Jackson Pollock appeared as patterns on everything from formica tabletops to handbags and fabrics. The strange organic and amoebic forms conjured up by surrealist Joan Miro inspired sculpted chairs, ovoid ceramics, and kidney-shaped tables. People's excitement about these styles soon gave way to another cycle of fashion. European-inspired, Danish modern furniture styles marked the next trend.

The home became a major recreation center with its modern technology and do-it-yourself projects. Amidst all the gadgets, barbecues, high-fidelity stereos, and swimming pools, however, the television set reigned supreme. Television programming proved so popular that it destroyed radio comedies and dramas and nearly ruined the motion picture industry.

Although television replaced radio as the omnipresent enter-

workers during World War II, those in the postwar work force were confined to dead-end, low-paying jobs in light manufacturing, office work, health care, and education. This job segregation helped keep women's earnings low. In fact, women's wages in manufacturing dropped from a high of about 67 percent of men's earnings to only 53 percent within a few years of the war's end. Still other women were forced out of their high-paying assembly line jobs and into lower-paying work as waitresses, clerks, or other service workers to clear slots for returning World War II veterans. And professional schools discouraged female enrollment, giving preference to the GIs, so there were fewer women doctors and lawyers in the 1950s than in previous decades.

Although millions of married women entered the labor market in record numbers, the "American way of life" still celebrated the middle-class suburban existence in which Mom stayed at home and Dad worked in the city. In these early housing tracts, women no longer had access to the corner store, nearby grandparents, or the convenient streetcar that they had relied on to ease the burden of shopping, housework, and child rearing. By making work outside the home

tainment source, it still faced stiff competition from newspapers, sports, movie theaters, concerts, and other forms of diversion. The surviving motion picture studios claimed the movies were better than ever. Bolstered by new projection techniques, the studios brought epic spectacles such as *Ben Hur* and *The African Queen* to the big screen, and celebrities like Clark Gable, Marilyn Monroe, and John Wayne remained popular. But high-priced admission tickets often drove customers to drive-in movies or the small screen at home. Inexpensive paperback publications proliferated, book clubs increased in number, and new magazines appeared.

Funny and absurd fads filled this era, too. Disneyland opened in 1955 in Anaheim, California, and the country seemed overall to be one big amusement park. On campus it was the decade of the panty raids, goldfish swallowing, and telephone booth jamming. People vied to see how many individuals they could pile on a mattress or how long they could play bridge or stay on a teeter-totter. Other fads became the rage; including Canasta, Hop-a-Long Cassidy, Davy Crockett coonskin caps, Hoola Hoops, flying saucers, 3-D glasses, Barbie dolls, and Scrabble. While the stylish danced the mambo and cha-cha-cha, teens rocked and rolled. And the growing popularity of outdoor activities like scuba diving, water skiing, surfing, tennis, and golf led to a booming new market for sporting goods.

increasingly difficult for women, suburban life further advanced traditional gender roles in postwar society. This sexual ideology was sustained by what feminist Betty Friedan called "the feminine mystique" in her best-selling 1963 book, which raised women's consciousness about the sexist system. Thus in the 1960s advertising increasingly was criticized for duping women into thinking that homemaking was the ultimate achievement in life.

The Generation Gap Opens Up

The emancipation of teenagers also began in the prosperous years after World War II. In the face of the traditional conservative values espoused by society as a whole, the more liberal youths sought to express their individuality. The rising postwar baby boom generation (or "boomers") could hardly be aware of what their parents and grandparents had endured during the lean years of the Depression and World War II.

a 2-quart cow can't produce a 4-gallon daughter

That is to say, blood will tell. We got the piquant aphorism from our bucolic-type grandpa out in the Middle West. The more we look around, the truer the truism seems—and we don't mean just down on the farm. A 2-quart cow can't have a 4-gallon calf—you said it. If Gimbels were a dainty little shoppe, Gimbels couldn't produce hairy-chested bargains. Leave it to a big store with a big frame (like Gimbels) and a mammoth buying power (like our'n) to come up with a real whopper of a bargain. Put the 4 huge Gimbels stores together, and nobody in creation beats us. Propagating fat rosy bargains just comes naturally to Gimbels. We do it every day. We've been doing it for 108 years. Ain't we plumb tuckered? Is it time to go moo in some grassy pasture? Shucks, son, we were just winding up—now watch our speed!

Figure 6.7   Beginning in 1941, copywriter Bernice Fitzgibbon created ads for Gimbels department store as one of the highest-paid women in advertising.

This new generation had more money to spend than in the past and more time to enjoy it. Teenagers adopted distinctive fashions to distinguish themselves from adults. Pony-tailed girls wearing the "raccoon look" of heavily mascaraed eyes, felt skirts with poodle appliques, bobby sox, and saddle shoes were one target of the growing cosmetics and beauty market. As for the newly affluent young men who could afford expensive hairstyling, cropped crew cuts were "cool," and slick-backed flattops and ducktails were "neat." Meanwhile "dungarees" became a wardrobe staple for both sexes.

The sound of rock 'n' roll provided the beat for the younger generation. This exciting new sound mixed elements of rhythm and blues, country western, and gospel. The postwar musical phenomenon began in 1952 when Cleveland disc jockey Alan Freed started playing records by such little-known musicians as Chuck Berry and Bo Diddley. Three years later, the Bill Haley and the Comets thunderbolt "Rock Around the Clock" helped inspire a musical revolution. But it was Elvis Presley who in 1956 shook up all the generations. His looks, dress, and gyrating hips made him the first rock star and the symbol of teenage liberation. Was it music or madness? Millions of delirious teenage fans bought his records as adults recoiled in horror. Such music, warned a psychologist, could induce "medieval types of spontaneous lunacy" and even "prehistoric rhythmic trances."[13] In any case rock music became linked with rebellion. An army of disc jockeys around the nation aired the popular music, while Dick Clark's "American Bandstand" televised performances.

For the first time advertising carefully cultivated an independent market of affluent teens who had increasing amounts of money to spend. Sales of radios, records, record players, teen magazines, cosmetics, and clothes soared as ads promoted these products as essential to teens. Soft drinks specifically targeted teens. For example, Seven-Up established a "going steady" theme with such headlines as "It's great to 'go steady' with this cool, clean taste!" (Figure 6.8). Although Coca-Cola featured youths in its ads, a rival soft drink now specifically focused on this market: "Pepsi, for those who think young." Such campaigns reflected the goal of conditioning the younger generation to the allure of the marketplace. Not only did the ads begin to establish consumerist attitudes at this early age, but sales to teens soared and in the future would yield an even greater "harvest."

It was also a time when a new breed of youth emerged. Frightened by nuclear weapons, alienated by modern technology, and disgusted by conspicuous consumption, these youths rejected the "soulless" American middle-class ideal. Beginning in the mid-1950s a small group of intellectuals used poetry and literature to mock mainstream values, which they believed embodied materialism, sexual repression, and spiritual emptiness. Led by Jack Kerouac and Allen Ginsberg the stereotypical "beat poet" dressed in black, wore sandals, sported a goatee, and idolized jazz musicians. These youths were called the "Beat Generation" or "beatniks," a term coined by San Francisco newspaper columnist Herb Caen, who combined the words "beat" and "sputnik." Over time the movement weakened, but it would abruptly appear again in the form of the "hippies" in the following decade.

Even as the beats challenged the established order, a separate subculture of rebellious adolescents also emerged in the form of the "rebel without a cause," as personified by James Dean. Many adults expressed concern about the younger generation's inability to conform to postwar societal patterns as the generation gap continued to widen.

It's great to "go steady" with this

cool, clean taste !

Nothing does it like Seven-Up !   You like it... it likes you!

Figure 6.8   This 1950s ad targeted the emerging teenage market with its "go steady" theme.

Civil Rights Become an Issue

Not all Americans enjoyed the benefits of the affluent postwar era. African Americans, Puerto Ricans, Mexican Americans, and Asian Americans continued to face discrimination in virtually every aspect of life—from housing, jobs, and education, to the political and legal systems.

The experience of World War II had given a fresh impetus to the struggle for civil rights. For much of the century, African Americans in the South had been denied the right to vote and to own land. They also had been forced to attend different schools, take rear seats or even stand on public transportation, use separate restrooms, and eat only at designated restaurants. During the war, however, African Americans served in the armed forces to preserve the ideals of freedom and equality. They returned from the war with a new sense of self and challenged segregation with lawsuits and boycotts. In 1947 Jackie Robinson broke Major League Baseball's color line by starring for the Brooklyn Dodgers. The next year President Harry Truman ordered the military integrated, and in 1954 the Supreme Court banned segregated schools. The Reverend Martin Luther King Jr. led the civil rights crusade that employed nonviolent tactics with the goals of full citizenship and total integration for all Americans.

From the standpoint of the advertiser, however, the prime market continued to be not city dwellers, but white suburbanites—the typical "average Americans" who also appeared in television, radio, and print advertisements. This well-off group read a lot of magazines and watched a lot of television, from which many took cues on how they should live. In short, they were ideal targets for advertising. Yet all the while advertising excluded not only African Americans but residents of ethnic urban neighborhoods, the single, the widowed, and single parents.

Advertising also continued to perpetuate racial stereotypes as imagined by white advertisers for a white audience. African Americans invariably were portrayed as smiling chefs or servants, from Aunt Jemima and the Cream of Wheat chef to Hiram Walker's butler and Pullman's train porters. Mischievous little African American children commonly appeared in ads as well, and an occasional endorsement featured an African American athlete or entertainer.

A few pioneering African American admen started their own agencies, including David Sullivan in New York (1943); Fusche, Young & Powell in Detroit (1943); and Vince Cullers in Chicago (1956). However, "they were limited to selling black products through black media to black consumers," concluded historian Stephen Fox. "At the major white agencies, apparently no black held a significant position until the 1950s."[14] The BBDO agency recognized the beginnings of a new economic opportunity, the black "special market," and started a unit of African Americans to sell to African Americans. In 1955 Young & Rubicam hired Roy Eaton, probably the first African American at any major agency to work in a creative function not limited to ads and products for African Americans. Fox provides a circular explanation for this racial imbalance on Madison Avenue: "Few were hired, so few applied, so few were hired."[15]

Advertising would become more sensitive to portraying stereotyped images as the civil rights movement began to challenge issues of housing and employment discrimination in the 1960s. In the meantime, however, advertisers continued with their never-ending exploration of new ways to reach consumers.

Vince Cullers

Chicago-based Vincent T. Cullers founded the first black-owned full-service advertising agency in 1956. Cullers began his advertising career at *Ebony* magazine, where he served as art director, and then started his own business as a way to reach the growing African American consumer market. At first, according to Cullers, white clients were reluctant to spend money promoting products for African Americans. During the 1960s, however, businesspeople began to recognize the substantial buying power of African American communities and found a need for special marketing programs targeted at this market. They then involved the forward-thinking Cullers, who managed to segment a part of the marketplace that previously had been ignored.

Culler's campaigns for Afro Sheen, Sears, and Amoco Oil created a positive image that reflected the emerging pride and heritage of African Americans. Cullers' agency has since grown to a staff of twenty-five employees and 1995 billings totaling $18 million. The firm also has represented Johnson Products, Coors beer, Kellogg's, Pizza Hut, and the Chicago White Sox.

New Ways of Selling

Advertising enjoyed flush times in the 1950s. Although no major agencies were launched during this decade, many organizations merged, opened offices overseas, and expanded their services. This trend toward mergers arose as clients demanded more services such as research, sales analysis, package design, and publicity. It also coincided with business expansion into the international arena, as agencies added new offices in Canada, Europe, Latin America, and other locales.

Previously the J. Walter Thompson agency had dominated the international advertising field. The company was already established abroad as the first American agency with foreign offices in Great Britain in 1899 and on the European continent in 1920s; General Motors took the agency into Latin America the following decade. By the end of World War II, the agency operated fifteen foreign offices and quickly added another fourteen. As for the other leading agencies, the Standard Oil account took McCann-Erickson into Europe during the 1920s and into Latin America the following decade. In the 1950s McCann-Erickson's international accounts included Bristol-Meyers, Colgate-Palmolive, Nestlé, and Westinghouse. One reason Coca-Cola shifted its business from D'Arcy to McCann-Erickson was the latter agency's global capacity. BBDO and Young & Rubicam, however, initially limited their efforts to Great Britain and Canada.

Competing in a Crowded Market

Advertisers competed in an increasingly cluttered marketplace as business boomed in the postwar era. For every new product four or five major competitors already existed. In order to sell more, businesses advertised more, but the ads also had to contend with more clutter in both print and broadcast media than ever before.

Advertisers still had much to learn about consumers and patterns of consumption. Marketing and advertising research departments had greatly improved their survey techniques since George Gallup began polling audiences in the 1920s. Admakers now claimed a scientific basis for their work based on demographic studies and statistics. Research departments expanded. Media departments obtained a more precise idea of which audiences various media reached by measuring readership of past and current ads. But the search continued for still more persuasive ways to compete in the crowded market of the 1950s. Now more than ever, ads had to catch attention.

A significant development was the emergence of "lifestyle marketing," the practice of segmenting the market based on the spending patterns of groups of consumers. Advertisers targeted specific income levels, consumer lifestyles, and interest groups, instead of directing their pitches at the broadest range of the buying public. New magazines provided vehicles for advertisers to reach these audiences, such as *Jet* (1951) for the African American community and *Playboy* (1953). Other special-interest periodicals found a popular market by focusing on hot-rodding, surfing, home decorating, and television.

One publication provided a key to understanding this market. Lloyd Warner's landmark book *Social Class in America* (1949) defined the social layers not only in terms of wealth and power but also on previously ignored aspects such as consumption patterns. "Middle majority woman is the target you are supposed to hit," claimed Warner. "Mrs. Middle Majority" occupied the combined social classes of white-collar workers, tradesmen, and skilled and semiskilled workers, who made up approximately 65 percent of the work force. Warner explained further that the typical American housewife lived in a very narrow world, tended to accept conformity, and built her whole life around the home.[16]

Where goods for the home were concerned, women represented a crucial market. Sales of household appliances were booming, and predictably the adman's obsession with the female consumer intensified. Ads showed wives overjoyed to own products and appliances for the kitchen, which was the center of their world. The number of ads personifying the idealized woman pampering her husband, chauffeuring the children, and scrubbing floors increased in proportion to the amount of advertising dollars spent.

Tapping into Consumers' Hidden Desires

Another new tool that had a major influence on advertising was motivation research (MR). Researchers had declared the old "reason-why" copy approach to be outdated for the new era of affluence and consumer products. This new MR methodology replaced the statistical techniques of polling and counting with concepts derived especially from psychology and psychoanalysis. Instead of accepting that people were rational beings who knew what they wanted, MR examined what triggered people to make choices on the subconscious and unconscious levels. Although admakers' use of psychology dated back to the 1920s, MR did not take root until the late 1940s and early 1950s.

Consumer researcher Ernest Dichter pioneered the MR approach. Dichter, noted for his work for Chrysler, deduced that more men bought a sedan even though they were attracted to a convertible because they associated the practical hardtop with their wife and the sportier vehicle with a mistress. Dichter also explained why domestic happiness was often tied to an endless inventory of big-ticket appliances and other items: "Marriage today is not only a culmination of romantic attachment . . . it is a decision to create a partnership in establishing a comfortable home."[17]

Focusing on what people really wanted, MR reduced this to two basic human motives: sex and security. Armed with this information, advertisers added psychological "value" to products to make them more appealing. For example, Camel cigarettes targeted women, claiming a scientific basis for the benefit of smoking. "It's a psychological fact: Pleasure helps your disposition," stated a 1955 advertisement. Advice from a respected authority further supported the claim.

Advertisers also focused on product features that implied social acceptance, style, luxury, and success, molding "symbols" to create products with vivid "personalities." For example, Ivory soap personified purity in picturing mother and child. David Ogilvy used an eye-patched patrician to sell Hathaway shirts. Leo Burnett built a distinct personality for a cigarette brand, the Marlboro Man. Other products began to take on new symbolic dimensions that appealed to individuals who aspired to climb the social ladder. For instance, Buick and Oldsmobile owners were status seekers striving to occupy the Cadillac class.

Maidenform based its eye-stopping campaign on what motivation research later considered to be the fulfillment of women's basic exhibitionist tendencies. One of a series of advertisements pictured an otherwise fully dressed woman wearing only a bra above the waist with the headline "I dreamed I was a Lady Ambassador in my maidenform bra" (Figure 6.9). Another showed a similarly clad woman stand-

Figure 6.9   This 1951 ad was based on what motivation research later concluded was women's subconscious or unconscious exhibitionist tendencies.

ing in front of a locomotive, with the headline "I dreamed I stopped them in my tracks in my maidenform bra." Maidenform offered a $10,000 prize to people who could come up with other "dream" situations for their campaign.

MR also enabled advertisers to understand why consumers avoided certain products, such as instant coffee, tea, and food mixes. Sales proved sluggish for new instant coffee despite its convenience and ease of preparation. Why? Most people said it was the taste. But researchers identified another reason: the product had an unfortunate association with lax housekeeping. Advertisers improved the image of Nescafé by stressing the phrases "100% pure coffee" and "you can serve it with pride." Tea had the image of mostly being consumed when someone was miserable, tired, or sick. To change people's perception of the brew, the Tea Bureau launched a new campaign: "Make mine hefty, hale and hearty."

Food mixes, particularly for cakes, encountered resistance as well. With the early ready-to-mix packages, users simply added water. Yet MR revealed that a woman making a cake symbolized the creative act of giving birth. If she used a quick mix, she felt guilty for being a lazy housekeeper. To solve this problem, manufacturers changed the directions to increase the involvement of the homemaker: "You add fresh eggs" or "You add fresh eggs and milk." Researchers also measured anxieties. In the early 1950s Jell-O produced ads featuring elaborate desserts made with the product, but research showed that housewives questioned their ability to duplicate the recipes. After Jell-O went back to simple, one-color molded mounds, women felt more confident about making the desserts at home, and sales improved.

Research also provided copywriter Shirley Polykoff, of Foote Cone & Belding, with a new approach for selling Clairol hair coloring (Figure 6.10). At the time only about 7 percent of all women admitted to using hair color; the general perception was that only society women, actresses, and women of questionable character colored their hair. Polykoff's five-word headline created a stir: "Does she . . . or doesn't she?" The answer: "Hair color so natural only her hairdresser knows for sure." Her male superiors at the agency initially questioned Polykoff's headline and withheld the ad from publication, believing that the copy was too suggestive. But women supported Polykoff's point of view, because they knew exactly what she meant (that even a woman's friends wouldn't be able to tell that she colored her hair). In the end the agency fought to run the ad, and the campaign led to substantial rewards. In six years Clairol's sales rose over 400 percent; and nearly half of adult women admitted to using hair-coloring products.[18]

Psychologists also teamed up with merchandisers. They gave packages bold new looks with eye-catching graphics that made full use of the advances in color printing. Illustrations presented the contents in a seductive manner. Color coding identified each of a line of products. Once designed, many new packages didn't hit store shelves until they had been tested. For example, eye-tracking tests, which were first used as part of the training of British anti-aircraft gunners during World War II, gauged the way the consumer's eyes traveled to the package on the shelf and the holding power of the design.

When Procter & Gamble updated Crisco shortening to look more contemporary, they recognized that color combinations stimulated moods or feelings about the package. They made the blue-and-white can look crisp and clean, just like the modern kitchen. They then took the same shortening and created a competing brand called Fluffo. For this package they simply added a warm, "golden" color and covered the can with a homespun, checkered-tablecloth label to conjure up images of grandma's kitchen.

MR was not without its critics. The strongest criticism centered on the premise that hidden motives extracted from individuals could

Does
she...
or
doesn't
she?

Hair color so natural only her hairdresser knows for sure!

She has a fresh, young way of looking—and of looking at things. Her naturalness, the way her hair sparkles and catches the light, its depth of color—as though she's found the secret of making time stand still. And in a way she has! With Miss Clairol, it's so easy to keep hair color young and radiant . . . to keep gray from ever showing! And *this* is why more women use it than all other haircolorings combined.

Hairdressers everywhere prefer Miss Clairol and always recommend it because it truly lives up to its promise. Not only is it the most beautiful, most effective way to cover gray but it keeps hair in wonderful condition—so silky, lively, completely natural-looking. Its automatic color timing is most dependable. So try Miss Clairol yourself. Today. Takes only minutes. Creme Formula or Regular.

MISS CLAIROL® HAIR COLOR BATH! THE NATURAL-LOOKING HAIRCOLORING

Figure 6.10 This 1955 ad with its suggestive headline "Does she . . . or doesn't she?" created a stir and boosted Clairol's sales.

be accurately applied to a mass audience. The publication of Vance Packard's best-seller *The Hidden Persuaders* (1957) informed the public about MR with this message: "Large scale efforts are being made, often with impressive success, to channel our unthinking habits, our purchasing decisions, and our thought processes by the use of insights gleaned from psychiatry and the social scientists."[19]

Packard claimed that two-thirds of the hundred biggest advertisers were using MR and subliminal advertising techniques.[20] The book, however, distorted the extent of psychological selling in this era. For example, Packard described a controversial six-week experiment in which the phrase "eat popcorn and drink Coca-Cola" was briefly flashed on the screen during the showing of the movie *Picnic;* sales of popcorn allegedly jumped immediately afterward. Not surprisingly, alarmists raised a fuss about the manipulation of people "against their will," and several states passed measures banning the practice. However, this experiment has never been replicated successfully.

Although Packard's book represented the most popular attack on advertising since the 1930s, other books and novels carried similar themes. For example, *The Hucksters* (which MGM turned into a movie), *Please Send Me Absolutely Free,* and *The Space Merchants* stereotyped admen as crass, materialistic, deceptive, and interested only in appearances.

Bringing Television to the Masses

After several false starts, American television began its explosive growth in 1948. Television grew far more rapidly than radio because the developers of the new medium tapped the experiences of the early radio broadcasters. Recognizing that the shoestring operations characteristic of many radio stations were no longer feasible, TV established networks of affiliated stations. Initially the national commercial networks were limited to the big three—CBS, NBC, and ABC. In 1946 the nation had fewer than 10,000 TV sets and only six stations, each of which broadcasted for 10 hours a week. Regular network service became available in the Midwest and on the East Coast in 1948 and on the West Coast in 1951. National network television soon would reach 60 percent of American homes.

As had been the case with radio, the television networks at first merely served as production and transmission facilities; the advertisers controlled the programs. By sponsoring programs, advertisers could control when and how commercials were inserted. Philip Morris cigarettes, for example, owned "I Love Lucy," General Mills sponsored "Betty Crocker's Star Matinee," and Dutch Master cigars funded the "Ernie Kovacs Show." Market research on which programs drew the most viewers—that is, potential customers—determined which programs aired. Sponsors hoped that the shows would create good feelings about their products so people would buy them.

Television soon offered everything from movie reruns, variety shows, and situation comedies to kiddie shows and quiz programs. NBC introduced "Kraft Television Theater" in 1947. Children enjoyed "Howdy Doody" in New York and "Kukla, Fran & Ollie" in Chicago. In 1948 "The Ed Sullivan Show" debuted on CBS. But it was "Texaco Star Theater," which debuted the same year, that became television's first sensation. To open the show, four Texaco gas station servicemen stood in front of a painted background and sang a song urging loyal viewers to "Trust Your Car to the Man Who Wears the Star"; the quartet then introduced the star, Milton Berle. At the end of each show, the servicemen returned to say good night.

Also in 1948 John Cameron Swayze started anchoring NBC's 15-minute "Camel News Caravan." The program speeded up news reporting and took people right to the spot to watch newsworthy events as they happened. For the next twenty years Swayze also hosted a variety of torture tests designed to demonstrate the strength of Timex watches: "They take a licking and keep on ticking."

By 1950 TV advertising revenues reached $100 million (a four-fold increase over the preceding year); soon thereafter TV revenues overtook radio's. By year's end 9.7 million TV sets had been sold, and about 9 percent of the nation's households owned sets. Four years later, in 1954, television became the leading medium for advertising. Newspapers and magazines had also found a new category of product to sell— television sets. A small TV set cost $200, and a fancy console model ran as high as $2500 (at a time when the average annual income was about $3000). By 1960 nearly every home had a television set.[21]

The first television ads were simply televised radio commercials, and sometimes the announcer could even be seen holding the script. These commercials, as well as most programming until 1957, aired live because videotape recording had not yet been invented. Of course, goofs did happen during live broadcasts. In a classic 1954 commercial celebrity spokesperson Betty Furness calmly explained why a new Westinghouse refrigerator was easy to use, all the while tugging on a refrigerator door whose latch was stuck.

Other credible spokespersons included Dinah Shore for Chevrolet, Polly Bergen for Pepsi, and Ozzie and Harriet Nelson for Coca-Cola. Viewers became used to seeing glamorous models and actors in commercials, so they took notice when offbeat animated spots appeared on the scene. In 1948 the Ajax Pixies for Ajax cleanser appeared as the first animated trademark characters on television. Other favorites included the bumbling businessmen Bert and Harry Piel for Piel's beer, the Hamm's beer Bear, and Tony the Tiger, who growled, "They're GR-R-REAT!" about Frosted Flakes. Animated commercials reached a zenith in the late 1950s, in part because they were less costly than other approaches.

Some of the most innovative television commercials of the era were for Chevrolet. Campbell-Ewald, Chevrolet's agency, employed special effects extensively to astound consumers and give the cars a special aura. One ad showed a man and a woman driving along the highway without a car, which gradually materialized around them. In another ad a flashy convertible zipped by without a driver.

Advertisers also targeted children as a specific market. In this pre-regulation era sponsors routinely used special effects to improve the appearance of toys or to depict children who acquired superhuman strength by eating certain breakfast cereals. Stars of programs also

Television Timeline

1920

Russian-American Vladimir Zworkykin, an engineer for Westinghouse, builds a crude all-electronic television system but immediately finds himself embroiled in a patent suit brought by Philo T. Farnsworth, among others.
1923

AT&T gives the first public demonstration of television, showing the image of Herbert Hoover.
1927

1926
Scottish inventor John L. Baird improves the system and shows clear images on his tube.

1939
RCA demonstrates television broadcasting at the New York World's Fair.

NBC broadcasts a big league baseball game in Brooklyn from their experimental station W2XBS.

pitched products and would interrupt the show to sell toys, cereals, and candies. For instance, Howdy Doody, Miss Frances of Ding Dong School, and Captain Midnight all sold Ovaltine. Captain Midnight also carried on a tradition that had originated on radio, offering Secret Squadron badges, membership cards, and rings that decoded the message of the day.

Late in the 1950s a staple of the era, the network quiz shows, was revealed to be largely rigged. Advertisers seeking the largest possible audiences had supplied the impetus for quiz rigging in order to keep appealing contestants on the air. By the time official confirmation of fraud came in 1959, the quiz craze had run its course, having earned millions of dollars for drug and cosmetic sponsors such as Geritol, Revlon, and Bristol-Meyers.

But the ensuing controversy provided the impetus for the networks to seize control of commercial entertainment from the advertising agencies. Full sponsorship, once the principle type of network advertising, faded from television during the 1960s when most advertisers decided that programs were too expensive to sponsor and strategically ran their messages on several other programs. When the networks took over the responsibility for programming from advertisers, they at first referred to advertisers whose commercials appeared during their programs as "participating sponsors." Today most broadcast advertising is sold simply as spot announcements or "spots"—that is, the breaks between programs.

As viewers and advertisers flocked to television, radio began to lose both talent and advertising revenue to the new medium. The answer to radio's crisis came in the late 1950s in the form of "Top-40"

Commercial television
broadcasting begins with NBC and
CBS competing for viewers.

Regular network service reaches
the West Coast, and national
The first TV commercial airs, for   network television is established.
Bulova watches, on station WNBT.
1941   **1951**

1948   **1966**
Regular network service is available   Color TV becomes a commercial
in the Midwest and on the East   reality.
Coast.

Television has its first smash hit, the
"Texaco Star Theater."

1970

programming, the practice of limiting disc jockeys to a specific playlist
of current best-selling popular records. In the process radio changed
from a mass medium to a specialized one, providing advertisers with a
consistent, specific audience segmented in terms of age, musical taste,
and geography.

As in other eras, advertisers tried a variety of approaches to sell
their products. Agencies competed fiercely to promote ever-expanding
product lines, to introduce new products, and to utilize new communications media.

Four Creative Philosophies

To understand the advertising of the era and the forces that shaped the
subsequent 1960s "creative revolution," we need to examine the work
of four leading admen—Rosser Reeves, Leo Burnett, David Ogilvy, and
Bill Bernbach. Reeves' work emphasized science and research, and his
ads typically featured simple repetition of a single theme. Throughout
this era comfortable ad designs associated products with the "good old
days" before the Depression and the war. Designers streamlined product forms and headline typefaces, while artists created literal representations. Despite the many new schools of art, the average American
preferred realism over abstract expressionism and pop art. In particular, Norman Rockwell's paintings depicting folksy scenes such as baseball games, a swim in the creek, and holidays at home enjoyed a wide
following.

At the same time, advertising's emphasis began to shift away from
product features and toward product image or personality. The striking

Favorite TV Jingles

Brylcreem

Brylcreem makes men's hair look neat, / smooth and lustrous, can't be beat. / Use it daily, just a bit, / Brylcreem always makes a hit. / Brylcreem, a little dab'll do ya, / Brylcreem, you'll look so debonair, / Brylcreem, the gals will pursue ya, / Simply rub a little in your hair.

Colgate Dental Cream

Brush your teeth with Colgate, Colgate Dental Cream. It cleans your breath (what a toothpaste), while it guards your teeth.

Bosco

I love Bosco, it's rich and chocolaty, / Chocolate-flavored Bosco is mighty good for me. / Mama puts it in my milk for extra energy. / Bosco gives me iron and sunshine Vitamin D. / Oh, I love Bosco. That's the drink for me!

Old Spice After-Shave

Old Spice means quality, said the captain to the bosun. / Ask for the package with the ship that sails the ocean. / Yo ho, Yo ho, Yo ho . . .

Gillette Razor Blades

To look sharp every time you shave, / to feel sharp, and be on the ball, / just be sharp, use Gillette Blue Blades / for the quickest slickest shaves of all.

Campbell Soups

M'm, M'm good/ M'm, M'm good/ That's what Campbell Soups are/ M'm M'm good!

Doublemint Gum

Double your pleasure, double your fun / with double good, double good, Doublemint Gum. / Double delicious, double smooth too, / Doublemint's double delightful to chew. / So double your pleasure, double your fun. / Get double everything rolled into one. / Oh, double your pleasure, double your fun / with double good, double good, / Doublemint Gum.

Chevrolet

See the U.S.A. in your Chevrolet. America is / asking you to call; drive your Chevrolet through the / U.S.A. America's the greatest land of all. / On a highway or a road along a levee, per- / formance is sweeter, nothing can beat'er, life is comple- / ter in a Chevy. So make a date today / to see the U.S.A. and see it in your / Chevrolet.

The Best TV Commercials

As part of a special spring 1995 issue, six editors of *Advertising Age* selected the "50 best" TV commercials. Compiled by decade, here's the list for the 1940s and 1950s.

1940s

Gillette An animated parrot entertains viewers.

Lucky Strike Cigarettes dance.

Texaco The men from "Texaco" sing.

1950s

Alka-Seltzer The Speedy Alka-Seltzer character is introduced.

Anacin A hard-selling spot features hammers pounding.

Chevrolet Dinah Shore sings "See the U.S.A. in your Chevrolet."

Timex A watch "takes a licking and keeps on ticking."

Speedy.

campaigns of Leo Burnett, David Ogilvy, and Bill Bernbach fueled the shift from pseudoscience and market research to art, inspiration, and personal expression.

Rosser Reeves—The Hard Sell

Rosser Reeves, of the New York–based Ted Bates agency, emerged as an influential advertiser. Reeves, however, represented a throwback to the days when the main goal of advertising was simply to grab attention, not to entertain people who might not even buy the product. Moreover, Reeves did not believe in overestimating the intelligence and attention span of his audience. Thus he utilized the simple repetition of a single theme to cut through the clutter of advertising messages. In his 1961 book *Reality in Advertising,* Reeves explained his guiding principle: "The consumer tends to remember just one thing from an advertisement—one strong claim, or one strong concept."[22]

In Reeves' ideal selling campaign, the pitch was a simple "Buy this product, and you will get this specific benefit." The selling point had to be a claim that the competition did not and could not make, and it had to "pull"—that is, penetrate the market. Reeves' philosophy was

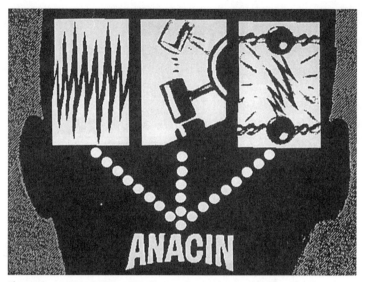

Figure 6.11   This 1950s ad by Rosser Reeves presented repetitive and unpleasant images—and helped boost sales of Anacin dramatically.

summed up in the idea of the "unique selling proposition" (USP). Reeves often brought in scientific evidence to demonstrate a point of difference. His commercials featured actors dressed in white coats and portraying doctors to amplify the evidence, or they discussed a special ingredient that only his product had. Here are some memorable ways in which Reeves employed the USP approach:

Wonder Bread helps build strong bodies in eight ways.

M&M's melt in your mouth, not in your hands.

Certs breath mints with a magic drop of retsyn.

Colgate cleans your breath while it cleans your teeth.

How do you spell relief? R-O-L-A-I-D-S.

Only Viceroy gives you 20,000 filter traps in every filter.

For Anacin, Reeves portrayed three boxes in the head of a headache sufferer; one contained a pounding sledgehammer, one a coiled spring, and one a jagged thunderbolt. But all three types of headache pain were relieved by little "Anacin" bubbles flowing up through the body from the stomach (Figure 6.11). The slogan read: "Anacin, the pain reliever that doctors recommend most." The ad was unpleasant, repetitive, and intrusive—and it helped boost sales dramatically.

According to Reeves' straightforward, hard-sell formula, an ad contained nothing—not even sex—that would distract people from the message. The key to maintaining focus became repetition. For instance, an ad for Fleischmann's margarine mentioned the USP "corn oil margarine" seven times. Reeves specialized in packaged goods and brought the Bates agency from $16 million in billings in 1945 to $130 million in 1960.

However, the ad industry had concerns about this "pseudoscientific" approach. Advertising's self-regulated National Association of Broadcasters' television code forbade TV commercials with men in white coats posing as doctors. Although the organization did not have the authority to enforce such regulations, the federal government did. The Federal Trade Commission issued many orders to agencies to drop certain claims and campaigns. Among these the Bates agency, Reeves' employer, received the most complaints and was forced to drop pitches for Carter's Little Liver Pills, Colgate Dental Cream, Blue Bonnet margarine, and Rapid Shave shaving cream.

Reeves also pioneered the use of the new medium of television as a force in American political campaigns. He sold a presidential candidate the same way he promoted toothpaste. In 1952, for example, the adman projected Republican presidential candidate Dwight Eisenhower's military experience in a series of newsreel-type commercials. The strategy was to spend about $2 million in the last three weeks of the campaign. At the time the American public was worried about U.S. military involvement in Korea. With this concern in mind, Reeves created this USP: "Eisenhower, man of peace." The spots opened with an announcer declaring, "Eisenhower answers the nation!" Ordinary citizens then asked Eisenhower questions, to which he responded not with typical detailed speeches, but with a 15-second statement. The competition was never mentioned at all.

Leo Burnett—"Inherent Drama"

In 1935 copywriter Leo Burnett opened his creative shop, Leo Burnett Co., in Chicago and set out to create better ads. Like Reeves, Burnett anchored his pitch on the product itself. Instead of resorting to the typical Depression-era devices of contests, premiums, sex, and gimmicks, Burnett focused on the product and sparked interest with good artwork, information, recipes, and humor.

Rather than relying on trickery or slick techniques, Burnett insisted on stressing the "inherent drama"—a particular way of looking at a product that could be found only in the product itself. His task, he argued, was identifying "the thing about that product that keeps it in the marketplace . . . capturing that, and then taking that thing—whatever it is—and making the thing itself arresting."[23] The best examples of Burnett's application of inherent drama are found in the food categories. One classic ad showed a multilayered Pillsbury cake with a slice cut out of it (Figure 6.12). The original ads for Green Giant peas contained the headline "Harvested in the moonlight" instead of

Got the notion? Why don't _you_ bake one of these terrific cakes?

Just add milk. You do it in minutes. You get something momentous.

Milk is all you add

No eggs, flavoring or extras of any kind required. These are complete mixes.

Pillsbury Cake Mixes

WHITE · CHOCOLATE FUDGE · GOLDEN YELLOW

Figure 6.12   In this 1950 ad Leo Burnett focused on the "inherent drama" of an appealing multi-layered cake made with a quick mix.

"Packed fresh." For the Meat Institute, Burnett photographed red, raw meat against a vivid red background.

Yet Burnett differentiated his approach from Reeves' scientific angle with his ability to empathize with the mass audience. Burnett often used a host of continuing characters called "critters," as well as jingles, in both print and television ads. For inspiration Burnett often drew on American history and folklore to create universal archetypes and symbols that helped "humanize" the product. For example, his Jolly Green Giant was in the Paul Bunyan mold. Other likable, animated characters created by Burnett included Tony the Tiger for Kellogg's Frosted Flakes and the elfish Snap! Crackle! and Pop! for Kellogg's Rice Krispies.

The Marlboro Man, however, became Burnett's most famous success. Traditionally the market for filter-tip cigarettes had been females. In the 1920s Marlboros had come in a white package and had featured a red paper "beauty tip" to conceal lipstick traces. Burnett's challenge was how to promote Marlboros as a brand a man would smoke. His first move was to redesign the package as a flip-top box with a bold red-and-white pattern. His first ad, which appeared in 1955, introduced a character who was to become a cultural icon—the Marlboro Man. Other ads featured a wide variety of rugged outdoorsmen—skin divers, football players, boxers, canoeists, and race car drivers—to suggest toughness and virility. These characters also had a tattoo on their hand or wrist to suggest an interesting past. But the campaign touting the most masculine cigarette on the market eventually returned to the familiar cowboy, the Marlboro Man, riding horseback, rounding up cattle, or relaxing beside the campfire. This archetypal figure, drawn from American history, hit a subconscious nerve in the public mind. Cowboys symbolized the most masculine type of man, and Burnett's ads evoked memorable imagery of real men in a man's world. The campaign became one of the all-time greats in advertising history.

David Ogilvy—Image and Science

When David Ogilvy set up shop on Madison Avenue in 1949 (later Ogilvy & Mather), he stood out as a maverick in a relatively dull industry. "I am an advertising classicist," Ogilvy said. "I believe that advertising has had its great period to which I want to return it."[24] A researcher turned writer, Ogilvy looked to Claude Hopkins' scientific claim school and Raymond Rubicam's image tradition for inspiration. From them Ogilvy learned that people might buy a product not for the product itself, but because they associate it with a particular image. "Try to give each advertiser a becoming style," explained Ogilvy about brand image. "To create the right individuality is a supreme accomplishment."[25]

Ogilvy honed his style on high-priced, high-status products. One of his most famous ads was for the Rolls-Royce; it headlined: "At 60 miles an hour the loudest noise in this new Rolls-Royce comes from the electric clock." The luxury car was shown in an elite setting with high-status people to further enhance its prestige (Figure 6.13). The ad followed the Ogilvy formula: a handsome picture, a long

The Rolls-Royce Silver Cloud—$13,995

"At 60 miles an hour the loudest noise in this new Rolls-Royce comes from the electric clock"

What makes Rolls-Royce the best car in the world? "There is really no magic about it— it is merely patient attention to detail," says an eminent Rolls-Royce engineer.

1. "At 60 miles an hour the loudest noise comes from the electric clock," reports the Technical Editor of THE MOTOR. Three mufflers tune out sound frequencies—acoustically.

2. Every Rolls-Royce engine is run for seven hours at full throttle before installation, and each car is test-driven for hundreds of miles over varying road surfaces.

3. The Rolls-Royce is designed as an owner-driven car. It is eighteen inches shorter than the largest domestic cars.

4. The car has power steering, power brakes and automatic gear-shift. It is very easy to drive and to park. No chauffeur required.

5. The finished car spends a week in the final test-shop, being fine-tuned. Here it is subjected to 98 separate ordeals. For example, the engineers use a stethoscope to listen for axle-whine.

6. The Rolls-Royce is guaranteed for three years. With a new network of dealers and parts-depots from Coast to Coast, service is no problem.

7. The Rolls-Royce radiator has never changed, except that when Sir Henry Royce died in 1933 the monogram RR was changed from red to black.

8. The coachwork is given five coats of primer paint, and hand rubbed between each coat, before *nine* coats of finishing paint go on.

9. By moving a switch on the steering column, you can adjust the shock-absorbers to suit road conditions.

10. A picnic table, veneered in French walnut, slides out from under the dash. Two more swing out behind the front seats.

11. You can get such optional extras as an Espresso coffee-making machine, a dictating machine, a bed, hot and cold water for washing, an electric razor or a telephone.

12. There are three separate systems of power brakes, two hydraulic and one mechanical. Damage to one will not affect the others. The Rolls-Royce is a very safe car—and also a very lively car. It cruises serenely at eighty-five. Top speed is in excess of 100 m.p.h.

13. The Bentley is made by Rolls-Royce. Except for the radiators, they are identical motor cars, manufactured by the same engineers in the same works. People who feel diffident about driving a Rolls-Royce can buy a Bentley.

PRICE. The Rolls-Royce illustrated in this advertisement—f.o.b. principal ports of entry—costs $13,995.

If you would like the rewarding experience of driving a Rolls-Royce or Bentley, write or telephone to one of the dealers listed on opposite page. Rolls-Royce Inc., 10 Rockefeller Plaza, New York 20, N. Y. Circle 5-1144.

Figure 6.13 In this 1958 ad David Ogilvy combined a handsome picture, an arresting headline, and straightforward copy to sell not a product, but an image.

headline, and straightforward, low-key copy. The visual and the copy contributed to the overall image of the brand. There was nothing amusing about an Ogilvy image ad.

Ogilvy also devised unique hooks to capture people's attention, and then he repeated these themes to link his campaigns together.

Figure 6.14   In this 1950s ad David Ogilvy used the unique look of the bearded salesman to introduce Schweppes tonic water to America.

One example was the bearded salesman from Schweppes, Commander Whitehead (Figure 6.14). But Ogilvy's biggest success depended on a smaller device. In 1951 the adman took on the account of an obscure line of shirts for Hathaway clothing. His approach differed from the traditional claim copy style in vogue at the time. In the campaign the model in the Hathaway shirt had a black patch over one eye and appeared in a series of situations from painting to playing the oboe. Nothing was wrong with the stylish model's eye; Ogilvy added the patch simply to give the man "story appeal." The advertisements ran only in *The New Yorker* magazine over the next four years, thus gaining additional prestige by association with an upscale periodical. In no time readers nationwide eagerly followed the dashing Hathaway man to see what he was doing from month to month. Sales for Hathaway shirts soared. Customers did not buy a shirt; they bought an image.

Figure 6.15   This 1951 ad by graphic designer Paul Rand reflected the influence of avant-garde European graphic designers.

Bill Bernbach—The "New" Advertising

The innovative approach of Bill Bernbach and his New York–based agency Doyle Dane Bernbach (DDB) represented another leading force in advertising. Bernbach's fresh style had its roots in his successful ads for second-rank retailers, services, and automobiles; he cleverly turned this second-rank status into an advantage. Bernbach implemented this contradictory approach within a very distinct format—clean and direct, yet often with a touch of humor.

Perhaps more than any other designer, the American Paul Rand influenced Bernbach's theories of visual communication. Inspired by modern European graphic design, Rand used collage techniques, universal symbols, dynamic composition, and modern typography (Figure

Figure 6.16 In this 1950s ad Bill Bernbach imaginatively remade the retailer's image as a cheap dress store into a shop that featured high quality at low prices.

6.15). As an art director at the Weintraub advertising agency in the early 1940s, Rand worked closely with Bernbach to create campaigns that integrated images and ideas, notably for Ohrbach's department store, Dubonnet, and Airwick. The ads for Ohrbach's featured puns and wordplay reinforced by a whimsical fusion of photos, illustrations, and logotype. This collaboration provided the prototype for the "creative teams" that Bernbach would later nurture at his own agency.

In 1949 Ned Doyle, Maxwell Dane, and Bernbach opened their Doyle Dane Bernbach agency in New York. Doyle was the account

GRANDMA MOSES PHOTOGRAPHED WITH A NEW POLAROID LAND FILM.

Figure 6.17   In this 1950s ad Bill Bernbach integrated attention-getting images and limited copy to suggest instant photography.

executive, Dane handled administration and finance, and copywriter Bernbach managed the creative area. His initial staff consisted of art director Bob Gage and copywriter Phyllis Robinson.

DDB's first client was Ohrbach's department store, an account Bernbach had worked on at the Weintraub agency. They needed a strategy to turn around the retailer's image as a low-priced dress shop. It was here that Bernbach made his major contribution. At most agencies copy preceded art. In contrast, with the Bernbach approach the artist and writer worked together as a team to produce the ads. "Two people who respect each other sit in the same room for a length

Starting
Dec. 23
the
Atlantic
Ocean
will be
20%
smaller.

for the inauguration of the first jet prop service across the Atlantic, introducing the Bristol Britannia, starting Dec. 23.

EL AL
ISRAEL AIRLINES

Figure 6.18 In this 1958 ad for El Al airline's trans-Atlantic flights, Bill Bernbach stopped readers cold with an image of a stormy sea.

of time and arrive at a state of free association," explained art director Bob Gage, "where the mention of one idea will lead to another idea will lead to another idea, and then to another."[26] With this collaborative approach, the art and copy became fused together as the artist suggested a headline and the copywriter an image.

In order to create a new image, Bernbach imaginatively packaged the message in an exciting new way. One of the series showed a man carrying his wife under his arm; the headline read: "Liberal Trade-In: bring in your wife and just a few dollars . . . we will give you a new woman." Perhaps the most famous was a 1958 ad headlined "I found out about Joan." The "catty lady" revealed how her friend Joan dressed so well—by buying high fashion at low prices at Ohrbach's (Figure 6.16). This success led to others. Bernbach's campaign for the new Polaroid instant camera cut out the step-by-step details to suggest instant photography (Figure 6.17). His ads for El Al airline's trans-Atlantic flights stopped readers cold with arresting images and succinct copy (Figure 6.18). Bold graphic images with strong lines characterized these classic campaigns. But it would be Bernbach's subsequent breakthrough work on a major national account for Volkswagen, a small German car, that would emerge as the agency's hallmark campaign.

The creative work of Leo Burnett, David Ogilvy, and particularly Bill Bernbach in the 1950s planted the seeds for a creative revolution in advertising that would flourish in the turbulent 1960s. In that decade advertisers realized that they were facing a very different buying public, and agencies recognized that they would have to change as well. In the process admakers broke with past conventions as they searched for new ways to communicate with a younger, more skeptical audience. In the next chapter we will examine the forces that shaped this exciting new advertising.

Part IV

Contemporary American Advertising

Think small.

Our little car isn't so much of a novelty any more.

A couple of dozen college kids don't try to squeeze inside it.

The guy at the gas station doesn't ask where the gas goes.

Nobody even stares at our shape.

In fact, some people who drive our little flivver don't even think 32 miles to the gallon is going any great guns.

Or using five pints of oil instead of five quarts.

Or never needing anti-freeze.

Or racking up 40,000 miles on a set of tires.

That's because once you get used to some of our economies, you don't even think about them any more.

Except when you squeeze into a small parking spot. Or renew your small insurance. Or pay a small repair bill. Or trade in your old VW for a new one.

Think it over.

1960

The Cuban missile crisis has the world on the brink of war for six days.
1962

John F. Kennedy's image outshines Richard Nixon's in the nation's first series of televised presidential debates.
1960

American troops are ordered into Vietnam.
1965

NBC drops its ban on comparative ads.

The Civil Rights Act becomes law.
1964

1963
Civil rights supporters march on Washington.

Feminist Betty Friedan publishes *The Feminine Mystique.*

President John F. Kennedy is assassinated, and Vice President Lyndon Johnson takes office.

1966
Mary Wells starts the first major ad agency headed by a woman, Wells, Rich & Greene (WRG).

1967
The media declares San Francisco's Haight-Ashbury district a "Hippie Haven," and thousands flock there for a "Summer of Love."

Chapter 7

1960–1975 The Creative Revolution

Cigarettes ads are banned from television.
1971

Neil Armstrong takes "one giant step for mankind" on the moon.
1969

U.S. involvement in the Vietnam War reaches its peak. Senator Robert Kennedy and Martin Luther King are assassinated.
1968

The Vietnam War ends.
1975

President Richard Nixon resigns, and Vice President Gerald Ford takes office.
1974

The Arab oil embargo causes shortages of gasoline and heating oil and plunges the economy into a recession.
1973

1972
After threats of lawsuits by the FTC, both ABC and CBS drop their ban on comparative advertising, and two years later, the advertising trade group AAAA follows suit.

Congress approves the Equal Rights Amendment and sends it to the states for ratification.

1975

Politics, culture, and technology helped shape advertising in the 1960s. Advertising faced a different audience than it had known in the previous thirty years. Americans were younger, better educated, and more mobile, and new technology accelerated the pace of their lives. They also represented a new kind of consumer, one in search of novelty and opportunities for individual expression. Even as advertisers were trying to connect with this new audience, the industry was undergoing a creative revolution. The results were new ways of doing business, a revitalized creative approach, and an emerging social consciousness.

America seemed poised on the verge of a "New Frontier" as the decade opened. The youthful president John F. Kennedy symbolized the exuberance of a prosperous, forward-looking nation convinced that anything was possible. Kennedy's platform called for an end to racial and social injustice, and idealistic young Americans responded by joining the Peace Corps and supporting the civil rights movement. Another important part of the president's vision was fulfilled when American astronauts set foot on the moon in 1969.

Meanwhile, a wave of new products and services gave evidence of the nation's overall affluence. Inexpensive chain restaurants like McDonald's, Burger King, and Kentucky Fried Chicken (later KFC) lured millions of customers. Prices of cameras, consumer electronics, and appliances dropped. Nearly every home had at least one radio and one television set. Many households also had "automatic servants" like garbage disposals, dishwashers, vacuum cleaners, and freezers, as well as luxury items like color TVs, campers and sports cars, and swimming pools.

Yet under the surface trouble was brewing. Despite the nation's prosperity the unemployment rate soared, in part due to workers who lost their jobs to newly automated manufacturing methods. The problem of poverty also persisted. On the international front Cold War tensions remained high, the threat of nuclear war loomed, and the conflict in Vietnam escalated. President Kennedy's assassination in 1963 seemed to mark the end of an "age of innocence." In the following years, sparked by civil rights activists, antiwar protesters, and feminists, profound social changes took place.

The Times They Are A-Changin'

Propelled into the presidency by Kennedy's assassination, Lyndon Johnson advanced Kennedy's dreams for a new generation. The Johnson administration enacted sweeping reforms that covered almost every phase of American life. Fueled by the ambitious goal of wiping out poverty and establishing a "Great Society," Johnson pushed through the Civil Rights Act, accelerated medical research, educated disadvantaged children, established Medicare for the elderly, and created many antipoverty programs.

Expressions of discontent with government's failure to relieve racial and social injustice had first became noticeable at the end of World War II. But during the early 1960s and 1970s, as the Vietnam War dragged on, millions of Americans banded together to make their voices heard on a variety of issues. In the process they would dramatically alter the social, political, and economic outlook for the nation, as well as reform advertising.

Power to the People

The first of many challenges to the established social order centered on the issues of civil liberties and academic freedom. The civil rights movement forced the nation to confront the continued oppression of African Americans, and marches, sit-ins, freedom rides, and registration at all-white schools became common events. Peaceful demonstrations, however, often met with violent retaliation from the white power structure.

The civil rights movement, led by Martin Luther King, had adopted a nonviolent protest technique, the "sit-in," to combat discrimination throughout the South. In 1960 African Americans who took seats at a segregated lunch counter were refused service; they responded by saying they would remain at the counter until served. Within a year, after sit-ins in more than a hundred cities, restaurants were desegregated, and African Americans and whites ate side by side.

The next major challenge was to integrate interstate bus terminals. "Freedom riders" traveling through the South on integrated buses deliberately disregarded signs that designated separate seating for whites and blacks to test southern compliance with recently enacted antisegregation regulations. As civil rights activists vigorously demanded further extensions of civil rights, the "dominoes" of racial discrimination began to tumble. Traditionally white southern universities integrated. Local officials and businessmen agreed to desegregate public facilities and to hire African Americans. And the Civil Rights Act, enacted in 1964, barred discrimination against minorities in employment and places of public accommodation, protected voting rights, and furthered advances in school integregation.

The renewed struggle for civil rights seemed to have a ripple effect. The movement was proof that other groups, including students, intellectuals, and African Americans, could organize to change society. An emerging counterculture challenged "the establishment"—the government, powerful businesses, and conventional hierarchies of authority—as domestic conflicts intensified and more and more American soldiers were dispatched to a seemingly futile war in Vietnam. Young people, not surprisingly, gave enormous spirit and energy to the social movements. In the early 1960s the postwar baby boom generation came of age, and nearly half of America's population was under age 25. As these baby boomers swarmed into the nation's institutions of higher learning, enrollment in many schools more than doubled over the decade.

The first major student demonstration took place at the University of California, Berkeley, campus in 1964. Students spanning the political spectrum from left to right challenged the university's ban on their right to make speeches, set up tables, and hand out leaflets on campus property. Within a few years campuses nationwide had become hotbeds of protest and demonstration. Students called for action on everything from curfews, dress, and cafeteria food to admissions practices and academic programs. But nothing galvanized young Americans more than the Vietnam War. The massive antiwar movement created battle lines between the generations and put tremendous pressure on government to bring American troops home.

By 1965 the nation had entered a seemingly unending period of national turbulence. Martin Luther King invoked the battle cry of the civil rights movement to muster support for registration of African American voters, declaring "We shall overcome." Days after the Voting Rights Act became law, pent-up frustrations with racial oppression, unemployment, inadequate housing, and poverty boiled over, as riots erupted in cities nationwide.

Many militant inner-city African Americans rejected King's non-violent tactics for more radical alternatives. The powerful Black Muslim leader Malcolm X led the separatist movement, and prominent African American leaders sought to establish a distinct identity for African Americans, apart from white America. Black nationalists advocated that African Americans found their own schools and businesses and, ultimately, their own nation. They also proposed alternatives to the term "Negro," including "black," "Afro-American," and simply "African." African Americans also reexamined their heritage and searched for a connection to their African past. Rejecting white standards of beauty, African Americans began to style their hair in Afros or braids, and many wore African jewelry, headgear, and other native garments (Figure 7.1). "Black is beautiful" became a common theme, as did "Be Black. Buy Black."

After assassins gunned down Malcolm X in 1965, the nonviolent civil rights movement became more militant. An extremist group called the Black Panthers armed themselves and provided African American communities with "protection" from the police. African Americans now demanded not just equality, but also economic and social justice. Thousands participated in the People's March on Washington, D.C., to call poverty to the attention of the American people.

Figure 7.1   This 1960s ad reflected the rejection by African Americans of white standards of beauty and the promotion of the "Black is beautiful" theme.

Other militants demanded African-American dormitories, courses, and even departments staffed solely by African American instructors.

When an assassin's bullet felled Martin Luther King in 1968, the hope for nonviolence as a means to social change seemed all but lost. Throughout 1968 protesters clashed with police, government, and college officials over the Vietnam War, the draft, and other issues. The Democratic National Convention in Chicago broke down in pandemonium as police battered thousands of antiwar protesters. Women, too, raised their voices to protest the injustices that they suffered due to

A Taste of the Times

As the 1960s began, the postwar emphasis on material acquisitions continued. A design elite still dictated style, and "keeping up with the Joneses" remained the order of the day. The new president's demure young wife, Jacqueline Kennedy, became the role model for style-conscious women with her Parisian couture, bouffant hairdos, and pillbox hats.

When the baby boomers came of age, however, a youth culture quickly took over and challenged social conventions. Teens embarked on their own pursuit of pleasure, surfing, skateboarding, cruising, and dancing the night away. Teen idols Frankie Avalon and Annette Funicello starred in movies like *Beach Blanket Bingo,* which glamorized a carefree lifestyle, deep suntans, and most important, a cool attitude. The clean-cut Beach Boys popularized the California scene in dozens of recordings, as they sang, "Everybody's gone surfin', surfin' U.S.A."

With a phonograph and a collection of 45s, teens turned the family recreation room into a dance floor. Everyone wanted to learn the newest dance craze. For instance, after singer Chubby Checker did a new dance—with no hands—on "American Bandstand," the twist became the rage. One psychologist concluded that this development represented nothing more than a return to the African ceremonial dances and would disappear in no time. But when the over-thirty crowd twisted, it was time for teens to take up something new. Overnight teens began dancing the mashed potato and then the frug, watusi, and swim. Skateboards, super balls, and frisbees were also in. Little girls adored Barbie, while young boys idolized the caped crusader Batman, masked Zorro, and suave James Bond.

By the mid-1960s the spirit of rebellion had swept over music, art, and apparel. It began in London boutiques along Carnaby Street, where a new generation of imaginative designers from working-class backgrounds reinvented the art of dressing. They searched for new styles and borrowed from every imaginable source, ranging from contemporary art to revivals of historic styles.

The "British invasion" imported these avant-garde looks to America in 1964. From England the mop-haired Beatles and the renegade Rolling Stones brought the mod style, or Carnaby Street look, which featured high boots, hip-hugging slacks, floral prints, wide belts, and fitted double-breasted sports coats. Meanwhile, hemlines rose high and higher. Across the country principals and college deans banned such "distracting" influences as long hair on boys and knees showing on girls—but to little avail. In subsequent years the clothes would get skimpier and the hair would grow longer; sideburns, beards, and mustaches would also become popular.

At the same time, American designers borrowed their motifs from the world of popular culture. They made outfits of paper, plastic, consumer packaging, metal, vinyl, and other industrial materials. The nation's obsession with space exploration also fostered futuristic fashions. The trendsetting designer André Courreges created space-age silver foil suits complete with visors, knee-baring skirts, and white ankle boots. And men's clothes were as outrageous as women's. The traditional muted tailored shirt burst into flashy colors, and jackets were made out of suede and velvet. The turtleneck showed up as formal wear, and designer Pierre Cardin introduced the upright-collared Nehru shirts and jackets. Rules were to be broken, and people discarded constraints of every kind, from neckties to bras, slips, and girdles. By the end of the decade, anything could be deemed fashionable.

Television, too, brought an array of far-fetched spectacles. "The Beverly Hillbillies" were unlikely hick millionaires settling in Beverly Hills, while "Green Acres" featured rich city folks transplanted to the farm. Witches, ghouls, genies, extraterrestials, and talking animals crowded the airwaves. A variety of heroes—from physicians and lawyers to espionage teams to the Caped Crusader—captivated viewers. At the same time, Hollywood introduced a vivid assortment of antiheroes that challenged the audience's preconceptions. Dustin Hoffman rejected the career track in *The Graduate*. Peter Fonda, Dennis Hopper, and Jack Nicholson searched for America on motorcycles in *Easy Rider*. And Warren Beatty and Faye Dunaway glamorized bank robbery in the Depression-era *Bonnie and Clyde*.

The decade also generated writers who delved into the lives of radicals and African Americans, as well as pop artists who created playful tributes to mass culture. The mordant humor was typified by Joseph Heller's *Catch-22* (1961), while the new African American militancy was reflected in Eldridge Cleaver's classic *Soul on Ice* (1964). Other books energetically combined reportage and fiction, including Truman Capote's *In Cold Blood* (1966), Norman Mailer's *The Armies of the Night* (1966), and Tom Wolfe's *The Electric Kool-Aid Acid Test* (1967).

Pop artists, too, rejected 1950s action painting and abstract expressionism. Instead, they looked to popular culture for new ideas, creating easily identified images based on everyday consumer items, ads, and comic books. For example, Andy Warhol painted Campbell soup cans and Brillo soap pad boxes. Jasper Johns created "Painted Bronze," depicting two beer cans. Roy Lichtenstein painted individual panels of action-packed comic strips on huge canvases. And "op" artist Bridget Riley delighted observers by painting optical illusions of an abstract nature. Such new art enticed the buying public, and art became big business.

their gender. At the annual Miss America contest in Atlantic City, feminists crowned a sheep and tossed bras, false eyelashes, and steno pads into "freedom trashcans" in the name of women's liberation.

Other previously neglected groups began to make similar demands for equal rights. Militant young Mexican Americans, or "Chicanos," demanded more educational opportunities and increased attention to their economic and social needs. Cesar Chavez fought for the rights of migrant farm workers. Native Americans also demanded equal rights and challenged policies concerning tribal land ownership and cultural life. And another minority fought back in 1969, when New York City police raided the Stonewall Inn, a Greenwich Village bar catering to homosexuals. Instead of peacefully submitting, the patrons chose to fight back. Thus began the gay rights movement, which sought to overturn generations of discrimination and abuse. Finally the nation's fastest-growing minority began to make themselves heard as senior citizens banded together to form the Gray Panthers.

A Nation Divided

When President Richard Nixon took office in 1968, he faced a badly divided nation. In his victory speech Nixon declared that the objective of the new administration was "to bring America together." But the escalating war in Vietnam served only to fuel the fire of the antiwar movement. Yet another shock staggered the nation when National Guardsmen gunned down students at both Kent State University in Ohio and Jackson State University in Mississippi. Student strikes disrupted or shut down colleges and universities across the nation. Protesters descended on Washington, D.C. Bombs demolished banks, computer facilities, ROTC centers, and other "establishment" buildings. The Vietnam War had come home to America.

By the end of 1969 the economy had slipped into a recession, the unemployment rate was rising, and inflation ran high. Yet more shocks followed. In Washington, D.C., the "Watergate" scandal began as a small news item; a security guard caught five men breaking into the Democratic National Committee headquarters in the Watergate complex to bug the phones and look for documents. Ultimately, after a two-year investigation of the break-in and subsequent cover-up involving FBI, CIA, and White House officials, the Nixon administration was in shambles. Although Nixon denied knowledge of any illegal activities, he faced almost certain impeachment and so resigned in 1974, the first American president in history to do so.

In the following year the Vietnam War came to an end when Saigon, South Vietnam's capital, fell to the North Vietnamese. But the ordeal had eroded national confidence and would haunt American society for years. Over 50,000 Americans had been killed in the war and hundreds of thousands more wounded. While direct war costs alone topped $137 billion, indirect costs may have been three to four times that amount.[1] These expenditures contributed greatly to the creation

New Brand Names

1960 Domino's Pizza delivers hot, fresh pies in Ann Arbor, Michigan.

1960 Etch A Sketch magnetic screen makes artists out of children and adults.

1962 Royal Crown Diet Cola is the first nationally marketed low-calorie soft drink, quickly followed by Coca-Cola's Tab and Pepsi's Patio Cola.

1963 The Corvette Sting Ray is one of the hottest cars on the road.

1963 Weight Watchers is founded by Jean Nidetch to help people take off pounds sensibly.

1964 Gatorade sports drink first appears on the sidelines at University of Florida Gators' football games.

1964 The Ford Mustang is introduced as a sporty, stylish car priced at just $2,368.

1968 The Big Mac appears on McDonald's fast food menu, featuring "two all-beef patties special sauce lettuce cheese pickles onions on a sesame seed bun."

1972 Nike launches an athletic shoe business.

1972 Celestial Seasonings steeps America with whimsical herb teas like Red Zinger, which comes in bright, psychedelic packages covered with proverbs.

1974 Yellow Post-It notes show up on documents, desks, and walls.

of large deficits in the federal budget and to the growth of inflation. Inflation had averaged only about one percent a year in the early 1960s, but during the 1970s annual inflation rates reached double digits, and unemployment rarely dropped below 7 percent. Food costs skyrocketed, and jobs became harder to find. The post–World War II boom had come to an end.[2]

On top of that, the nation faced another shortage of one of its most basic commodities—oil. When OPEC, the oil-producing nations' cartel, raised prices drastically, it precipitated the 1973–74 oil crisis. Home fuel heating bills doubled and even tripled. Panicked motorists began lining up at gas stations; and once at the pumps, they faced soaring prices. To save energy, the government reduced the speed limit from 70 miles per hour to 55. Many commuters carpooled or bicycled to work. Other Americans turned to fuel-efficient foreign cars, pushing the automotive industry into a deeper slump. Although OPEC lifted the oil embargo in 1974, prices remained high.

The inflated energy prices, the lingering costs of Vietnam, and other factors exacted a long-term toll on the economy. Domestic automakers, hit by plunging sales, cut production and laid off workers. These reductions quickly spread to other industries such as rubber, steel, and glass. By 1975 the economy was in its worst slump since the Depression. At the same time, prices continued to spiral upward. The combination of stagnant growth and inflation, or "stagflation," became the norm of the decade.

In such a turbulent social and economic atmosphere, change was inevitable. As women and minority groups became empowered, as social institutions changed, and as sexual and behavioral norms loosened, advertisers recognized that they, too, would have to change. Thus was born the creative revolution.

The Creative Revolution

The phrase "creative revolution" was first coined in 1965, and by the time *Newsweek* magazine featured the trend in its cover story in August 1969, the revolution was complete.[3] For many individuals in the 1960s, social activism provided a sense of purpose and a feeling of community that previously had been missing. The resulting spirit of personal liberation spawned a new generation of artists who used music, fashion, and art to assault conventional values or simply to shock. America had changed so fast that even cutting-edge admakers did not fully grasp the extent to which the nation was transformed. How did this happen?

Several factors accounted for this complete shift in mainstream conventions. Advertisers' audience had dramatically changed when the postwar baby boom generation came of age. Most advertisers began to slant their campaigns toward the nation's teenagers and young adults, because marketers discovered that those individuals controlled great amounts of money. Youthful models replaced elegant middle-aged ones, and to be over age 30 was considered to be "too old." The new national goal was to be youthful, slim, and active.

Another traditional feature of American life also changed. The Puritan ideal, which stressed the importance of hard work and just rewards, had gradually dropped out of favor with youths and given way to pleasure seeking. The widespread availability of birth control also contributed to this new sense of personal freedom. The increased acceptance of sexual license in motion pictures, literature, and dress reflected this trend. When Dr. Alfred Kinsey published his 1948 *Sexual Behavior in the Human Male,* the uproar was volcanic. But William Masters and Virginia Johnson's 1966 *Human Sexual Response,* a far more intimate and revealing study, hardly created a stir.

Still another social transformation involved the communications revolution. With astounding speed new and more potent communications media projected to more homes and in more ways than ever before. The generation gap widened as young people lacking traditional cultural roots became the first consumers raised on television and movies, not books, magazines, and other reading matter. In fact, more than 90 percent of American homes had one or more television sets by the mid-1960s, compared to a mere 10 percent of homes in the early 1950s.

According to art critic Robert Rosenblum, the "unbelievably rapid tempo of information" had an effect on most people. The nation shifted from a "literary culture" toward a more "visual culture." "The fact is that most people have stopped reading, or being involved with any high-minded cultural activity that takes too long a time," explains Rosenblum. "People's attention span in the late 20th century is very, very short . . . people register things very quickly. It's kind of instant gratification."[4] Conventional advertising would have to find new ways to communicate with a young and questioning audience.

Tune In, Turn On, Drop Out

Even as the antiwar and civil rights movements stirred passions among the nation's youths, an opposite trend away from political activism emerged. A new breed of alienated youths called "hippies" formed a counterculture based on the ideals of love and peace and the rejection of materialism. The hippies followed Timothy Leary's advice to "tune in, turn on, drop out"—that is, to take drugs, raise one's spiritual consciousness, and drop out of school, work, and society. Hippies and nonhippies alike experimented with drugs such as marijuana and LSD. In 1966 *Newsweek* described Berkeley, California, as "a turned-on town where marijuana and LSD are plentiful. . . . More than half the student body have probably tried marijuana at least once, and maybe a third have gone back for more. Youth were convinced drug trips were no worse than the alcohol and barbiturates the grown-ups were using."[5] Similar trends were observed in cities and on campuses nationwide. The hippie scene culminated in 1967 with the "Summer of Love" in San Francisco; and in the summer of 1969, some 400,000 music fans flocked to Woodstock to celebrate rock music, sex, and drugs.

With the mind-enhancing drugs came a creative counterculture that also had a considerable influence on youths. "Do your own thing" became the slogan of the day. Youths pieced together outfits from clothing found in secondhand stores, attics, and funky shops. The basic look featured bell-bottoms, tie-dyed shirts, fringed jackets, and Victorian shawls, to which were added love beads, peace symbols, headbands, and lots of flowers. Youths hung out at city parks and staged "love-ins," "be-ins," and "happenings." And as the media asked, "Is God dead?" the Beatles helped popularize Eastern mysticism, and young people explored nontraditional spiritual and religious beliefs. Psychedelic colors, day-glo dance halls, strobe lights, Zen, macrobiotic diets, herbal tea, tarot cards, body painting, folk music—all were "in."

Figure 7.2   This detail from illustrator Peter Max's 1972 "Life is beautiful" antismoking poster captured the vibrant neo–art nouveau style.

Neo–art nouveau became the visual accompaniment to the hippie movement, and intricate, elaborate posters were used to promote pop concerts and records. The vibrant style of Peter Max perfectly expressed this new movement (Figure 7.2). The youth culture also sponsored a range of alternative magazines, including *Oz* and *IT,* that promoted the same visual styles as the posters. A succession of popular styles emerged that incorporated elements from Victorian and Edwardian to art nouveau, exotic Hollywood, and art deco. For example, small Victorian prints decorated furniture, tea cloths, and curtains alongside "pop" and "op" art patterns, while rustic pine furniture and hand-crafted textiles, jewelry, metalwork, ceramics, and glass objects became popular.

The Underground Goes Mainstream

As youthful mod and hippie "street styles" emerged as a strong force, styles were influenced by sources from all over the cultural landscape. Instead of a design elite dictating what "proper" fashion should be, marketing and mass media performed the function of disseminating styles. Color advertisements, magazines, television, and chain stores promoted the latest trends in fashion and lifestyle accessories.

Moreover, by the mid-1970s the marketing of design had become one of the most clearly visible and influential aspects of contemporary mass culture. Even furniture and electronic equipment had strong fashion elements built into them, emphasizing that they were not intended to last forever. Never had fashions changed so rapidly or reached such eccentric extremes. In the absence of traditional fashion rules, people expressed themselves in what they wore. Hot pants, platform shoes, clogs, stretch pants, bell-bottoms, fake furs, miniskirts, calf-length midis, mood rings, and the ultimate 1970s fashion statement, the polyester leisure suit—all added up to a certain outrageous tackiness.

Marketers also promoted stylish "throwaway" furniture for the young mass market. Bright colors and simple forms characterized cardboard and blow-up plastic chairs, and couches were covered with "fun" fur. Playful "pop" imagery derived from comic books, science fiction, and advertising soon covered the surfaces of everything from furniture to textiles, ceramics, clocks, and trays. Popular patterns included flags, bull's-eyes, stripes, and other pop art motifs.

In the 1970s, with the economy in recession, the fun-loving atmosphere of the previous decade faded away. However, many aspects of alternative 1960s life became mainstream attitudes in the 1970s. The rebellious obsessions of youths evolved into a set of styles widely used in advertising graphics, store interiors, and fashion-conscious homes. Unisex hairstyles and dress became the norm. For women the miniskirt, the no-bra bra, and pants became wardrobe staples. Hollywood geared films mainly to younger audiences. This general trend also became visible in the widespread acceptance of other "counterculture" ideas: health foods, macrame, tie-dye textiles, hot tubs, waterbeds, acupuncture, astrology, transcendental meditation, encounter groups, sensitivity training, and nude streakers, to name just a few. And advertisers, ever attuned to the tenor of the times, created new images and crafted their messages in exciting new ways.

Inspiration, Intuition, and Creativity

The old rules and old ways of fantasy-filled advertising no longer seemed appropriate. As the conventional advertising industry faced increasing pressure to communicate in new ways with a young and more skeptical audience, new, more creative agencies appeared, and established agencies began to put more importance on their creative output, many at the insistence of their clients. As a result advertising changed dramatically.

The creative revolution swept aside many conventions. In step with the times, strict adherence to scientific methods gave way to inspiration, intuition, and creativity. Energetic young art directors and copywriters worked together in teams as equals where previously they had worked independently. Agencies began to recruit a new breed of unconventional and nontraditional employees, including Italians, Jews, and Greeks, instead of Eastern establishment types with Ivy League roots and WASP affiliations. Talent now became the only credential that mattered. Blue jeans were in and suits were out. Other long-standing traditions began to fall. For example, Ogilvy & Mather agreed to work for a fee instead of the usual 15 percent commission. Two years later, starting with Papert Koenig Lois (PKL), agencies went public by issuing stock. And DDB's Avis campaign broke the taboo against comparative advertising.

The "New" Advertising

A number of long-established advertising agencies operated successfully at this time, including McCann-Erickson; J. Walter Thompson; Batten, Barton, Durstine, & Osborne (BBDO); and Young & Rubicam. Over the next few years three other agencies joined the select ranks of top-billing agencies: Leo Burnett, Ogilvy & Mather, and Doyle Dane Bernbach (DDB). They did this by recognizing that the most important thing they had to sell was not market research, media analysis, or other support services, but the making of an ad itself.

Traditionally the objective of most ads had been to gain attention and interest, but now the emphasis shifted to the product. This new approach drew inspiration primarily from three people: Leo Burnett, David Ogilvy, and in particular, Bill Bernbach at DDB. Although their creative approaches differed significantly, their focus was identical. Burnett's folksy credibility, Ogilvy's classicism, and Bernbach's humor all reflected the same precept: the product must be the centerpiece of the advertisement.

In one of the most successful campaigns in history, beginning in 1964, Leo Burnett used real cowboys, not models, to urge viewers to "Come to where the flavor is. Come to Marlboro Country." And when the tobacco industry was pressured into dropping broadcast ads in 1971, the theme successfully translated to print. Subsequent Marlboro advertising included mailings, store displays, sponsorships of sports events, billboards, and colorful magazine spots. By 1972 Marlboro was the top-selling brand internationally, and three years later it overtook Winston for first place in the United States, a position it still holds.[6]

Burnett also accumulated a growing menagerie of cartoon critters and continuing characters. Poppin' Fresh, the bashful Pillsbury

Memorable Slogans

Beanz meanz Heinz.

It's finger-lickin' good. (Kentucky Fried Chicken)

Put a tiger in your tank. (Esso)

Someone, somewhere, wants a letter from you.
(U.S. Postal Service)

Don't ask a man to drink and drive. (public service campaign)

Things go better with Coke.

Try it—you'll like it. (Alka-Seltzer)

I can't believe I ate the whole thing. (Alka-Seltzer)

We try harder. (Avis rental cars)

Come to where the flavor is. Come to Marlboro Country.
(Marlboro cigarettes)

You've come a long way, baby! (Virginia Slims cigarettes)

We make it simple. (Honda automobiles)

From Protest Campaigns

Ban the bomb.

Black is beautiful.

Make love, not war.

Power to the people.

™ The Pillsbury Doughboy.

Doughboy, sold Pillsbury refrigerated dough. Charlie the Tuna, the beatnik fish, tried to show Starkist he had good taste but was informed: "Sorry Charlie. Starkist doesn't want tuna with good taste. It wants tuna that tastes good." Finicky Morris the Cat approved of little other than Nine Lives' cat food. All the while, the lonely Maytag Repairman waited patiently, and sometimes not so patiently, for customers to call and request repairs for their Maytag washing machines.

The Shell Oil account, a book, and a merger pushed David Ogilvy to prominence. The Shell campaign did not make wild claims, but rather provided a dignified explanation of what was being sold. With no visual gimmicks to distract the reader, one dense newspaper ad started: "Shell recommends 21 ways to make your car last longer."

Ogilvy also published his theories of advertising in the best-sellers *Confessions of an Advertising Man* (1962) and *Ogilvy on Advertising* (1983). The tell-all book covered topics ranging from managing an agency to writing effective copy. Two years later, Ogilivy's agency merged with Mather & Crowther to form Ogilvy & Mather, whose combined billings made the new organization one of the world's top ten agencies.

Although Ogilvy's work proved among the most original in the 1950s, most creative types in the 1960s sought to emulate Bill Bernbach's fresh approach. Among the DDB agency's award-winning campaigns, many considered the Volkswagen (VW) campaign to be not only the best of the decade but among the best of all time. The account arrived at DDB in 1959, a time when America was still infatuated with tailfin styling. The admakers took an offbeat approach to turn the VW's apparent shortcomings into well-crafted virtues. The style and candor transformed the utilitarian, low-power "bug" into a unique, high-quality product with a sensible price tag (only "$1.02 per pound," or about $1595). Due to the work of copywriter Julian Koenig and art director Helmut Krone, the VW ads seemed as unusual as the car. The most famous ad in the series, "Think Small," featured a tiny image of the car with oceans of white space and austere sans serif type (Figure 7.3). Another brilliantly written ad gave straightforward facts. The headline simply said, "Lemon," while the text stated, "This Volkswagen missed the boat. The chrome strip on the glove compartment is blemished and must be replaced. . . . We pluck the lemons, you get the plums" (Figure 7.4).

The hundreds of print ads and television commercials that sold the bug to America reflected the work of many other creative teams. Each ad focused on the selling of a single advantage, featured a simple picture, and included terse, straightforward copy explaining why consumers should buy the car. Moreover, the ads all left the reader smiling. One ad explained the tough decision the Hinsleys of Dora, Missouri, had to make: "To buy a new mule. Or invest in a used bug. . . . When a mule breaks down, there's only one thing to do: Shoot it." But a VW dealer was nearby, if and when their bug broke down. Another ad compared the unique shape of the VW to an egg: "Some shapes are hard to improve on." The copy went on to explain: "Ask any hen. You just can't design a more functional shape for an egg. And we figure the same is true of the Volkswagen. Don't think we haven't tried. (As a matter of fact, the VW's been changed nearly 3,000 times.)." Yet another ad showed a lunar landing vehicle instead of the car and had but one line of copy: "It's ugly, but it gets you there."

Avis, a car rental company, also shifted its account to DDB in 1962. At the time Avis found itself falling further behind Hertz, the industry leader. The maverick agency proposed a new campaign that shifted Avis into high gear. At the time, nobody had ever seen advertising like this. Imagine a company admitting that it ranked only second in its in-

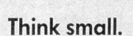

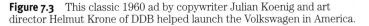

Figure 7.3   This classic 1960 ad by copywriter Julian Koenig and art director Helmut Krone of DDB helped launch the Volkswagen in America.

dustry. Furthermore, the scrappy ads broke the taboo against comparative advertising (Figure 7.5). The first candid ad opened with "Avis is only No. 2 in rent a cars. So why go with us?" The answer: "We try harder. . . . We just can't afford dirty ashtrays. Or half-empty gas tanks.

Lemon.

This Volkswagen missed the boat.

The chrome strip on the glove compartment is blemished and must be replaced. Chances are you wouldn't have noticed it, Inspector Kurt Kroner did.

There are 3,389 men at our Wolfsburg factory with only one job: to inspect Volkswagens at each stage of production. (3000 Volkswagens are produced daily; there are more inspectors than cars.)

Every shock absorber is tested (spot checking won't do), every windshield is scanned. VWs have been rejected for surface scratches barely visible to the eye.

Final inspection is really something! VW inspectors run each car off the line onto the Funktionsprüfstand (car test stand), tote up 189 check points, gun ahead to the automatic brake stand, and say "no" to one VW out of fifty.

This preoccupation with detail means the VW lasts longer and requires less maintenance, by and large, than other cars. (It also means a used VW depreciates less than any other car.)

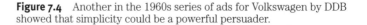

We pluck the lemons; you get the plums.

Figure 7.4 Another in the 1960s series of ads for Volkswagen by DDB showed that simplicity could be a powerful persuader.

Or worn wipers. Or unwashed cars. Or low tires. Or anything less than seat-adjusters that adjust. Heaters that heat. Defrosters that defrost." And try harder they did. The campaign hammered home the scrappy spirit theme over and over with lines like these: "When you're only No. 2 you try harder. Or else . . . we'd be swallowed up"; "Avis can't afford

Avis is only No.2 in rent a cars. So why go with us?

We try harder.

(When you're not the biggest, you have to.)

We just can't afford dirty ashtrays. Or half-empty gas tanks. Or worn wipers. Or unwashed cars. Or low tires. Or anything less than seat-adjusters that adjust. Heaters that heat. Defrosters that defrost.

Obviously, the thing we try hardest for is just to be nice. To start you out right with a new car, like a lively, super-torque Ford, and a pleasant smile. To know, say, where you get a good pastrami sandwich in Duluth. Why?

Because we can't afford to take you for granted.

Go with us next time.

The line at our counter is shorter.

Figure 7.5 This 1962 ad by DDB broke the taboo against comparative advertising.

dirty ashtrays"; and, "Avis can't afford unwashed cars." Ironically the award-winning campaign almost didn't run. Research indicated that it would fail miserably, but Bernbach sold the idea anyway. Overnight the ads became a hot topic nationwide, and the phrase "We try harder" entered the everyday language. Within two years Avis increased its market share by 28 percent.[7]

The successful VW and Avis campaigns brought DDB major national accounts, including such big-ticket businesses as United Airlines, Seagram, Heinz, Sony, UniRoyal, Lever Brothers, Gillette, Bristol-Myers, and Mobil Oil. DDB also helped less well known brands like Chivas Regal Scotch whisky achieve prominence (Figure 7.6). Its total billings reached $174 million in 1965, moving DDB into the ranks of the top agencies.[8]

Figure 7.6   With this 1960s ad DDB helped Chivas Regal achieve national prominence as a premium Scotch whisky.

Creative Boutiques

The ad business opened up to more than new people; it also opened up to new agencies. Advertisers moved their business away from the established old-line agencies to small, innovative "boutique" agencies. These agencies proved fast, flexible, and enormously successful. They spent huge sums on in-house research, hired specialists on every aspect of the marketplace, and built in-house television production facilities and packaging laboratories.

Of course, such services didn't mean much to advertisers; what they cared about was creativity. Thus success was equated with origi-

If you spent 40 days in the sun you'd be rosy and plump, too.

Hunt's tomatoes spend their lives lolling in the sun. Then when they have a nice color, are firm and vine-ripened, we stuff as many as two pounds of them into each bottle of Hunt's Catsup.

Hunt's CATSUP

So the catsup is thick, rich with big tomato taste. There's nothing like a well-rested tomato to make a lively CATSUP. HUNT-WESSON FOODS FULLERTON, CALIFORNIA.

Figure 7.7   This 1968 ad used a bright, playful image to promote Hunt's Catsup.

nality. Understandably ads grew more outrageous to catch attention. The watchword became novelty. Innovation became the ideological commodity. Realistic art gave way to collages, psychedelic images, pop art blowups, and camp art parodies. Ads grew more daring in an effort to sell everything form cars to catsup (Figure 7.7).

The new agencies boasted an array of outstanding talent, including George Lois, Julian Koenig, Mary Wells, Carl Ally, Jerry Della Femina, and Howard Gossage. Account man Fred Papert, copywriter Julian Koenig, and art director George Lois of DDB opened for business as Papert Koenig Lois (PKL) in 1960, one of the first of the hot new creative shops. Although Lois had worked for only a year at DDB, he had garnered three prestigious awards for art direction. In his own

Figure 7.8 This 1960s ad combined slick graphics and humorous, suggestive copy to sell vodka.

shop Lois sought to emulate the DDB style, from its creative teams to its informal working methods. In a series of ads for Wolfschmidt vodka, PKL combined slick graphics with humorous, sexually suggestive copy (Figure 7.8). Another memorable PKL commercial demonstrated how easy it was to operate a new technology, the Xerox machine. The first television spot showed a little girl making copies, but complaints surfaced concerning the accuracy of the degree of difficulty demonstrated. The agency responded by creating a new spot showing a chimpanzee making copies. PKL also combined images and copy beautifully in campaigns for Allerest, Coty Cremestick, and Naugahyde vinyl material. This highly creative agency, however, did not survive the decade.

Carl Ally left the PKL group in 1962 to establish another agency with Amil Gargano and Jim Durfee. Also steeped in the DDB creative tradition, Ally opened for business with the Volvo account, turning out headlines like "It'll last longer than the payment book" and "Drive it like you hate it" (Figure 7.9). One of the agency's most famous cam-

It'll last longer than the payment book.

It takes about three years to go through a payment book.
It takes about eleven years to go through a Volvo.
That eleven years, incidentally, is based on the average life of a Volvo in Sweden, where there are no speed limits on the highways, where there are over 70,000 miles of unpaved roads, where driving is virtually a national pastime.
You may not want to keep your Volvo eleven years, but if you do, nobody will be the wiser. We don't follow the wasteful practice of making new models look different just to make old models look obsolete.
But no matter how long you keep your Volvo, you won't tire of it. A Volvo will run away from every other compact in its class, yet deliver over 25 miles to the gallon, even with automatic transmission.
Drive a Volvo at a nearby dealer. And don't look at it merely as a superb automobile.
Look at it more as a way to get out from under car payments into swimming pool, boat, or vacation house payments. After all, there's more to life than owning the newest car on the block. Even for us. **VOLVO**

Figure 7.9 Steeped in the DDB tradition, Carl Ally grabbed attention with arresting headlines, strong images, and straightforward copy.

paigns was in response to the Avis spots by DDB, which had taken away customers from Hertz and lowered its morale. With slashing copy the new Hertz campaign confronted "No. 2's" sales argument. One ad featured the headline "Hertz has a competitor who says he's only No. 2. That's hard to argue with." The copy listed five claims by Hertz, to which No. 2 weakly responded, "We try harder," point after point (Figure 7.10). The clever campaign helped Hertz recover a large share of the market.

Copywriter Mary Wells, who trained at McCann-Erickson and DDB, became one of the most successful figures in the creative revolution, starting one of the first major agencies ever headed by a woman. In 1963, while working at Jack Tinker Partners, she produced one of the most memorable commercials of the decade for Alka-Seltzer: "No matter what shape your stomach is in." The spot, which

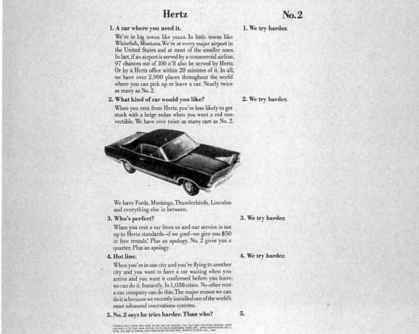

Hertz has a competitor who says he's only No. 2. That's hard to argue with.

Hertz	No. 2
1. A car where you need it.	**1. We try harder.**
We're in big towns like yours. In little towns like Whitefish, Montana. We're at every major airport in the United States and at most of the smaller ones. In fact, if an airport is served by a commercial airline, 97 chances out of 100 it'll also be served by Hertz. Or by a Hertz office within 20 minutes of it. In all, we have over 2,900 places throughout the world where you can pick up or leave a car. Nearly twice as many as No. 2.	
2. What kind of car would you like?	**2. We try harder.**
When you rent from Hertz, you're less likely to get stuck with a beige sedan when you want a red convertible. We have over twice as many cars as No. 2.	
We have Fords, Mustangs, Thunderbirds, Lincolns and everything else in between.	
3. Who's perfect?	**3. We try harder.**
When you rent a car from us and our service is not up to Hertz standards—if we goof—we give you $50 in free rentals.* Plus an apology. No. 2 gives you a quarter. Plus an apology.	
4. Hot line.	**4. We try harder.**
When you're in one city and you're flying to another city and you want to have a car waiting when you arrive and you want it confirmed before you leave, we can do it. Instantly. In 1,038 cities. No other rent-a-car company can do this. The major reason we can do it is because we recently installed one of the world's most advanced reservations systems.	
5. No. 2 says he tries harder. Than who?	**5.**

Figure 7.10   In this 1968 ad Carl Ally counterpunched DDB's campaign for Avis.

showed jiggly bellies of all shapes and sizes, was an instant success; the TV jingle even became a hit record. For Braniff International Airlines' "Flying Colors" campaign, Wells painted the planes pastel shades, dressed the stewardesses in Pucci outfits, and lured businessmen with exotic appeals. One of the most effective TV spots, "The Air Strip," showed a stewardess greeting passengers dressed in one outfit and then slipping into a hostess outfit for dinner; the spot then announced that "on those long flights she'll slip into something a little more comfortable."

Wells left Jack Tinker with the Braniff account later in the decade and started her own agency, Wells, Rich & Greene (WRG). The agency's flair for theatrics made it stand out. Notably WRG produced other humorous TV spots for Alka-Seltzer: "I can't believe I ate the whole thing" and "Try it, you'll like it." In another landmark campaign WRG broke a cardinal rule of advertising when it wittily presented the many supposed disadvantages of smoking Benson & Hedges 100's. For example, the extra-long cigarette ripped a too-small pocket, burned a newspaper, set a man's beard on fire, got caught in an elevator door, and mashed against a shop window.

The Delehanty, Kurnit & Geller agency also turned out landmark work. The group hired top young talent like copywriter Jerry Della Femina and art director Ron Travisano (who later teamed up to form Della Femina Travisano & Partners in 1967). Although produced on a very small budget, the agency's campaign for Talon zippers played a major role in having shoppers actually seek out garments displaying Talon ID tags on their merchandise. The ads used a humorous touch to memorably get the message across that one could be sure that the Talon zipper would stay up. One ad showed the bare back of a well-dressed woman with a popped zipper: "Last Night Mrs. Mary Powers Opened on Broadway." Other zippers didn't perform for a hardhat worker, "a prominent stockbroker [who] just went public," and "baseball players of all ages" (Figure 7.11).

Much of Howard Gossage's work involved what today is called "direct response" advertising, creating relations between his clients and their customers. Although Gossage's copy was zany, measured results proved that his ads hit the intended target. Gossage put his humor to the test by integrating coupons and write-ins into almost every ad he created. One of Gossage's most famous promotions was an Eagle shirt campaign that featured a color-naming contest resulting in some of these winners: See Red, Favor Curry, Holler Copper, Free Loden, Robert Shaw Coral, Lawsy Miss Scarlett, and 'Enry 'Iggins Just You White. Other ads offered readers special gifts such as Eagle labels and shirting samples called "Shirtkerchiefs" (Figure 7.12). Gossage's agency also turned out brilliant copy for the Sierra Club, Beethoven sweatshirts, and Land Rover cars.

The Loss of Creative Momentum

In less than a decade the creative revolution had gathered momentum and flourished, but external events caused it to falter. One factor was the 1965 Highway Beautification Act, which prohibited commercial signs within 660 feet of all federally funded highways. This put an end to the golden age of outdoor advertising (1920–1965). But the 1970s recession was the most significant factor. Artistic creativity gave way

Figure 7.11 This low-budget 1960s ad used humor to increase consumer identification with garments made with Talon zippers.

to the hard-sell approach deemed more appropriate for the tight economy. On television advertisers communicated their messages in seconds, not minutes. In 1970 the 30-second commercial replaced the standard 1- and 2-minute spots that had been the perfect creative vehicle during the golden age of television commercials (1964–1970).

By the end of the 1970s, the small, flexible idea-houses had become bloated and sluggish. Agencies faced the constant dilemma of how to grow and still keep that "creative spark," and few did so successfully. Many agencies had plowed their enormous profits back into

*OVER

[cont. from preceding page]

SEND FOR YOUR FREE EAGLE SHIRTKERCHIEF (SHIRTKIN?) (NAPCHIEF?)

AS far as we know this is a brand new invention. Perhaps you will be able to figure out how to realize its full potential. ★ It all started when we tried to devise something to send you—short of an actual shirt—to illustrate a few of the fine points of fine shirt making. A sample to take with you when you go shirt shopping. ★ So first we hemmed a piece of fine shirting; *20 stitches to the inch,* just like in our shirts. At this point you could still call it a handkerchief. ★ But it did seem a shame not to show one of our threadchecked buttonholes, so we did. It makes a pretty good shirt protector: just whip it out of your breast pocket and button it on the second from the top to avoid gravy spots. Good. And tuck your tie in behind it. ★ But then somebody in Pockets said, "Look, if you let us sew a pocket on it, it will show how we make the pattern match right across, no matter what." ★ So if anyone knows what you can use a pocket in a handkerchief/napkin for we will be glad to hear. We will give a half-dozen shirts for the best answer. Make it a dozen.

Eagle Shirtmakers, Quakertown, Pa.
Gentlemen :
Please send me whatever it is. (Signed)_____
Address_____ City_____ State_____

Figure 7.12 This ad for Eagle shirts by Howard Gossage had a front and back page and included a special gift offer—a "shirtkerchief."

in-house research departments. But in the lean times of the 1970s, the newly expanded agencies suffered losses, lost accounts, became more conservative, or simply disappeared.

Magazine publishers also had become rich with ad money, which supported a great number of periodicals. However, for some time now network television had been attracting the kind of large national audience traditionally enjoyed by the mass-circulation magazines. Although some of the giant periodicals had paid circulations in the millions, advertising revenues were no longer sufficient to subsidize rising production and distribution costs. Publishers tried offering cut-rate subscriptions to maintain those numbers, which allowed them to charge advertisers a higher rate; others even limited readership. But nothing worked. Dozens of magazines folded, including *Colliers* and *Women's Home Companion* in 1957, the *Saturday Evening Post* in 1969, *Look* in 1971, and *Life* in 1972 (the magazine was reborn as a monthly in 1978).

As these big general-interest magazine giants toppled, publishers responded by developing special-interest magazines with well-defined audiences, including *Sailing World* (1962), *Runner's World* (1966), *Weight Watchers* (1968), and *Rolling Stone* (1967). Advertisers turned to these publications as a choice vehicle for reaching audiences of a specific age or interest. Thus, despite the casualties in the ranks of the big general-interest publications, magazines continued to flourish. But with the end of the creative revolution, the advertising world was ripe for yet another wave of reform.

Reform Sweeps Madison Avenue

The legacy of the 1960s was far more than a new wave of advertising. By the early 1970s the spread of new social values had begun to transform the workplace, creating new demands for equal rights in hiring and promotion. Multiculturalism, feminism, and environmentalism all became potent forces as well. Thus, for the first time, social events forced Madison Avenue to address long-deferred issues. "At the height of its powers, in the 1920s, advertising had been a primary, independent force in the molding of American culture and mores," observed historian Stephen Fox. Since then, "advertising has increasingly functioned more as a mirror than mindbender, responding to American culture more than shaping it."[9] But the general course of American life typically outstripped advertising's reflection of it, especially regarding the most important changes related to cultural diversity and feminism. However, under pressure the industry gradually demonstrated a new social consciousness.

Minority Groups Demand a Piece of the Pie

Ethnic stereotypes died hard in the advertising industry. Advertisers continued to fantasize about a mythical middle America populated by white people and guided by traditional values. Yet such cultural homogenety had never existed. Following World War II vast numbers of African Americans had migrated from southern to northern states, and waves of immigrants from Latin America and Asia continued to arrive in America. Yet advertisers typically avoided controversial and political issues and feared breaking the color line. African Americans literally disappeared from print ads and TV commercials in the 1950s and 1960s, and other minority group members rarely appeared; Hispanic Americans were particularly invisible.

More than anything, the civil rights movement enlightened the nation and led to more cultural diversity throughout the advertising industry. African Americans upgraded their employment status and demanded less stereotyped ad images of themselves. The DDB campaign for Levy's bread became a model with its "You don't have to be Jewish to love Levy's" ads (Figure 7.13). This series of ads and posters pictured members of a variety of ethnic groups, including African Americans, Asian Americans, and Native Americans. The desire to include more diversity eventually extended to nationwide advertising. For example, in 1963 Lever Brothers, one of the largest

You don't have to be Jewish

to love Levy's

real Jewish Rye

Figure 7.13   This 1960s ad was one of a series by DDB that acknowledged America's cultural diversity by including images of African Americans, Asian Americans, and Native Americans.

advertisers on TV, announced that it would picture more blacks. And the first spots for All detergent showed Art Linkletter talking with an African American housewife about her laundry problems.

Yet the pace of progress remained slow. Shows featuring African American performers found it difficult to attract sponsors. In 1964 General Motors threatened to withdraw its sponsorship of the popular Western television series "Bonanza" should an episode feature an African American guest star. Under pressure from NBC and the NAACP and facing considerable negative publicity, however, GM later reversed its position. As late as 1968, Chrysler complained openly about "Petula," a variety show that it sponsored. Chrysler did not approve when the show's star, the popular British singer Petula Clark, held the arm of her guest star, black singer Harry Belafonte. Chrysler deemed it far too intimate a pose to appear on camera.[10] By decade's end, however, several shows starring African Americans met with unprecedented approval, including "Julia," "The Bill Cosby Show," and "The Flip Wilson Show."

The degree to which African Americans were excluded from mainstream advertising has been extensively documented. For example, Harold Kassarjian examined twelve national magazines from 1946 to 1965 and found that blacks appeared in less than 1 percent of the ads.[11] The New York City Commission on Human Rights monitored commercials from forty agencies for a one-year period from 1966 to 1967 and found that blacks appeared in only about 4 percent of the commercials.[12] And in 1968 the federal Equal Employment Opportunity Commission (EEOC) held hearings investigating the number of minority group members in advertisements. All of this contributed to a considerable growth in the number of African Americans appearing in mainstream advertising.

Only a few mass market advertisers had mounted specialized campaigns aimed at African Americans prior to this era. Advertisers simply adopted campaigns for white-oriented media by substituting nonwhite models and running the ads in African American–oriented media such as *Ebony* (1945), *Tan* (1950), and *Jet* (1951). In fact, this technique is still used today.

For some personal care products like Clairol hair coloring, however, it made more sense to create nonwhite advertising. At the time Clairol targeted only two shades to the African American market—black velvet and sable brown. Clairol also faced two sensitive issues. It had to overcome the idea that "good women" did not color their hair, and it had to convince nonwhite women that hair coloring could naturally flatter their complexions. To solve these problems, Clairol put out a series of trade advertisements to condition hairdressers. It also ran consumer advertising in African American media to explain to nonwhite women that hair coloring was as natural to use as other cosmetics. Although Clairol ran ads with its famous "Does she . . . or doesn't she?" line with an attractive African American model, it also introduced a new theme specifically for this market: "If you want to . . . why not?" The pictures showed African American models with hair colored from brunette to blonde. Through this targeted advertising Clairol developed an entirely new market for their product.

Yet the most noticeable reform involved the "role" of African Americans portrayed in ads. Instead of presenting demeaning, stereotyped images, admakers cast African Americans in a range of normal occupations and tasks. Uncle Ben's chef disappeared for a time, while Aunt Jemima's "mammy" character slimmed down, discarded her

handkerchief head covering, and donned
pearl earrings. And African American
celebrities pitched products to the mass
market, including Lena Horne for Sanka
coffee and Bill Cosby for Jell-O.

However, efforts to hire more
African Americans for important positions
in advertising lagged. In the early 1960s few
African Americans worked on Madison Avenue in
any capacity, professional or clerical. In 1966 the Equal Employment
Opportunity Commission (EEOC) surveyed sixty-four New York
ad agencies and found that only 2.5 percent of white-collar employees were African Americans. In response to these findings and to pressure from concerned organizations, the racially unbalanced industry
began consciously to address this imbalance. Agencies created new
training programs and white-collar positions, and by 1969 minority
employment had risen to 10.5 percent at the fifteen largest New York
agencies.[13]

At the same time, several national African American agencies
opened. In 1956 Vince Cullers had started the nation's first African
American–owned, full-service agency. The introduction of Burrell,
Inc., in 1971 (now Burrell Communications Group) and UniWorld,
headed by Bryon Lewis, inspired new concepts about the portrayal of
African Americans in advertising and a better understanding of the
African American consumer market. Burrell believed that ads targeted
to African Americans must reflect their culture and pioneered the
concept of "positive realism." In other words African Americans could
be seen in common everyday settings—brushing their teeth, washing
their hair, going to work, driving cars, taking vacations, and so on. The
idea caught on in the industry, and Burrell has since grown into the
nation's largest African American–owned agency, targeting special-
interest markets. By the 1970s over a dozen such agencies had opened
to tap into the lucrative African American consumer market.

Although a considerable amount of research segmented mainstream America into different demographic categories (for example,
based on sex, age, income, family structure, and educational levels),
no differences among African Americans were noted. "All 'Negroes'
were perceived to be the same: They supposedly aspired to the same
goals, came from the same backgrounds, and desired the same products," explains Gail Baker Woods, author of *Advertising and Marketing to the New Majority*.[14] Yet in reality the buying patterns of the
emerging African American middle class were not much different from
those of their white counterparts. Over time marketers increasingly
geared programs to this audience, as well as to the emerging Hispanic
American and Asian American consumer markets. Overall, however,
the extent to which advertisers cultivated the African American

The Best TV Commercials

As part of a special spring 1995 issue, six editors of *Advertising Age* selected the "50 best" TV commercials of all time. Here's the list for the 1960s:

1960s

Maxwell House A perky jingle simulates percolating coffee.

Lyndon Johnson A girl picks petals from a daisy juxtaposed against a nuclear countdown.

Marlboro The rugged cowboys of "Marlboro Country" ride the range.

Noxzema A woman urges a shaver to "take it off, take it all off."

Cracker Jacks Comedian Jack Gifford delivers a deadpan routine.

Hertz The company wants to "put you in the driver's seat today."

Benson & Hedges Amusing scenes demonstrate the "disadvantages" of 100-millimeter cigarettes.

Alka-Seltzer Even the distress caused by a "spicy meatball" can be relieved.

consumer remained relatively small in relation to the efforts to influence the white audience.

Stereotypes of other ethnic groups also came under pressure. For example, Mexican Americans charged one of the nation's leading ad agencies, Foote Cone & Belding, with creating an unflattering stereotype, the Frito Bandito character. The smirking, gun-toting Pancho Villa look-alike held up supermarkets, picknickers, and the like in search of his favorite snack. The character was retired in 1970. Similarly Funny Face fruit drink for children transformed the ethnic characters originally used to promote the product. "Chinese Cherry" became "Choo-Choo Cherry," while "Injun Orange" became "Jolly Olly Orange." Italian Americans, too, often were cast as stereotypical spaghetti-serving mommas, seductive men, or gangsters.

Even an American staple like Jell-O displayed racial stereotypes. In Young & Rubicam's award-winning 1959 commercial "Chinese Baby," a Chinese-accented narrator described a baby who could not eat his slippery gelatin with his chopsticks: "But, ah! Mother brings great Western invention—the spoon! Spoon was invented to eat Jell-O, Chinese Baby velly happy!" The commercial was an unintentional reminder to members of the Chinese-American community of the difficulty they had learning to speak the language. In any case advertisers

Favorite TV Jingles

Oscar Mayer Wieners

Oh I wish I were an Oscar Mayer Wiener. / That is what I'd really like to be. / 'Cause if I were an Oscar Mayer Wiener / Everyone would be in love with me.

Armour Hot Dogs

Hot dogs, Armour hot dogs / What kind of kids love Armour hot dogs? / Big kids, little kids, kids who climb on rocks, / fat kids, skinny kids, even kids with chicken pox / love hot dogs, Armour hot dogs, / the dogs kids love to bite!

Pepsi-Cola

There's a whole new way of livin'; / Pepsi helps supply the drive. / It's got a lot to give / to those who like to live / 'cause Pepsi helps 'em come alive. / It's the Pepsi generation / comin' at ya, goin' strong. / Put your self behind a Pepsi. / If you're livin' you belong. / You've got a lot to live, / and Pepsi's got a lot to give. / You've got a lot to live, and Pepsi's got a lot to give.

in general had become more culturally sensitive about presenting stereotyped images to capture a mass market.

You've Come a Long Way, Baby!

Women also took a cue from the successes of the civil rights movement and began raising their voices. Relatively quiet since the 1920s, the feminist movement came to life again in the 1960s. Feminists not only addressed the old issues of pay inequities and a lack of opportunities but also challenged the roles assigned to women in a male-dominated society. They argued that society conditioned females from childhood to think of themselves only as wives and mothers. In contrast, males were taught to believe that they would do a "man's work" and become leaders in business and politics. Such conditioning, wrote Betty Friedan in *The Feminine Mystique* (1963), limited women's chances to achieve their full potential. Furthermore, Friedan concluded, most women were unfulfilled and had to develop their own identities.

Modern feminists formed small consciousness-raising groups across the country and urged women to resist being treated as sex objects, to reject sexual competition, to boycott beauty pageants, and to combat female passivity. To the delight of some and the horror of others, women tossed their miniskirts and confining undergarments away for politically correct pants and the no-bra bra. As feminists mobilized into an array of national organizations and publications, they asked questions like these: Why are women usually paid far less than men for the same work? Why are women forbidden to drink at some bars? Why do flight attendants lose their jobs when they have children? And why are there so few women in Congress?

The National Organization for Women (NOW), founded in 1966, sought to eliminate gender stereotypes and to acquire political and economic power for women. With affirmative action goals were set for businesses, schools, and universities to bring qualified women and minorities into the labor force. And even though the Equal Rights Amendment was not ratified by the requisite number of states to become law, its approval by Congress reflected the improving status of women.

At the same time, the social forces of feminism hit Madison Avenue. The women of the 1960s were a new phenomenon, better educated and more socially and politically aware. They also represented almost half of the total work force in the country. Although many women held "traditional" secretarial, sales, teaching, and nursing jobs, the nation also saw its first female firefighters, airline pilots, construction workers, and telephone linepersons. More and more women joined the professional ranks of engineers, doctors, lawyers, bank officers, and advertising and public relations executives. Although many advertising agencies employed women, some creative agencies like Leo Burnett did not accept women in higher positions. DDB led the way with a substantial creative staff of women, including Phyllis Robinson, Mary Wells, Paula Green, Judith Protan, Lorie Parker, and Rita Selden. The agency also hired its first woman account executive, Marcella Rosen, in 1962. At Ogilvy, Rita Korda wrote copy for Schweppes, Dove, and Pepperidge Farm. Benton & Bowles also hired women as art directors.

What did all this mean in terms of marketing and advertising? "It means that today's woman is not going to be influenced by the same advertising and promotional message that may have motivated her a few years ago, " declared Tina Santis, Colgate-Palmolive's public relations representative, in 1974. She explained that women confronted all new issues that were unheard of a century earlier: "Should she go to work . . . should she have children if she doesn't want them . . . should she go back to school and get that degree . . . should she give her teen age daughter The Pill?"[15]

Women began to express their emerging sense of self by making their own decisions whether to accept or reject traditional absolutes related to women's appearance, social roles, and life choices. No longer did women accept that they had to get married, start a family, and dedicate themselves to homemaking; nor did they accept that

How to wind up a doll for Christmas!

Figure 7.14 This 1962 ad for Evans furs helped perpetuate the stereotyped image of women as dependent on men.

they had to be pretty, sweet, and demure. But advertisers continued to address women in terms of "idealized roles" rather than "reality situations," because they had narrow ideas of what they thought reached women. The credibility gap between fantasy and reality in advertising widened even further as advertisers continued to perpetuate stereotypes.

Admakers repeatedly used images of women as sex objects, brainless housewives, and other traditional stereotypes (Figures 7.14 and 7.15). One of the most successful fantasy commercials was for Ajax. In 1964 the Ajax White Knight—every woman's dream in his shining

Figure 7.15   Despite the inroads made by the women's movement, this 1971 ad for National Airlines used sexist—and sexually suggestive—appeals.

armor—rode in and turned laundry pure white with the touch of his wand. Ads depicting women with freshly shampooed hair, a whiter-than-white smile, sweet-smelling breath, and smooth skin all ended with marriage, because advertisers believed that's what reached women. Once married, women clad in Dior gowns extolled the virtues of everything from refrigerators to dishwashing detergents. And, of course, housework was reserved for women, as a 1965 Vel dishwashing liquid ad showed. In this commercial a husband and wife "played house" together at the kitchen sink; however, he wasn't washing the dishes, but simply showing her how to do it.

Feminist criticism did not abate until the advertising industry recognized its insensitivity to its prime audience: women. NOW and *Ms.* magazine confronted the agencies themselves. "Advertising is a very important form of education," remarked feminist Gloria Steinem. "It is estimated that 40 percent of all of our subcultural intake comes from advertising."[16] Ads like Shirley Polykoff's Clairol spot ("Does she or doesn't she?") received a NOW "Barefoot & Pregnant" award. Another prize went to a Geritol ad in which the man stated: "My wife, I think I'll keep her." Feminists also placed "This ad insults women" stickers on billboards, recaptioned posters, blacked out offending pictures, and distributed "Plastic Pig" awards to companies that portrayed women in a demeaning manner.

Meanwhile, a number of studies related to the issue of gender in advertising were published. In one influential study, *Gender Advertisements,* Erving Goffman explained that advertisements represented men as heads of the household. Ironically "an appreciable amount of the advertising aimed at selling supplies for women's household work employs males in the depicted role of instructing professionals."[17] Another way of portraying women as subordinate to men involved what Goffman called the "ritual of subordination," or "that of lowering oneself physically in some form of prostration." For example, sultry spokesperson Joey Heatherton lay atop Serta mattresses in her nightgown, caressing the springs to demonstrate their responsiveness. Like beds, floors represented another place where women appeared in a subordinate position, doing chores like scrubbing floors and bathtubs. Moreover, Goffman explained, "floors are also associated with the less clean, less pure, less exalted parts of a room, for example, the place to keep dogs, baskets of soiled clothes, street footwear, and the like."[18]

Another study, Alice Courtney and Thomas Whipple's *Sex Stereotyping in Advertising,* showed how advertising divided women into working and nonworking categories. The nonworking women appeared in home-based contexts. In 1958 advertising portrayed most working women as secretaries; in 1970 most appeared as entertainers; and two years later, most were "decorative objects."

The industry eventually began to pay attention to feminists' concerns with gender issues. One of the most popular ways to deal with the issue was with checklists that admakers consulted to avoid sexism and gender stereotyping in their ads. By the mid-1970s admakers had begun to "power-dress" women and to cast them in business and managerial roles.

Three ad campaigns reflected this change in society's attitude toward women. The pre–women's liberation Maidenform campaign had shown women acting out their supposedly exhibitionist fantasies

The Gender Issue

The following checklist, produced by the National Advertising Review Board, gave admakers a set of questions to ask themselves to monitor potentially sexist and gender-stereotypical content in their ads.

Am I implying in my promotional campaign that creative, athletic and mind-enriching toys and games are not for girls as much as for boys? Does my ad, for example, imply that dolls are for girls and chemistry sets for boys, and that neither could ever become interested in the other category?

Are sexual stereotypes pepetuated in my ad? That is, does it portray women as weak, silly, and overemotional? Or does it picture both sexes as intelligent, physically able, and attractive?

Are the women portrayed in my ad stupid? For example, am I reinforcing the "dumb blonde" cliche? Does my ad portray women who are unable to balance their checkbooks?

Women who are unable to manage a household without the help of outside experts, particularly male ones?

Does my ad use belittling language, for example, "gal friday" or "lady professor"? Or "her kitchen" but "his car"? Or "women's chatter" but "men's discussion"?

Does my ad make use of contemptuous phrases such as the "weaker sex," the "little woman," "the ball and chain," or "the war department"?

Do my ads consistently show women waiting on men? Even in occupational situations, for example, are women nurses or secretaries serving coffee to male bosses or colleagues? And never vice versa?

Is there a gratuitous message in my ads that a woman's most important role in life is a supportive one, to cater to and coddle men and children? Is it a "big deal" when the reverse is shown, that is, very unusual and special—something for which the woman must show gratitude?

while displaying their Maidenform bras (Figure 7.16). However, with women's liberation women turned these dreams into reality by penetrating traditionally male-dominated domains and situations. And by the late 1960s many women were burning their bras or at least not wearing them, so Maidenform discarded the campaign. Meanwhile, Virginia Slims cigarettes targeted women buyers and launched one of the longest-running, most successful campaigns in advertising history. With its slogan "You've come a long way, baby" and comparative photographs, the campaign contrasted women of today with those of ear-

I dreamed
I took the bull
by the horns...
in my
maidenform bra

Figure 7.16 With this 1962 ad Maidenform continued its "I dreamed" campaign from the 1950s, which tapped into women's supposedly exhibitionist tendencies.

lier eras. But the turning point came in 1973 when Revlon's Charlie perfume campaign displayed confident, pant-suited young women pursuing traditionally male-oriented activities (Figure 7.17). By the end of the decade marketers also recognized that growing numbers of women were earning higher salaries. Thus ads now not only depicted the professional woman at work but also increasingly pitched her cars, homes, and insurance.

Figure 7.17 This 1973 ad built on the themes introduced in the Virginia Slims campaign by portraying the confident, independent "Charlie girl" making her way in a formerly male-dominated world.

By the late 1970s many women had opened their own agencies. Among these were Shirley Polykoff (from Foote Cone & Belding), Jane Trahey (from Neiman-Marcus in Dallas), Paula Green (from DDB), Jo Foxworth (from Calkins & Holden), Lois Geraci Ernst (who created the "I'm going to have an Aviance night" slogan for Aviance perfume), Jacqueline Brandwynne, Janet Marie Carlson (who sold Cole's ladies' swimsuits), Faith Popcorn (who wrote the *Popcorn Report*), Adrienne Hall and Joan Levine, and two African American adwomen, Joyce Hamer and Caroline R. Jones. Also, Jane Maas (who directed the "I Love New York" program at WRG) went on to head the Muller Jordan Weiss agency.

More Issues Explode Advertising's Dream World

Advertisers faced still other challenges on a number of fronts, including the rekindled controversy over subliminal advertising, the health hazards associated with tobacco, a revived consumerism, and controversy over the role of advertising in the public service sector and politics. In 1964 the surgeon general announced that cigarette smoking was a "health hazard of sufficient importance to the United States to require remedial action." For advertisers this meant two things. First, warning notices had to be printed on every pack: "Caution: Cigarette smoking may be hazardous to your health." Second, cigarettes could no longer be advertised on television and radio. In response the tobacco companies shifted their focus to magazines and newspapers and to sponsorship of sporting events such as the Virginia Slims tennis tournaments and the Winston Cup auto races. Although magazines like *Reader's Digest, Good Housekeeping,* and *The New Yorker* refused to run cigarette ads, advertisers simply funneled ever-increasing revenues into other promotional vehicles.

Like the tobacco industry other industries met mounting political and consumer pressures. Rachel Carson's *Silent Spring* (1962) exposed the health and environmental hazards of DDT and other pesticides and helped launch the environmental movement. Meanwhile, the quality of American-made products seemed to be declining and pride in workmanship often seemed a thing of the past. To counter criticism of lack of their social accountability, corporations spent more and more dollars on advertising, public relations, and snazzy designs. However, an increasingly educated and skeptical public, led by consumer advocate Ralph Nader, wasn't buying it.

The automobile industry also emerged as a major source of controversy. Ralph Nader revealed what many had long suspected about American cars in his book *Unsafe at Any Speed* (1965). The safety, environmental impact, reliability, and fuel efficiency of the huge, finned American cars came under attack. In response the government passed the Highway Safety Act, which established federal safety standards for automobiles and tires, provided federal funds for state highway programs, and funded research into new and safer automobiles. The auto industry also was staggered by the 1970s oil crisis, as consumers increasingly purchased the smaller, more reliable, and more fuel-efficient Japanese cars.

Even the public service sector came in for its share of resentment. For example, critics charged the Ad Council, established during World War II, with taking on causes that were already won or too superficial to justify the expenditures. This resulted in the peacetime council committing itself to specific causes such as curbing smoking, combating drunk driving, and registering voters. And public institutions like the American Lung Association, the Sierra Club, the U.S. Postal Service, the armed services, and the immigration service all began to advertise their services and polish their images.

William Bryan Key

Journalism professor William Bryan Key, a critic of advertising, rekindled the controversy over subliminal manipulation in his books *Subliminal Seduction* (1973) and *Media Sexploitation* (1976). In the tradition of Vance Packard's *Hidden Persuaders* (1957), Key sought to demonstrate how certain ads incorporated subliminal stimuli to manipulate, control, and direct the public's buying behavior. Throughout his books Key speculated on how sex was embedded in everything from ads for Ritz crackers and Camel cigarettes to the front-page photographs documenting the Vietnam War in *The New York Times*. According to Key, "Embedding refers generally to the practice of hiding emotionally loaded words or pictures in the backgrounds of ads."[a]

Key explained that sexual embedding could be accomplished with several techniques, photographically or artistically. For example, a photographer could first take a photo of a model and props; then a double exposure could be made in which only the word "SEX" was photographed as a faint impression across a portion of the original picture. The word could be used dozens of times in a layout to create a "SEX" mosaic. Or photographs could be retouched so that the word "SEX" was lightly etched across the photoengraving plate. Also, skilled artists could embed "SEX" into props or ad designs.

Key cited a curious example in a 1971 *Time* magazine ad for Gilbey's London Dry Gin as a "classic design of subliminal art." Key suggested viewing the ad while relaxed, for at least thirty seconds, to assimilate consciously the imagery. Key claimed that three of the ice cubes in the glass next to the bottle contained images that spelled out the word "SEX." But that was not all. Key also claimed that images of three women and two men appeared in various parts of the ad. For instance, the top ice cube contained a face peering down at the spelled-out "SEX"—and winking

---

Political parties in this era increasingly relied on the booming medium of television to promote candidates. The first televised series of presidential debates appeared in 1960. Many critics believe that John F. Kennedy's narrow victory over the previously favored Richard Nixon was the result of the debate. Although both men handled themselves well, Kennedy simply looked more vigorous and healthy on television, than did the swarthy, sweating Nixon. In the 1964 election the Democrats generated controversy with a spot created by the Doyle Dane Bernbach agency that aired only once. An angelic little girl was shown picking the petals from a daisy one at a time while counting backwards from ten. The countdown ended in a nuclear explosion

Break out the frosty bottle

GILBEYS

LONDON DRY

GIN

and keep your tonics dry!

To some observers this 1971 ad was a classic example of subliminal manipulation.

one eye at the reader. The bottom ice cube contained another face, one of a woman with long hair, appearing to look in the direction of the bottle cap. The reflections of the bottle and the bottle cap could be interpreted as another man's legs and partially erect genitals, and the drops of melting ice on the frosty bottle could suggest seminal fluid. Finally female genitalia appeared in the reflections of the tonic glass and of the bottle. The subliminal message? Gilbey's gin promised a "good old-fashioned sexual orgy" for those who broke out the bottle.[b]

Although Key's interpretations often stretch the limits of the imagination, his publishing success evidenced a large readership willing to believe even the most suspect attacks on advertising.

[a] William Bryan Key, *Subliminal Seduction: Ad Media's Manipulation of Not So Innocent America* (New York: Signet, 1974), 108.
[b] Key, *Subliminal Seduction*, 3–8.

with a final warning from President Lyndon Johnson: "The stakes are too high for you to stay at home." The publication of Joe McGinnis' tell-all book *The Selling of the President 1968* also generated an uproar. The newspaper reporter concluded that advertising and public relations had proved very influential in Richard Nixon's victory over Hubert Humphrey. Advertising has been involved in the political process since ancient times, but now more than ever politicians dared not ignore its power.

Yet another hot topic was the large volume of television advertising directed toward children. By the early 1970s advertisers were spending over $400 million a year advertising on children's programs, and in 1977 the average child was exposed to more than 20,000 television commercials. The bulk of these spots pitched sugared foods, which posed a threat to children's well-being. For example, over the first nine months of 1975, only 4 commercials appeared for any "nutritional foods," compared with 7066 for sugary cereals, candies, snacks, and fruit drinks. Also, children presented advertisers with a uniquely receptive audience. "As a psychological matter," observed Peggy Charren, founder of the consumer group Action for Children's Television (ACT), "children are cognitively incapable of understanding all television commercials directed toward them." Impressionable young minds often could not tell the difference between a commercial and the program, and elves, wizards, and other attention-getting cartoon figures tended to be perceived as real.[19]

In 1972 the Federal Trade Commission (FTC) issued new regulations stipulating that children were "not to be exposed to 'disguised' and 'hidden' advertising." The FTC cited one curious case illustrating how impressionable children can be. In January 1965 on his morning children's show, the performer Soupy Sales suggested to his young viewers that they find the wallets of their sleeping fathers and take out "some of those funny green pieces of paper with all those nice pictures of George Washington, Abraham Lincoln, and Alexander Hamilton, and send them along to your old pal, Soupy, care of WNEW, New York." It worked. According to reports it was "the biggest heist since the Brink's robbery."[20]

Five years later the Better Business Bureau formed the Children's Review Unit, which compiled a list of thirty advertiser "Can't Do's." For instance, the unit instructed advertisers to reduce the number of commercials on Saturday mornings and banned hosts and stars from pitching products in a manner that blurred the line between advertisement and program. The unit also cautioned against exaggerating the size or speed of a toy and admonished advertisers not to foster the idea that a child would gain prestige or a special skill by owning the product. Finally advertisers were enjoined not to urge children to ask their parents to purchase the product.

The industry's own self-regulating organizations also advocated tighter controls on advertising. One of the most important developments was the establishment of the National Advertising Review Board (NARB) in 1971. The NARB aimed to speedily resolve advertising disputes through two operating arms. One directed its efforts primarily at untruthful advertising; the other reviewed decisions of the National Advertising Division, a unit within the Better Business Bureau that monitored advertising to detect unfairness and that processed complaints of unfair advertising. For example, concern about the claims Listerine made led the FTC to order the manufacturer to spend $10 million on corrective advertising ("Listerine will not help prevent colds or sore throats or lessen their severity"). The FTC also ordered Anacin to spend $24 million on ads disclosing that the product would not relieve tensions as previously pitched. In sum, by the mid-1970s advertising found itself closely policed both within the industry and outside by government agencies, consumer-protection legislation, and consumer groups.

The mid-1970s were tough times all around. The Watergate scandal and the disgrace of President Nixon had eroded Americans' faith in the political system. The oil crisis and the recession had likewise eroded their faith in the economy. And on the cultural front disco, mood rings, and leisure suits seemed appropriate symbols of the times. Advertising, too, had suffered a severe fall from grace with the collapse of the creative revolution and the increase in public suspicion and cynicism. But over the next decade or so, as we will see in the next chapter, advertising would regain its creative vision.

The Supreme Court declares state bar associations' ban on advertising by attorneys to be unconstitutional; the American Bar Association issues advertising guidelines for attorneys.
1977

Apple Computer company is founded, heralding the start of the personal computer age.
1976

The National Association of Broadcasters abolishes guidelines that cautioned advertisers against discrediting competitors.

AIDS (acquired immune deficiency syndrome) becomes a deadly new health peril.

The FCC rescinds its ban on program-length commercials on radio.
1981

1975

1980
Inflation hits 13.5 percent, the worst since 1946, creating tremendous economic anxiety.

1982
The FTC allows physicians and dentists to advertise.

USA Today is introduced as a full-color, national newspaper.

London agency Saatchi & Saatchi begin a series of acquisitions in pursuit of a global communications organization.

Chapter 8

1975–1990 From Positioning to Image Building

The FCC rescinds its ban on program-length commercials on television.
1984

Sally K. Ride is the first American female astronaut as a crew member of the space shuttle *Challenger.*
1983

The stock market plunges more than 500 points in one day.
1987

1986
Three major ad agencies merge to create the largest agency in the world: BBDO, Doyle Dane Bernbach, and Needham Harper Worldwide.

1989
London-based WPP acquires both J. Walter Thompson and the Ogilvy group.

The Berlin Wall falls, and communist regimes crumble in Eastern Europe.

The World Wide Web is first proposed as a means to search for information in databases on selected workstations.

1990

In the late twentieth century technological advances propelled America into the "Information Age." As the pace of scientific inquiry accelerated, important breakthroughs were made in the fields of medicine, robotics, computers, and automation. Scientists split genes, space flight became routine, and high-tech automation spurred productivity. But some of the greatest innovations came in computerization. With the invention of the silicon chip microprocessor, computers became smaller, more powerful, and more affordable. Individuals now could use their personal computers, cellular phones, and fax machines to quickly access a broad spectrum of information and services. Computers also speeded up the pace of advertising design at an unimaginable rate.

Advertising agencies grew rich in the 1960s and early 1970s as corporations poured money into bright, playful ad campaigns. But that trend changed in the mid-1970s, when a severe recession and double-digit inflation stifled the economy. In manufacturing, massive military spending had diverted resources from the development of new consumer products. Although the wizardry of American electronics manufacturers made possible "high-tech" military products, their expertise did not readily transfer to the production of high-quality, competitively priced home electronics, automobiles, and machine tools. Thus Western European and Asian manufacturers stepped in to satisfy consumer demands, undercutting prices and often surpassing the quality of American-made products.

Such foreign competition, combined with escalating wages and energy prices, led to a decline in corporate profits and a return to the product-oriented selling characteristic of the 1950s. American corporations also searched for ways to lower their manufacturing costs. Some firms moved their operations from the more expensive northeastern "Rust Belt" states to the "Sunbelt" states extending from Virginia south to Florida and west to California. Other firms moved their production facilities abroad to take advantage of the cheap, nonunion labor available in Latin America and Southeast Asia. As more and more sophisticated components were produced in low-wage foreign factories, traditional American industries, such as automobiles, garments, electronics, steel, and printing, declined. In this tight economy advertisers resurrected the hard-sell approach, shifting from entertaining consumers to doing more market research, making specific product claims, and comparing products.

Nevertheless, the stagnant economy of the 1970s gave way to a boom period in the 1980s. The Reagan administration slashed federal spending on social programs, lifted pollution controls, and cut income taxes. The money freed by "Reaganomics" was intended to encourage investment and build up the military, thus stimulating growth; the ensuing profits were expected to "trickle down" from the upper to the lower classes. Until 1988 the plan seemed to work. Tax cuts and military contracts stimulated business, new jobs were created, deregulation brought consumer prices down, and the economy picked up.

Dramatic changes in the American economy also led to an American working class of incredible ethnic diversity. Early in the twentieth century European immigrants had filled millions of factory jobs. Now, in the 1970s and 1980s, huge numbers of Asian and Hispanic immigrants flocked to America to fill the millions of new service, retail, clerical, and light manufacturing jobs. Between 1983 and 1992 America experienced one of the heaviest floods of immigration in its history. As many as 8.7 million immigrants came to live in this country, the highest number in a ten-year period since 1910, and an estimated 5 million more newcomers slipped across the border without documentation. For many of these people, even minimum-wage work in America paid five or ten times more than they could earn in their homelands. As the foreign-born pursued the American Dream, they re-created the sights and sounds of their homelands in self-contained, self-supporting communities. Although agencies like Caroline Jones Advertising helped pioneer multiethnic marketing, advertisers' awareness of this important demographic trend lagged behind the course of events.

Like other American firms advertising agencies "went global" in the 1980s, building gigantic ad empires to service international clients. Glamour, wealth, and style were back in vogue. In turn, this upscale trend spawned new advertising styles and approaches; advertisers again moved away from hard-sell tactics to build more esoteric brand images for cosmetics, perfumes, fashions, home electronics, and cars. Before we trace that development, however, we must return to the mid-1970s, because the increased reliance on research and technology in that era is reflected in today's advertising.

The Late 1970s: Advertising Isn't Fun Anymore

With the onset of the recession in the 1970s, manufacturing costs skyrocketed and the flow of dollars for corporate promotions slowed. For a time, the increase in advertisers' billings did not match the rate of inflation. The advertising business was in trouble.

In this new climate tight budgets and cautious clients substantially changed the way Madison Avenue operated. In an attempt to make ends meet, many agencies pared their staffs. For example, a 1976 survey of seventy-seven major agencies reveals that they employed approximately four staffers for every $1 million in billings, compared with an average of six staffers in 1970. Although the largest agencies, such as J. Walter Thompson, Young & Rubicam, and

Caroline R. Jones

Caroline R. Jones, president and creative director at Caroline Jones Advertising in New York, helped pioneer multiethnic marketing, offering advertising, public relations, direct marketing, and special events promotions to domestic and international clients. Jones went into business with the late Frank Mingo in 1977; together they provided services for Pepsi and Disney and created the "We do chicken right" slogan for Kentucky Fried Chicken. After Mingo's death, the company split into the Mingo Group and Caroline Jones Advertising. Jones' agency opened its doors in 1987 with the following mission: "To sell products, through advertising and promotion, by accurately reflecting the colors and cultures of the consumers who buy those products." The company has represented Anheuser-Busch, Chemical Bank, Clorox, McDonald's, and USA Network.

McCann-Erickson, generally maintained their standing, other agencies suffered losses, lost accounts, and even shut down.[1]

Demanding clients, who faced consumers more wary than ever before, now judged advertising campaigns based on sales figures, not creative awards and entertaining ideas. Consequently they insisted on more market research. Agencies responded by hiring MBAs who understood pricing, distribution, and packaging strategies and by plowing an enormous percentage of their profits back into in-house research with a focus on audience analysis. Common research techniques included focus groups; motivational studies; measurement of brain waves, perspiration rates, and pupil dilation; and computer models. By the end of the 1970s the small, flexible idea-houses had become large and sluggish. "Advertising isn't fun anymore," said leading New York adman Jerry Della Femina about the trend. "Everything is tested, usually in small cities instead of big markets to hold down advertising expenditures."[2]

Positioning: The New Game on Madison Avenue

Della Femima was hardly alone in his assessment of mid-1970s advertising. "Today creativity is dead," wrote Al Ries and Jack Trout, who ran a small New York agency, in a series of articles for *Advertising Age* that later evolved into a book. "The name of the game on Madison Avenue is positioning."[3] Of course, this was not a new idea. The concept had been developed in the late 1950s by divisions of General Foods—quick, simple, aggressive pitches that cut through the competition. But the Trout & Ries agency best articulated the strategy. "Positioning is thinking in reverse," stated Ries and Trout. "Instead of starting with yourself, you start with the mind of the prospect."[4] The first step in the process was to give the product a memorable name. The next step was to find some specific selling point (like Rosser Reeves' unique selling proposition or USP) and repeat it to the point of monotony. Humor, mood, and aesthetics only diverted attention from the product. The admakers and their clients called this approach "realistic," "tough," or "consumer-oriented," but in reality it was nothing more than the traditional hard sell.

In their 1981 book *Positioning: The Battle for Your Mind,* Ries and Trout advocated comparative ads as the best way to "position" a product against the competition in consumers' minds. By then a number of larger agencies had adopted the comparative positioning technique. Print ads became wordier to combat consumer skepticism. For example, whereas earlier auto ads had contained few words and said little more than that the cars were beautiful, the new ads were crammed full of facts about mileage, disk brakes, engine design features, and so on. Taking aim at Anacin and Bufferin, Tylenol—"for the millions who should not take aspirin"—became a leading pain reliever. The success of Scope, which didn't taste "mediciney," prodded Listerine to produce a better-tasting mouthwash. Even the Doyle Dane Bernbach agency resumed its "We try harder" pitch for Avis after a six-year hiatus.

Hard-sell devices stressing repetition also appeared in commercials. As television production costs rose, the standard 60-second commercial increasingly was replaced by repetitive messages crammed into 30-second spots. Television advertising also relied on pretesting that favored hard-sell, reason-why content. Creativity had turned into a rational, quantifiable science. One of the most conspicuous "realistic" approaches was exemplified by Foote Cone & Belding's vignette, "Want a Tough Stain Out?" to which the commercial loudly answered, "Shout It Out" with Shout laundry stain remover. Then there were the straightforward Alka-Seltzer jingles ("Plop, plop, fizz, fizz, oh, what a relief it is") created by Wells, Rich, & Greene, a far cry from the award-winning work the same agency had turned out for the same product a few years before. The Purina Kitten Chow commercial managed to mention the product "Meow Mix" no less than a dozen times with a cat singing "Meow, Meow, Meow . . ." Then there were the old-fashioned slice-of-life vignettes and celebrity testimonials pitching everything from cars to colognes.

The positioning approach also spawned a variety of creative styles that managed a more entertaining hard sell. These ads had one thing in common: they used more product-oriented pitches to explain what the product did or why it was better than the competition. For instance, the new agency Scali, McCabe, Sloves developed a memorable series of ads designed to bring brand names to the poultry business. For Perdue chicken they featured plucky-voiced Frank Perdue telling

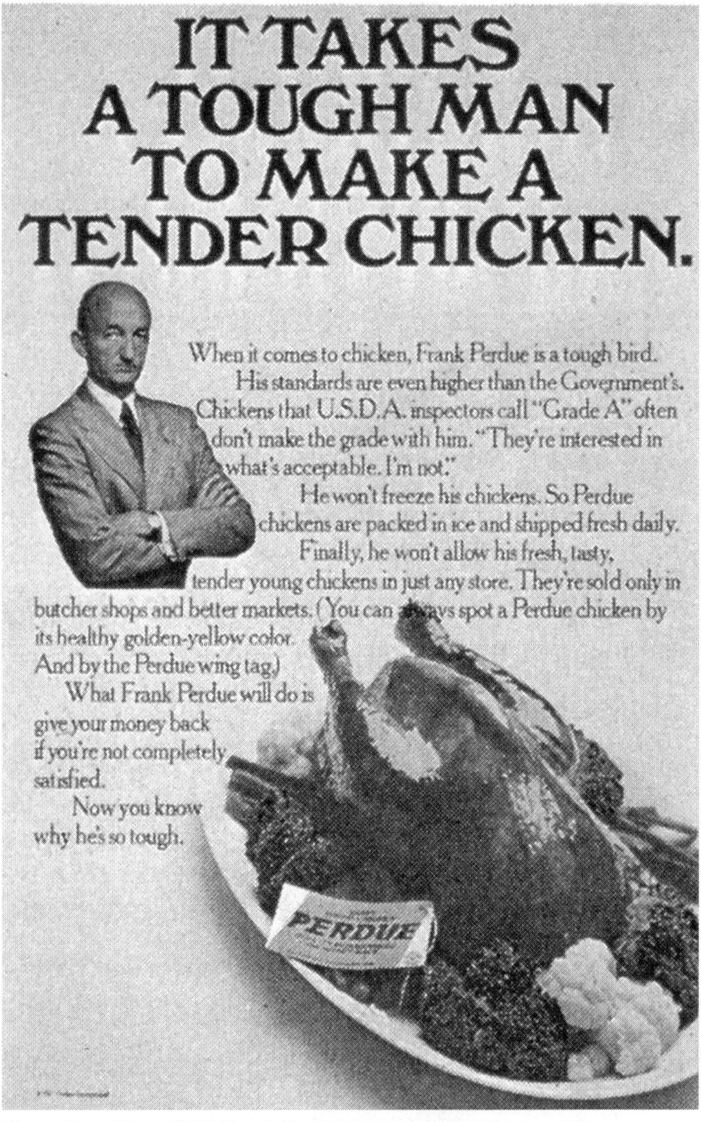

IT TAKES
A TOUGH MAN
TO MAKE A
TENDER CHICKEN.

When it comes to chicken, Frank Perdue is a tough bird.
His standards are even higher than the Government's.
Chickens that U.S.D.A. inspectors call "Grade A" often
don't make the grade with him. "They're interested in
what's acceptable. I'm not."
He won't freeze his chickens. So Perdue
chickens are packed in ice and shipped fresh daily.
Finally, he won't allow his fresh, tasty,
tender young chickens in just any store. They're sold only in
butcher shops and better markets. (You can always spot a Perdue chicken by
its healthy golden-yellow color.
And by the Perdue wing tag.)
What Frank Perdue will do is
give your money back
if you're not completely
satisfied.
Now you know
why he's so tough.

Figure 8.1   Since 1971 Frank Perdue has appeared in over 175
commercials and is one of the most successful corporate spokespersons
in American business history.

consumers that it "takes a tough man to make a tender chicken" (Figure 8.1). Other ads simply started out, "My Chickens Eat Better Than You Do," suggesting that Perdue chickens were more pampered than the people who ate them. The agency also triumphed with ads like the one for Volvo that stated: "It shouldn't take an act of Congress to make cars safe."

Although comparative advertising had been used obliquely before, the government did not allow direct comparison until 1981. Previously the major agencies and trade groups had generally avoided comparing products and services specifically by brand name, considering it "gauche," "unsportsmanlike," and even risky. In contrast, to consumers comparative selling pitches offered verifiable facts instead of overblown generalities. The Federal Trade Commission agreed, stating that comparisons might lead to better products and lower prices but that ads could make only truthful, scientifically verifiable claims. NBC television had first dropped the ban on such comparative ads in 1964. In 1972 ABC and CBS did so as well, but only after the FTC threatened legal action over restraint of trade. Soon thereafter, the National Association of Broadcasters abolished guidelines that cautioned advertisers against discrediting competitors, and the American Association of Advertising Agencies followed suit.

Marketers soon were hammering one another's products in comparative ads that named names. Of the campaigns the bruising soft drink and fast food TV commercials were especially noteworthy. The fast food wars demonstrated how a touch of humor could take the edge off these assaults on competitors. Burger King's research, for example, uncovered negative feelings about the inflexibility of fast food menus, even if customers wouldn't actually ask for modifications in their burgers. Burger King responded with the "Have It Your Way" and "Your Way Right Away" ad campaigns. In another commercial Burger King took on McDonald's by interviewing a real-life family, the McDonalds, who were so embarrassed to admit that they preferred Burger King that they actually wore disguises.

The suspicion remained, however, that comparisons could also work against the advertiser. As David Ogilvy observed, "There is a tendency for viewers to come away with the impression that the brand which you disparage is the hero of your commercial."[5] Despite such risks the Ogilvy & Mather agency broke with its longstanding opposition to comparative advertising in 1981, stating that the practice could be a successful, "short-term tactical weapon."[6] Today advertisers name names in print and over the airwaves more than ever before.

The Soft Drink Shootout

Other admakers followed David Ogilvy's approach to positioning. To Ogilvy the concept of positioning was important to the extent that it identified what the product did and who would buy it. Most ads traditionally had directed their pitch at the largest segment of the buying public, but now they targeted specific socioeconomic or interest groups. The soft drink industry provides an excellent example of such lifestyle marketing ideas, as Coca-Cola, Pepsi, and 7-Up battled it out for market share.

Most soft drink advertising is about creating a distinct product personality. After all, how much can you say about carbonated water, sugar, and citric acid? In the past Coca-Cola had tried to associate it-self with motherhood, the flag, and country sunshine—"It's the real thing." Meanwhile Pepsi had appropriated an entire age group, the "Pepsi Generation," by tying itself to free-spiritedness, youth, and California girls in the 1960s and 1970s. But Pepsi wanted a campaign that would move even more product, so it turned to a product superiority claim—something the bottler had dared not do previously.

Pepsi's plan was simple: it conducted hidden-camera, blind taste tests against Coke which showed that a consistent majority of taste testers preferred Pepsi. The Pepsi Challenge hit the air in 1975 (Figure 8.2). "More people prefer the taste of Pepsi to Coke," the spots claimed. And as viewers watched people taking the challenge, they'd hear: "They pick Pepsi, time after time after time." Oddly, despite glowing sales reports, the Pepsi Challenge remained essentially a local marketing device and was never made the basis of a national advertising blitz. Coca-Cola struck back in a 1983 commercial with Bill Cosby mocking the Pepsi Challenge taste tests. Focusing binoculars on a Pepsi booth, the popular comedian announced, "I'm looking for the Coke drinker that Pepsi guys never show on TV." The Pepsi challenge was soon discontinued.

In 1979 the McCann-Erickson agency signed Mean Joe Greene, the Pittsburgh Steelers' future Hall-of-Fame defensive tackle, to deliver a sentimental pitch when he shared his football jersey—and a Coke—with a young fan. The immensely popular commercial performance was continued in the 1982 made-for-TV movie *The Steeler and the Pittsburgh Kid,* the first feature film based on a commercial. In another advertising first Coke gave us Max Headroom, the computer-generated spokesperson who later "starred" in his own television show. In a surprise move in 1985, Coca-Cola made an unprecedented announcement that it was dropping its popular century-old formula for Coke and reformulating it to make it sweeter. Although spokesperson Max Headroom was popular, the "New Coke" was not. Consumer complaints numbered as many as 1500 per day following the introduction of New Coke, and a newly formed organization of Coca-Cola drinkers demanded the return of old Coke. Amazingly, less than three months later, Coca-Cola announced that it was reviving the old brand under a new name, "Coca-Cola Classic." Company president Donald Keough appeared in Coca-Cola television spots apologizing to consumers for having seriously underestimated their passion for the drink. Apparently the strong test market success of the sweet Cherry Coke had convinced the firm to roll out the new Coke product before its market research was completed. Coca-Cola found that it simply couldn't sell a product to consumers that they didn't want.

In response, Pepsi ran ads poking fun at the confusion the move caused. One ad headlined: "Old Coke? New Coke? New Old Coke? New Classic Old Coke? Now more than ever, it's Pepsi, the choice for a new generation." Pepsi then showed just what money could buy, trotting

Figure 8.2 Beginning in 1975 Pepsi challenged consumers to compare the beverage to Coca-Cola.

out a line of celebrity spokespersons from Michael Jackson to Lionel Ritchie to Madonna. In their efforts to outsell each other and get their message across, the cola giants produced ever more fanciful and fantastic ads.

Figure 8.3   With this 1968 ad 7-Up positioned itself as the fresh alternative to Coca-Cola and Pepsi.

Meanwhile, 7-Up was sneaking up on the dueling titans. Since it had been created in 1929, the beverage had suffered from a series of identity problems, starting with its original name, "Bib Label Lithiated Lemon-Lime Soda." Despite a name change to 7-Up, early advertising for the drink limited its appeal, talking it up as "The Cure for Seven Hangovers." But in the 1960s 7-Up sought to change its image from a medicinal specialty drink or cocktail mixer to another appealing soft

Figure 8.4   In the 1970s 7-Up shifted advertising strategies to associate the beverage with an active, healthy lifestyle.

drink option. Advertisers repositioned it in 1968 as an alternative to Coke and Pepsi with an "Uncola" theme in tune with the rebellious times (Figure 8.3). Sales more than doubled, making 7-Up the number-three soft drink in the country, albeit still far behind Coke and Pepsi. At the same time, however, Dr. Pepper began national distribution, and lemon-lime-flavored Sprite and Mountain Dew cut into 7-Up's share of the market.

To head off the onslaught, 7-Up created new campaigns. In the 1970s the soft drink tried the lifestyle approach with its "America's turning 7-Up" theme (Figure 8.4). The advertising then aggressively shifted focus to provide a rational reason to buy the product. Interestingly research showed that consumers perceived colas as containing unhealthy ingredients. In one comparative commercial deep-voiced actor Geoffrey Holder cast a sour look at cans of Pepsi, Coca-Cola, and others and chided the bottlers for their use of artificial colorings and flavors: "Don't you feel good about 7-Up?" A simple, strong idea proved the best way to sell the product.

In the 1970s computer-generated animated graphics also began to be seen on television commercials. Robert Abel and Associates' Hollywood studio pioneered the new look. At the time, television viewers had seen nothing quite like the dazzling 1974 7-Up commercial "Bubbles," in which winged fantasy females swam through the carbonated drink. Abel's out-of-this-world animation also enlivened a 1977 Kawasaki motorcycle commercial entitled "The Ultimate Trip," which duplicated the view of passing scenery seen by the motorcyclist—but the gray asphalt turned a brilliant yellow, the green trees turned bright orange, and so on. The distorted, glowing imagery also simulated the psychedelic experience that ended Stanley Kubrick's film *2001: A Space Odyssey.* Both ABC and CBS, alarmed by what they saw, censored the commercial for allegedly "contributing to the use of drugs by motorcyclists."[7] Abel also produced another computerized commercial, the landmark "Brand Name" spot for Levi-Strauss, that same year. The Foote Cone & Belding spot followed the surreal adventures of a "pet" Levi's trademark that frees itself from its leash and frolics up a magical sidewalk filled with people in Levi's fashions.

As ads like these demonstrated, creativity was still alive on Madison Avenue. In fact, in many ways America was poised to emerge from the doldrums of the 1970s. With a resurgent economy, a wave of new products, and an enthusiastic consumer base, America would once again undergo a metamorphosis.

The 1980s: Let's Make a Deal

In spite of advertisers' continued reliance on research, the hard-sell, product-oriented tactics of the 1970s gave way to a focus on more esoteric aspects of building a brand image in the 1980s. Yet again, agencies would respond to changes in the American way of life.

The Ultraconsumer

The same economic factors that devastated the country's industrial heartland gave the United States an aura of prosperity throughout the 1980s. Defense spending, foreign investment, and the maturation of the baby boom generation sent the real estate, finance, retail trade, and high-tech manufacturing industries soaring. Deregulation of the banking industry and the stock market also touched off a wave of financial speculation.

In 1982 stock prices began a long, seemingly endless climb, due in part to the trend toward corporate mergers. Financial raiders realized huge profits acquiring companies, breaking them apart, and selling the

Figure 8.5 In a series of 1980s ads *Rolling Stone* attempted to lure "ultra-consumers" by trumpeting its new upscale image.

pieces one at a time. This financial speculation also generated hundreds of thousands of high-paying jobs for young bankers, lawyers, MBAs, and stockbrokers. As long as the market kept going up, the baby boomers apparently would enjoy splendid prosperity, except perhaps for employees of corporations that were restructured or broken up. In 1984 it was estimated that the 25- to 35-year-old group controlled an astonishing 23 percent of the country's disposable income. At the outset of their careers, these baby boomers became a new American social phenomenon, the young urban professional or "yuppie."

"Greed is good," assured actor Michael Douglas as Gordon Gekko in the movie *Wall Street.* The beneficiaries of the new wealth reveled in their new status. Trend-setting yuppies flooded into cities and brought new life to decaying residential and industrial neighborhoods. In the process of gentrification, gourmet shops, upscale restaurants, and trendy boutiques replaced mom-and-pop businesses. Rental apartments were converted into high-priced condominiums. Even the former countercultural magazine *Rolling Stone* reworked its image to attract this upscale group (Figure 8.5). These young professionals seemed to have an unlimited appetite for consuming premium goods—that is, the best that money could buy. In 1986 Grey Advertising heralded new research identifying "The Ultra Consumer," who had

A Taste of the Times

In 1975 *New York* magazine ran a feature article by social critic Tom Wolfe reporting a shift in how Americans viewed life. The article, entitled "The Me Decade," recounted how many people who formerly had supported political and social causes were now throwing their energy into a wide variety of self-help programs and disciplines. Millions of people took up jogging both to stay fit and to experience a runner's high. Health spas, fitness centers, and diet clinics boomed. Brown rice, tofu, and alfalfa sprouts became staples of many Americans' diets.

At the same time, many Americans donned hot pants and leisure suits and flocked to the discos and singles' bars in pursuit of a relationship. The flashy sounds of Donna Summer, the Bee Gees, and the Village People urged everybody to "Dance! Dance! Dance!" The hit movie *Saturday Night Fever,* starring John Travolta, captured the essence of the scene.

Still other Americans turned to new forms of psychotherapy and new approaches to spirituality. The human potential movement spread as self-seekers plunged into gestalt therapy, primal scream therapy, Zen meditation, and so on. Books like psychiatrist Eric Berne's *Games People Play* (1964) and Thomas Harris' *I'm OK—You're OK* (1969) helped people "to get in touch with themselves." Thousands of people discovered drugless "highs," practicing transcendental meditation (TM), shaving their heads and becoming Hare Krishnas, or "turning on to Jesus."

In tune with the times, directors like Francis Ford Coppola, Steven Spielberg, and George Lucas redefined American film with blockbusters like *The Godfather, Jaws, Close Encounters of the Third Kind,* and *Star Wars.* Television shows with a social conscience also appeared. The megahit "Roots," a 12-hour epic of slavery in America, mesmerized the country. "All in the Family," "Maude," and the irreverent "Saturday Night Live" found an audience—while "The Brady Bunch" idealized the family.

The styles of the early seventies—hot pants, platform shoes, polyester—fell out of favor as a newfound soberness began to infect the fashion world. Men wore "dress for success" three-piece suits. Although the Farrah Fawcett blow-dried hairstyle remained popular with women, the trend was toward a serious, no-

"seemingly unlimited appetites for acquiring premium goods that ooze with sensational immediacy and impact." Grey predicted that this "massive" segment was "here to stay."[8] Advertising explored new ways to court the ultraconsumer, ranging from corporate sponsorship to promotion of new technology.

nonsense look characterized by tailored clothing and conservative-length skirts.

"High tech," the term coined by designer Susanne Slezen in her 1978 book *High Tech Living,* became the new aesthetic. In sharp contrast to the postwar pursuit of novelty in the home, the watchword became "less is more." Industrial objects made their appearance in bland, pin-neat homes whose walls were painted white, gray, and other low-key monotones.

In the 1980s glamour, wealth, and power were back in style. Well-heeled, well-traveled consumers expected quality goods, fashions, furniture, and architecture. They drank Perrier, ate sushi, and worked out in designer sweats. Every jacket, polo shirt, and pair of jeans seemed to be stamped with a designer logo, and people bought expensive watches and anything by Ralph Lauren, from knit sport shirts to bed linens. "Power dressing" became an important part of the climb up the corporate ladder. Armed with expensive briefcases, women went to work in Donna Karan suits, while men purchased tailored fashions by Georgio Armani, Perry Ellis, and Calvin Klein. Looking sexy was also in. Chanting the slogan "no pain, no gain,"

legions of fitness addicts sweated and grunted their way to slimness, strength, and beauty. Jane Fonda and Richard Simmons became gurus of fitness. Exorbitantly priced activewear and athletic shoes became stylish street clothes as fitness buffs and nonexercisers alike tried to look chic. But it was primarily BMWs, Mercedes, and other costly automobiles that became the badge of their success.

"Cocooning," a term coined by trend-watcher Faith Popcorn, described people who stayed at home playing Trivial Pursuit and watching movies on their VCRs. Meanwhile, rafters shot the rapids, bungee-jumpers and skydivers plunged earthward, mountain bikers hurtled down rocky trails, and daredevils whizzed by on rollerblades.

In tune with the times, home and office interiors displayed a new look. The boring "less is more" formula of bland interiors and furnishings abruptly evolved into new decorative styles. Postmodern edifices avoided "pain-neat" minimalism and featured eclectic combinations of bright colors, signs of decay, and sometimes outrageously surrealist classical allusions. Clearly the marketing of design had become one of the most

(Continued)

And Now, a Word from Our Sponsor

Corporate sponsorship became big business in the 1980s, and it continues to grow today. Americans' passion for sports—and increasingly for tours, festivals, and the arts—provided businesses with a powerful

A Taste of the Times
(Continued)

visible and influential aspects of contemporary mass culture.

In the 1980s home was not complete without an entertainment center, including stereo, television, and VCR. The emerging video technology was epitomized by MTV, which premiered on cable television in 1981. How an artist looked became as important as the sound. The fame of such pop idols as Michael Jackson and Madonna reached extraordinary proportions through music videos and media blitzes, while rap, classical, and country-western music also promoted musicians as pop stars and celebrity product endorsers.

Rapt viewers caught glimpses of their favorite celebrities in television shows like "Lifestyles of the Rich and Famous" and in high-gloss fashion magazines like *Harper's Bazaar, Vogue,* and *Gentleman's Quarterly (GQ).* Not surprisingly, the not-so-wealthy became caught up in the quest to "have it all." Many people wanted at least to look as if they were rich and powerful. The upscale trend even trickled down to department and discount stores, which built strong fashion ele-

ments into their merchandising. J. C. Penney promoted a private-label polo shirt, sporting a fox emblem, and claimed parity at a better price than the best-selling Izod line; their slogan, "See you later, alligator," was an allusion to that brand's symbol. Model Cheryl Tiegs lent her name to a clothing line for J. C. Penney, and actress Jacklyn Smith did the same thing for Kmart; Martha Stewart endorsed a line of lifestyle accessories.

The picked-up pace also had its costs. Many young professionals drove themselves too hard, working long hours in the relentless pursuit of success. Leisure time became an extension of work. Eating in restaurants, vacationing at spas, and exercising at fitness clubs all provided opportunities to make business contacts, or "network." There never seemed to be enough money, and upscale lifestyles often were built on a mountain of debt. Two novels captured this spirit of hedonism— Tom Wolfe's *Bonfire of the Vanities* (1987) and Jay McInerney's *Bright Lights, Big City* (1984). One Alka-Seltzer campaign was specifically aimed at these overachievers, offering the product as a remedy "for the stress of success."

advertising opportunity. Sponsorship of an event could make people think more favorably of a company and provide an opportunity for the sponsor to enhance its image. But successful businesses wanted to know what they were going to get out of their sponsorship dollars before they spent them. Many companies initially didn't see much justification for the practice because sports organizations proved slow in using research to measure the value of the sponsorships.

In the 1970s most companies had limited sponsorships of charitable events. However, in the 1980s the number of companies involved went up as firms set out to enhance their image and increase sales. Miller Brewing Company of Milwaukee emerged as one of the most active sponsoring companies in the United States, particularly for sporting events. The firm believed that sports fans were more inclined to purchase beer, and so Miller used its sports sponsorships to reach these beer drinkers by boosting its image and increasing brand awareness. Since the 1950s Miller has sponsored football, basketball, and auto racing. And the brewer's sponsorship of pro beach volleyball beginning in the 1980s also helped change it from a regional sport into an international one. In addition, the company currently sponsors coverage of hockey, soccer, golf, tennis, and other sports.

Most sports, however, do not currently provide what auto racing offers—fans who are extremely loyal to the sponsors. These events significantly impact what spectators and home viewers buy and don't buy. For example, drivers can display as many as ten or more trademarks on their racing suits, shoes, and helmet, and, of course, on the car. Even the race car's interior provides an opportunity to display brand names, which are captured on film as cameras cover the racing scene from the driver's point of view. And research has shown that when a motor oil or tire company stops sponsoring a popular driver, thousands of fans switch to other brands. "NASCAR is family for these people," explains Performance Research vice president Bill Doyle. "If you're a sponsor, you're part of that family. People don't notice sponsors jumping in and out of the Olympics."[9]

The Indianapolis 500, the world's premier racing event, is owned by IndyCar racing teams, which recruit their own sponsors, unlike other forms of racing. IndyCar has a full-time, in-house market research department that helps identify the most appropriate sponsors. For example, Pittsburgh Paint and Glass (PPG), the world's largest paint and finishes manufacturer, is the title sponsor. Other companies involved in racing sponsorship include Kmart, Target, Ford, Kellogg's, DuPont, and Kodak, to name just a few. Tobacco companies, barred from the television airwaves, also turned to event marketing. These companies managed to skirt the TV ban and sneak on the air by sponsoring an event like the Winston Cup series of stock car races, a Marlboro car at a race, or a sign on a scoreboard. The cost of this type of advertising depends on the number of disclosures of the product name.

On the whole sports fans understand and accept corporate sponsorship as economically beneficial to the communities in which the events are held and as a means of keeping ticket prices down. Popular forms of corporate sponsorship include giveaway promotional items bearing a company logo, sponsored events (fan photo nights, banner days, and so on), company logos on racing boats and cars, advertising

Figure 8.6   In a series of ads, including these two from 1984 (top) and 1989 (bottom), Benetton promoted racial harmony with its "United Colors of Benetton" theme.

on beverage and food containers, signs, title sponsorship, company identification on athletes' clothing, and company brochures.

Besides sponsoring pro sports teams, other companies swear by their backing of ski areas, concerts, and festivals. For example, JVC, an electronics manufacturer, sponsors the annual JVC Jazz Festival with sites in Newport, New York, and Europe. This sponsorship successfully created a link between the brand name and jazz. Advertising also waged successful public service campaigns against smoking, drinking and driving, and unsafe sex; as part of the latter effort, a taboo-breaking condom ad appeared in a 1986 issue of *Cosmopolitan* magazine, targeting a female audience. Other companies, like the Italian knitwear firm Benetton, used the power of advertising to involve the public in the fight against racism. The campaign presented images of individuals all races and ages, backed by the theme "The United Colors of Benetton." Although this campaign increased racial awareness, it also generated a great deal of controversy (Figure 8.6).

Putting a Human Face on Technology

The materialism of the 1980s was also aided by the transfer of emerging technologies from the labs of engineers and technicians to the public at large. In both the workplace and the home, high technology transformed Americans' lives in a remarkably short period of time. As in most areas of industry, the role of advertising here was to educate the public and to encourage a belief that these innovations would somehow make life better.

Like the telephone, radio, and television in previous generations, the computer was the communications breakthrough of this era. "The electronic computer has become one of the most distinctive and potent inventions of the twentieth century," states historian R. A. Buchanan.[10] The first truly automatic digital computer came into operation in 1943. This highly complex machine, called "Colossus," was used to decipher enemy secret codes during World War II. After the war a second generation of computers was made available to businesses and offices. Users hired time from manufacturers of room-size "mainframe" machines and fed in their own information, which was stored on punched cards or paper tape. The next big breakthrough came with the first patent for an integrated circuit in 1959. An array of minute transistors were printed or etched on a piece of semiconductor, which could then perform all the functions of the large-scale systems. And in 1971 the invention of the silicon chip microprocessor enabled the development of even smaller, cheaper, and more powerful computers.

These emerging technologies also gave rise to the next generation of computer, the personal computer. It began with a gathering of electronic buffs called the "Homebrew Club" in a Menlo Park, California, garage in 1975. The excitement generated by a series of how-to articles in *Popular Electronics* on the Altair 8800, a somewhat limited personal computer, led to Steve Wozniak's work on his own machine in Steve Jobs' garage. Their first machine, intended only for sophisticated hobbyists, was merely a bare board without a cabinet, monitor, keyboard, operating system, disk drive, or any other way to load a program. The following year Jobs and Wozniak unveiled the Apple II, the first mass-marketed personal computer able to generate color graphics (Figure 8.7). Their company, Apple Computer, became one of the fastest-growing companies in American history.

In retrospect both Apple and rival IBM faced the herculean challenge of selling the idea that the slightly intimidating machines had a place not only in the office or studio but also in the home. Early on they recognized that their presentations had to be "user-friendly" to allay the skepticism of a wary buying public. One tactic was to use familiar spokespersons: Dick Cavett for Apple commercials, Bill Cosby for Texas Instruments, William Shatner for Commodore, and Alan Alda for Atari. None of these presenters, however, had the impact of Charlie Chaplin's endearing tramp, who became the mascot for IBM.

How to buy a personal computer.

Suddenly everyone is talking about personal computers. Are you ready for one? The best way to find out is to read Apple Computer's "Consumer Guide to Personal Computing." It will answer your unanswered questions and show you how useful and how much fun personal computers can be. And it will help you choose a computer that meets your personal needs.

Who uses personal computers.

Thousands of people have already discovered the Apple computer—businessmen, students, hobbyists. They're using their Apples for financial management, complex problem solving—and just plain fun. You can use your Apple to analyze the stock market, manage your personal finances, control your home environment, and to invent an unlimited number of sound and action video games. That's just the beginning.

What to look for.

Once you've unlocked the power of the personal computer, you'll be

using your Apple in ways you never dreamed of. That's when the capabilities of the computer you buy will really count. You don't want to be limited by the availability of pre-programmed cartridges. You'll want a computer, like Apple, that you can also program yourself. You don't want to settle for a black and white display. You'll want a computer, like Apple, that can turn any color tv into a dazzling array of color graphics.* The more you learn about computers, the more your imagination will demand. So you'll want a computer that can grow with you as your skill and experience with computers grows. Apple's the one.

How to get one.

The quickest way is to get a free copy of the Consumer Guide to Personal Computing. Get yours by calling 800/538-9696. Or by writing us. Then visit your local Apple dealer. We'll give you his name and address when you call.

Figure 8.7 In 1977 Apple introduced the personal computer to the general public.

When IBM launched its new personal computer aimed at the mass market in 1981, it needed an advertising campaign that would attack the problem of computer fright. The Madison Avenue firm of Lord, Geller, Federico, Einsteing had mulled over the idea using the Muppets or mime Marcel Marceau, but the agency and IBM eventually

The Best TV Commercials

As part of a special spring 1995 issue, six editors of *Advertising Age* selected the "50 best" TV commercials of all time. Compiled by decades, here's the list for the 1970s and 1980s.

1970s

Budweiser A commercial serves as a corporate Christmas card.

Volkswagen A man's frugality, embodied by his VW Beetle, is rewarded by his rich uncle.

Miller Lite Former pro athletes make a lower-calorie beer appealing to male drinkers.

Xerox A monk performs a "miracle" with a Xerox copier.

Life Two boys foist a cereal on little Mikey, but to their surprise, "he likes it!"

American Express "Don't leave home without" travelers' checks, urges the actor Karl Malden.

Dannon Longevity is linked to eating yogurt in a spot filmed in what was then Soviet Georgia.

Southern Airways A hilarious parody of the differences between coach and first class amuses viewers.

7-Up The "Uncola" shows off the "Uncola nut"—a lemon and a lime fused together.

Sunsweet A product improvement is heralded—"Today the pits, tomorrow the wrinkles."

Polaroid Mariette Hartley and James Garner promote cameras.

Chanel An avant-garde spot urges consumers to "share the fantasy."

The Energizer Bunny.

1980s

Bartles & Jaymes The folksy duo introduces a wine cooler.

Chrysler Lee Iacocca asserts, "If you can find a better car, buy it."

Wendy's An elderly woman bellows, "Where's the beef?"

Eastman Kodak A father recalls his daughter's childhood at her wedding.

Energizer A battery-powered bunny spoofs spots for other products.

(Continued)

The Best TV Commercials
(*Continued*)

Federal Express A fast-talking man quickly lists Fed Ex's attributes.

Ronald Reagan An emotional paean to "morning in America" helps re-elect a president.

Coca-Cola Mean Joe Greene tosses his football jersey to a boy who gives him a Coke.

AT&T A woman cries when her son calls "just to say, 'I love you, Mom.'"

Isuzu Joe Isuzu tells outrageous lies about the car.

Nike Bo Jackson and Bo Diddley play an improbable duet.

Cheer A low-key demonstration of a detergent's prowess breaks conventions.

Apple Macintosh A spot inspired by George Orwell's *1984* promotes computers.

Pepsi-Cola Michael Jackson pitches "the choice of a new generation."

Calvin Klein Brooke Shields models jeans.

California Raisins An animation technique called claymation brings a product to life.

concluded that Chaplin's "Little Tramp" character, with his ever-present rose, would help the PC open up a new technological world for the nontechnician. The campaign was so successful that it completely revamped IBM's formerly stuffy image (Figure 8.8).

Meanwhile, Apple allowed the Chiat/Day agency the creative license to produce what *Advertising Age* called the best television commercial ever made. In 1984 the first Macintosh was unveiled at a shareholders' meeting; the price was a hefty $2,495. Apple's willingness to take risks gave the computer company and its advertising a distinctive panache and image, a combination of counterculture appeal and cutting-edge technology. Apple stunned the advertising world with its legendary "1984" television commercial, which ran just once during the 1984 Super Bowl. Aimed directly at IBM, the Chiat/Day spot boldly proclaimed that because of the innovative new personal computer, "1984 won't be like 1984." The idea of smashing the Orwellian image of Big Brother seemed to tap into the antigovernment mood of the Reagan era. Apple had projected sales of 50,000 units for the first 100 days; actual sales reached over 72,000 units.[11] The spot also created a new category of commercial—"advertising as an

Figure 8.8 In 1981 IBM put a human face on the personal computer with its Chaplinesque "Little Tramp"; the character reappeared in this 1993 French ad.

event"—and established the Super Bowl telecast as the venue of choice for campaign launches.

Yet the legendary commercial almost landed on the cutting room floor. Although Apple had signed for a 30-second version, a longer 60-second version ran solely on the authorization of Chiat/Day copywriter Steve Hayden. "Apple was appalled," recalls Hayden. "The only reason '1984' aired was because we were unable to sell off $500,000 worth of Super Bowl time and had to fill 60 seconds with something."[12] The one-exposure spot succeeded through a combination of promotional daring, startling creativity, and ingenious media scheduling. The following year Apple premiered its "Lemmings" spot, which depicted a long line of working men and women marching trancelike off a cliff as a voice-over suggested that they switch from IBM to Apple computers.

At the same time, new methods of rapid pictorial duplication developed. The process of xerography had been invented in the 1930s; social historians have since dubbed the introduction of the Xerox 914 office copier the most spectacular single technological innovation of the twentieth century. Prior to the early 1980s the office copier had sold well simply through a demonstration of the machine in action.

Figure 8.9   This 1986 ad reminded the public of how seemingly miraculous an invention the Xerox machine was.

Only when Xerox faced new competition, however, did the company really begin to advertise. Like IBM, Xerox put a human face in its celebrated advertising campaign, featuring devout monks reminding us what a miraculous invention the Xerox really was (Figure 8.9). The product has become so popular that the name Xerox is synonymous with photocopying, as Xerox reminds us in its advertising: "There Are Two R's in Xerox" (the second one being the circled "R" for registered trademark) and "You can't Xerox a Xerox."

Most people overcame their ambivalence and quickly took advantage of the new technologies to communicate, to produce, and to entertain themselves. Remarkably innovations like voice mail, pagers, cellular telephones, copiers, fax machines, and personal computers quickly became new necessities of life. Yet another set of products were developed for the home. Microwave ovens heated meals in minutes. Vinyl records and transistor radios gave way to portable stereo radio-and-cassette players complete with earphones, to even bigger radios called "boom boxes," and later to compact discs (CDs). Viewers armed with remote controls "zapped" from one TV channel to another without leaving their armchairs. Videocassette recorders became both affordable and easier to use. Then came laptop and hand-held computer systems and other marvels of electronic miniaturization. The technology for instantaneous global communication had developed from a sophisticated curiosity to a commonplace commodity.

Ad agencies also adopted computerization for communications, administration, and design. The capabilities of computers to manipulate typography, graphics, and photography seemed endless. Instead of going through hand-sketched layouts and cut-and-paste production, art directors now went from "thumbnails," or small sketches of a proposed ad, to computer-generated "comps," or full-color comprehensive finished presentations, to give clients an impression of what the final ad would look like. Typefaces could be changed, distorted, and moved around the layout. Colors could be altered and night turned into day and back again at the press of a button. Images could be transmitted through a phone line, checked, altered, and returned in minutes. Once the client approved the laser-printed comp, the image was finalized and forwarded on disk or over a modem to the printer, with copy typeset electronically and color separations already made. In short, the production process speeded up at an unimaginable rate.

Global Brands and Global Advertising

The newest challenge facing advertisers was not just coordinating extensive advertising on a national scale, but developing campaigns in a number of foreign markets. In the 1980s global marketers pushed international advertising expenditures to unprecedented levels. In fact, advertising in foreign markets has outpaced the growth in the U.S. market since the mid-1980s. In 1989, for example, foreign advertising expenditures increased 12 percent to $136 billion while spending in the United States increased only 5 percent to $123 billion. The leading advertisers were Unilever, which spent more than $1 billion in 24 countries; Procter & Gamble, which spent over $900 million in 18 countries; and Nestlé, which spent about $600 million in 19 nations.[13] Among the agencies Tokyo-based Dentsu Inc. emerged as the leader in worldwide billings, followed by U.S.-based McCann-Erickson Worldwide and J. Walter Thompson Co.

Several factors account for the enormous growth in international advertising during this period, including the increased number of multinational companies and global brands, improvements in living standards, and innovations in communication and transportation. Multinational corporations with significant operations and marketing activities outside their home country first became a global force in the 1960s. Now companies like Exxon, IBM, Mobil, Citicorp, Gillette, Xerox, and Dow Chemical make more than half of their sales abroad.[14] Coca-Cola also anticipates the day when foreign sales will account for as much as 75 percent of its earnings, because there will be many more young people abroad than in aging America.[15]

As international ventures became less attractive to U.S. companies in the mid-1970s—due in part to the energy crisis, inflation, and currency devaluation—foreign multinational corporations began to operate in the American market. Americans began driving more Hondas, Nissans, and Toyotas from Japan and more BMWs, Mercedes, and Volkswagens from Germany. They loaded Konica cameras from Japan with Fujitsu 35mm film and wore more clothes from Taiwan and Korea. They watched more Sony and Panasonic televisions and listened to more Pioneer and Sanyo stereos from Japan. They drank more beer from Canada, Holland, China, Japan, Germany, Australia, and many other countries.

At the same time, people in other countries smoked more Marlboro, Winston, and Salem cigarettes. They also used more IBM and Texas Instruments computers, sipped more California wines, shopped for food in 7-11 stores, watched more Clint Eastwood movies, and wore Levi's blue jeans. And they ate more McDonald's hamburgers and Kentucky Fried Chicken and drank more Coke, Pepsi, and Dr. Pepper.

Globalization of marketing became so important that a number of foreign firms made significant investments in U.S. companies. Foreign-based multinational corporations even began manufacturing their products entirely in the United States, such as the Honda Accord in Marysville, Ohio. Other global corporations acquired shares in such major retailers as Fedmart, A&P, F.A.O. Schwartz, and Gimbels. Such investments are made all around the world. In fact, some analysts predict that there will be only a few automobile manufacturers by the end of the century and that the cars they produce will be global brands. The recent operations of Toyota and Honda in America may be the first step.

In developing a marketing strategy, advertisers have two basic options: a global strategy or a multinational marketing mix. The global strategy adopts a standardized marketing program with minimal modifications for different localities. For example, Benetton, with its well-known line of Italian knitwear and cosmetics, targets the same customers worldwide—young, affluent shoppers with trendy tastes. The visual images in its ads appeal to consumers in New York, Tokyo, and Paris; the only modification is translation of the copy into different languages. This approach has also worked for Levi's jeans, which have a universal appeal, and for Kodak (Figure 8.10). Similarly Coca-

Figure 8.10   As part of its global advertising strategy, Kodak presented the same images to consumers from New York to Paris to Tokyo.

Cola uses the same TV ads with local languages dubbed in, successfully implementing "one sight, one sound, one sell" around the world.[16] At a cost of $5 million, archrival Pepsi debuted its 2-minute "Make a Wish" commercial featuring pop singer Madonna in 1989. The ad appeared on the top-rated evening show in various countries, airing first in Japan and then following the time zones around the world, and ultimately reaching 250 million viewers.

Most firms, however, found it necessary to customize their approach for each marketplace. With this multinational marketing strategy, each market is assumed to have different cultures and competitive situations. For example, Tang sold successfully in America as a substitute for orange juice. However, because the French don't drink orange juice for breakfast, admakers repositioned Tang in France as a refreshing drink. In a campaign for Lux soap that appeared in Germany ads showed a celebrity about to enter a shower while ads in the United Kingdom pictured the same woman using the soap in a bathtub. This reflected the fact that the Germans are more likely to take a shower while the British prefer to bathe.

Other advertisers used a combination of the multinational and global approaches. For example, when Scott Paper entered the European market, it created a consistently warm, cuddly advertising image in the form of a labrador puppy to tell consumers that their product was soft yet strong. But Scott shot the series of ads in different settings; in Spain the living room had Spanish-style furniture, in Great Britain the setting was a traditional English country garden, and in Italy the living room featured an Italian decor. Likewise, ads for General Motors trucks that ran in Arab countries showed the vehicles at work in the desert (Figure 8.11).

Global Challenges

When global advertisers developed international campaigns, they faced a number of challenges. Among these was the need to understand and appreciate cultural differences. Even the most seemingly innocent uses of colors, numbers, shapes, sizes, symbols, body language, and so on were potentially offensive to a given culture. For example, a firm had to change the models in an advertisement in Thailand from a boy and girl holding hands to two girls doing so because the former approach was considered offensive. And an American shoe manufacturer insulted Southeast Asians by showing bare feet in its advertisements.

Firms also had to make a special effort to ensure that they were correctly translating the intended message. A poorly chosen name or a bad translation could undermine the credibility of the product. For example, when General Motors introduced the Chevy Nova automobile in South America, it did not sell well—the name meant "It won't go." The Ford Pinto flopped in Brazil—the name meant "small male appendage" in Portuguese slang. Even Coca-Cola suffered translation problems. Translated into Chinese characters, the brand name sounded like "Coca-Cola," but unfortunately the rendering meant "Bite the wax tadpole." Coca-Cola subsequently changed to a set of characters that mean "Happiness in the mouth."

Although American advertisers quickly adapted to global styles of advertising, foreign media proved another challenge. With the explosion of cable television and satellite receivers, viewers could watch channels from around the world. This transformed television from a mass medium to a global medium. But governments controlled most broadcast media, and many did not permit commercials—yet the message somehow managed to spread. Most Europeans now owned televisions, but in less-developed countries only the well-off could afford

Figure 8.11 As part of its multinational marketing strategy, General Motors adapted its ads for the Arab market by placing the trucks in desert settings.

this luxury, and even then, coverage generally was limited. Lower literacy and education levels in some countries also restricted the use of print media. Among those countries with national newspapers, advertisers typically found the circulation limited to upper-class, well-educated people. To reach this audience, auto manufacturers successfully used TV and magazine advertising, while companies like Coca-Cola and Pepsi successfully reached the lower-income market through radio and billboards. Movie advertising, too, could reach urban markets where TV ownership rates were low.

With the spread of multinational corporations and the explosive growth of communications technologies, advertisers faced unprecedented numbers of potential consumers. In this fertile environment

International Mistranslations

Literal translations and mistranslations of English advertising copy into other languages can send the wrong advertising message or no message at all. Here are some classic examples of mistranslations and faulty word choices.

Kentucky Fried Chicken's slogan "finger-lickin' good" translated into Chinese as "eat your fingers off."

In Taiwan Pepsi's slogan "Come alive with the Pepsi Generation" read, "Pepsi will bring your ancestors back from the dead."

Perdue Chicken's slogan "It takes a tough man to make a tender chicken" appeared on billboards in Mexico as "It takes a hard man to make a chicken aroused."

Schweppes Tonic Water translated into Italian as "Schweppes Toilet Water."

Braniff promoted its upholstery with "Fly in leather," but in Spanish it read as "Fly naked."

The Coors slogan "Turn it loose" read in Spanish as "Suffer from diarrhea."

Puffs introduced its tissue product in Germany, only to discover that "puff" in German is slang for "whorehouse."

Clairol introduced the "Mist Stick," a curling iron for hair, in Germany, only to find that "mist" in German is slang for "manure."

the seeds of the next creative revolution were sown; the harvest would feature image building, sex, and symbolism.

The Next Creative Revolution

When the London advertising agency Saatchi & Saatchi acquired Compton Communications in 1982, it looked like another case of a big agency wanting to take over another agency's blue-chip, packaged-goods accounts. But the mega-merger and partnership activity that followed dramatically altered the advertising industry. Pursuing a vision of a global "supermarket" communications organization, Saatchi & Saatchi added Dancer Fitzgerald Sample, Backer & Spielvogel, and Ted Bates Worldwide over the next four years. Other mega-mergers soon followed. For example, the Omnicom Group linked up with BBDO International, Doyle Dane Bernbach, and Needham Harper Worldwide; D'Arcy MacManus Masius and Benton & Bowles merged; and Chiat/

Table 8.1   Top Ten U.S.-Based Consolidated Ad Agencies, by Billings, 1995

Rank	Agency	Total Worldwide Billings (in billions)
1.	McCann-Erickson Worldwide	$1.20
2.	BBDO Worldwide	1.14
3.	Young & Rubicam	1.12
4.	J. Walter Thompson Co.	1.05
5.	DDB Needham Worldwide	1.05
6.	Ogilvy & Mather Worldwide	0.89
7.	Grey Advertising	0.83
8.	Leo Burnett Co.	0.80
9.	Saatchi & Saatchi Advertising	0.77
10.	Foote Cone & Belding Communications	0.76

Source: *Advertising Age* (April 15, 1996).

Day combined with Australian-based Mojo MDA. By 1988 the number of multinational agencies had dropped from twelve to eight, and that group increased its share of total advertising revenues from 12 percent to 20 percent.[17] The 1989 acquisition of both J. Walter Thompson and the Ogilvy Group by the London-based WPP group represented the final act in this merger-mad period (Table 8.1). Of the fifteen largest agencies at the beginning of the decade, only four emerged with the same structure at the end of the decade: Young & Rubicam, Leo Burnett Co., Grey Advertising, and McCann-Erickson Worldwide. (Note, however, that McCann-Erickson had long been part of the Interpublic Group, created in the 1960s.)

The mega-merger activity also signaled the growing importance of putting worldwide capabilities in place to handle global clients. A merger was one way to consolidate media-buying operations and to remain competitive in the emerging European media and marketing scenes. One of the farthest reaching changes was probably the shift to the European style of media buying, in which the buyer purchased time in bulk and resold it at a discount. (Recall that the J. Walter Thompson agency, the oldest continuing agency, had started as a wholesale buyer of space.)

Yet the new world of advertising was not without problems. As the business homogenized, there were fewer opportunities for unique, midsize agencies, such as specialists in packaged goods or business-to-business advertising. The global clients also were leery of the agency mega-mergers, questioning whether the gigantic ad empires could offer economies of scale and cross-agency services and at the same time keep client information confidential. In fact, this concern

Figure 8.12   With images of celebrities like Ella Fitzgerald, American Express's "portraits" campaign emphasized that "Membership Has Its Privileges."

led to clients shifting more than $500 million worth of business.[18] Deal making also reshaped clients and the media industry. Of the 100 leading advertisers listed in *Advertising Age* in 1980, one-third had ceased to exist a decade later.[19] By 1988 eleven of the top twenty broadcast companies had changed hands or merged, and newspapers and other print publications suffered the same fate.

Image Building

Despite rising production costs and an increasingly cluttered marketplace, some admakers overcame the obstacles and created new styles and approaches to sell their products. The trade publication *Advertising Age* had announced in a 1980 article that the industry was on the verge of "a new creative revolution." That statement turned out to be prophetic.

In the following years manufacturers spent a great deal of money on image building for cosmetics, perfumes, and fashions. Style reigned over substance. Advertisers no longer described how their products worked; customers were left to fill in the reasons for the purchase based on their feelings about the product line, its image, and the attractiveness of the models showing it. For example, the L'Oreal hair color campaign theme touted individual self-fulfillment, "Because I am worth it." Nearly 90 percent of the advertisements for cars used the

Memorable Slogans

Tell 'em Charlie sent you. (Star-Kist tuna)

It's going to be an Aviance night. (Aviance perfume)

Heineken refreshes the parts other beers couldn't reach.

I thought . . . until I discovered Smirnoff.

Click, click, every trip. (use seat belts)

Porsche: There is no substitute.

We bring good things to life. (General Electric)

The real thing. (Coca-Cola)

Just for the taste of it. (Diet Coke)

The heartbeat of America. (Chevrolet)

I want my MTV!

Give yourself a Dannon body. (Dannon yogurt)

The incredible edible egg.

Where's the beef? (Wendy's)

Drink your vegetables. (V8 vegetable juice)

Button your fly. (Levi's blue jeans)

We make it simple. (Honda)

You asked for it, you got it—Toyota.

The ultimate driving machine. (BMW)

Charlie the Tuna.

same self-fulfillment theme. Few described why their car was better or different; it simply was. And fewer ads featured comparisons with competitors, explained a product's unique features, or offered consumers specific reasons to make a purchase. Powerful images alone were expected to evoke confidence in the brand.

A campaign for American Express launched in 1987 reflected the new emphasis on esoteric image building; *Advertising Age* named this the print campaign of the decade. One of the reasons for its success was the compelling Annie Liebovitz photographs of celebrities, ranging from Thomas "Tip" O'Neill to Ella Fitzgerald (Figure 8.12). The print component of the "portraits" campaign reflected an overall marketing strategy emphasizing the umbrella theme "Membership Has Its Privileges." Previous print ads had touted the card with an elitist pitch, made famous in the "Do You Know Me?" campaign. David Ogilvy

Figure 8.13 Jerry Della Femina's 1986 pop-up 3-D ad for TransAmerica Insurance ran only once in a 1986 issue of *Time* but still yielded a remarkable 96 percent recall rate.

then shifted the tone of the marketing message to address a change in consumer values. "Prestige for prestige's sake is a rather empty feeling that to have meaning, prestige needs to be identified with values," said Kenneth Chenault, president of AmEx's Consumer Card Group. "The individuals portrayed aren't merely celebrities, they stand for achievement, reaching for the best."[20] One of the most successful spots brought together two extremes, the pint-sized jockey Willy Shoemaker and basketball's Wilt "the Stilt" Chamberlain.

Gimmicks were also in. Some of the decade's most heralded commercials featured Spuds MacKenzie, the original party animal for Budweiser beer; Joe Isuzu, a lying car salesman; and a fast-talking executive for Federal Express. These campaigns set the stage for a new breed of cartoonish characters in exaggerated situations. In a Wendy's hamburger spot who could forget Clara Peller bellowing, "Where's the beef?"—a line that has since entered the national lexicon.

Other ad designers tried dramatic variations in new printing techniques to set their ads apart from the pack. The perfume scratch-n-sniff fragrance strip first appeared in 1984, followed by samples containing lipstick, mascara, nail polish, dish soap, and hand lotion. And in 1987 Rolls-Royce ran an ad in *Architectural Digest* featuring a peel-and-sniff strip that gave off the scent of leather upholstery, standard in the model's interior. In addition, there were pop-up, three-dimensional ads. One ad in particular got readers' attention—Jerry Della Femina's pop-up image of downtown San Francisco, which appeared only once in a 1986 issue of *Time* magazine but still yielded a remarkable 96 percent recall rate (Figure 8.13). Other pop-ups gave us a cartoon Joe Camel and a paper Apple II computer.

A celebrated campaign for Absolut vodka dramatically mixed art and advertising. Drawing on a technique first used in the 1890s, Absolut commissioned contemporary artists such as Keith Haring, Kenny Scharf, and Andy Warhol to create vivid, full-color paintings to give the vodka a unique, upscale image. And each holiday season Absolut vodka produced ads featuring Christmas cards with microchips that played music, a bottle insert filled with floating snowflakes, and other three-dimensional images.

For the first time, New York City no longer dominated the creative scene, and marketers now looked beyond Madison Avenue for advertising. They found it at the offices of West Coast agencies like Chiat/Day, Hal Riney, and Foote Cone & Belding, all of which produced award-winning ads. Other innovative agencies began to spring up in cities such as Minneapolis, Dallas, Atlanta, and Portland, Oregon. New York agencies still controlled the major share of ad dollars spent in the United States each year (Table 8.2). But the flood of creativity from the West Coast agencies became so powerful that they grew at twice the rate of their New York counterparts from 1977 to 1982, and their billings skyrocketed more than 120 percent. As a result California overtook Chicago as the number two advertising locale in the country.[21] Much of this growth was due to California's overall business boom, fueled by the emergence of the Pacific Rim countries as major trading partners. Perhaps more than anything else, the California advertising growth stemmed from the success of Silicon Valley, as most of these agencies counted at least one high-tech company among their clients. Perhaps reflecting their improbable success, these technology and other start-up companies generally were willing to take chances.

The West Coast agencies also tended to operate in a more relaxed manner than their East Coast counterparts. California-based Chiat/Day, named the top creative agency for the 1980s, was typical. At Chiat/Day everyone working on the same account sat together, and anyone, even the lowest-ranking member of the team, could talk to anyone at the client's office, including the company president. "This is the easiest way to stimulate creative exchanges and foster new ideas," explained founder Jay Chiat. The creative product of this corporate counterculture succeeded in increasing the shop's billings ten-fold during the 1980s, from $100 million to $1.3 billion; by decade's end the firm also employed a staff of 1200 and had acquired Australian-based Mojo MDA.

Table 8.2   Top Ten U.S. Metropolitan Areas by Advertising Billings, 1995

Rank	City	Total Local Shop Billings (in billions)
1.	New York	$29.93
2	Chicago	9.50
3.	Los Angeles	6.23
4.	Detroit	5.72
5.	San Francisco	3.63
6.	Minneapolis	2.56
7.	Boston	2.38
8.	Dallas	2.37
9.	Connecticut	1.35
10.	Atlanta	1.18

Source: *Advertising Age* (April 15, 1996).

Early in the decade, Chiat/Day created attention-getting campaigns for smaller accounts such as Fotomat, Olympia beer, Yamaha motorcycles, and USA snowmobiles. It also grabbed national attention with a handful of striking ads, including billboards for Nike athletic apparel that featured blowups of star athletes and little else (Figure 8.14). But the public really took notice when the agency created the surrealistic "1984" TV ad for Apple Computers and then a lively campaign for California Coolers. At the time two competitors, Gallo and Seagram, also were developing advertising campaigns for wine coolers. The Chiat/Day concept was to present a product that apparently had come from nowhere. As it turned out, the wine cooler did indeed have a heritage. The admakers explained how they overcame the obstacle and found their tale: "People had been concocting this stuff in tubs on the beaches of California before it was ever bottled. So we talked to these people, watched old surf movies, listened to rock 'n' roll and drank a cooler or two. Then we wrote about what we learned."[22] The resulting campaign, aimed at the younger drinker, was heralded as one of the best of the decade.

Rival agency Hal Riney & Partners, which also had a wine cooler account, took a different approach, one that garnered the agency a best-of-the-decade award. The classic campaign for the Bartles & Jaymes' wine cooler talked about product differences but simultaneously built an image (Figure 8.15). To sell the brand, Riney created folksy Frank Bartles and Ed Jaymes, usually seen sitting on a porch chatting. The first commercial spoof had Ed writing to Harvard for an MBA so that the two could go into business. Every week the message changed but closed on a personal note: "We thank you for your support." Many people thought that there really were a Bartles and

Figure 8.14 This striking billboard by Chiat/Day helped build an image for Nike.

Jaymes. Actually the cooler was produced by the giant vintner Gallo, and it soared to the first place in the market.

Riney has been based in San Francisco for his entire career. He started in the mailroom at BBDO, worked for Botsford Ketchum, and then moved on to Ogilvy & Mather's San Francisco branch office, which he purchased in 1986 to form his own agency. Riney's ads do not make a flat-out pitch that a product is the best, the finest, or the greatest, nor do they feature heavy-handed comedy. The "Rineyesque" slice-of-life spots do more than add humor to advertising; they also humanize it. As Riney observes: "I think to touch people, you have to involve them. And involving people requires that you let them make up their own minds about what you've said. That means you leave out product features and communicate through suggestion."[23]

Whether he's promoting beer or presidential candidates, Riney's words and visuals embrace the audience. His feel-good approach worked in promoting Henry Weinhard beer, Perrier water, and President Ronald Reagan. The Reagan spots were simple and reassuring. They recited Reagan's accomplishments, focusing on the line "More families will go to work today than at any other time in our country's history" while shooting warm, emotional visuals of mornings, weddings, grandpas, and kids. Reagan was reelected in a landslide.

Another notable San Francisco–based shop attracted attention with two campaigns that wowed the industry. Foote Cone & Belding

Thank you for your support

Figure 8.15   Hal Riney created folksy characters Frank Bartles and Ed Jaymes to build a down-home image for the wine cooler.

brought an MTV-style look to Levi-Strauss's "501 Blues" spots, which evolved in step with the moods and styles of young people. The agency also gave viewers something to smile about. When the dancing California Raisins, with their wrinkled bodies, black stick legs, and white gloves debuted on television, they belted out Marvin Gaye's classic "I Heard It Through the Grapevine." In 1988 the "grape hit" was named the best television commercial of the year, and a line of tie-in merchandise soon followed. The California Raisins were old enough to have wrinkles but young enough to rock 'n' roll—one of the many "grape facts" to bombard the public.

Sex and Symbolism

After the 1970s battle of the sexes, a spirited new sensibility in male–female relationships evolved in the 1980s. The 1973 Charlie fragrance ads had introduced the attractive, independent woman who needed no one else in her life, and these values began to reassert themselves in sexually charged advertising for everything from perfume to blue jeans (Figure 8.16). For example, Lois Geraci Ernest of Advertising to Women presented strong but sexy women for Jean Naté ("Take charge

New Brand Names

1975 Sony videocassette recorders (VCRs) invade the home.

1975 Pet rocks do not need to be kept on a leash.

1977 Apple II takes the world by storm as the first personal computer that can generate color graphics.

1978 Ben and Jerry sign up for a $5 correspondence course in ice-cream making.

1979 The Walkman portable stereo with headphones first sells as the "Soundabout" in the United States.

1979 Black & Decker's Dustbuster vacuums those hard-to-get-at places.

1980 Gloria Vanderbilt and Calvin Klein market designer jeans.

1981 MTV launches a music video channel and helps revive the pop music industry.

1981 IBM's PC is the long-awaited version of the personal computer.

1981 Nintendo releases the video games Donkey Kong and later Super Mario for arcade and home use.

1981 Nutrasweet sweetens foods with no calories and no bitter aftertaste.

1983 Swatch Swiss watches sell style and reliability for $40.

1984 Apple unveils the Macintosh personal computer for $2495.

1985 The Discover credit card is issued by Sears, Roebuck & Co.

1985 New Coke is marketed, but customer complaints force Coca-Cola to bring back the original formula under the name Coca-Cola Classic.

1989 Nissan Infiniti's initial ad campaign introduces the luxury car by not showing it.

of your life"), Rive Gauche (a woman "having too much fun to marry"), and Aviance perfume ("It's going to be an Aviance night").

In the 1980s other advertisers altered their portrayals of women due to the forces of feminism and the increasing number of women entering the work force.

As the climate for women in American society changed, so did Betty Crocker. General Mills updated her portrait to reflect the new roles women were accepting outside the home. The seventh portrait (1986) depicts Betty as comfortable in the board room as she is in the dining room (Figure 8.17).

The fresh approach was best captured in an ad for Johnnie Walker scotch that featured two bikini-clad women joggers and the headline

The Charlie perfume woman had been one of the earliest (in 1973) to show a confident working woman striding purposefully through a male world. The ad here was refused by the New York Times for being sexist and "in poor taste," but eleven women's magazines accepted and ran it and the publisher of Ms. called it "light-hearted." "It's kind of fun to see a couple where the man is not the tall, powerful one," she explained. The ad still "works" and the image was still being run in 1988.

Figure 8.16   This 1988 ad for Revlon's Charlie perfume portrays the confident, independent woman.

"He loves me for my mind. And he drinks Johnnie Walker." Other fashion marketers were breaking the mold and redefining the way they advertised to the confident new woman. To enhance the allure of their products, however, few advertisers explained the unique features or gave consumers a rational reason to buy the product. Instead, the emphasis was only on the effect. The ads simply hinted at an experience, showing fantasy or dream sequences resulting from using the product.

1936   1955   1965   1968

1972   1980   1986   1996

Figure 8.17   As American society changed, General Mills updated Betty Crocker's portrait to reflect contemporary women. Since her creation in 1921, Betty Crocker has provided tips, meal plans, and products to American families.

"The most risque copy I have seen was for Paco Rabanne men's cologne," says David Ogilvy.[24] One of television's sexiest 30 seconds, called "Man in Bed," opened with a French-accented man stirring himself awake as the telephone rang. "Hello" he yawned into the phone. "You snore," a women's voice informed him. "And you steal the covers," he responded jokingly. As the conversation continued, paintings and discreet camera angles hid his nudity; we never saw the woman. In a gender-role reversal it was now the woman who rose at daybreak to go on a business trip, leaving the lovesick man in bed. A two-page print ad also ran, showing the man in bed, with the commercial script expanded and printed alongside (Figure 8.18). As a promotional stunt department stores across the country hired actors to lie on beds placed in store windows and talk with passersby who called from extension phones placed on the sidewalk. Sales for Paco Rabanne went up 25 percent, and the advertisement, created by Ogilvy & Mather, was voted the best to appear in magazines in 1981.

Another fragrance, the pricey Chanel No. 5, used surreal imagery to create an upscale appeal with its sexually charged "Share the

Figure 8.18   This 1981 ad by Ogilvy & Mather reflected a fresh approach to male–female relationships.

Fantasy" commercials. The imagery was a visual feast. Beside a blue swimming pool, which perhaps represented nothing more than a day-dream, a woman dropped her robe and sat; as she reclined, a mysteri-ous man materialized, and she spread her legs to greet him. All the while the woman's voice was heard: "I am made of blue sky and golden light and I will feel this way forever." This foray into sexual adventur-ism continued with Calvin Klein's promotion of Obsession perfume, whose ads suggested that an erotic fantasy world awaited consumers. The scintillating campaign shot the unknown perfume to the top of the market within months. The firm spent $17 million to launch Obses-sion, and within one year it was selling $40 million worth of it.

Using sex to sell to teens also became a common image-building tactic. The once humble "dungarees" became big fashion and big news. For example, in 1980 Sergio Valente, Bon Jour, Calvin Klein, Gloria Vanderbilt, and Jordache spent nearly $40 million in advertis-ing. When Calvin Klein introduced his jeans campaign in 1981, contro-versy arose over the sexy ads and commercial spots featuring teen star Brooke Shields seducing audiences with her provocative "Know what comes between me and my Calvins? Nothing." Three network-owned stations in New York banned the ads. Nevertheless, sales of the

Figure 8.19 Despite offending some people, this ad reflected a triumph of modern-day advertising—overpriced designer jeans.

expensive jeans jumped nearly 300 percent following the first wave of commercials.[25] In another controversy that same year, the Chicago Transit Authority pulled hundreds of bus billboards for the Bon Jour brand due to citizen complaints. The ads showed a model's torso with her jeans unzipped far enough to hint that she was not wearing underwear. And Jordache ran ads of blouseless young women astride similarly clad young men. Many people objected to the sexy jean ads, but before long, people paid extravagant sums for denims that displayed designers' names on their backside (Figure 8.19).

The recession of the late 1980s caught many Americans by surprise—they had thought the good times would go on forever. But the massive cuts in military spending shrank the defense industry. Foreign competition and deregulation of the savings and loan, railroad, utility, and airline industries led to a decline in corporate profits. Mergers and leveraged buyouts led corporations to adopt "lean and mean" strategies, and few new jobs were created. Instead, waves of reorganization and layoffs swept through middle management. Finally there was a downturn on Wall Street. For example, in 1987 the Dow Jones plunged 508 points, almost double the record set in 1929. In sum, the high-flying spirit of the 1980s was gone. The sobering realization was that the "good life" was out and the "simple life" was in, at least for a while. The next chapter explores how this far-reaching trend continued into the 1990s and sent shock waves through the advertising industry.

got milk?

McDonald's opens a restaurant
in Moscow.
1990

Presidential candidate Ross Perot
catapults the infomercial into
prominence.

After four white police officers are
acquitted on all charges but one in
the beating of African American
motorist Rodney King, riots erupt
in Los Angeles.
1992

1991
Iraq's invasion of Kuwait results in
the Persian Gulf War.

The Soviet Union breaks up as
republics declare independence.

Chapter 9

1990s and Beyond The Media Revolution

Programs are released for home computers to access the World Wide Web through on-line service providers such as Prodigy and America Online.

Manhattan-based Green Team bills itself as the first and only New York agency to specialize in environmental issues.

Programs are released for home computers to access the graphical portion of the Internet, called the World Wide Web.

New guidelines for food labels require that amounts of fat, sodium, cholesterol, and protein be printed on the label; foods with terms such as "light" and "low fat" must meet certain criteria.

1993

The first baby boomers turn 50.

1996

1995
HotWired is the first Web site to use the traditional magazine format, placing ads on certain pages among editorial matter.

The O. J. Simpson "trial of the century" begins.

2000

Emerging technologies, globalization, and fluctuating economies have dramatically impacted the modern advertising industry. In the 1990s the number of new product annual introductions has doubled. The proliferation of cable television, satellite receivers, videocassette recorders, and electronic mass media has transformed communications. Worldwide markets have grown due to improved economic conditions and a desire for expansion. Advertising is no longer a Western phenomenon; it is now global. Countries like China and the former Soviet Union once condemned advertising as a capitalist evil, but billboard images of Kentucky Fried Chicken in Beijing and McDonald's in Moscow have become the norm. And with the collapse of the Soviet Union, Eastern European nations are encouraging private enterprise and acknowledging the benefits of advertising.

Internationally minded marketers have spurred an explosive growth in advertising with their aggressive campaigns outside the United States, following the lead of American films, television, and music. Coca-Cola, McDonald's, and, most recently, Microsoft have created truly global brands. By the year 2000 consumers may well shop for cosmetics at The Body Shop, rent a video at Blockbuster, or dine at Planet Hollywood in almost any part of the world.

Global competition also has put American corporations under pressure to restructure, consolidate, and simplify. The overall U.S. economy has shifted from an industrial base toward one rooted in information technology and services. Firms have pared down their organizations to an essential core, slicing away layer after layer of the work force through "rightsizing," "reengineering," and "downsizing." In place of large corporate staffs, firms are hiring temporary workers on a project-by-project basis.

Lifestyles have changed along with the economy and the work world. Many Americans suffered in the economic downturn of the early 1990s. Real estate prices stagnated on both coasts, the savings and loan industry fell on hard times, and the national debt reached a staggering $4 trillion. Though the economy stabilized and even improved by 1995, it had already led to a massive shift in consumer behavior and buying patterns.

In this new era selling has become more complicated. Advertisers face an increasingly fragmented audience and diverse emerging markets, ranging from the vast aging baby boomer generation to environmental crusaders. But the creative process hasn't changed much at all. Centuries-old ideas that worked for newspapers, magazines, and broadcast media have been applied to an enormous range of new media, from movie theater screens to shopping carts.

Today's Consumers

Advertisers now face their most diverse audience in modern times. The economic realities of the 1990s, combined with changing demographics and lifestyles, have created a new breed of consumer who eschews advertising. Across all income groups consumers are more selective in their buying behavior. They are skeptical of product claims, doubt they will be as well-off as their parents, and want the most out of every hard-earned dollar they spend.

To further complicate the issue, mass marketers have found that they can't identify their target audience through demographics alone. The 1950s axiom "Mrs. Middle Majority is the target you are supposed to hit" (referring to middle-class white women age 25–49) no longer applies. The baby boomers represent perhaps the last dominant WASP generation as America becomes more racially and ethnically diverse. Now consumers might be baby boomers, generation Xers, teens, older Americans, gays, African Americans, Hispanics, Asian Americans, and so on. And all these different groups are composed of people with varied incomes, education, and life experiences.

One message won't work for all people, because new generations of consumers react differently to commercial messages. Many marketers have made the mistake of trying to reach the largest segments based on demographics such as age and income, ignoring geographics, psychographics, and market fragmentation. As a result different brands of a given product come to resemble one another, competing on value and price. But some companies created great advertising when they recognized that within each of these segments, the market also contains consumers with highly different lifestyles and values.

The Money Is in the Middle

Marketers have kept their sights on the now middle-aged baby boomers, a lucrative market ever since the boomers were born. For example, Walt Disney, the Gap, and McDonald's joined the trend toward marketing with more mature consumers in mind. Disney targeted the over-40 crowd with ads that showed Disney World as an adult playground. The apparel retailer Gap cut back its teen marketing to address the boomers. But in the fast food industry, no one has spent more than McDonald's expected $200 million to introduce a fast food product—the Arch Deluxe burger aimed at adults.[1] The venture even risked the franchise's positioning with kids. The series of ads, launched in 1996, spoke directly to adults by featuring icon Ronald McDonald basically looking and acting adult, grooving to disco, shooting pool, and wearing a business suit—practically everything short of smoking.

Yet the boomers have done more than acquire gray hairs; they also have altered their buying habits. The recent recession was the most serious economic setback in the boomers' adult life. It drove home the message that the seemingly unending abundance was in fact finite.

The classic American Dream that hard work brings rewards was fading. For the first time a generation may not surpass or even match its parents' standard of living. Several factors account for these diminished expectations. Skyrocketing real estate prices vastly inflated the financial worth of many older Americans and placed home ownership out of the reach of many younger people. The shrinking industrial and manufacturing base resulted in the loss of many high-paying, mass-production jobs. And two-paycheck households became the norm; by 1992 three of five women with children held jobs outside the home.[2]

Not surprisingly, this downward mobility has prompted many boomers to curtail their spending. Some cut up their credit cards while others traded in their expensive cars for cheaper models. Dressing down became fashionable. Chains like WalMart, Target, and Taco Bell that delivered value enjoyed increased sales. Hordes of bargain hunters shopped at a new breed of superstores such as Toys "R" Us, CostCo/Price Club, Circuit City, and Home Depot. Although consumers still shopped the upscale downtown stores it was the superstores that rang up the big sales.

These emerging trends also coincided with the baby boomers settling down and starting families of their own, as well as often shouldering the burden of caring for their aging parents. Convenience, simplicity, and affordability became watchwords. Advertisers addressed the new realities of the American family, pitching long-lasting value, time-saving features, and rock-bottom prices, as well as wholesomeness to health-conscious parents. And more and more ads for everything from deodorant to cellular phones included images of working women and single mothers (Figure 9.1).

Women Wield Their New Power

For most of the twentieth century advertising portrayed women in narrow roles—as dim-witted sex objects, as perky young things in search of a man, or one-dimensional homemakers eager to serve their husbands. Now advertising showed women in two different worlds: the traditional one, a rerun of the 1950s with stay-at-home moms, and a modern one filled with working women. In the traditional ads women were depicted putting dinner on the table, caring for the children, and cleaning the house. In some ads the homemaker derived pleasure only from pleasing others. Such ads for household cleaners, foodstuffs, and over-the-counter drugs were still effective with the modern, working woman, for whom the tableaux may have mirrored real life. Apparently the ad industry has recognized that women are still responsible for most household purchases, as well as for most of the cooking, shopping, and cleaning.

At the same time, other marketers have tried to go beyond old stereotypes and redefine the way they advertise to women. Advertisers have made major efforts to court the "new" modern woman, who holds a job, has career goals, and derives pleasure outside the home. In

I need to learn how to multiply.

Take one woman.

Add job.

Add boss.

Add husband.

Add children.

Add promotion.

Add overtime.

Add daycare.

Add pressure.

Subtract time.

Divide attention.

How does this equal one woman?

You can't be in ten places at once, but you could get a Motorola cellular phone. It's easy to use, hard to hurt and small enough to fit right in your pocket. Multiply yourself with Motorola. The best-selling, most-preferred cellular phones in the world. For more information, call 1-800-331-6456.

MOTOROLA

Figure 9.1   This ad for Motorola's cellular phone targeted working women.

some ads for products traditionally targeted at women, no women even appeared. Commercials for Motrin IB, for example, mirrored the trend that fathers were participating more in child care. Ads for Cheer laundry detergent used a bald man to demonstrate the product's cleaning power. General Foods introduced a new Betty Crocker image that blended the features of seventy-five real women to better represent the 1990s homemaker (Figure 9.2). Other ads creatively addressed such women's issues as maintaining control without being a super-woman, combatting fatigue, balancing family and work, and so on.

Some marketers reshaped their ads aimed at women purely for economic reasons. Consumer research indicated that women exuded more influence than men over most household purchases for products like groceries, children's clothing, and toys, as well as swaying 80 percent of car purchases. Agencies like J. Walter Thompson Co.

Figure 9.2 In 1996 General Foods introduced the new Betty Crocker as the symbol of the 1990s American homemaker—a composite portrait of dozens of real women from different backgrounds.

(JWT) monitored these trends to better understand how the agency should advertise to women. "With the exception of some categories, like feminine hygiene and cosmetics, the idea of gender will disappear," pointed out Peter Kim, former director of strategic planning at JWT. "We are going to find a repositioning where the thrust of advertising is to position tools that empower women rather than as something to enhance self-esteem or make her a better housewife."[3] The bottom line was finding the approach that would sell more products.

Because more women now hold key marketing and advertising positions, they have impacted the basic promotional appeal for many accounts, too. They are drawing attention to the underlying drives that contribute to women's buying actions and developing campaigns that establish emotional ties with consumers.

When Foote Cone & Belding launched Levi's award-winning print ads using Matisse-like drawings of women in 1991, they created the smartest, artiest, and most sensitive campaign ever for female jeans wearers (Figure 9.3). Several years later, stunning television commercials brought the drawings to life. The animated spots had virtually no copy, no voice-over, and no slogans. Instead, they simply conveyed emotional truths about women's lives, touching on such "hot buttons" as men, love, pain, and food. Pop-up titles included "Women Not Feeling Blue," "Women Finding Balance," "Women Finding Love," and "Women Getting Things Off Their Chest." Women identified with this type of product advertising that did not use the "too-perfect" model. This Levi's campaign proved inspiring, uplifting, and even empowering.

In addition, for the first time, other male-targeted products such as athletic shoes, cars, condoms, and beer were marketed with the lucrative female audience in mind. These advertisers recognized that they simply could no longer afford to alienate women. For example, Nike's athletic shoe ads offered women a nurturing message and encouragement (Figure 9.4). Ford Motor Company went the extra mile to make its vehicles attractive to both sexes and specifically targeted women with advertisements in magazines such as *Ladies' Home Journal*.

Beer advertising visibly changed, too. Although traditionally the typical beer drinker had been a man age 21–35, increasing numbers of women were drinking beer. As a result many advertisers stopped showcasing women as sex objects and featured them as equals. For instance, Barton Brands reversed St. Pauli Girl's decision to print the image of a buxom German girl with more cleavage. The 1991 Old Milwaukee beer commercial retired the semi-naked Swedish Bikini Team. Also, Miller Lite abandoned the "just-us-guys" approach and showed men and women socializing together. However, supporters of the Dangerous Promise Coalition believed that the real message in alcohol advertisements and similar ads was "that young men who drink alcohol will attract beautiful, sexually available women."[4] The group aimed to put an end to alcohol ads that were demeaning to women and that could encourage violence against women by dehumanizing them. Their 1994 campaign set up billboards across the country with the headline "Quit using our cans to sell your cans."

At the same time, a new genre of advertisements emerged that focused on the sensibilities of a new breed of women by fostering the image of "reverse sexism." Marketers started to tap into women's "I-don't-need-a-man" attitude by portraying men in the same negative ways that women had been featured for years. In an upbeat parody one such print ad pictured a set of headlights, door knockers, and melons—all ridiculous images men have used to describe women's breasts—with the kicker tag line "Bamboo Lingerie, a company owned by two women. Put that in your pipe and smoke it."

Figure 9.3   A series of ads for Levi's featuring Matisse-like drawings was the smartest, artiest, and most sensitive campaign ever for female jeans wearers.

Figure 9.4 Nike encouraged women to "just do it."

Some ads were far more explosive. Bodyslimmers lingerie showed a woman from the neck down wearing a one-piece undergarment; the copy read: "While you don't necessarily dress for men, it doesn't hurt, on occasion, to see one drool like the pathetic dog that he is" (Figure 9.5 on page 390). Another ad for Hyundai cars featured two women arguing that men buy powerful cars because they are worried about the size of their penis—but the word is never spoken. One read: "He must be overcompensating for a . . . shortcoming." When a handsome man drove up in an economy Hyundai Elantra, the second woman mused: "I wonder what he's got under the hood?" Of course, this mind-set was not shared by all women, so admakers continually faced the challenge of how to reach a new balance, adjusting approaches in favor of women and following the currents of the culture.

"X" Marks the New Target

In the 1990s advertisers started looking past the dominant baby boomers to target the boomers' children—the 18- to 29-year-olds known as "generation X," a term coined by Douglas Coupland in his

A Taste of the Times

The economic crunch of the 1990s helped create a new breed of consumer. Fewer people believed that the status-symbol products characteristic of the conspicuous 1980s were worth their price. High-end designers introduced moderately priced lines, and fashions became plain, simple, and rugged. In home decor just about anything was acceptable as a means of self-expression, in distinct contrast to the traditional idea that everything had to match. Checked gingham was juxtaposed with floral patterns, and faded blue denim covered elegant gilded armchairs. The new eclecticism also reflected how collecting had become a middle-class phenomenon. Instead of buying seven-piece matching bedroom suites the way their mothers and grandmothers had, people acquired singular pieces of furniture at retail outlets, antique stores, and even flea markets. In restaurants the hottest look was a different china pattern at every place setting. And in lieu of expensive restaurants, coffeehouses provided a comfortable place to meet, play chess, listen to poetry readings, make business contacts, or sign deals.

In the media a new breed of television show mixed news with entertainment. Outrageous and combative talk show hosts titillated audiences with sensational investigations into and debates on AIDS, incest, abortion, and transsexuals. Shows like "A Current Affair" took their cue from the tabloids, and slice-of-life shows like "Cops" and "Rescue 911" proved to be hits. Semi-autobiographical TV movies based on sensational headlines proliferated. Dramas added more realism, and popular sitcoms like "Roseanne," "Married with Children," and "The Simpsons" gave viewers a whole new version of the American family.

New technology promised interactive TV, movies on demand, and an all-in-one computer, telephone, and TV set. Yet, instead of cutting into the numbers of

novel *Generation X* (1991). Cars, magazines, music, clothing—it was hard to name a category in which marketers were not chasing this prized audience.

Yet generation Xers had little in common with their boomer parents, who came of age in the reactionary 1960s. These younger adults watched less network television, read different magazines, and were frustrated that the American Dream seemed beyond their reach. A dollar simply wouldn't buy as much as it had for their parents twenty or thirty years earlier. These young people, who made up 23 percent of the work force in 1993, earned nearly one-third less than their par-

moviegoers, the at-home video provided another movie-going option. Although young adults still preferred to get out of the house and see a film when it opened, family-oriented movies were more likely to ring up big box office sales. With expanded profits linked to the merchandising of videos, clothes, toys, books, and other licensed spin-off products, box office smashes like *Jurassic Park, Batman,* and *Lion King* proved extremely lucrative.

The explosion of new technology also made it possible for people to shop, bank, travel, work, and entertain themselves without interacting with other individuals. Consumers could pay for almost anything by simply inserting a credit card or ATM card into a machine. Computer-controlled reading devices allowed consumers to buy food, gasoline, tickets to movies and sporting events and countless other goods that were delivered overnight, not in days. But a growing number of overworked Americans also found the emerging technologies to be invasive. Pagers, cellular phones, and laptop computers extended their work week far beyond the traditional 40 hours. The fast pace of change and the overwhelming amount of information emitted from televisions, radios, computers, and electronic mail further added to the overload.

Not surprisingly, many people sought a return to a simpler life. These "New Agers" explored paths ranging from astrological spiritual quests to holistic medicine, crystal healing, pilgrimages to Egyptian monuments, and more. They adopted regimens of yoga, meditation, acupressure, and visualization, as well as color and sound therapy. Robert Bly's *Iron John* (1990) led men on a quest for their lost maleness, and Jungian analyst Clarissa Pinkola Este's *Women Who Run with the Wolves* (1992) helped women connect with their creative drive. In medicine the New Age movement stirred interest in Shiatsu massage, reflexology, homeopathy, aromatherapy, and soothing, melodic music.

ents had at the same age. In 1973 the typical man age 25–34 earned nearly $30,000 a year; in 1993 he earned only $21,604 in inflation-adjusted dollars.[5] Advertisers recognized that in these tight times the marketing message had to be one of long-lasting value to help consumers justify their purchases. For these consumers quality, durability, and reliability dictated their buying decisions. They also expected advertisers to represent products truthfully and to provide generous warranties that would be honored. In turn, admakers relied less on the old ways of advertising to reach this savvy audience, which questioned the sincerity of advertisers' pitches.

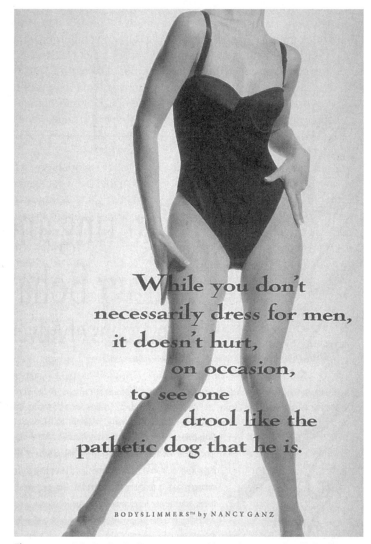

Figure 9.5 Ads for Bodyslimmers tapped into the emerging "I-don't-need-a-man" attitude.

Marketers who understood the postboomer market quickly changed their fashion, furniture, and automotive advertising. The look in youth fashions became antifashion. An inner-city style called "hip-hop" emerged. Teens adopted a new look featuring oversized jeans, T-shirts, hooded sweatshirts, flannel shirts, and hiking boots that has since spread into the middle-class suburbs. When the twenty-something crowd adopted the "grunge" look, a 1992 issue of *Business Week* called the long hair, torn sweaters, and body piercing a "slovenly, asexual, antifashion" statement.[6] Nevertheless, the grunge

Figure 9.6 Levi's targeted generation Xers with its 501 reasons to purchase the jeans.

look made its way onto fashion runways and into style-setting fashion magazines.

The moody rhythms of Foote Cone & Belding's landmark Levi's "501 Blues" spots gave way to conspicuous statements of brand benefits. In a knockoff of talk show host David Letterman's Top 10 list, the 1995 campaign gave 501 reasons young people should wear the original button-fly jeans. Among the best reasons for owning 501s: Reason No. 002, "That's a dangerous place to put a zipper," (Figure 9.6) and Reason No. 031, "They're even better the second day." And in a TV spot a young man tooling around the Eastern European city of Prague emerged from the car wearing only a nylon jacket and boxer shorts. Why no Levi's? Reason No. 007, "In Prague, you can trade them for a car." Interestingly there was no number-one reason; the numbers and reasons were arbitrarily chosen by the agency.

Cosmetics in particular became a tough sell to the younger set, which eschewed the bold use of cosmetics. The minimalist "waif look" dominated beauty and fashion magazines, so the image-driven beauty industry had to face up to slow sales of lipstick, nail enamel, mascara, and makeup. Some advertisers responded with aggressive campaigns that emphasized price. For example, Revlon compared its Almay line to the department store brand Clinique: "Just because it's more expensive doesn't mean it's better."

Other campaigns helped justify this generation's choice of major investments, including such big-ticket items as furniture and automobiles. Furniture sellers pitched lower prices, too. For example, Ethan Allen dropped its image of "your grandmother's furniture store." One campaign for the retailer's low-priced contemporary furniture pitched the line as collectible investments and showed their retail prices. It worked so well that the retailer marketed other contemporary lines in the same way.

Automakers also made substantial changes in their pitches to emphasize value and quality. For instance, the advertising agency Wieden & Kennedy developed a series of commercials for Subaru of America that pitched generation X by stressing product features over image. For one spot the voice-over read:

> *I want a car. . . . Don't tell me about wood paneling, about winning the respect of my neighbors. Tell me it has special lash adjusters like the [Subaru] SVX. So there's no more valve adjustments. Tell me it has air bags. Tell me. I have the money. I want to know what to drive. SVX. What to drive.*

The advertising agency Hal Riney & Partners understood these cynical young consumers as well as any agency. Riney helped propel General Motors' Saturn automobile, which debuted in 1990, to a position of popularity among younger buyers. To reach them, the agency meticulously crafted Saturn's down-home image and promoted its unintimidating approach to car selling (Figure 9.7). The ads emphasized straight talk. Red cars were "red," not "ruby red," and customers did not have to haggle over price with high-pressure salespeople; even dealers were called retailers. One commercial aimed directly at the person who wanted a small, economical, safe, affordable, and attractive automobile. In it a young woman setting out to buy her first new car got a lot of advice from her father about handling pushy salesmen. But she didn't need his advice when she entered the Saturn showroom

ALTON SMITH *has always loved cars. He first turned his backyard hobby into a full-time occupation in 1964, when he took a job on the line inspecting brake drums, fittings and gears. He remembers being gung-ho "because the guys depended on you." After nineteen years in the business, Alton talks about being gung-ho again. This time as a tool and die maker, building a brand new car called Saturn in Spring Hill, Tennessee.*

"... My best buddies in high school were twins. A couple of guys named Hugh and Hugo. We all had cars. And every Saturday we'd tear something down and put it back together just for the fun of it. So it's no big surprise that we all ended up in the car business.

But those guys wouldn't ever believe I just picked up and went to work for a car company that's never built a car before.

Well, what I'm doing now here at Saturn is something completely different.

Here, we don't have management and we don't have labor. We have teams. And we have what you call consensus. Everything's a group decision. **In the last seven months, I've only had a few days off here and there. But this is where I want to be. This is living heaven.**

You work through breaks and you work through lunch. You're here all hours and even sometimes Saturdays. And you don't mind. Because no one's making you do it. It's just that here you can build cars the way you know they ought to be built.

I know the competition's stiff. I was out in California for a family reunion and everything was an import. Hondas, Toyotas. Well, now we're going to give people something else to buy.

I wouldn't be working all these hours if I didn't think we could....**"**

A DIFFERENT KIND *of* COMPANY. A DIFFERENT KIND *of* CAR.
If you'd like to know more about Saturn, and our new sedans and coupe, please call us at 1-800-522-5000.

Figure 9.7   Hal Riney pitched the Saturn to younger consumers with straight talk about value, quality, and low-pressure sales tactics.

because she found the staff to be service oriented, not sales oriented. Saturn's philosophy and values struck a chord with younger people, who were less inclined to engage in price haggling.

Increasingly marketers also targeted preteens and teens, who wielded enormous purchasing power. Schools represented a key marketing vehicle. For example, at Palmer High School in Colorado Springs, kids found yellow school buses decorated with Burger King logos, hallways plastered with advertising banners from Mountain Dew (with a "Dew the Springs!" promotion), and a break room spruced up with a Frito-Lay display ("Enter the Crunch Zone!"). Branded refrigerators sold Snapple and Pepsi. The ad-supported national network Channel One reached an audience of over 8 million children, running 12 minutes worth of 30-second spots each day. Among the marketers were Pepsi, M&M/Mars, Procter & Gamble, Reebok, and Nintendo. Marketers also bought access to students by supplying everything from athletic warm-up gear to computers. And local retailers urged youth to use student discount cards to buy food, books, and clothing in the hope that these young consumers would stick with the products as they got older. Naturally marketers also hoped that their in-school ads would influence parents' purchasing decisions.

People Don't Die Away at 49

Youth-obsessed advertisers have tended to ignore one of the most important segments in America, the 50-plus market. And as the boomer generation ages, this market is growing. People age 50 and older currently represent 25 percent of the U.S. population, and by the year 2000 this group is expected to grow an additional 20 percent. Meanwhile the number of young adults age 18–34 is expected to decline. This older segment wields tremendous buying power, accounting for half the discretionary income in the United States and the majority of personal assets, stocks, real estate, and savings.

Advertising has been slow to recognize that a woman can be beautiful at 40, 50, and even older. One study, for example, found that only 5.9 percent of ads in seven national magazines showed the face of anyone over age 40. Among these Revlon signed 1970s supermodel, 50-something Lauren Hutton for a skin-care line. Another middle-aged beauty, 50-something French actress Catherine Deneuve, appeared for Chanel perfume. Nevertheless, young, waiflike models dominate the skin-care, scent, and cosmetic ads in national magazines. Similarly youth-obsessed TV advertisers have concentrated on people age 18–34, who, they say, buy most of the sponsors' products, including cars, software, and fast food. Another study found that a mere 7 percent of television commercials showed mature people. Paradoxically, although people over 40 are the fastest-growing segment of the population, their image is underrepresented in advertising.[7]

In the mature market Grey Advertising has identified two groups who offer opportunities for advertisers. The "Master Consumers," half of whom are still working, are fit, active, secure, and fulfilled; the "Maintainers" are more likely to be retired, yet also healthy and financially well-off. These mature adults buy everything from pets, toys, and playground equipment to luxury cars, spa memberships, and first-class travel. With America graying, questions about retirement, leisure, health, and living costs also are taking on new importance; advertising can address these issues (Figure 9.8).

Unfortunately other advertisers have insulted this market by perpetuating some ageist stereotypes, especially of women. Ads typically depict senior citizens as passing their time away in rocking chairs, as old fools, or as feeble (as in the "I've fallen and I can't get up" commercial). Other ads go to the opposite extreme, featuring almost superhuman seniors. For example, one of Nike's "Just Do It" commercials showed an 80-year-old man who ran a daily marathon. How did he keep his teeth from chattering on a cold day? He left them at home.

Professor Bonnie Drewniany suggests several types of strategic approaches appropriate for the mature market. These include casting models who represent the age the target audience sees itself as (ten

Figure 9.8 This ad for V8 Plus, approved by the American Heart Association, targeted mature Americans with informative, upbeat copy and images.

or fifteen years younger than the actual age), showing older people in ads across the product spectrum even if they don't buy these products, and showing older people setting out to do new things.[8]

Signs of the Times

With these demographic shifts have come dramatic changes in consumer attitudes and values. Savvy marketers have taken advantage of these opportunities to build lasting relationships with their customers by relating their brand to valued interest or cause, such as public smoking bans, environmental issues, and spectator sports.

Cigarette smoking, for example, now is no longer fashionable as Americans have confronted the harsh truths about the associated health hazards. Proposals were floated to regulate cigarettes as a drug, and legislation banned cigarettes from most workplaces and even bars and restaurants. Although burdened with curbs on advertising and the stigma of smoking, tobacco companies have become expert at making their customers "feel good" through clever and entertaining ads.

Philip Morris, for example, changed its advertising approach for its Benson & Hedges brand. Admaker Leo Burnett U.S.A. developed an empathy campaign that satirized the new constraints on smoking. Print and outdoor advertisements addressed the real world with this theme: "The length you go to for pleasure." One ad pictured smokers perched on the wing of an airplane. "Have you noticed all your smoking flights have been cancelled?" it asked. "For a great smoke just wing it." Another ad reached out to smokers who were forced outdoors to smoke due to restrictive policies in the workplace. It showed smokers seated at desks protruding outside office windows. "Have you noticed finding a place to smoke is the hardest part of your job?" the headline asked. "For a great smoke, put in for a window office." Smokers chuckled at these ads because they were living with these restrictions.

Philip Morris also added to its legions of Marlboro smokers by offering lower-priced cigarettes and merchandise promotions. The "Marlboro Adventure Team" contest became the most effective effort, and smokers also could cash in on merchandise like T-shirts, caps, jackets, and other items carrying the Marlboro logo. The firm shipped out approximately 19 million items in 1994, making Philip Morris the nation's third-largest mail-order house for a time.[9]

"Green marketing" represents another concerted effort by major advertisers to distinguish themselves from the competition. Green marketing was the direct result of consumer demands for more environmentally responsible products and packaging. Environmental crusaders pressured fast food chains into abandoning Styrofoam packaging, persuaded the tuna industry to quit buying from fishermen who snared dolphins in their nets, and diverted trash from landfills to recycling centers. Businesses responded with concentrated detergents and household cleaners to reduce waste, while packaging and paper produced from recycled materials became the norm. When Hugh Houghton opened the Manhattan-based Green Team Advertising Agency in 1993, he billed it as "the first and only New York advertising agency to specialize in the marketing and promotion of environmentally responsible products and services." The agency handled clients like Greenpeace and the Endangered Species Coalition. The Kamber Group, a Washington marketing firm, also specialized in environmental campaigns.[10]

American companies have learned that concern for the environment also can be good for business. In fact, green marketers have sought ways to connect themselves in a positive manner with wildlife and nature for decades. As far back as the 1880s, for example, boxes of Arm & Hammer baking soda carried this message: "For the good of all, do not destroy the birds." Companies sponsored environmental programs to conserve everything from wildlife to wetlands, backing up their donations with extensive TV and print campaigns. For example, Cadbury Beverages featured a promotion with the theme: "Keep animals free." For every 25-cents-off product coupon redeemed, the company made a matching donation to the National Park Foundation and supported the program with a stuffed animal giveaway. Cosmetic company Bonnie Bell ran a series of print ads that solicited teen support for a wildlife refuge in southeastern Ohio. Also, signs for Wal-Mart's new, environmentally friendly store in Lawrence, Kansas, carried such messages as "Reuse, reuse, recycle" and "We're committed to the air, land, and water."

However, savvy consumers often are skeptical about the amount of publicity that companies try to derive from such campaigns. For example, General Motors faced criticism when the automaker's fuel-efficient Chevrolet Geo line sponsored a program to plant 150,000 trees. Groups such as Greenpeace expressed concerns about GM's involvement in such a worthy cause, given that GM had lobbied against improved fuel efficiency in cars, one of the primary factors in the greenhouse effect.[11]

Meanwhile, in the realm of athletics the growing popularity of pro football, basketball, and baseball and of motor sports has led to the proliferation of the sports celebrity. Of course, the use of celebrity product endorsements is hardly a new concept. In the 1920s cigarette consumption skyrocketed when baseball player Ty Cobb and comedian Charlie Chaplin endorsed their favorite brands. More than ever, however, brand identity has become one of the primary reasons that advertisers so closely link their products with sports; fans seem to identify as closely with the sponsor as with the sport itself. Basketball's Michael Jordan popularized Nike's "Air Jordan" shoe. And after leading his team to a Super Bowl victory, quarterback Joe Montana responded to a commentator's question about what he was going to do next by exclaiming, "I'm going to Disneyland." NASCAR joined with Kellogg's to promote the Winston Cup auto racing series on the backs of 20 million cereal boxes; the spots featured Terry Labonte, who has competed in every Winston Cup race since 1979. This trend will more than likely accelerate as the athletes sign multimillion-dollar contracts and become as famous as movie stars.

As America ages, it also is becoming more diverse racially and ethnically. However, advertising has lagged behind the times. Not only are minorities underrepresented in ads, they are severely underrepresented in the industry itself.

The Minority Marketplace

Marketing to minorities will become even more critical as the buying power of racially and ethnically diverse consumers increases. By the year 2000 almost half of all Americans under age 20 will be ethnic minorities.[12] As the population grows more diverse, the special challenges of advertising to minority markets grow. Although advertising firms specializing in designing ads for minority markets have been around for some forty years, they have not grown the way their general audience counterparts have. According to the 1993 listings in the *Standard Directory of Advertising Agencies,* 105 firms specialized to some extent in minority markets. Of that number 24 reported expertise in working with the African American segment, 12 dealt with the Asian American segment, and 69 specialized in the Hispanic American segment (Table 9.1).

Table 9.1 Top U.S.-Based Ethnic Ad Agencies by Specialty, 1994

	Billings (in millions)
African American	
Burrell Communications Group	$89.9
Vince Cullers Advertising	18.0
Hispanic American	
Font & Vaamonde	65.0
Berry Brown	51.4
Conill Advertising	40.0
Casanova Pendrill Publicdad Inc.	40.0
Castor	39.0
Agencies U.S.A.	20.0
Asian American	
King & Lee	30.0
LLT International	22.0
AdLand	16.8
Multiethnic	
Uniworld	125.0
Mendoza, Dillon & Asociados	68.0
Mingo Group	53.0
Muse Cordero Chen	27.0

Source: *Standard Directory of Advertising Agencies* (1996).

Figure 9.9 General Mills targeted the growing African American middle class by presenting positive family images.

More and more advertisers have begun to turn to general agencies with specialized departments or to minority agencies for expertise in reaching this lucrative audience. In the past many advertisers lumped African Americans together as a single market segment, but research provided evidence of an emerging African American middle class. In 1980 *Black Enterprise* magazine coined the word "buppie" to describe the 21 percent of college-educated African Americans who lived in suburban areas and had upscale tastes in food, fashion, and lifestyles (Figure 9.9). A decade later, nearly 32 million African Americans had an estimated purchasing power of between $170 and $300 billion, and by the year 2000 that amount will almost triple to $889 billion.[13]

Figure 9.10   Ray Charles and the "Uh-Huh" girls sang the praises of Pepsi.

Elements of African American culture also were incorporated into a number of successful campaigns. For example, commercial jingles were based on rap and hip-hop music, and images associated with African Americans often conveyed what was considered "hip," "cool," and rebellious. Jell-O used television star Bill Cosby for a spokesperson. Music legend Michael Jackson earned an estimated $6 million to sing for Pepsi. Blues singer Ray Charles and the "Uh-Huh" girls promoted Diet Pepsi (Figure 9.10). Also, immediately identifiable African American athletes pitched everything from fried chicken to athletic shoes to car mufflers. These included basketball players Michael Jordan and Shaquille O'Neal and heavyweight boxers Evander Holyfield and George Foreman, to name just a few.

However, the emergence of the "ethnic market" did not mean that more minority images were used in general advertising. Instead, ethnic minorities were used in separate ad campaigns. "The advertising was targeted outside the general markets in black and Latino-oriented media," according to Mark Green in the 1991 study *Invisible People,* conducted by the New Department of Consumer Affairs.[14] Among the worst offenders were upscale, mainstream magazines *Esquire, Vogue,* and *Gentleman's Quarterly.* The African Americans who did appear in ads typically were athletes, entertainers, laborers, or children.[15] However, the emerging African American media has played an important role in helping African Americans to develop positive images, with publications like *Jet, Ebony,* and *Black Enterprise* and the Black Entertainment Television network leading the way.

Yet African Americans remain heavily underrepresented in the advertising profession. In 1992 *Advertising Age* ran an article entitled "The Ad Industry's Little Secret." The story reported that African Americans, who accounted for 10.1 percent of the total work force, filled only 5.2 percent of all positions in the nation's advertising, marketing, and public relations companies. And among managers and professional-level employees the figure was a minuscule 2.1 percent.[16]

Mainstream advertising also struggled with ways to sell to the newcomers who hadn't yet learned the language, especially the growing Hispanic and Asian markets. Hispanic Americans were virtually nonexistent in advertising until the mid-1980s, when advertisers began to recognize the potential of this market. Hispanic Americans are the fastest-growing ethnic minority in the nation. The group increased from 9 million to 23.7 million people between 1970 and 1989, and by the year 2000 there will be an estimated 41 million Hispanic Americans. Their buying power has dramatically increased as well, surpassing $200 billion in 1994.[17]

Although Hispanic Americans are linked by a common language—Spanish—they also represent many different nationalities: Mexican, Puerto Rican, Cuban, and so on. Due to the resulting diversity of buying behavior, lifestyles, and cultures, marketers have found it difficult to reach this segment with traditional wide-reaching campaigns. More than any other ethnic group, advertisers could reach the Hispanic American audience through a well-established media system, including the Spanish International Network, which includes Spanish-language television and radio stations and publications (Figure 9.11). UniVision is another Spanish-language television network operating in major markets such as Miami, Fresno, San Francisco, and Phoenix.

The fragmented Asian American market also presents particular challenges. The 5 million Asian Americans currently spend an estimated $35 billion annually, and the Asian American population is projected to nearly double by the year 2000. Like Hispanic Americans, Asian Americans represent a variety of nationalities, including Chinese, Japanese, Koreans, Pacific Islanders, Filipinos, and Vietnamese.[18] Each of these groups has unique backgrounds, traditions, and

Figure 9.11   Honda tooted its environmental horn in this ad targeted at the Hispanic American market.

dialects. For instance, a Chinese immigrant from Bejing who speaks the Mandarin dialect may not be able to communicate with someone from Hong Kong who converses in Cantonese. Thus, word of mouth was less important in disseminating product information than the well-established Asian-oriented magazines, newspapers, and television networks. Nevertheless, few national campaigns were targeted directly at Asian Americans.

Another historically ignored group is gays and lesbians. Attracted by these affluent, well-educated, and brand-loyal consumers who want quality products, many companies have expanded their campaigns to include the gay community, selling everything from beer and books to automobiles to this new target audience. But some advertisers, such as for packaged foods, cosmetics, over-the-counter drugs, and financial services, appear not to have recognized this group as a niche market.[19]

One recent national survey, by the market research firm of Yankelovich Partners, found that people who identify themselves as gay or lesbian account for approximately 6 percent of the U.S. population.[20] To reach this segment, some marketers have portrayed openly gay people in their advertisements. For example, AT&T mailed brochures that pictured three smiling couples in affectionate poses— two men, two women, and a man and a woman—along with the slogan "Let Your True Voice Be Heard." Companies also created images for this group that were very different from the usual heterosexual ads.

Figure 9.12   This 1995 ad for Saab automobiles is one in a series that features the central theme "Find Your Own Road."

American Express advertised traveler's checks with the signatures of two men or two women. For Ikea, a home furnishings store, the Deutsch agency created a spot in which a couple shopped for furniture; the hook was, this couple was composed of two men. The commercial showed the two men joking about shopping for furniture and its implications for a long-term relationship.

Other companies reached out to these consumers without using overtly gay images. A 1993 issue of *Out* magazine carried an Apple Computer Powerbook advertisement, the first for a high-tech marketer in publication aimed at a gay audience. The following year, Saab became the first automaker to specifically address homosexuals, running ads in *Out* and *Genre* identical to those appearing in publications like *Fortune* (Figure 9.12).

Not only are advertisers facing an increasingly diverse public; they also have to operate in the heady atmosphere of the media revolution. The old methods don't necessarily work, and the new communications technologies must be accounted for.

The Media Revolution

The technological explosion of the 1980s fragmented both the mass market and the mass media. Advertisers and agencies realized that consumers were becoming harder to reach with traditional mass media campaigns. "Is Advertising Dead?" asked the cover story of a 1994 issue of *Wired* magazine. The future-oriented publication reported on a major shift in the industry away from traditional media such as magazines and network television to emerging new forms: "The future of media is the future of advertising; the future of advertising is the future of media. The fundamental difference, however, is that the design philosophies of digital media will exert a greater influence on traditional advertising."[21]

Indeed, the proliferation of specialized magazines, cable television, satellite receivers, videocassette recorders, and computer technology has fragmented traditional mass media. Advertisers and agencies now realize that they can't get their messages across with one medium. Previously they might have run some television and print advertising to introduce a new product. However, with the media revolution they now use multiple media and innovative techniques to reach their target customers. This trend also has had a far-reaching effect on the way advertising agencies do business, forcing them to move beyond simply creating ads for placement in the media. But advertising's main purpose—to persuade and inform—remains the same.

The Total Communications Package

Each of the new communications technologies offered new opportunities to reach consumers. In 1970 there were only a handful of television networks and major magazines. Now television is fragmented into network, syndicated, and local TV, as well as cable; in addition, satellite receivers enable people to pick up broadcasts from around the globe. Specialized magazines are aimed at every conceivable interest group. Even national magazines publish editions for particular geographic regions. And nontraditional media have proliferated, ranging from videos and movie theater screens to blimps, balloons, and T-shirts.

To complicate things even more, advertisers often pay for ads that target consumers never see or hear. With a multitude of choices, readers now choose from many media options, selectively reading only sections of magazines or newspapers and flipping past the clutter of ads, avoiding television commercials by switching channels or muting the sound, and flipping around on the radio dial. As a result media

Memorable Slogans

Can't beat the real thing. (Coca-Cola)

Always Coca-Cola.

Just for the taste of it. (Diet Coke)

The best stuff made on earth. (Snapple)

Just do it. (Nike)

Another day. Another chance to get healthy. (Evian water)

Got milk? (California Milk Advisory Board)

Nothing outlasts Energizer batteries. They keep going and going.

All day long. All day strong. (Aleve pain reliever)

For your 2001 body parts. (Lever 2001 soap)

Intel's inside. (Intel microprocessor)

A new kind of company. A new kind of car. (Saturn)

Find your own road. (Saab)

Come see the softer side of Sears.

planning has become even more critical as the complexity of options has increased and costs have skyrocketed.

In turn, cost-conscious clients have put pressure on agencies to be more than efficient. They want creative buys. Complex media packages often employ nontraditional media such as public relations, sales promotion, direct marketing, personal selling, and any other tool to make contact with customers—everything from packaging and shopping bags to community events. This approach requires a consistent program of "integrated marketing communications" (IMC). The concept of preparing and presenting a total communications package evolved from the idea that a cohesive media package would be more effective than a series of independent shots, which might send out conflicting messages.

IMC programs actually are a new expression of an old school of thought. Agencies simply applied the concepts of consistency, clarity, and continuity to a wider range of media. This unified-image approach made Marlboro a leading brand with its Western theme. Hallmark used the idea "The Very Best" to tie a marketing program to the company's umbrella theme: "When you care enough to send the very best." IMC also worked for Apple, Honda, Nike, and Banana Republic. And it worked especially well for Coca-Cola.

In 1993 Coca-Cola used dazzling visual techniques to grab viewers' attention with the state-of-the-art animated "Always Coca-Cola" campaign. The ad industry especially took notice because Coca-Cola bypassed traditional agency sources to sign up Hollywood talent shop Creative Artists Associates (CAA) to create an unprecedented twenty-four elaborate commercials. Two other commercials were made by Coke's long-standing agency, McCann-Erickson Worldwide, which was also credited with the "Always Coca-Cola" theme.

The visually stimulating spots dared to break with the tradition of point-and-pitch repetition from previous Coca-Cola ads. Following the global trend toward fragmented media, Coca-Cola replaced its "one sight, one sound" approach in favor of saying different things to different audiences, in different media, and even in different seasons. Since Coca-Cola's introduction in 1886, its ever-cheerful ads had made "refreshment" the central theme and had tried to link the product with the pleasant things of life. For this campaign Coca-Cola updated the old idea, employed new media, and created commercials that looked completely different from anything on TV. A neon sign flashed the "Always Coca-Cola" message; a glassblower fashioned a Coca-Cola bottle; and polar bears romped in the snow and ice. The highly popular polar bears spot, said to have cost between $600,000 and $800,000, also provided Coca-Cola with opportunities for merchandising stuffed polar bears.[22] Although each commercial was different, each featured three images that reinforced the integrated marketing approach: the red disk (which first appeared in layouts in the 1930s), the unique contour bottle (shaped in 1916), and the "Always Coca-Cola" theme.

What is significant here is that advertising agencies recognized that they had to go beyond their specialty of creating ads to place in the media. Marketers provided the impetus for agencies to expand their range of services as they shifted more advertising dollars into promotion. In 1992 sales promotion expenditures accounted for 73 percent of the ad promotion budget, compared to 27 percent for advertising. Sensing an opportunity to win more business from clients, most major ad agencies restructured with an emphasis on research and technological resources to support IMC programs. They became generalists—advertisers, sales promoters, public relation firms, direct marketers, and managers of other communication services—directing and coordinating multiple-marketing programs in which individual teams worked on different IMC components.

The Printed Page

Magazine and newspaper publishers aggressively looked for ways to compete against other media, especially advertising publications, free weekly newspapers, and direct mailers. They succeeded by applying new printing techniques and technology to an old medium.

A growing number of magazines and newspapers started carrying fold-out print ads that delivered a poster-size message for products ranging from cosmetics and audio equipment to automobiles and cigarettes. For example, agencies produced fold-out ads for L'Oreal cosmetics, Calvin Klein jeans, and Tanqueray gin. The idea was to involve readers, increasing the chance they might absorb—or at least notice—the message. Pull-out, tear-out posters on larger, heavier paper simply represented another way to break through the clutter.

Like magazines, newspapers were already compatible with the emerging digital media, so that the writing, editing, and layout functions were performed electronically. Also, publishers now produce electronic newspapers on cable television, and virtually all the leading U.S. newspapers offer digital on-line versions whereby readers can use a personal computer and modem to access a large computer system where the newspaper information is stored. Other on-line systems, such as Prodigy, America Online, and CompuServe, offer text and graphics supplied by daily newspapers that enable readers to choose sections, topics, or headlines and to customize the layout, often before they are even available in print form. And experts predict that by the end of the decade, newspaper readers will be able to request specific stories and more information about a topic or an advertisement simply by pushing a few buttons on hand-held personal digital assistants.

Another practice, called "wild posting," was popular among fashion companies such as Georgio Armani, Calvin Klein, and Benetton. Formerly used by rock concert promoters, nightclub owners, and record companies, this practice involved pasting up promotional posters on construction sites and abandoned buildings in inner cities.

The "Noncommercial" Commercial

Television networks, cable operators, movie producers, and others also are experimenting with various ways to reach people with specialized media and creative messages. Experts predict that as commercials become larger and more entertaining, it will become more difficult to tell the difference between an ad and a program.

Advertisers have found that the key to effective televised commercials lies in making the pitch both entertaining and credible. For example, Campbell Soup sponsored a series of 85-second spots on the TV Food Network; the vignette "meals to prepare in a hurry" suggested different ways to use the soups. Among the Game Show Network's offerings were vintage game shows featuring original sponsors like Geritol, Remington, Revlon, and Bristol-Myers. A series of fast-paced MTV-style ads for Chevy's Mexican restaurant featured another first—"same-day advertising." The commercials aired the same day of production, highlighting that the restaurant's tortilla chips were also made fresh every day. Even the popular Energizer Bunny kept bursting into commercials that initially seemed to promote another product entirely. Though this upbeat parody did not look like a commercial, it did deliver a strong selling message about the long-lasting Energizer alkaline battery: "It keeps going and going."

At the same time, "ad plugs," or product placements, were on the rise. The appearance of a product in a program can be a powerful form of endorsement if it's placed in the hands of the right character. In television, however, the show's producers decide whether any branded goods will appear on screen, because federal regulations forbid any form of payment by product manufacturers. In the top-rated sitcom "Seinfeld" a Junior Mint candy ended up inside a character on the operating table. At the end of the episode, the surgeon accepted a Junior Mint and said, "These can be very refreshing." About 14 million viewers saw the show. And most famously, Elizabeth Taylor worked her way through four CBS sitcoms to push her Black Pearls fragrance. Other programs plugged brands simply by showing a logo or product package without even mentioning the name. Certain products were clearly identifiable by virtue of their distinct design, like the pink packages of Sweet 'n' Low sweetener, the red tag on Levi's blue jeans, and popular brands of athletic shoes and cars.

In film product placements are a different story, because advertisers are allowed to pay for placements. A typical charge for a visible placement is $40,000, and sometimes even larger sums are involved. Typically the fee takes the form of merchandise, as when Ford Motor supplied ten Explorers in the 1993 smash hit *Jurassic Park.* Nor is product placement a new phenomenon. In the 1950s the famous New York jewelry store got a free plug in *Breakfast at Tiffany's.* In 1980 Richard Gere appeared in *American Gigolo* wearing Armani suits. And two years later the little alien nibbling on Reese's Pieces in Steven Spielberg's *E.T.* established the candy as a major rival to M&Ms. Product placements also became common sights in music videos, syndicated TV shows, game shows, cooking shows, and even commercials for other products.

The Super Bowl has emerged not only as the most-watched TV program of the year but as a showcase for big-ticket advertisers' commercials, cross-promotions, and product tie-ins. The Super Bowl is the only time when advertisers can reach such a broad audience, cutting across gender, age, and ethnic lines. The 1996 Super Bowl set a record by charging an average of $1.2 million for each 30-second spot. Upwards of 60 percent of adults age 25–54 watched the game, as well as commercials by Anheuser-Busch, McDonald's, Nike, Frito-Lay, and Pepsi, among others.[23] The previous year the media had touted the Super Bowl as the "World Series of Advertising," and major newspapers scored the commercials as winners and losers, just as in movie reviews. The ads made more of an impression than the football game's half-time extravaganza.

When the Federal Communications Commission (FCC) did away with commercial time limits on television in 1984, it created still another new vehicle for advertising. In the absence of any guidelines, "infomercials," or program-length commercials, were introduced. Half-hour infomercials evolved from amateurish pitches for food choppers, car waxes, and spray-on hair to slick, fast-paced programs for a wide variety of products. The format worked for actress Jane Fonda's treadmill, fitness guru Susan Powter's weight-loss regime ("Stop the insanity"), and major marketers like Avon, Revlon, GTE, Volkswagen, Saturn, and Microsoft. Also, Apple Computer aired an innovative 30-minute advertisement entitled "The Martinettis Bring Home a Computer" that boosted sales for its Macintosh Performa multimedia computer line. Unlike most infomercials the program employed a "storymercial," with a beginning, middle, and end. The program told viewers the story of how a family found uses for its new computer.

Another challenge facing broadcast advertisers was competition from the rented home video. Ever since Pepsi sponsored the successful video release *Top Gun* in 1986, more advertisers have been placing commercials on videos. In one spot a woman going to the kitchen for a Pepsi encountered a series of adventures similar to those of Indiana Jones. Pepsi clearly understood the power of entertainment. One study showed that the majority of video renters watched the commercial that preceded the film—sometimes more than once. This will more than likely become a standard medium.

Other marketers already had found that the format enabled them to deliver effective product presentations in a longer form, called "direct-mail video" or "video catalogs." For about $2 a cassette, advertisers target their videotape messages to demographically desirable audiences without having to buy expensive commercial time on network or cable stations. Video advertising communicates messages in ways that other forms can't; the medium is ideal for demonstrating a product or stirring emotions. Videotape pitches date back to the early 1980s, when Soloflex, the exercise machine manufacturer, began mailing 22-minute tapes called "video brochures" to an estimated 3 million people. Production advances have speeded duplication, and new, lightweight cassette shells keep mailing costs down, so the trend could well accelerate.

If things weren't already confusing enough for viewers, television programmers now are developing shows that target advertisers as well as viewers. Already magazines have reinvented themselves as television projects, from "Elle TV" and "Woman's Day" to "Martha Stewart Living." The annual Clio Awards, the ad industry's version of the Academy Awards, showcase the year's best TV spots as selected by the ad industry. A one-time-only special, "And Now a Word from Our Sponsor," featured a variety of spots from around the world, and its producers even pitched the show as a prime-time weekly series. And

H. Ross Perot

H. Ross Perot.

In 1992 independent presidential candidate H. Ross Perot catapulted the program-length advertisement, or "infomercial," into prominence. Perot sat down in front of a TV camera for 30 minutes with homemade flip charts and a down-home pitch; a month later he garnered 19 percent of the vote. Interestingly *Advertising Age* named Perot its "Adman of the Year" for his unconventional and highly effective use of the media. The $65 million campaign enabled Perot to sell himself to a large portion of the American public and dramatically changed political marketing.

In the process Perot exploited free TV and radio time with appearances on live talk shows and ran eleven revolutionary 30-minute infomercials interspersed with more conventional 30- and 60-second spots. These ads positioned Perot as a public servant more than a product. "What we wanted to do was communicate with the American people," Perot explained. "And what I liked about [the infomercials and the commercials] was that they were me, like them or not. At least you knew what you were getting. It wasn't like pitching a product. I felt strongly that when we are talking about our country . . . it should be handled in a different way."[a] Perot may not have won the presidency, but he reawakened politicians and advertisers to the power of the media to promote candidates and causes.

---

[a] "Ross Perot: A Winner After All," *Advertising Age* (December 21, 1992), 16–18.

another special about the ad industry appeared on ET cable television: "Sex, Sizzle, and Sales."

Advertising On-Line

Some observers predicted that printed publications were doomed as a new generation of computer technology transformed the visual communications field. The new electronic communications network, called the "information superhighway" and "cyberspace," contains vast

The Best TV Commercials

As part of a special spring 1995 issue, six editors of *Advertising Age* selected the "50 best" TV commercials of all time. Compiled by decade, here's the list for the 1990s.

1990S

Bud Light A hapless impostor, when challenged about his identity, declares, "Yes I am!"

Hallmark A 2-minute spot features a not-so-surprise birthday for a woman who is turning 100.

Levi's for Women Jeans for women are sold with animation.

Coca-Cola Polar bears proclaim that it's "Always Coca-Cola."

amounts of information and continues to grow exponentially. In the next century home viewers will have access to every movie ever made. Books, magazines, and print-on-paper publications may be a thing of the past, and writers may simply publish on a computer network.

In this environment the rush is on to produce interactive multimedia advertising. This one-on-one form of advertising allows individuals to interact with the content of the ad. Usually the ad is electronic and distributed on videos, diskettes, multimedia CD-ROMs, and even video games. Alternatively the medium could be television, a kiosk, or even a digital page on the World Wide Web.

Interactive television actually has five distinct components, each of which offers something different. Advertisers can choose among video games; information services such as Prodigy; choice systems for pay-per-view service; "play-alongs" that let consumers play along with game shows, answer quiz questions, and request coupons or information; and "personalized TV," which allows advertisers to run more than one ad at one time. With this new medium advertisers can customize their message. For example, while watching an interactive Adidas TV spot, a viewer could choose between running shoes and tennis shoes using a hand-held remote control. Similar free-standing systems already are in place at kiosks in shopping centers, which provide information on everything from restaurant menus to restroom locations; in merchandise displays within stores; and on grocery shopping carts, highlighting weekly specials.

Computer games are another part of the growing effort to reach an audience of hard-to-get, affluent, technologically oriented young males. It began in 1987 when General Motors' Buick division pioneered the use of computer diskettes in auto marketing to provide visuals and information. The next generation of commercials looked nothing like an advertisement. Rather, they played like video games as simulations blended the medium with the message. For example, a game offered by the Chrysler Corporation challenges players to navigate through a rugged national park to photograph wildlife and beat a deadline using a camera, guide, map, cellular telephone, and Jeep Grand Cherokee. Similarly a Sega video game featured 7-Up's Cool Spot character (Figure 9.13).

The World Wide Web, the graphical portion of the Internet, has emerged as the fastest-growing portion of the electronic communications network. On-line computer systems date back to the 1960s, but recent innovations have made the Web's vast data resources accessible to millions of personal computer users. By "hypertext linking," or simply clicking on key phrases or icons, users can bring up a page of information, which likely includes more links to information. All the major on-line service providers including America Online, Prodigy, GEnie, Delphi, and CompuServe, deliver Web access.

Only computer-related businesses initially advertised their goods and services on the Web, but increasingly peripheral companies have been getting on line. Publishing companies, restaurants, music stores, television networks, florists, airlines, and so on all are recognizing the possibilities of the medium and mounting Web sites that provide information about services and products (Table 9.2). The cost of developing a Web site ranges from $5000 to $150,000. Users can log onto their computers and order everything from pizza to computer gadgets, cars, real estate, airplane tickets, and diamonds (Figure 9.14).

The 1995 launch of on-line magazines (or "e-zines") such as *HotWired, Vibe,* and Time Warner's *Pathfinder* provided advertisers with a way to reach a new generation of young, affluent consumers who had access to the Internet. In turn, cyberspace spawned a host of upstart agencies offering to build sites on the Web. Compared to traditional agencies, they were quick-moving, technically savvy, and

Figure 9.13   A Sega video game featured 7-Up's Cool Spot as the lead character.

Table 9.2   World Wide Web Advertising Sites

Address	Company/Product/Service
http://www.zima.com	Zima
http://www.eat.com	Ragu
http://www.planetreebok.com	Reebok
http://www.saturn.cars	Saturn
http://www.volvocars.com/	Volvo
http://www.AdMarket.com	Advertisers and marketers on the Web
http://www.stoli.com/#vod	Stolichnaya
http://www.spe.sony.com/pictures/ sonytheatres/theatres/theatres.html	Sony Pictures
http://www.InternetMCI.com	MCI's on-line magazine and marketplace
http://www.mastercard.com/	Mastercard
http://www.sprint.com/L	Sprint

Source: "Cyberspace Spawns Cottage Industry," *San Francisco Chronicle* (June 12, 1995), B1.

steeped in the culture of the Internet. For example, *HotWired* (the on-line magazine of the print publication *Wired*) became the first Web site to use the traditional magazine model, placing ads on certain pages among editorial matter. It then sold these spots to advertisers like Network MCI, AT&T, and IBM. *HotWired* also reported to its advertisers the exact number of people who visited the page (termed "hits"), their sex, and other information they filled out on a membership form. Ads not tied to on-line publications like *HotWired* are sometimes more difficult to find. A computer user has to type an address or use a software program that searches for an ad by topic.

The new on-line resources have given marketers an opportunity to extend brand images by integrating both digital and traditional forms of advertising. Advertisers combine ideas from print, radio, and television in this new medium. For example, the Ragu spaghetti sauce site offers a fictional spokeswoman, recipes, production information, travel tips, and even a brief Italian lesson. The Volvo site displays pictures of various car models, along with a list of dealer locations around the country and an electronic service center where users can get answers to questions about their cars. Some sites have developed a cult following, like the one for Stolichnaya vodka. Once at the site, visitors can assemble a puzzle, download a screensaver, or compete in a weekly recipe competition.

All of these developments have taken communications one step closer toward fully interactive television. Home shoppers now can call

Figure 9.14   This ad for Apple Computer displayed the advantages of advertising on the World Wide Web.

in and place orders for or even talk to a host about everything from top designer fashions to furniture. The next wave of home shopping will bring upscale merchandise from retailers such as Macy's, Nordstrom, and Williams Sonoma, to name a few. Soon viewers will be able to click on the television tube; find a shopping program; punch in their size, height, weight, and favorite color; and see how an ensemble looks on a model with their body size. They might even shop in a virtual super-market, pull a cake mix off the shelf, turn it around, and read the preparation instructions and ingredients. Or they might visit an auto center, pick out a car, arrange for a test drive, punch in the options, and see the sticker price plus finance options. Although interactive television isn't available for living rooms yet, industry analysts predict that it will be a major new medium in the near future.

Advertising for Today and Tomorrow

In the 1990s advertising agencies faced the decision whether to con-tinue building enormous ad empires, as did many firms in the 1980s' merger mania, or to become specialized. With the interest in global media and multimedia approaches, most major ad agencies restruc-tured with an emphasis on research and technological resources to integrate advertising with other marketing communications. At the same time, the economic crunch and the wave of new technology also made specialization a viable choice for midsize and small agencies. And some of the biggest agencies were spinning off divisions focusing on such strengths as direct marketing, sales promotion, or industrial clients. Foote Cone & Belding Communications, for example, created FCB Direct and FCB Healthcare, which were staffed to fill client requirements rather than provide full services. Some agencies also dropped certain services like media buying.

To stay viable, future-oriented Jay Chiat, founder of Chiat/Day/Mojo, had another solution—he created the world's first "virtual agency" in Venice, California. The high-tech organization cut down on face-to-face meetings, needless commutes, overstaffing, and paper clutter as Chiat employees brainstormed by electronic mail and video conferencing. Concierges helped settle staff members into appropriate spaces as needed, such as meeting rooms, art studios, postproduction facilities, and study carrels (called "pods"), where they could log onto a computer, plug in a laptop, or use a telephone. Kiosks around the agency provided access to a CD-ROM library to call up data and even past ads developed for a given account. As Chiat explained, the agency "is simply providing their staff with a resource and the support systems to work in bursts of energy for one week on a quick media plan or to produce an ad or for three months, if they are pitching new business."[24]

Agencies also added a new service called "account planning" to bridge the gap between the traditional agency research, account management, and creative departments. Account planning already had become a well-accepted function by the mid-1970s at British agencies like Boase Massim Pollit (BMP) and J. Walter Thompson/London. In the 1980s Chiat/Day/Mojo became among the first American agencies to provide the service.

Account planners studied consumers through interviews, phone surveys, and focus groups. For the Porsche's North American account, for example, Goodby, Berlin, & Silverstein (later Goodby Silverstein & Partners) conducted a thousand interviews with current and prospective drivers to understand their attitudes, feelings, language, and habits. This enabled the account planners to represent the consumer's point of view, encouraging ads that were creative, relevant, and on target.

Talking Smart

Smaller agencies dramatically altered the advertising culture of the multinational, New York–based powerhouse agencies. Madison Avenue lost more than 13,500 jobs between 1990 and 1993 when clients such as Coca-Cola defected to smaller creative agencies, Hollywood agents and producers, and specialists in video games, infomercials, and interactive media.[25]

What set agencies like Goodby Silverstein & Partners, Wieden & Kennedy, and Deutsch apart was not so much a particular style as a general approach that relied on ingenuity, got into the consumer's psyche, and engaged the viewer in a "smart dialogue."

Jeff Goodby formed the San Francisco–based agency in 1983 with partners Rich Silverstein and Andy Berlin. When Berlin left the firm in 1992, it became known as Goodby Silverstein & Partners. The agency, which *AdWeek* magazine called the nation's best, has won a number of awards for work on behalf of Norwegian Cruise Lines, the California Milk Advisory Board, and Sega of America, and others. The group translated sophisticated account planning into smart, funny, and irreverent ads that maintained a childlike sense of play. In the award-winning "Got Milk?" commercials, the agency discovered through focus groups that people never thought of milk until they were about to run out of it, and they only drank it with something else, such as a brownie, cereal, or a cookie (Figure 9.15). With this premise the agency created one spot in which a young man has just taken a big bite out of a peanut butter sandwich when the phone rings. "For $10,000, can you name the man who shot Alexander Hamilton?" He reaches for the milk to wash down the sandwich, but there are only a few drops left. He knows the answer—Aaron Burr—but all he can say is, "Awan Baa."

Goodby's agency made an impression with a number of other campaigns. The soft-sell vignettes for Norwegian Cruise Lines oozed sensuality as they reached for the under-50 crowd. Shot in black and white, the ads offered alluring invitations. "There is no law that says you can't make love at 4 in the afternoon on Tuesday," read one of the spots. Another proclaimed, "It's different out here." Their campaign for Foster Farm chickens featured two fugitive hens. In one spot they crossed the California border and were stopped by a highway patrol officer, who shone a flashlight into the car and said, "Foster Farm chickens are never frozen. This looks like freezer burn to me." "No!" squawked one of the birds, "it's a curling iron accident." Their "See what develops" campaign for Polaroid proved popular (Figure 9.16). And their cutting-edge work for video giant Sega of America helped push its sales to the top. These outrageous, flashy commercials ended with what is now considered the trademark Sega scream.

The Portland-based Weiden & Kennedy agency also managed to effectively connect with 1990s consumers. The agency's highly successful "Just do it" campaign for Nike spoke to a broader slice of America than just sports-crazed males. It tapped into consumer wants, motivating guilt-ridden Americans who didn't exercise to just go ahead and *do it*. One ad stated: "Can't decide to run, cycle, or play basketball? Just do it—and it wouldn't hurt to stop eating like a pig, either." In another triathlete Joanne Ernst asked, "So you want to get in shape?" The ads had one common denominator, the kicker tag line "Just do it" (Figure 9.17). The agency also developed a series of Nike ads positioning women positively and establishing emotional ties with women.

Figure 9.15 This ad for the California Milk Advisory Board promoted milk by portraying something people associate with the product.

Stylistically the work of the Deutsch agency was the opposite of the polished, high-tech approach. These reality-style commercials were usually shot on a low budget, featured "real people" instead of actors, and were rough around the edges. In place of jingles and sales, there was spontaneous dialogue and action, so some ads resembled a documentary more than a typical commercial. Ads poked fun at such American icons as Nike athletic shoes. "Your mother wears sneakers," yelled one Deutsch ad for competing British Knights shoes, suggesting that the top brand was uncool. Deutsch's quirky style has attracted other clients such as Lilyette lingerie, Oneida silverware, and

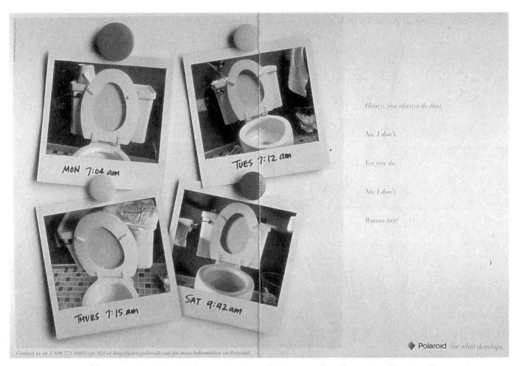

Figure 9.16   Polaroid boosted sales with its popular "See what develops" campaign.

Tanqueray gin (Figure 9.18). While some saw this style as a gimmick, Deutsch contended that this reality genre mirrors the sensational tabloid TV programming that is bombarding consumers every day.

Zipping, Zapping, and Channel Surfing

Consumers increasingly are tuning out sales pitches, as well as opting for discounted, private-label brands. Cable TV viewers armed with a remote control, VCR, and decades of media savvy have become too smart, too quick, and too elusive for the slow-moving conventional advertiser.

Television viewers annoyed with or sickened by commercials are zipping through with a remote control or even electronically eliminating them with a novel device called the "commercial brake." This high-tech zapper senses commercials and automatically skips over them when the tape is played back for viewing—saving up to 200 hours a year, the amount of time the average person spends watching commercials. Another company released a new software program, called "Internet Fast Forward," that blocked advertising from showing up on World Wide Web pages.

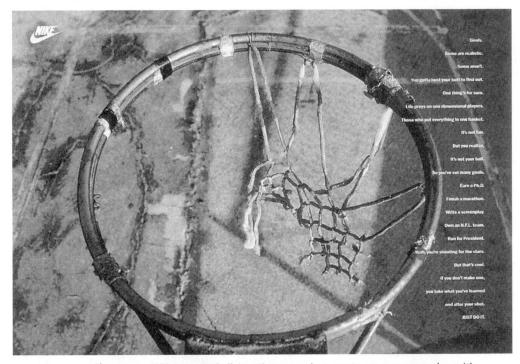

Figure 9.17 Nike targeted all Americans, not just sports-crazy young males, with its "Just do it" campaign.

What had sold a decade ago wasn't selling now. Video Storyboard Tests had been tracking viewers' responses to current advertising, and in 1993 the media research firm reported radical changes in which television commercials grabbed viewers' attention. For example, original music scores were out and well-known pieces of music were in. Prices appeared on everything from fast food specials to luxury automobiles. And multimillion-dollar athletes more than show biz celebrities were the spokespersons of choice.

Bizarre ads became another way to lure young consumers. Some observers described such ads as outrageous and even offensive; others suggested that this strange new direction represented a backlash against puritanical, political correctness. Among these ads one for Rib Ticklers barbecue sauce began with an ode to barnyard animals, until a barbecue grill appeared on the horizon. "Hey! Here's an idea," said the announcer. "Let's eat 'em!" In 1993 Protest Clothing, maker of a line of "grunge wear" for young men and women, aired three commercials that featured self-mutilation as an advertising event and defined a new genre. "Call it 'ad noir,'" said advertising critic Barbara Lippert. "It's based on speed, shock, new music, and a readable logo."[26]

Perhaps no advertiser sparked more controversy than Benetton, the trendy Italian clothing manufacturer. Under the umbrella theme

Figure 9.18   Tanqueray's campaign featured hip "Mr. Jenkins" in a series of quirky settings.

"The United Colors of Benetton," the company shifted from promoting harmony to presenting sobering social issues that snagged people's attention. A 1994 issue of *Colors,* the company publication, was devoted entirely to AIDS. The publication carried the poster image of former President Ronald Reagan accompanied by a sarcastic mock obituary. It began, "When former U.S. president Ronald Reagan died from AIDS complications in February of last year, the world lost a courageous

New Brand Names

1990 The Saturn automobile promotes an unintimidating approach to car selling.

1990 Apple's Powerbook laptop computer is introduced.

1992 The Newton Message Pad, a personal, hand-held digital assistant, recognizes handwriting.

1994 Apple's Power PC is the first computer to run both Mac and Windows applications.

1995 Flavor-Saver tomatoes are genetically engineered to stay vine-ripe fresh longer.

1995 Microsoft's Windows 95 is heralded as one of the most anticipated product launches since New Coke and the Macintosh computer.

1996 McDonald's Arch Deluxe is the burger with the grown-up taste.

1996 For her new Black Pearls fragrance, Elizabeth Taylor appears on an evening of TV sitcoms.

leader." Critics believed that the advertiser's editorial content should be kept separate from the clothing line. Yet Benetton insisted that the intent of *Colors* was not to sell sweaters, but to educate young people about AIDS.

This was not the first time that Benetton had used human tragedy and suffering to sell clothes. Earlier that year, Benetton had made a radical statement about the civil war in Bosnia with an ad entitled "The Known Soldier." It pictured the blood-soaked T-shirt and pants of a dead Croatian soldier. Newspapers like the *Los Angeles Times* refused to run the ad. Other controversial Benetton advertisements featured a priest kissing a nun, a man's arm tattooed with the words "HIV Positive," and two young men handcuffed, one black and the other white.

Such creative risks became increasingly important to generate brand awareness in fashion. Manufacturers of designer jeans like Joop and Diesel found that the ensuing controversy over their supposedly satirical ads helped garner publicity despite relatively small advertising budgets. And Calvin Klein, who long had used sexually provocative ads to promote perfumes, jeans, and underwear, was accused of crossing the line from provocative to pornographic. One 1995 ad featured a young boy who wasn't wearing jeans at all, just underpants and a vest; another showed underwear beneath drooping jeans. While adults protested, teens kept buying. In fact, back-to-school sales for the designer jeans proved the best in years. While Calvin Klein explained that he offered a "positive message" to the youths of today, the withdrawal of the campaign was precisely timed to coincide with the end of the back-to-school selling season. Such controversy was not new to Calvin Klein. Earlier ads had featured the well-developed rapper Marky Mark in briefs and waif-thin model Kate Moss in provocative poses with a large dog.

Recycling Old Campaigns

Advertisers also were reviving decades-old slogans, jingles, and trade characters, a process called "retro-marketing." From Coca-Cola's Santa Claus to Borden's Elsie the Cow and the percolating Maxwell House coffee jingle, advertisers discovered the strong affection baby boomers felt for the commercials of their youth.

While recycling old campaigns may not be creative, it is often savvy business. In an era of dozens of television channels and diverse audiences, these revived ads can recapture a time when families nationwide could be counted on to gather around the tube and watch the big three networks. These ads had a familiarity and comfort level that reminded baby boomers of the good times when they were young. The return of straightforward messages also came at a time when marketers were tightening their ad budgets; thus reviving old ads also made business sense.

Everybody remembers a good line, say marketers. After over a decade-long break, Timex again announced: "Takes a licking, but keeps on ticking." Coca-Cola updated its famous 1971 "Hilltop" spot featuring many of the original cast, this time with their own children. Oscar Mayer carried a jingle well known to anyone in the 1960s with children singing "I wish I were an Oscar Mayer wiener" and "My bologna has a first name, it's O-S-C-A-R." Even trendy, image-conscious liquor companies found that nostalgia sells. The House of Seagram put out ads for Glenlivet featuring the distiller's Scot stillman, "the father of all Scotch." This campaign stemmed from research showing that Seagram's audience considered heritage a strong product benefit.

Advertising characters, too, had a strong appeal to aging baby boomers. Fast food franchise Jack in the Box's clown had been blown up in an early 1980s commercial, but it was resurrected as a clown with a giant Ping Pong ball for a head. Borden readopted Elsie the Cow (dropped in 1966) to symbolize wholesome, country goodness for its line of dairy products. The new Elsie wears a fresh flower necklace and a sparkling white apron covering a blue, green, or purple blouse (Figure 9.19). And Little Miss Coppertone, the advertising symbol for Coppertone sun-protection products, appeared with a hat, T-shirt, and bottle of sunscreen lotion in her new role in ads and educational materials promoting the National Weather Service's new UV index, which indicates the risk level posed by the sun's ultraviolet rays.

Figure 9.19 Tapping into baby boomers' nostalgia for the commercials of their youth, Borden brought back the popular Elsie the Spokescow.

Still other advertisers celebrated milestones as a marketing opportunity. When Maypo, the instant maple-flavored cereal, turned 40 in 1993, the brand connected anew with the baby boomers who had grown up with Maypo and their spokesperson Marky. So Maypo issued this invitation: "If you or a friend turn 40 this year, just send in your or their name, address and birthday, and Maypo will mail a special 'I'm turning 40 and I want my Maypo' birthday present including a card from Marky, a vintage Marky Maypo refrigerator magnet and a Maypo coupon." The following year, the country celebrated Smokey the Bear's fiftieth birthday. The same year, the Campbell Kids were featured in a 125th anniversary commemorative campaign, appearing in a "Souper New Year" color calendar, ads, and offers for other special edition collectibles. Marketers will continue to find ways to give old products a new spin as the baby boomers age.

Even as consumers have grown nostalgic for the innocence and simplicity of their childhood, they are also looking ahead to the new millennium. The marketplace continues to fragment due to emerging technologies, growing global markets, and the proliferation of new products. Yet marketers and advertisers are slow to adapt to these trends. Companies need to keep pace with technological innovations and focus on producing enduring brands—a problem evidenced in the number of product failures. For example, although the number of new products introduced was up 41 percent in 1996, in general only one out of five new products succeeds.[27]

The most effective advertising strategies today are those that blend nostalgia, beauty, and familiarity with new technologies. Messages also must translate across national borders and address environmental issues. And, of course, advertisers must maintain the interest of target audiences.

Consumers are becoming aficionados of the new media. At the same time, the consumers who embrace the new technology are making choices about how and when they receive product information. This provides the forward-looking agencies an opportunity to reach segmented audiences by integrating their messages through print ads, direct mail, sales promotions, public relations, and other traditional media, as well as through satellite and cable TV, CD-ROMs, electronic publishing, interactive video, and the Internet. In the process the purpose of advertising will remain the same—to inform, persuade, and entertain.

Epilogue

As advertising has grown and prospered over the course of the twentieth century, no single institution has played a greater role in both reflecting and shaping American life. Throughout the seventeenth and eighteenth centuries, enterprising promoters used advertising to lure settlers to America with promises of gold and silver, fountains of youth, and, of course, "free" land. The New World became synonymous with wealth and opportunity; it was, in short, the American Dream. America, in the words of advertising, was branded.

This image of America, reinforced year after year by one of the first sustained advertising campaigns, captured Europeans' imagination and persuaded millions of people to leave their native land for America. The image epitomizes the power of advertising and, in time, became part of our national consciousness and culture.

The relationship between advertising and society has always been complex. As has been noted previously, advertising both mirrors a society and creates a society. Consider that the printing press, the Industrial Revolution, and urbanization eventually led to the emergence of advertising agencies a little more than a hundred years ago. Moreover, shifts in advertising practices can be linked to military conflicts; nothing seems to create such dramatic changes in ad styles, the advertising profession, and the advertisers themselves as does war. After the Civil War, for example, advertising grew in several ways—in size, scope, style, and boldness.

As an economic force, advertising became a dynamic, necessary part of consumer capitalism, stimulating the buying and selling of brand-name packaged goods. Ads convinced the public to buy food in tin cans instead of the traditional cloth bag or folded box. So important had advertising become to the culture and economy of the growing nation that by the 1880s virtually every widely accepted product had been promoted through advertising. Advertising's financial support of newspapers and magazines also powered the publishing and later broadcast industries—our primary sources of ideas, news, and entertainment.

Advertising may have exaggerated claims and made false promises, but that in no way diminishes its impact on society. Advertising made its greatest contributions by informing people about an endless stream of new products and, in the process, shaping mass behavior and desires—the driving forces in a capitalist consumer economy.

Advertisers also raised the consciousness of their readers. For example, copywriters helped educate women on their primary role in twentieth-century society. At a time when women's primary function was as mother and homemaker, ads gave female readers a model to emulate, as well as practical information on home management and home economics. Ads featured floor plans for well-designed houses, suggestions for furnishing the fashionable home, and devices that promised to eliminate the drudgery of household work. Ads provided tips for child-rearing, sew-at-home fashions, comparative prices for the smart shopper, and recipes for meal planning. Young women also could write to Betty Crocker or Dorothy Dix for counsel on courtship and marriage, cooking and cleaning.

In addition, ads countered the notion that newfangled products like motorcars were an expensive luxury rather than an emerging necessity. Advertising also spurred the phenomenal growth in sales of cameras, bicycles, and safety razors in the first quarter of the century. And as in the Civil War, advertising during the first World War fell into step with the war effort, fostering patriotism, selling bonds, and recruiting soldiers.

Yet it was in the 1920s that advertising reached a peak of influence on American life, shaping the products Americans bought, the fashions they wore, and the personal habits they acquired. Ads targeted newly emancipated women, selling them cigarettes, cosmetics, and fashionable ensembles. Ads introduced new modern art styles to audiences who never had been in museums. Ads promoted devices such as toasters, dishwashers, and refrigerators. Ads even altered people's lives down to the smallest details, shaping such daily habits as drinking orange juice, brushing one's teeth, taking a bath, and using deodorant.

From advertising's peak in the 1920s, the institution has since been constrained by government regulations and a more sophisticated and skeptical public. The federal government and the consumer movement forced strong corrective measures on the excesses of advertising; subsequently advertisers began to police their own industry, assuring the public of honest pitches. But as always, critics suggested that advertisers knew too much about Americans due to the vast amount of time, money, and effort they spent counting, categorizing, and analyzing the public's buying habits.

Advertising again played an important role in World War II. Advertisers proudly supported the conservation effort at home, explained how their products were vital to the war effort, and even went so far as to suggest that women work in factories to free men for duty at the front. After the war advertising still affected society, playing an important role in how Americans spent their money and occupied their newfound leisure time. Ads displayed suburbs, shiny automobiles, and television sets, which since have become staples of American culture. At roughly the same time, the advertising industry was undergoing a creative revolution.

The cataclysm in American culture that attended the civil rights movement and the Vietnam War shook advertising as well. One happy result was renewed creativity and a willingness to break with convention. Bill Bernbach, among others, helped reshape how advertising business was conducted and how ads looked. The creative revolution, as practiced by George Lois, Mary Wells, and Jerry Della Femina, freed advertising from many of the formulaic practices it had acquired. Also, emerging publications as diverse as *Ebony, Playboy,* and *Rolling Stone* enabled advertisers to tap into markets that traditionally had been shunned.

Nor did advertising ignore serious issues. In the 1960s and 1970s controversial images of feminism and minorities helped bring the issues of equal rights and empowerment to the forefront and began to remake the face of advertising. Advertising helped get out the vote and shaped the national debate on environmental issues, alcohol abuse, cigarette smoking, and, later, AIDS. Many advertising agencies came to see their role as supportive, helping their community through political campaigns, public service ads, and sponsorship of events. In conjunction with community services, advertising continued to provide vital information about such practical concerns as health care, education, and finances.

Today advertising in America is more varied than ever. Ads appear in newspapers and magazines, in television and radio commercials, on billboards and packaging, on T-shirts and shopping bags, and so on. And yet as advertising becomes more ubiquitous, the public has grown more sophisticated and skeptical. When the total number of messages increases, duplication is bound to occur. Consequently people screen the clutter more carefully and tune in to only a few messages. But an advertising innovator can still push a new or obscure product to prominence. In the past decade alone agencies as diverse as Hal Riney, Goodby Silverstein & Partners, Weiden & Kennedy, and Deutsch have shaped new messages—sometimes courageously, sometimes brilliantly—and challenged the dominance of Madison Avenue.

Advertising offers persuasive information on fashion, home management, and cars, but now it also guides us into the new millennium. Advertisers are already fueling a media revolution, sponsoring new forms of communication as diverse as satellite and cable TV, CD-ROMs, and the World Wide Web.

As a whole, then, advertising is a necessary force in the American economy and a sponsor of the most important sectors of the nation's marketplace of ideas, information, and entertainment. In the process the highly visible institution has played a varied role—as salesperson, tastemaker, educator, creator of popular culture, and historian—reflecting and shaping American life. On occasion the commercial message may interfere, but consider the alternative. A world without advertising would offer a far narrower range of goods, services, and entertainment—and conceivably a nation without a clear idea of the American Dream.

Notes

Introduction

1. Quoted in Daniel Pope, *The Making of Modern Advertising* (New York: Basic Books, 1983), 4.

Chapter 1

1. James Burke, *The Day the Universe Changed* (Boston: Little, Brown, 1985), 91–92.

2. Thomas Hine, *The Total Package: The Evolution and Secret Meanings of Boxes, Bottles, Cans, and Tubes* (Boston: Little, Brown, 1995), 46.

3. Frank S. Presbrey, *The History and Development of Advertising* (New York: Doubleday, 1929), 20.

4. Presbrey, *History and Development of Advertising,* 52.

5. R. Atwan, B. Orton, and W. Vesterman, *American Mass Media: Industries and Issues* (New York: Random House, 1986), 34.

6. Herbert G. Gutman, ed., American Social History Project, *Who Built America, Vol. 1* (New York: Pantheon Books, 1992), 45.

7. H. J. Bass, G. A. Billias, and E. J. Lapsansky, *America and Americans, Vol. 2* (Morristown, NJ: Silver Burdett, 1983), 49–50.

8. Marilyn Kern-Foxworth, *Aunt Jemima, Uncle Ben, and Rastus: Blacks in Advertising, Yesterday, Today, and Tomorrow* (Westbury, CT: Praeger, 1994), 3.

9. Phillip P. Meggs, *History of Graphic Design* (New York: Van Nostrand Reinhold, 1992), 112.

10. Hine, *Total Package,* 71.

11. Michael Schudson, *Advertising, the Uneasy Persuasion: Its Dubious Impact on American Society* (New York: Basic Books, 1984), 161.

12. Gutman, *Who Built America,* 22–23.

13. Presbrey, *History and Development of Advertising,* 250–51.

14. Bass et al., *America and Americans,* 32.

15. Presbrey, *History and Development of Advertising,* 281.

16. Stephen Fox, *The Mirror Makers: A History of American Advertising and Its Creators* (New York: Vintage Books, 1983), 19.

Chapter 2

1. H. J. Bass, G. A. Billias, and E. J. Lapsansky, *America and*

Americans, Vol. 1 (Morristown, NJ: Silver Burdett, 1983), 413.

2. U.S. Bureau of the Census, *Historical Statistics of the United States from Colonial Times to 1970* (Washington, DC: Government Printing Office, 1975), 855–56.

3. Frank S. Presbrey, *The History and Development of Advertising* (New York: Doubleday, 1929), 361–63.

4. Thomas Hine, *The Total Package: The Evolution and Secret Meanings of Boxes, Bottles, Cans, and Tubes* (Boston: Little, Brown, 1995), 57–65.

5. Stephen Fox, *The Mirror Makers: A History of American Advertising and Its Creators* (New York: Vintage Books, 1983), 27.

6. Amy Janello and Brennon Jones, *The American Magazine* (New York: Abrams, 1991), 198.

7. Ernestine G. Miller, *The Art of Advertising* (New York: St. Martin's Press, 1982), introduction.

8. Presbrey, *History and Development of Advertising,* 386.

9. *Printers' Ink* (June 28, August 23, 1893).

10. *Printers' Ink* (March 18, 1903).

11. Richard Scheffel, ed., *Discovering America's Past* (Pleasantville, NY: Reader's Digest Association, 1993), 114.

12. Daniel Pope, *The Making of Modern Advertising* (New York: Basic Books, 1983), 113.

13. Charles A. Bates, *The Art and Literature of Business* (New York: Bates, 1909), 35 (first published 1902).

Chapter 3

1. U.S. Bureau of the Census, *Historical Statistics of the United States Colonial Times to 1970* (Washington, DC: Government Printing Office, 1975), 855–56.

2. Ralph L. Nelson, *Merger Movements in American Industry 1895–1965* (Princeton, NJ: Princeton University Press, 1963), 67–68.

3. U.S. Bureau of the Census, *Historical Statistics,* 855–56.

4. H. J. Bass, G. A. Billias, and E. J. Lapsansky, *America and Americans, Vol. 2* (Morristown, NJ: Silver Burdett, 1983), 59.

5. Richard Tedlow, *New and Improved: The Story of Mass Marketing in America* (New York: Basic Books, 1990), 191.

6. Tedlow, *New and Improved,* 182–258.

7. Quoted in Jackson Lears, *Fables of Abundance: A Cultural History of American Advertising* (New York: Basic Books, 1995), 209.

8. Lears, *Fables of Abundance,* 209.

9. *Printers' Ink* (April 19, 1899).

10. Hal Morgan, *Symbols of America* (New York: Penguin Books, 1986), 52.

11. Lears, *Fables of Abundance,* 309.

12. *Printers' Ink* (July 17, 1907).

13. Claude Hopkins, *Scientific Advertising,* 1927 (Lincolnwood, IL: NTC Books, 1986).

14. Quoted in Stephen Fox, *Mirror Makers: A History of American Advertising and Its Creators* (New York: Vintage Books, 1983), 81.

15. Frank S. Presbrey, *The History and Development of Advertising* (New York: Doubleday, 1929), 442–43.

16. Suellen Hoy, *Chasing Dirt: The American Pursuit of Cleanliness* (New York: Oxford University Press, 1995), 87–122.

17. Jane and Michael Stern, *Auto Ads* (New York: Random House, 1978), 14.

Chapter 4

1. U.S. Bureau of the Census, *Historical Statistics of the United States, Colonial Times to 1970* (Washington, DC: Government Printing Office), 855–56.

2. *National Markets and National Advertising* (New York: Crowell, 1929), 9.

3. Albert D. Chandler Jr., *Giant Enterprise* (New York: Arno, 1980), 5.

4. H. J. Bass, G. A. Billias, and E. J. Lapsansky, *America and Americans, Vol. 2* (Morristown, NJ: Silver Burdett, 1983), 63.

5. Bass et al., *America and Americans,* 66.

6. Richard L. Scheffel, ed., *Discovering America's Past* (Pleasantville, NY: Reader's Digest Association, 1993), 55.

7. Bass et al., *America and Americans,* 64.

8. *Printers' Ink* (November 7, 1929).

9. Roland Marchand, *Advertising the American Dream* (Berkeley: University of California Press, 1985), 33. Here Marchand references *Who's Who in Advertising* (1931) and notes that the directory had included sketches of only 126 women in a volume that gave profiles of 5000 advertising men.

10. Marchand, *Advertising,* 35.

11. Suellen Hoy, *Chasing Dirt: The American Pursuit of Cleanliness* (New York: Oxford University Press, 1995), 141.

12. Julian Watkins, *The Hundred Greatest Advertisements* (New York: Dover, 1959), 73.

13. *Printers' Ink* (November 10, 1927).

14. Albert Lasker, *Lasker Story* (Chicago: Advertising Publications,1963), 89.

15. Richard S. Tedlow, *New and Improved: The Story of Mass Marketing in America* (New York: Basic Books, 1990), 310.

16. Stephen Bayley, *Harley Earl and the Dream Machine* (London: Weidenfeld & Nicholson, 1991), 37.

17. Frank Rowsome, *The Verse by the Side of the Road: The Story of Burma Shave Signs and Jingles* (Brattleboro, VT: Stephen Greene Press, 1965).

18. William F. Aarens and Courtland L. Bovee, *Contemporary Advertising* (Burr Ridge, IL: Irwin, 1994), 445.

19. Sydney W. Head and Christopher H. Sterling, *Broadcasting in America: A Survey of Electronic Media* (Boston: Houghton Mifflin, 1987) 54–55.

20. *Printers' Ink* (April 13, 1922).

21. *Printers' Ink* (March 5, 1931).

22. Normand C. Lumina, *Living in America* (New York: Van Nostrand Reinhold, 1970), 349.

Chapter 5

1. Herbert G. Gutman, ed., American Social History Project, *Who Built America, Vol. 2* (New York: Pantheon Books, 1992), 321.

2. Gutman, *Who Built America,* 319.

3. H. J. Bass, G. A. Billias, and E. J. Lapsansky, *America and Americans, Vol. 2* (Morristown, NJ: Silver Burdett, 1983), 65.

4. Bass et al., *America and Americans,* 274.

5. Bass et al., *America and Americans,* 271.

6. *Printers' Ink* (July 5, 1934).

7. *Printers' Ink* (September 17, 1932; February 17, 1934).

8. Quoted in Stephen Fox, *The Mirror Makers: A History of American Advertising and Its Creators* (New York: Vintage Books, 1983), 166.

9. David Ogilvy, *Ogilvy on Advertising* (New York: Vintage Books, 1983), 196.

10. Julian Watkins, *The Hundred Greatest Advertisements* (New York: Dover, 1959), 227.

11. Erik Barnouw, *The Sponsor: Notes on the Modern Potentate* (New York: Oxford University Press, 1978), 27.

12. Sydney W. Head and Christopher H. Sterling, *Broadcasting in America: A Survey of Electronic Media* (Boston: Houghton Mifflin, 1987), 67.

13. Barbara Leaming, *Orson Welles* (New York: Viking Penguin, 1985).

14. Head and Sterling, *Broadcasting in America,* 72.

15. *Advertising Age* (January 13, 1941).

16. John Heskett, *German Design 1870–1918* (New York: Taplinger, 1986), 149.

17. Michael Horsham, *'20s & '30s Style* (London: Grange Books, 1994), 18.

18. Jane Stern and Michael Stern, *Auto Ads* (New York: Random House, 1978), 32.

19. Head and Sterling, *Broadcasting in America,* 76.

Chapter 6

1. Paul C. Light, *Baby Boomer* (New York: Norton, 1988), 20.

2. Herbert G. Gutman, ed., American Social History Project, *Who Built America, Vol. 2* (New York: Pantheon Books, 1992), 524.

3. Gutman, *Who Built America,* 525.

4. H. J. Bass, G. A. Billias, and E. J. Lapsansky, *America and Americans, Vol. 2* (Morristown, NJ: Silver Burdett, 1983), 49–50, 418.

5. Thomas Hine, *Populuxe* (New York: Knopf, 1986), 20.

6. Christopher Pearce, *Fifties Source Book: A Visual Guide to the Style of a Decade* (Secaucus, NJ: Chartwell Books, 1990), 10.

7. Jack Mingo, *How the Cadillac Got its Fins* (New York: HarperBusiness, 1994), 197–200.

8. Hine, *Populuxe,* 12.

9. Stephen Bayley, *Harley Earl and the American Dream Machine* (London: Weidenfeld & Nicholson, 1991), 69–70.

10. Bayley, *Harley Earl,* 93.

11. Daniel Yergin, *The Prize: The Epic Quest for Oil, Money & Power* (New York: Simon & Schuster, 1992).

12. Charles Goodrum and Helen Dalrymple, *Advertising in America* (New York: Abrams,1990), 77.

13. Clifton Daniel, editorial director, *Chronicle of America* (Mount Kisco, NY: Chronicle Publications, 1989), 775.

14. Stephen Fox, *The Mirror Makers: A History of American Advertising and Its Creators* (New York: Vintage Books, 1983), 278.

15. Fox, *The Mirror Makers,* 279.

16. W. Lloyd Warner, *Social Class in America. A Manual of Procedure for the Measurement of Social Status* (Chicago: Science Research Associates, 1949).

17. Quoted in Vance Packard, *The Hidden Persuaders* (New York: Pocket Books, 1957), 108–10.

18. Fox, *The Mirror Makers,* 293; Shirley Polykoff, *Does She or Doesn't She?* (New York: Doubleday, 1975).

19. Packard, *The Hidden Persuaders,* 110.

20. Packard, *The Hidden Persuaders,* 2.

21. P. J. Bednarksi, "TV Arrives and the Future Begins," *Advertising Age* (July 31, 1995).

22. Rosser Reeves, *Reality in Advertising* (New York: Knopf, 1960), 34.

23. Michael L. Ray, *Advertising & Communication Management* (Englewood Cliffs, NJ: Prentice-Hall, 1982), 286.

24. David Ogilvy, *Ogilvy on Advertising* (New York: Vintage Books, 1983), 203.

25. Ogilvy, *Ogilvy on Advertising,* 230.

26. Fox, *The Mirror Makers,* 253.

Chapter 7

1. H. J. Bass, G. A. Billias, and E. J. Lapsansky, *America and Americans, Vol. 2* (Morristown, NJ: Silver Burdett, 1983), 463.

2. Herbert G. Gutman, ed., American Social History Project, *Who Built America, Vol. 2* (New York: Pantheon Books, 1992), 611.

3. Cover story, *Newsweek* (August 18, 1969).

4. Robert Rosenblum, "Towards a Definition in New Art," in Andreas Papadakis, ed., *New Art* (New York: Rizzoli, 1991), 44–45.

5. Quoted in Paul Sann, *Fads, Follies and Delusions* (New York: Bonanza Books, 1967), 312.

6. *The New York Times* (August 27, 1995), F11.

7. Stephen Fox, *Mirror Makers* (New York: Vintage Books, 1983), 258.

8. "Burnett—An Enduring Culture," *Advertising Age* (July 31, 1995).

9. Fox, *Mirror Makers,* 272.

10. J. Fred MacDonald, *Blacks and White TV* (Chicago: Nelson-Hall, 1992), 88–89.

11. Marilyn Kern-Foxworth, *Aunt Jemima, Uncle Ben, and Rastus: Blacks in Advertising, Yesterday, Today, and Tommorow* (Westbury, CT: Praeger, 1994), 133.

12. Kern-Foxworth, *Aunt Jemima,* 136. See also Fox, *Mirror Makers,* 281.

13. Reported in *Advertising Age,* October 30, 1967; January 22, 1968; November 3, 1969.

14. Gail Baker Woods, *Advertising and Marketing to the New Majority* (Belmont, CA: Wadsworth, 1995), 22.

15. Quoted in *Advertising Age* (March 18, 1974).

16. Quoted in *Advertising Age* (May 22, 1972).

17. Erving Goffman, *Gender Advertisements* (New York: Harper & Row, 1976), 32.

18. Goffman, *Gender Advertisements,* 41.

19. FTC, "Federal Trade Commission Staff Report on TV Advertising to Children," *Advertising Age* (February 27, 1978).

20. FTC, "Staff Report."

Chapter 8

1. *AdWeek* (June 12, 1976).

2. *Advertising Age* (April 12, 1976).

3. Al Ries and Jack Trout, *Positioning: The Battle for Your Mind* (New York: McGraw-Hill, 1981), 228.

4. Ries and Trout, *Positioning,* 219–20.

5. Quoted in "Advertisers Remove the Cover from Brand X," *U. S. News & World Report* (December 19, 1983).

6. Quoted in "The '80s: What a Decade!" *Advertising Age* (January 1, 1990), 19.

7. Jim Hall, *Mighty Minutes* (New York: Harmony Books, 1984), 138.

8. "The Decade of the Deal," *Advertising Age* (January 1, 1990), 4.

9. "And Now, a Word from Our Sponsor," *Marketing Tools* (June 1995), 50.

10. R. A. Buchanan, *The Power of the Machine* (1992), 165.

11. Buchanan, *Power of the Machine,* 12.

12. "From Apple to 'Where's the Beef?' 12 Campaigns That Shook the Decade," *AdWeek* (July 9, 1990), 34.

13. "Euro, Pacific Spending Spree: Ad Budgets for '89 Lag in U.S.," *Advertising Age* (April 10, 1989), 4, 55. See also "Unilever Triumphs as Top Ad Spender," *Advertising Age* (December 4, 1989), S1.

14. "The 100 Largest U.S. Multinationals," *Forbes* (July 23, 1990), 362.

15. "How Coke Runs a Foreign Empire," *Business Week* (August 25, 1973), 40–43.

16. "Coke Spins Same Sell All Around the World," *USA Today* (December 28, 1988), B6.

17. "Decade of the Deal," 3.

18. "The '80s: Invasions Topple Madison Ave.'s Crown," *AdWeek* (December 11, 1989), 18.

19. "Decade of the Deal," 4.

20 "Decade of the Deal," 12.

21. "The Advertising Game Tilts Toward the West," *Newsweek* (March 4, 1985), 41.

22. *AdWeek* (July 9, 1990), 21.

23. Quoted in "On Top of His Game," *San Francisco Focus* (March 1994), 46.

24. David Ogilvy, *Ogilvy on Advertising* (New York: Vintage Books, 1983), 28.

25. "The '80s: What a Decade!" 18.

Chapter 9

1. Cover story, *USA Today* (May 9, 1996).

2. *Washington Post,* national weekly edition (February 15–21, 1993).

3. "Narrowcast in Past, Women Earn Revised Role in Advertising," *Advertising Age* (October 4, 1993), S10.

4. "Community Agencies Join to Battle Sexist Advertising," *San Diego Union Tribune* (January 27, 1994).

5. "Getting Your Slice of the Pie," *San Francisco Chronicle* (October 14, 1994).

6. *Business Week* (December 14, 1992), 77.

7. Bonnie Drewniany, "Writing to Reach the 50-Plus Market," in A. Jerome Jeweler, *Creative Strategy in Advertising* (Belmont, CA: Wadsworth, 1995), 311.

8. Drewniany, "Writing," 311.

9. "Uncle Sam Is No Match for the Marlboro Man," *New York Times* (August 27, 1995), 3–1.

10. "The Media Business," *New York Times* (August 8, 1995), C18.

11. "Greenhouse Marketing," *Advertising Age* (June 28, 1993), S2.

12. Gail Baker Woods, *Advertising and Marketing to the New Major-*

ity (Belmont, CA: Wadsworth, 1995), 22.

13. Woods, *Advertising and Marketing,* 38–39.

14. Quoted in Marilyn Kern-Foxworth, *Aunt Jemima, Uncle Ben, and Rastus: Blacks in Advertising, Yesterday, Today, and Tomorrow* (Westbury, CT: Praeger, 1994), 142–43.

15. Kern-Foxworth, *Aunt Jemima,* 28.

16. "The Ad Industry's Little Secret," *Advertising Age* (June 16, 1992), 18.

17. Woods, *Advertising and Marketing,* 38.

18. Woods, *Advertising and Marketing,* 46–49.

19. "The Media Business," *The New York Times* (September 29, 1994), C16.

20. "More Advertisers Reaching Out to Gay Consumers," *San Francisco Examiner* (October 9, 1994), B3.

21. "Is Advertising Dead?" *Wired* (February 1994).

22. "The Coke Saga," *Advertising Age* (October 4, 1993), 22.

23. *The New York Times* (January 26, 1996), C3.

24. "Welcome to the Club House in the Virtual Office," *AdWeek* (November 22, 1993), 38.

25. "Toppling the Madison Avenue Giants," *Los Angeles Times* (June 5, 1994), 12.

26. "The Pain Principle," *Advertising Age* (August 16, 1993), 23.

27. "New Products, Same Old Mistakes," *Advertising Age* (October 7, 1996), 60.

Acknowledgments

p. 306, Fig. 7.4: Reprinted by permission of Arnold Advertising and Volkswagen of America.

p. 309, Fig. 7.7: Reprinted by permission of Hunt-Wesson, Inc. All rights reserved.

p. 311, Fig. 7.9: Reprinted by permission of Volvo Cars of North America.

p. 321: Lyrics are reprinted courtesy of Armour Swift-Eckrich, Downers Grove, IL.

p. 323, Fig. 7.14: Reprinted by permission of Evans, Inc., Chicago, IL.

p. 327: Ad is reprinted by permission of Maidenform, Inc.

p. 340, Fig. 8.1: Reprinted by permission of R. C. Auletta and Company, Inc.

p. 344, Fig. 8.3: 7UP, Seven-Up and the Spot Character are registered trademarks in the United States of Dr Pepper/Cadbury North America, Inc.

p. 345, Fig. 8.4: 7UP, Seven-Up and the Spot Character are registered trademarks in the United States of Dr Pepper/Cadbury North America, Inc.

p. 347, Fig. 8.5: Advertisement by Fallon McElligott, by Straight Arrow Publishers, Inc. All rights reserved. Reprinted by permission.

p. 352, Fig. 8.6, photo: O. Toscani, courtesy of United Colors of Benetton.

p. 355: Energizer Bunny is used by permission of Eveready Battery Co., Inc.

p. 357, Fig. 8.8: Reprinted by permission. Copyright © 1993 by International Business Machines Corporation.

p. 358, Fig. 8.9: Reprinted by permission of Xerox Corporation.

p. 366, Fig. 8.12: Reprinted by permission of American Express.

p. 367: Charlie the Tuna trademark is owned by Star-Kist Foods and is used by permission.

p. 368, Fig. 8.13: Reprinted by permission of Transamerica Corporation.

p. 376, Fig. 8.18: Used by permission of Paco Rabanne, Paris.

p. 383, Fig. 9.1: © 1992 Motorola, Inc. Reproduced with permission from Motorola, Inc.

p. 384, Fig. 9.2: Used by permission of General Mills.

p. 395, Fig. 9.8: Used by permission of The Campbell Soup Company.

p. 412, Fig. 9.13: 7UP, Seven-Up and the Spot Character are registered trademarks in the United States of Dr Pepper/Cadbury North America, Inc.

p. 414, Fig. 9.14: © Apple Computer, Inc. Used with permission. Apple® and the Apple logo are registered trademarks of Apple Computer, Inc. All rights reserved.

p. 417, Fig. 9.15: Got Milk?® California Milk Processor Board.

Index